T0326729

Colonial Fantasies

Post-Contemporary Interventions
Series Editors: Stanley Fish and Fredric Jameson

Colonial Fantasies

Conquest, Family, and Nation

in Precolonial Germany, 1770–1870

Susanne Zantop

Duke University Press   Durham and London 1997

© 1997 Duke University Press
All rights reserved
Printed in the United States of America on acid-free paper ∞
Typeset in Sabon by Keystone Typesetting, Inc.
Library of Congress Cataloging-in-Publication Data appear
on the last printed page of this book.

Contents

Preface and Acknowledgments   vii
Introduction   1

I Armchair Conquistadors; or, The Quest for "New Germany"   17

1 *Tiranos animales o alemanes*: Germans and the "Conquest"   18
2 A Conquest of the Intellect   31

II Colonizing Theory:
Gender, Race, and the Search for a National Identity   43

3 Gendering the "Conquest"   46
4 Racializing the Colony   66
5 Patagons and Germans   81

III Colonial Families; or, Displacing the Colonizers   99

6 Fathers and Sons: Donnerstag and Freitag, Campe and
   Krusoe   102
7 Husbands and Wives: Colonialism Domesticated   121
8 Betrothal and Divorce; or, Revolution in the House   141

IV Virgin Islands, Teuton Conquerors   163

9 The German Columbus   166
10 The Second Discovery   173
11 Colonial Fantasies Revisited   191

Epilogue: Vitzliputzli's Revenge   202

Notes   211

Bibliography   263

Index   287

Preface and Acknowledgments

It is always curious to note to what extent our critical interests are tied to, or emanate from, our autobiographies. As is by now well known, more often than not we choose our subject matter and approach not by an act of free will but because of historical experiences and chance encounters beyond our control. This is certainly the case with this study.

When I conceived of an investigation into German fantasies of South America, I was, on the surface at least, finally connecting two of my long-standing academic interests, an interest in eighteenth- and nineteenth-century German history and literature with an interest in everything Latin American, from politics and literatures to the many diverse cultures. Little did I realize then that I was also, in a way, reproducing my own geographic and intellectual trajectory and, at the same time, attempting to exorcize some of the demons I had collected along the way: the trajectory from Berlin, Germany, to the United States, and from there to South America, then Spain, and finally back to the United States, first as a student, then as the wife of an employee of U.S. mining companies, then as an academic; and the trajectory from a self-satisfied anti-imperialist sixties radical, to a guilt-ridden, reluctant participant in U.S. imperialism, to a critic of the culture of imperialism and my own involvement in it. The questions that arose in my mind as I examined my own contradictions form the understory, the backdrop against which this study developed and which it constantly engages, albeit on a subliminal level: how as a student in Germany, I had cheered the Chinese Cultural Revolution as "the end to all bureaucratic os-sification"; how my husband and I, living comfortably off salaries provided by American companies in Costa Rica, had demonstrated against "Mamita Yunai," the United Fruit Company; or how I was siding with the "oppressed" in the safe haven of New England academe. As I was exploring "German" fictions of otherness, I was asking myself to what extent my vision, my questions and hangups, had been shaped by growing up in a German cultural environment and to what extent I was unwittingly reproducing what I was analyzing: the exoticist fascination with South America, the condescending, although well-meant, paternalist assimilation fantasies, the self-righteousness with which the writers and critics I examined claimed the right to speak "for" others and to integrate and subsume others into their racial or moral categories.

As Thomas Pavel has recently reminded us, "political critics" run the risk of getting "carried away by commitment to their own concerns," neglecting, as a consequence, "the text's own effort to mold their attention and lead their gaze"[1] — a useful reminder. Although one could, of course, retort that this risk is shared by all of us who interpret texts, and that nonpolitical criticism tends to overlook important textual components as well. The "colonial interpretation" of *The Tempest* could only be "first invented by the *supporters* of British imperialism" (125), because Caliban's position in the drama of the encounter allowed for such an interpretation. Likewise, it is only possible to discover illiberal, colonialist undertones in seemingly liberal, anticolonialist texts if they are *there*.

In order to avoid (too) one-sided readings and facile conclusions, I have consulted with many friends and colleagues. To all of them who were willing to read the totality or portions of this study and to challenge me in discussions, I am deeply grateful: Michael Ermarth, Sara Friedrichsmeyer, Gerd Gemünden, Marianne Hirsch, Robert Holub, Mary Kelley, Lawrence Kritzman, Sara Lennox, Silvia Spitta, Leo Spitzer, Virginia Swain, Diana Taylor, and Daniel Wilson. My dear colleague Walter Arndt took great pains to reproduce in English, rhyme and all, some of the most awful poems and colonialist propaganda. His impish humor helped sustain me in my more depressed moments. It is indeed a pleasure and a privilege to be surrounded by such a community of scholars and friends.

I also want to thank my former students who assisted me in the bibliographical work over the years, and with cleaning up the manuscript, Mark Buschmann, Lisa Gates, Roland Schweighöfer, and Rebecca McCallum — and the three staff persons in the Baker Library at Dartmouth College who were instrumental in locating obscure texts: Patsy Carter, Marianne Hraibi, and Lois Krieger. And last, but not least, I want to express my appreciation for the Howard Foundation, the National Endowment of the Humanities, the Marion and Jasper Whiting Foundation, and the John Carter Brown Library for providing me with grants to support me during my years of primary research.

No effort of this sort can be sustained without moral and logistic support from one's most immediate surroundings. As I was working on familial fantasies of colonial relations and on colonialist perversions of the familial model, I became keenly aware of how wonderfully supportive and nurturing even the much-maligned nuclear family can be. This book is therefore dedicated to them: to my mother, Marianne, whose unshaking faith in my ability to finish projects energized me throughout my life; to my father, Joachim, whose enthusiasm for cannibals and Amazons translated into many visits to libraries and much epistolary exchange on the subject matter; to my daughters, Veronika and Mariana, who bore with me through thick and thin, with leniency, love, and good humor; and to Half, in more than one sense my better half. Without them, this project would neither have been started nor completed.

Introduction

Do not laugh at the visionary who expects the same revolution to occur in the phenomenal realm as has happened in the realm of the mind. Thought precedes action as lightning precedes thunder. German thunder, of course, being German, is not very agile, and rolls along rather slowly; but it will arrive in due course, and when you hear such a crash as has never yet been heard in the history of the world, then you will know that German thunder has finally reached its goal. When its sound is heard, the eagles will drop down dead from the sky and the lions in the remotest deserts of Africa will draw in their tails and creep into their royal caves. A play will be performed in Germany, compared with which the French Revolution will seem a mere inoffensive idyll. — Heinrich Heine, On the History of Religion and Philosophy in Germany, *1834*[1]

On April 24, 1884, Bismarck, chancellor of the then thirteen-year-old German Empire, sent a cable to the German consul in Cape Town to proclaim "imperial protection" over the territories the Bremen tobacco merchant Lüderitz had acquired from African chiefs in South-West Africa. Although this "protective" paternal gesture is generally considered the first official act in the history of German imperialism, all observers agree that the German Empire's claim to its "place in the sun" did not come about all of a sudden. In fact, the short history of Germany's imperialism — from the establishment of colonies in South-West Africa, Togo, Cameroon, East Africa, and the Pacific in the 1880s to the loss of these colonies as a result of World War I — was preceded by a long history of small-scale colonial ventures, large-scale colonialist theories, and a myriad of colonial fantasies, from the sixteenth century onward. The famous telegram that made German imperialist claims manifest to the world thus marked not so much the beginning as the end in what Mary Townsend termed a "distinct colonial cult," a cult that had characterized much of German public discourse during the two previous, "precolonial" centuries.[2]

Colonial Fantasies

Germany's "distinct colonial cult" is the focus of this book. Rather than study the debates in the 1870s and 80s about colonial expansion, as Townsend did, I go back to the times before a united German Empire engaged in imperialist endeavors, and to texts whose connection to colonialism is less obvious. More concerned with the emergence of "latent colonialism," as an unspecific drive for colonial possession, than with "manifest colonialism" targeted at a specific object, I explore how a colonialist subjectivity emerged in Germany as early as the 1770s, during the so-called coloniopolitical half of the eighteenth century, and how it grew into a collective obsession by the late 1800s.[3] The desire to venture forth, to conquer and appropriate foreign territories, and to (re)generate the self in the process formed in subtle and indirect ways. Ironically, it often appeared under the guise of an anticolonialist stance. Indeed, the drive for colonial possession — and by this I mean actual control over territories and resources as well as control over the body and labor of human beings — articulated itself not so much in statements of intent as in "colonial fantasies": stories of sexual conquest and surrender, love and blissful domestic relations between colonizer and colonized, set in colonial territory, stories that made the strange familiar, and the familiar "familial."

As stories of sexual or familial encounters, these colonial fantasies could take on any generic form. They were cast as children's books or entertainment for adults, as narratives, poetry, or drama. They were inserted into anthropological, philosophical, or political treatises, in the form of tropological ministories (e.g., "Virgin Islands," "marriage of cultures," "daughter colony"), or as illustrative anecdotes. They even appeared in travel literature that purports to represent an experienced reality, not the fantasy life of the traveler. As both full-fledged stories ("fantasies") and a peculiar imaginative configuration ("fantasy") informing other forms of discourse, colonial fantasies were ubiquitous.

In my analysis of German colonial fantasies, I therefore draw from a variety of texts — tales, novels, and plays; scientific articles; philosophical essays; and political pamphlets. All of them, in one way or another, expand on the colonial urfantasy of the encounter between European and "native," which they recast to meet particular ideological needs. All of them build on one another, creating a network of implicit references, which reinforce their message and anchor it in the minds of their readers. Together, they create a colonialist imagination and mentality that beg to translate thought into action.

By using the term "fantasy" rather than "fiction" or "myth," I want to highlight two important aspects of these colonialist stories: their purely imaginary, wish-fulfilling nature and their unconscious subtext, which links sexual desire for the other with desire for power and control.[4] Unlike the violent "male fantasies" of the Freikorpsmen, which, in Klaus Theweleit's cogent analysis, reveal their pathological grounding in sexual anxieties, the colonial fantasies of sexual bliss cloaked their obsession with conquest and appropriation in cross-cultural, cross-racial romances.[5] As seductive master fantasies, German fantasies of colonial mastery continuously rewrote the colonial history made by others: they created an imaginary German colonial history on paper and in the minds of their readers; they were recycled, over and over again, until they acquired the status of factual "reality." Proliferating in the late 1700s and early 1800s, by the 1880s they had become so firmly entrenched in Germany's collective imagination that they formed a cultural residue of myths about self and other(s) that could be stirred up for particular political purposes — progressive as well as reactionary ones — whenever the need arose. Their significance as a corollary to the more official colonial-scientific discourse, as its subtext or, occasionally, countertext, should therefore not be underestimated.

Curiously, the colonial imagination and hence colonial fantasies as I define them have been largely ignored in Germany. Historians deemed them unworthy as historical documents; literary scholars dismissed them as "literature"; and to philosophers and anthropologists alike, they seemed to be lacking in complexity and profundity.[6] As Sara Lennox has recently suggested, Germany's specific postcolonial situation may account for its scholars' relative reluctance to tackle the German colonialist imaginary.[7] The shortness of the colonial period, the absence of vocal "colonial subjects" in the German "metropolis" (the lack of a metropolis, for that matter), and the preponderance of the Holocaust in all post–World War II discussions have obscured the significance of colonial fantasies in the formation of German national identity and of race relations within Germany. As I argue, however, the undefined status and the slippery position of colonial fantasies both inside and outside the canon, inside and outside of texts, and somewhere in between well-defined literary genres — as well as their pervasiveness — make them crucial markers, even agents in cultural history. More than any statements of intent or any complex work of high art, colonial fantasies provide access to the "political unconscious" of a nation, to the desires, dreams, and myths that inform public discourse and (can) propel collective political action.

I use the terms "desire" and "unconscious" metaphorically, not in their strictly psychoanalytic context, since I am less concerned with the fantasies and the unconscious of individuals than with a collective mentality, whose object "escapes historical individuals, because it reveals the impersonal content of their thought."[8] However, fantasy does provide a link between individual and collectivity, the individual subconscious and the political subconscious of a society. Through allegory and symbol, fantasies can and did suggest a collective individuality; they forged a national identity, producing not just a "family" of likeminded readers, but the illusion that when it came to colonial expansion, the nation was driven, like an individual, by one will, one desire. Fantasies are simultaneously the vehicle of, and the driving force behind colonialist ideology. They provide, through representation, the parameters for the "lived relation between men and their world," the framework for their (desired) identity and relationship toward others.[9]

In his landmark study *Orientalism,* Edward Said alluded to the "battery of desires, repressions, investments, and projections" that, in combination with scholarly or economic-utilitarian interests, contributed to the production of a colonialist mentality.[10] As critics have pointed out, however, Said did not explore this realm of what Homi Bhabha calls "unconscious positivity."[11] His investigation focused on the representation of the Oriental other and on the collusion between knowledge and power, not on the formation of the colonizing subject — "that 'new product' of the dynamogenic effects of self-endangering and self-renewal," as David Trotter characterized it.[12] Yet as both Trotter and Bhabha indicate, and as this study insists, it is necessary to explore the complexities and ambivalences of the nation's imagination in order to understand the lure of the colonial "adventure," particularly for those who, like the Germans, had been excluded from it. It is important to investigate, in Trotter's words, "the ideals and fantasies which made it [colonialism], for so many people, the right (indeed the only) vocation to pursue," and to dwell on the tension between desire and fear, attraction and repulsion, incitement and interdiction which is operative in the imagination of would-be colonizers.[13] An analysis of these tensions will help us understand the seductive power exercised by colonialist ideology. To focus on fantasies rather than on statements of opinion or intent may provide us with tentative answers to questions cultural historians have been posing for a long time: What were the "desires, repressions, projections, and investments" that fueled colonial discourse? Did they change over the course of centuries, or did they remain constant? Why did the drive for colonies become so powerful in late nineteenth-century Europe, despite internal resistances to colonialism, and despite evidence that colonies did not really "pay off"? And how or why does one discourse gain hegemonic status over others? In other words, what must the political, economic, or social conditions be if they are to foster the emergence of one particular master fantasy and its preponderance over others?

To Homi Bhabha, the "colonial stereotype" provides access to the "royal road to colonial fantasy."[14] Bhabha locates the stereotype in "racial" difference, whereas sexual difference, as Robert Young has noted, does not enter his analysis. Sexuality, if it appears at all, is only used metaphorically.[15] Issues of gender and sexuality are also conspicuously absent from Said's *Orientalism,* an oversight Said himself later acknowledged yet diffused by relegating gender analysis to analogous structures (patriarchy), rather than exploring gender dynamics within Orientalism itself.[16] Recent studies of British imperialism, such as those by McClintock and Young, have shown, however, that sexuality plays a crucial role, if not *the* crucial role in colonial fantasies. In fact, racial and sexual stereotypes intersect and overlap in the colonialist imaginary, creating the peculiar dynamics of attraction and repulsion within colonialist subjectivity identified by Bhabha and others. This was also the case in Germany. As the eighteenth-century German colonial fantasies under scrutiny make painfully clear, the concept of "race," in its modern, biological definition, emerged at the same time as modern gender roles were conceived. Indeed, it was in the late 1700s — and not in the late nineteenth century — that "race" became defined as a series of immutable physical properties, accompanied by equally immutable intellectual and moral characteristics, and that "gender" was constituted as a naturally hierarchical difference between the sexes.[17] This construction of a race-gender model occurred within a decidedly "colonial" context. Only by recourse to colonized peoples, to men and women of color, whom they displaced or desired, could white European males define themselves as the White European Male, predestined by biology to a position of physical and cultural dominance.

From its very inception in the imaginary, the colonial project encompassed both the foreign and the domestic sphere. Eighteenth-century stories not only gendered master-slave relations, but racialized domes-

tic arrangements when they defined both women and colonized subjects as immature "children," bound to their masters in loyalty and
obedience, or when they depicted domestic and colonized women as a
savage "dark continent" in need of cultivation and enlightenment.[18]
They renegotiated gender distinctions at home as loving "master-slave"
relations, while they recast master-slave relations in the colony in terms
of familial paternalism. As John Gabriel Stedmann, the protagonist of
one of the popular German plays of the period, says to his beloved
future wife, the slave Cery: "If you weren't a slave, my eye would not
find you half as lovable."[19] (Hetero)sexual desire across a racial divide
had to legitimize and veil the libidinal drive for possession of foreign
territory and the power relations within the European bourgeois household. Existing conditions in the colony or "at home" (in the state and in
the family) were thus recast in and through colonial fantasizing; the
"reality" of one became the metaphor for the other, and vice versa.

Peter Hulme has suggested that the production of colonial fantasies
was an all-European endeavor. His fascinating study of colonial encounters, as they were emplotted in the tales of Prospero and Caliban, John Smith and Pocahontas, Robinson Crusoe and Friday, and
Inkle and Yarico, however, concentrates exclusively on the imaginary
reworkings of Columbus's first encounter with "Indians" within an
English-American cultural tradition. Hulme does not address either
national specificities or the intersection of a colonialist with a nationalist discourse or project. Similarly, McClintock's and Young's studies of
colonial desire do not cast more than a fleeting glance at the mainland.
When it comes to postcolonial theory, Germany remains a marginal
"other." Yet for the European context, particularly at the turn of the
eighteenth century, attention to national specificity is crucial. German
colonial fantasies were different even when they imitated or rewrote
those of other European nations. By virtue of existing in the "pure"
realm of the imagination, "untainted" by praxis, German fantasies
were not only differently motivated, but had a different function: to
serve not so much as ideological smokescreen or cover-up for colonial
atrocities or transgressive desires, but as *Handlungsersatz,* as substitute
for the real thing, as imaginary testing ground for colonial action. By
commenting upon and criticizing the colonial ventures of others, individuals and nations; by building on, revising, and amending the theories developed outside German borders by foreign discoverers; and,
above all, by imagining colonial scenarios that allowed for an identification with the role of conqueror or colonizer, Germans could create a

colonial universe of their own, and insert themselves into it. Their writings did not just produce "the rest of the world" (Mary Louise Pratt) like those of other West Europeans, but a world with a specific place for the German colonizer in it. The re-presentation of past heroic ventures and the critique of the "excesses" committed by others provided Germans with spaces for the inscription of their own identities as "different" (= better) colonists, anticipatory identities into which they could slip once the economic and political conditions permitted state-sponsored colonial activity or imperialist expansion on a grand scale. Furthermore, by inscribing Germans into a colonial script, German writers were able to define what was "German" and what was "un-German." German protagonists could be pitted against various *native* others (blacks, Amerindians, "mulattoes") with whom they interacted; Germans and their "Germanic" national characteristics could be contrasted with those of other Europeans, with whom Germany competed for moral, economic, or political supremacy. The plot "resolutions" in turn would give an indication how Germans imagined ideal colonial relations. In short, colonial fantasies provided an arena for creating an imaginary community and constructing a national identity in opposition to the perceived racial, sexual, ethnic, or national characteristics of others, Europeans and non-Europeans alike. As Germans imagined their others both outside and inside Germany, they created themselves. The "colony" thus became the blank space for a new beginning, for the creation of an imaginary national self freed from history and convention — a self that would prove to the world what "he" could do.

In contrast to Said, who has argued that the lack of colonies made German colonialist discourse more abstract, scholarly, and by implication, less powerful, I propose that it was precisely the lack of actual colonialism that created a pervasive desire for colonial possessions and a sense of entitlement to such possessions in the minds of many Germans.[20] Since a colonial discourse could develop without being challenged by colonized subjects or without being tested in a real colonial setting, it established itself not so much as "intellectual authority" (Said) over distant terrains, than as mythological authority over the collective imagination.[21] The power of colonial fantasies, which developed in the abstract, was such that they would eventually eclipse colonial reality. For example, even when German colonialists such as Carl Peters in East Africa, or von Trotha in South-West Africa engaged in the violent displacement of native populations and genocidal massacres, the "colonial legend" [*Koloniallegende*] of the German as "the best

colonizer and cultivator" (Simonsfeld) prevailed, coloring representations of Germany's colonial past in novels and schoolbooks well into
the 1950s and 60s.[22]

The question this study raises is not whether Germans were in fact
different from other European colonial powers, that is, whether or not
they pursued a pernicious *Sonderweg,* a separate course, even in their
colonial policies. I am less concerned with the colonial reality of the late
nineteenth century than with the formation of a sense of German difference that grew out of specific historical realities in the late 1700s and
early 1800s and that manifested itself in Germany's colonial fantasies.
Thus, the fragmentation of Germany in the eighteenth century, which
enforced colonial abstention, produced a sense of moral superiority, a
moral highground for judging the performance of others. The battle
against French "imperialism" during the Napoleonic Wars, in turn, pro-
moted a sense of identification with the colonized underdog and hence
fantasies replete with compassion and self-pity. The battle of the late-
comer for national unity, finally, which was waged mostly in the realm
of the symbolic, created particularly ethnocentric, exclusive, eventually
even aggressive fantasies. In other words, I do not compare Germany's
colonial performance to that of other nations. Instead, I analyze why
and how a sense of exclusivity and moral superiority was constructed in
the writings of eighteenth- and nineteenth-century authors, to form part
of Germany's colonial imagination and its nationalist-colonialist ideology — and why and how this sense of specialness was challenged by a
few writers who were sensitive enough to see through the tangle of
myths and interests.

The question of a distinction between colonialism and imperialism,
which forms the point of departure for most historical studies and
which was most recently raised in Said's *Culture and Imperialism,* is of
limited relevance for this exploration of the German colonial imagination. Said reverses the conventional sequence, maintained by Marxist
philosophers, historians, and economists (Lenin, Hobson, Herzberg, et
al.), whereby traditional "colonialism" culminated in aggressive economic "imperialism" at the end of the nineteenth century. He redefines
the concepts in terms of the relative distance between colonizer and
colonized and the difference between theory and practice: " 'Imperialism' means the practice, the theory, and the attitudes of a dominating
metropolitan center ruling a distant territory; 'colonialism,' which is
almost always a consequence of imperialism, is the implanting of settlements on distant territory."[23] Imperialism thus encompasses both

thought and action, colonialism only the latter, the actual taking possession and settling of the land.

Despite the inclusiveness of Said's use of "imperialism," I prefer to use the terms "colonialism" and "colonial fantasies," for they correspond to the peculiar situation Germans faced in the late eighteenth and nineteenth centuries: the lack of a nation state before 1871 and of a colonial policy before the 1880s. My focus is on imaginary formations created at a time when Germany was *not yet* an empire nor controlled any foreign lands excepting, of course, Prussia's expansion into eastern and western territories. Since I focus on fantasies, not actions, and since these fantasies are informed predominantly by a settlement rather than an economic exploitation ideology, "colonial" seems to be the more appropriate label.[24]

However, as the preferred metaphors for colonial takeover — "rape," "conquest," "surrender," "marriage" — suggest, the difference between colonialist and imperialist fantasies is only one of degree. Their ubiquity and interchangeability, their common basis in sexuality, in a universe experienced and represented as gendered, divided, and potentially violent, blurs the distinctions. How easily one or the other fantasy could be called upon became obvious, for example, when in the early 1880s German advocates of economic imperialism evoked the picture of peaceful colonial farm families in order to sway a conservative nationalist electorate, interested in agrarian settlements, in favor of aggressive expansion.[25] As the experience of Germany shows, colonialist desires could be instrumentalized for imperialist purposes, since they had taken hold of the imagination long before any state-sponsored expansion was even considered. Imaginary colonialism anticipated actual imperialism, words, actions. In the end, reality just caught up with the imagination.

Germany's Occidentalism

All of the texts analyzed in this book relate to Latin America and the Caribbean, to territories and islands south of the Rio Grande, to "South America." The use of this term is not coincidental. It does not so much demarcate a geographic region as the "surprising contrast" (Hegel) between north and south, that is, the symbolic opposition between "North America" (= *Amerika*) and "South America" as it was constituted in the German imagination. This mental division occurred after 1776, when North America, the liberated colony, became associated with youth and dynamic energy ("the land of the future"), whereas the backward South, lingering under disintegrating colonial rule and engaged in mostly futile uprisings, came to hold an ambiguous status as object of both contempt (its supposed decadence) and desire (its colonial potential). The north-south divide was accentuated by topographical symbolism — the clear distinction between the north as the upper parts of the continental "body" (head and chest — intellect and feelings) and the south as the lower parts (sexuality) — and by a gendered imagery (the north as "virile," the south as "effeminate"), which eighteenth- and nineteenth-century writers frequently alluded to. Gustav Siebenmann has rightly pointed to the sloppy, unfocused use of the term *Südamerika* in German discourse, to its "stereotypical undertone" — its association with native festivities and adventure, with crooks, impostors, and, more recently, Nazi war criminals.[26] It is precisely the multivalent, unspecific, and multiply invested nature of the term "South America," in quotation marks, that makes it appropriate for an exploration and critique of the fantasy world of eighteenth- and nineteenth-century Germans.

Given Germany's colonial acquisitions in Africa and the Pacific in the late nineteenth century, a concentration on South America fantasies may seem far-fetched. However, the New World's[27] southern hemisphere was not only the first object of German colonial desire, it remained the German colonialist dream even after the German Empire actively supported settlement in Africa.[28] The continued fascination with things South American manifested itself in countless travel collections, reeditions and translations of factual and fictional reports, odes to Columbus, conquista dramas, operas, ballets, and novels, throughout the eighteenth and nineteenth centuries and well into the twentieth.[29] It produced what I would call in analogy to Said's Orientalism a German Occidentalism.

The attraction of South America rather than Africa for colonial imaginings may have been due to differences in accessibility.[30] Until late in the eighteenth century, the Spanish colonial powers kept their South American viceroyalties under lock and key, permitting only a few foreigners access to coastal towns. The idea of "hidden treasures" in someone else's possession may have provided a powerful stimulus for the imagination. Africa, on the other hand, was *terra incognita* not because some European colonial power prohibited entry, but because the exploration and appropriation of interior territories were hampered by insurmountable physical difficulties — the stifling climate, the diseases, the poverty of the land, the ferocity with which its inhabitants defended their lives and habitats against foreign predators.[31] The supposed scarcity of resources, the apparent lack of wealthy, that is, pillageable "kingdoms" may have contributed to the moderate enthusiasm for the exploration of Africa until well into the nineteenth century. In the words of the geographer E. A. W. von Zimmermann, whose musings on the reasons for the European predilection for the Americas over Africa introduced his eighteenth-century re-vision of the conquest:

> Africa placed major obstacles in the way of European penetration. Its soil was burning hot, vast expanses were desert sand, the banks of the large rivers as well as the low countries were enormously populated. . . . The Negro, furthermore, was much more manly, much more violent than the West Indian: the continued bloody wars with his kin, the slave-trade he had been engaged in since way back, had transformed many of these nations under the burning sky into wild and cruel peoples. . . . How different, how much more agreeable to the European were things in the West.[32]

Zimmermann's words suggest that in addition to the hostility of the territory and its inhabitants, there were other obstacles to blissful fantasies of colonial appropriation. The "manliness" with which African nations defended their lands precluded their feminization and the generation of fantasies of sexual appropriation so common for the South American context.[33] Furthermore, the incipient racism, apparent in the aesthetic debates on "Hottentots" and in the new anthropological and physiognomic theories enhanced the "repulsion" felt by "civilized" whites for "primitive," "ugly" blacks.[34] South America, with its promise of gold, moderate climates, abundant vegetation, and the relatively easy subjection of its inhabitants to foreign rule appeared both more known and more knowable; gentle American "redskins" with their "noble" features and beautiful bodies more desirable. By the eighteenth century, images of threatening "cannibals" that had populated the early accounts had receded into the background in favor of a more alluring picture of the natives. When the Latin American colonies shook off Spanish colonial rule in the early 1800s, the territory seemed once again available to other European competitors ready to act out colonialist fantasies in a neocolonialist environment. The former existence of highly developed, splendid pre-Columbian states, of local aristocracies and priest castes and a refined system of social stratification may have contributed to making these territories and their "noble savages" attractive to colonizers, would-be conquerors of Virgins of the Sun, bent on finding at least vestiges of the familiar in the unknown.

The interest in South America as the elusive and alluring object of desire and conquest encompassed all of Europe. In the competitive climate around the turn of the century, writers in many western European states, particularly in France and England, developed intellectual (and practical) strategies of appropriation of South American realities. To Germans, however, the continent held a particular attraction: as a missed opportunity, as the recollection of colonial failure, as a lost object to be regained through renewed efforts. Indeed, the "New World" had offered Germans their first opportunity at overseas colonization when Charles V granted the Welser merchant company the right to appropriate and explore vast territories on the South American continent, in what is now Venezuela and parts of Colombia. This first attempt at establishing a German colony was ill fated and badly executed: the Welsers were deprived of their possessions after long court battles in which they were charged with mismanaging finances and committing atrocities. The failed venture became, however, a kind of colonial primal scene, an *Urerlebnis,* that would haunt generations to come. Whereas the knowledge of German participation in massacres of native peoples was repressed or displaced by the "Black Legend," which postulated a specifically *Spanish* propensity for cruelty, memories of adventures in South America lingered on. They were retrieved and reinterpreted by nineteenth-century colonialists in search of a colonial tradition that would preordain Germany's special propensity for colonizing. The almost ritualistic revisiting and re-vision of Germany's colonial "first" throughout the latter part of the nineteenth century and the repeated attempts to cleanse Germans of any guilt suggest that the fixation on South America may also have a traumatic component.

In order to demonstrate the mechanisms at work in these colonialist re-visions and their impact on the collective unconscious, I have chosen texts that rewrite — "Germanize" — foreign texts on South America by introducing German protagonists or a peculiarly Germanic perspective and that had an impact on a wide range of German audiences. To distinguish between literary and nonliterary works or between genres did not seem productive, partly because these distinctions were not pronounced in the eighteenth century — which subsumed everything under literature — and partly because fantasies about colonial relations permeated all texts, irrespective of their intent, subject matter, or form, thus creating a network of references, an intertext that gained cultural currency.[35]

The texts range from philosophical treatises such as Corneille de Pauw's *Philosophical Investigations* (1768–1769), which was based on Buffon's *Natural History* and which left its pernicious traces everywhere, to novels for young audiences, such as Joachim Friedrich Campe's rewrite of Defoe's *Robinson Crusoe,* entitled *Robinson der Jüngere: Ein Lesebuch für Kinder* (1779–1780), a book that educated whole generations of Germans in colonizing skills. I have included plays — for example August von Kotzebue's sentimental takeoff from Marmontel's *Les Incas,* which rocked all of Europe — as well as tales and poems that represent slave rebellions or conditions in the colonies from a decidedly Germanic perspective. I examine purely fictional texts, dreamed up by armchair conquistadors, and contrast them with texts based on supposed personal experiences, in order to assess to what extent colonial fantasies came to shape even the most factual accounts of colonial "reality" by the end of the nineteenth century.

While the colonial encounter is represented as a cross-cultural, cross-racial, cross-gender romance throughout the two centuries, there are significant differences that locate the texts in their respective historical contexts. The assimilationist educational model embodied by Campe's Robinson and Friday, which sublimates sexual attraction into an eros of "cultivation," is clearly the by-product of early Enlightenment colonialism (1740–1770). The fantasy of "love at first sight" and of the voluntary surrender of Indian princesses to superior European conquerors emerges in the context of the disintegration of Spanish colonial rule and challenges to European absolutist rule in the late Enlightenment (1770–1789). It suggests a natural patriarchal order both within the absolutist state and between nations, an order the "weaker" not only accepts, but cherishes. The fantasy of legitimate bonds between colonizer and colonized ("marriage"), on the other hand, is intimately tied to times of colonial suspicion, when "slave" uprisings undermine the authority of "great white fathers" on both continents (1789–1804); whereas the fantasy of a breakup between (unequal) partners, a separation of table and bed, becomes imaginable only *after* the first instances of successful decolonization have occurred (1804–1820). The return of rape fantasies in the late 1800s, after a period of renewed interest in "discovery" and exploration of "virgin territory," finally, must be read within the context of neocolonialism and the buildup of aggressive imperialist desire. These rape fantasies could be (re)mobilized, I argue, because the idea of rape was contained, in the Hegelian sense of *aufgehoben,* in the colonial fantasies all along.

Significantly, the subconscious desire for colonies is present even in texts with an avowed anticolonialist stance, texts that denounce the cruelties committed during the conquest, such as Campe's, or texts that denigrate South American "savages," such as de Pauw's. While de Pauw's denigration of the New World and its inhabitants and Campe's exhortations on the pernicious impact of conquest on the character suggest an ideology of "Stay home and flourish" similar to Voltaire's "Il faut cultiver notre jardin," the overt sexualization of the conquest in the case of de Pauw, and the erotics of pedagogy in the case of Campe, undermine their expressed purpose. As I suggest, these texts as well as many others instill in their readers a colonialist mentality that, through their very narrative, comes "home" to roost.

Occidentalisms-Orientalisms

The connections between the "over there" and the "over here," between the colony and the home, the other and the self, are of course at the heart of all colonial fantasies. The "other" is not just out there, but forms an integral part of the self and its self-perception. The dialectics of self and other are external as well as internal; they affect the collectivity as well as the individual. This connection is not abstract or timeless, but profoundly historical and time-specific. As this study emphasizes, de Pauw's 1768 fantasy of the bearded "natural conqueror" must also be (and was) read as an antiaristocratic diatribe; Christoph Meiners's insistence in the 1790s on the natural superiority of the Germanic races over peoples of color was a wish-fulfilling dream at a time when France threatened to overtake Germany politically and culturally. Campe's education of Robinson Krusoe was also a model for domesticating little "savages" in Germany; and Kotzebue's cross-continental matrimonial fantasy expressed not just colonial desires but the German bourgeois dream of climbing socially by "conquering" a noble (but impoverished) native princess. Kleist's "earthquake in Chile," finally, shook Europe just as much as it shook the New World. Although escapist, wish-fulfilling, or universalizing, these fantasies were fully anchored in their historical reality, which they produced and reproduced.

While it is important to take note of the dialectics of self and other and the metaphorical overlap between home and abroad, such a binary approach misses the complexities of multiple positioning and the contradictions within Occidentalist discourse itself. The "discovery," in 1492, of a whole new continent to the west of Europe and Africa had already forced the "Occident" to abandon its exclusive focus on the east and south. It had expanded any simple self–other, Occident–Orient dichotomies, to include not just many others, but multiple, multivalent, constantly shifting "occidents." The discovery of Occidentals with a "new" skin color and different cultural practices from those already known had undermined the existing race geography, creating a need for new racial-cultural mappings and classifications. This need was also felt by "disinterested" German Occidentalists in the eighteenth century, who, in their attempt to position themselves vis-à-vis a variety of Oriental and Occidental, northern and southern others, sought to produce complex ideological structures: overlapping triangles and squares, with Europe/Germany at one corner, the Orient, Africa, and the Americas at the others, hierarchies of civilization, and models of organic development. They also generated a new libidinal economy that played one "other" against "an-other" — American Indians against Africans, Africans against Arabs, Arabs against Indians, Indians against Germans — and that imagined the most varied color schemes produced through "cross-breeding." The obsession with "miscegenation," with skin color variations and "improvement of the races," translated into fantasies about successful or unsuccessful "marriages" of cultures and races. The anxieties about origin, cultural status, and stages of acculturation became apparent in the discussions over a special affinity between "Germans" and "Indians," "Germans" and "Patagons," as opposed to specific disaffinities between "Germans" and "Jews," "Germans" and "Gypsies." To introduce a third, fourth, or fifth into the Occident–Orient dyad thus not only rendered the categories more dynamic; it also reinforced the notion of ambivalence, the anxieties that were operative in the colonialists' mind, anxieties about loss of sexual, racial, cultural, or recently acquired political identity.

It would be wrong to assume that the representational practices of German Occidentalist writers were monolithic; they were not, at least not at the start. Historical events such as the Haitian and French Revolutions, or political-personal circumstances inserted into their discourse a disruptive element, an element of "colonial suspicion" (Said) that undermined any facile triumphalism or any totalizing perspective. This colonial suspicion, apparent, for example, in texts by Heinrich von Kleist, Heinrich Heine, or Gottfried Keller, challenged the idea of a blissful marriage between colonizer and colonized early on, replacing it with images of deception, brutal warfare, or international "cannibalism." That the critique of the colonialist discourse and of colonial master fantasies would come from the margins (sexual, ethnic, geographical), and that it was neither recognized nor accepted, but marginalized itself, should not surprise anyone familiar with German history after 1848.

Likewise, it would be wrong to conceive of colonial fantasizing in terms of a linear, teleological development that began with a genuine curiosity about difference and ended in the Herero massacre of 1906 and the extermination of the Jews in the Third Reich. Of course there is always a danger of reading German history backward from the Holocaust. By the same token, the Holocaust has taught us to take the first stirrings of racism seriously, and to look for powerful ideological undercurrents even in times of relative tolerance and stability, undercurrents that can be activated in times of crisis. While the Holocaust was certainly not the only possible outcome of German eighteenth- and nineteenth-century history, it is the outcome with which we must contend. We need to analyze and explain why it was not the enlightened models of tolerance and assimilation that prevailed, but racism, xenophobia, sexism, and aggressive expansionism. If we concentrate on colonial fantasies rather than on the colonialist debates; if we take the stories of conquest and mastery seriously, even if they come in the guise of benign paternalism; if we are willing to explore popular writings, children's literature, and so-called *Trivialliteratur* that reached all ages and classes of German society—then we may discover that racist, xenophobic, and sexist models for action did not emerge in a vacuum, but were firmly implanted in the imagination of "precolonial" Germans, as they were reconquering their own national territory and before they would follow their "natural urge" (Friedrich Naumann)[36] to "colonize" the rest.

Armchair Conquistadors; or, The Quest for "New Germany"

Bestir yourselves, then, doughty Germans, take ye care that henceforward there be found on the map, besides New Spain, New France, New England, also New Germany. Ye are no more deficient in understanding or resolve to do such things than other nations; in truth, ye have everything that is needful for this: ye are soldiers and peasants, watchful and hard working, industrious and unflagging; ye are able to do many good things at once, through an exemplary life and good order, towards turning the Indians into friends and civilized folk, aye, mayhap even into Christians. — Johann Joachim Becher, Politischer Discurs, 1669[1]

Without a doubt Columbus's "Discovery" of the "New World" is the single most important event in the history of early modern Europe. In fact, the discovery of unknown, unheard-of lands heralded the beginning of European modernity. It literally opened up new horizons for Europeans: "virgin territories" were to be possessed and exploited; "different" realities were to be taken in, surveyed, and described; "strange" peoples were to be understood, integrated into existing categories, and subjected to European needs. The Discovery (re)generated desire: for gold, spices, land, power, the unknown; it infused the Old World with energy, with a drive for conquest. Simultaneously, however, the violent incorporation of new territories and the subjection of their peoples also produced shock and fear. As the conquest proceeded with increasing brutality and as most of the native populations were annihilated in the first years of colonial rule, many observers began to have second thoughts about the moral right to conquer and subjugate others, and to question the validity of such simple, self-serving oppositions as civilized versus barbarian, human versus inhuman, Christian versus heathen.[2] Globally speaking, the conquest was thus a process of material/physical, epistemological/intellectual, and emotional appropriation that triggered complex processes of reorientation, of spatial and ideological repositioning — not just among Europeans in contact with Native Americans, but also among Native Americans in contact with Europeans.[3] And not just among those directly involved in the conquest, but also among European bystanders, such as the Germans.

1

Tiranos animales o alemanes: Germans and the "Conquest"

Y con qué se recompensarán tan innumerables ánimas como están ardiendo en los infiernos por la cudicia e inhumanidad de aquestos tiranos animales o alemanes. — Bartolomé de las Casas, Brevísima relación, 1542¹

Ambrosius battled there with truly Swabian strength,
Albeit himself unconscious of the goal,
For Germany's cause — a hero lost to fame.
But where he planted deep the blunt end of his spear,
And where his valorous breast did bleed its last,
To the New World we reaped a rightful claim.
— *Adolph Seubert, "Ambrosius Alfinger," 1887*²

Almost from its inception, individual Germans took part in the conquest of the new territories — as adventurers or mercenaries in Spanish or Portuguese expeditions (e.g., Ulrich Schmidl, Hans Staden); as merchants outfitting and equipping ships or trading in slaves (e.g., the Welsers); as scientists, explorers, or interpreters in the service of German, Dutch, or other officials or companies.³ According to Viktor Hantzsch, thousands of German men went to the Americas, irresistibly drawn by stories of unheard-of adventures and riches — or pushed out by dire economic conditions at home.⁴

With few exceptions there existed no state-sponsored colonial enterprises. Most of the three hundred some states that comprised the Holy Roman Empire ("of German Nation") were far too small or far too poor to engage in such activities. And even the few colonial endeavors that were undertaken were short-lived and produced little revenue. The "German" colony Tobago, which Duke Jakob I of Courland had supposedly purchased from England in the mid-1600s (1634 or 1654), lasted until 1659, when it was returned to British possession; its settlers never managed to produce profitable crops for export.⁵ The trading post on St. Thomas, which the Great Elector of Brandenburg, Friedrich Wilhelm, established through negotiations with the island's Danish "owners" in 1685, had to be closed in 1731 after repeated conflicts with the Danes.[6] Friedrich Wilhelm's and his successors' further attempts to negotiate purchases or occupy islands by force as bases for their slave trade — Tobago, St. Croix, St. Eustache — were unsuccessful. Likewise, Bavarian-Dutch and French-Bavarian colonization projects in Guyana (1664–1665), and a colonial treaty between the Duke of Hanau and the Dutch West India Company for a colony between the Orinoco and the Amazon ("Hanauisch-Indien," 1669) never materialized.[7] There were various reasons why these ventures failed, among them the reduced financial means of the German principalities after the Thirty Years War and fierce competition from other colonial pretenders. Throughout the sixteenth, seventeenth, and eighteenth centuries, the German states were first and foremost struggling to establish control over their own territories, if they were not engaged in more localized "colonizing" eastward.[8] While the wealthy merchant houses of the Fuggers and Welsers lacked the political authority of a state (or the will) to claim so-called unclaimed territories, and resorted instead to indirect colonizing through financing the ventures of others, the small principalities lacked the organization, the ports, and the means to outfit fleets or send troops to conquer territories abroad. Throughout the centuries, however, while material realities precluded colonial ventures for German states, and despite considerable opposition to colonialism among some rulers, the wish to conquer, own, and exploit a tropical island grew into what Volberg termed an "obsession."[9]

The ill-fated, albeit profitable, colonial episode of the Welsers in Venezuela (1528–1555) is perhaps most indicative of the nature of German colonialism in South America during the early phases of European expansion.[10]

In 1528, the wealthy southern German merchant and banking company Bartolomä Welser, which had lent Charles V vast sums to finance his election as emperor of the Holy Roman Empire, negotiated a treaty for colonial possessions with the Spanish government. Although the South American territories remained in principle closed to foreign colonizers,[11] the Welsers were given exceptional status: they would be allowed to conquer, settle, rule, and exploit a hitherto unknown region located between the province of Santa Marta and Cabo de la Vela in the west and the Cabo Maracapaná in the east, and from the Atlantic Ocean in the north to the "South Sea" in the south — roughly the territory of today's Venezuela and part of Colombia. The wealthy financiers would thus help the Spaniards expand and secure their colonial holdings, while doing some colonizing and profiteering on the side. In a series of (unconnected) subcontracts, the two agents of the Welsers, Heinrich Ehinger and Hieronymus Sailer, focused on three areas: mining, slave trade, and settlement. The company agreed to hire fifty German miners as instructors and administrators to improve mining in the Caribbean region; they received license to import and sell four thousand black slaves to increase the labor force in the area; and they agreed to bring over a determined number of colonists to work the newly "acquired" South American territories. In order to carry out this task, Charles V granted the Welsers the privilege, under Spanish sovereignty, to choose governors and military (*capitán general*) and administrative heads (*alguacil, adelantado mayor, teniente*) for the new acquisitions, to appropriate twenty-five Spanish square miles of land for their own use, and to collect, in addition to the salaries for the administrators, 4 percent of the profit that was to be transferred to the Crown. In order to establish the colony economically, they were freed from taxation for eight years and from paying the "fifth" for precious metals for three years.[12] In exchange for these privileges, the new rulers agreed to settle the colony within two years, found two settlements with three hundred inhabitants each, erect three forts, and establish a functioning colonial administration.

All contemporary historians agree that a host of factors ensured the failure of this colonial venture from its inception. Competition between the Welsers and the Spanish colonial administration—the Real Audiencia in Santo Domingo, the Consejo de Indias in Spain, and the Spanish Crown—between Spanish and German administrators and governors in the colony, and between the interests of the German merchants and those of the predominantly Spanish settlers led to physical and legal power struggles.[13] Keen on making quick profits and fully aware that their presence in Venezuela might be short-lived since it depended on the goodwill of the Spanish authorities, the Augsburg merchants did not so much support a peaceful, long-term settlement policy as a series of destructive and disruptive sallies into the interior in search of "El Dorado." When the explorers, notably the governors Ambrosius Alfinger,[14] Nikolaus Federmann, and Jörg Hohermuth von Speier (Jorge de Espira), failed to discover and loot wealthy "Indian kingdoms," secure a flow of precious metals, and appease the settlers with quick profits, they turned increasingly to capturing and selling Indians as slaves to make up for the loss in anticipated colonial revenue. As a consequence, remnants of the oppressed Indian tribes, ever more suspicious of any foreign settlement, withdrew from the coast into the less accessible interiors. Without gold, without tradable goods, and without slave labor, the German colony of Venezuela eventually collapsed, and, although a series of law suits did not confirm allegations of financial or legal wrongdoings, had to be returned into Spanish possession in 1555.[15]

In the imagination of subsequent generations of Germans, this ill-fated, poorly executed colonial enterprise with its many near-discoveries of fabulous peoples (dwarves, Amazons)[16] and rich "king-doms" gained special status as a kind of colonial "urnarrative." Particularly for nineteenth-century colonialists, the Welser episode became the story of the origin of the German colonial movement, a "German" first. It marked the moment when a German conquistador — the elusive Ambrosius Alfinger from Ulm — "planted deep the blunt end of his spear" into the virgin soil of South America, as Seubert's poem of 1887 puts it, and in which a German martyr, by fertilizing the foreign soil with his blood, established German paternity/property rights over the new territories. As a story of copulation between German conqueror and native soil this urnarrative became the urfantasy underlying all future German colonial fantasies directed at South America. Significantly, in the imagination of its nineteenth-century narrator, "Germany's" first encounter with the New World was not so much a romance with a female other, as the story of lone heroism and sacrifice, a *Blut und Boden* soldier's tale of male (re)generation through contact with foreign soil. As a story of failure ("a forgotten hero"), failed paternity so to speak, the story of the Welser's conquest raised a series of questions that were implicitly alluded to in future colonial fantasies.

The failure of the German colony in Venezuela produced in subsequent generations of German colonialists a nagging frustration for having arrived "too late" on the colonial scene. Federmann reached the land of the *Muiscas* in the Andes shortly after Gonzalo Jiménez de Quesada had invaded and laid his hands on that advanced, wealthy civilization. Likewise, the German princes never found a territory or an island that did not yet "belong" to Spain, Portugal, England, France, Denmark, or the Netherlands. And in the nineteenth century, when massive state-sponsored colonial expansion finally seemed possible, it was feared that the world had already been subdivided and "given away," as a line in Schiller's famous poem "The Partition of the World" suggested, leaving no more space for the establishment of a "New Germany" abroad.[17]

The shock of having come too late was reinforced by doubts as to Germans' ability to colonize. The loss of colonies Germans had actually possessed would lead to a continued preoccupation with the causes of that loss in the nineteenth century: Had the Welsers lost the colonies because of the "envy" of other colonial powers and because of lack of strength to defend their own entitlements? Or had they lost them because of concentrating too much on looting and trading and too little on establishing viable long-term agricultural settlements? The answers to these questions depended on the political agenda of those who asked. Advocates of economic imperialism tended toward the foreign competition argument (e.g., Hübbe-Schleiden, Hassert, Hantzsch);[18] advocates of settlement or emigrationist colonialism toward a critique of military expansionism at the expense of peaceful colonization (Simonsfeld). However, both positions were often alluded to simultaneously (Fabri, Peters) to garner widespread support for a repeat of the colonial performance.[19]

The third cluster of concerns that appears as a leitmotiv throughout the centuries has to do with the question of Germany's share in "colonial guilt," that is, German participation in the enslavement, mistreatment, and annihilation of the indigenous populations. The issue was first raised by Bartolomé de las Casas in his *Brevísima relación sobre la destruición de las Indias,* written in 1542 and published in 1545, during the last stages of the Welsers' colonial experiment in Venezuela. The discussion of the role some Germans had played in the conquest — or the careful sidestepping of that discussion — is indicative of how the Welser narrative served not just as colonial urnarrative, but as linchpin in the formulation of German national character. The telling and retelling of the story, and the subtle and not so subtle maneuvers to exonerate "Germans" produced, in fact, a discourse of Germanness.

Las Casas, the Spanish Dominican friar and later bishop of Chiapas, provided the first impetus for a nationalization of the question of colonial guilt. In his *Brevísima relación* he had denounced not only the cruelty of the Spanish conquistadors, but that of the "animales alemanes," the German animals or bestial Germans. The German merchants were, he affirmed, even more cruel, more ferocious, more greedy than their Spanish counterparts:

> Those merchants, upon entering the land with three hundred or more men, encountered people as tame as sheep, as were all the native peoples in the Indies everywhere, until they suffered injury at the hands of the Spaniards.

And here [in Venezuela] were committed, I believe, incomparably more cruelties than those we have described, acts more irrational and ferocious than any inflicted by the most ferocious lions and tigers and rabid wolves. Because the actions were carried out with more avidity and blind greed, with more subtle determination to rob the Indians of their gold and silver than all the tyrants who had gone before.[20]

While the friar's apparent hostility against the "Lutheran heretics" served to explain the vehemence of his denunciation, the facts he reported — the burning and beheading of resisting natives, the chaining, branding, and selling of Indian slaves — were powerful spiritual weapons to contend with.[21] His verdict forms the backdrop of subsequent attempts to assess German colonizers in relation to others: were they worse, were they better, or were they like everyone else? Whoever retold the story of the Welser colony felt called upon to respond — overtly or covertly — to what Juan Friede termed the "Black Legend" against all German conquistadors: the fear of a specific German proneness for cruelty.[22]

The general political context and the interest of the writers determined the strategies of denial, repression, or denunciation they employed. In the years of the Dutch uprising, the German participation in colonial violence was played down till it almost got lost in the larger Spanish-Dutch, or Catholic-Protestant conflict. During the Enlightenment and late-eighteenth-century revolutions, Las Casas's denunciation fused with the universal moral verdict against tyrants and barbarians of all nations. In the years of rising German nationalism and growing colonial interest, it was "contextualized" or simply brushed aside, to be replaced by a counterstory: the story of Germany's specific propensity for colonizing based on superior qualifications — and on a history of colonial innocence.[23]

The first German translation of the *Brevísima relación,* which appeared in 1597 and was reprinted in 1599, with slight changes in 1613 and 1665, already displaces the German share in colonial guilt by focusing almost exclusively on Spanish atrocities.[24] Its anti-Spanish thrust — the address to the reader rallies support for a Dutch rebellion against Spain — manifests itself, for example, in the summaries of the arguments in the margins of the text. Whereas the text clearly refers to the German merchants as "demonios encarnados" [devils incarnate], the marginal notes, more often than not, attribute the atrocities to the Spanish settlers alone: "Spaniards catch the ruler in Venezuela and kill the Indians mercilessly"; "Spaniards gobble up what the Indians had stored"; or "Spanish ungratefulness toward the Indians." Even in the last paragraph, which addresses the Welsers' slave trade, the commentary integrates, once more, the German actions into the larger Spanish picture, thereby diluting the attack: "Unheard-of tyranny of Spaniards and Germans" (79). The translator employs the passive voice frequently to obfuscate agency. Unlike the Spanish original, he often leaves open who did what by cutting connections between nouns and pronouns or by generalizing.[25] He also omits Las Casas's aside against the German Lutheran heretics, which might have placed Las Casas in the Catholic camp, undermining his credibility for Protestant readers and hence the translator's "protestant" project. The illustrations to the text which, like broadsides with captions, are appended to the text separately, depict only Spanish atrocities. Subsequently integrated into the text itself (but not in the chapter on Venezuela), they do not underscore Las Casas's contention that the Germans were incomparably more cruel than all the other conquistadors, but reinforce the Black Legend vis-à-vis Spain: the Spaniards are the true devils incarnate.

German atrocities toward the indigenous, particularly the Amerindians', enslavement, are indirectly alluded to in two texts that are not translations of Las Casas's but colonial projects whose ideological direction connects them with the Early Enlightenment: Johann Daniel Kraft's memos on a future "East- and West Indian Company of High-German Nation" of 1666 and Johann Jakob Becher's 1669 treatise on mercantilism and colonialism, *Politischer Discurs.*[26] Both of them delineate an ideal German colony, populated by honest, hardworking settlers who work the soil and produce agrarian products for export (97, 157), gaining riches not through exploitation of the natives or futile search for gold and silver, but through their own labor. Becher's treatise consciously departs from the Welserian models and espouses the perspective of Las Casas insofar as he advocates leaving the native population in peace. Instead of a systematic Christianization of the Indians, he suggests that settlers serve as role models so that the Indians will eventually assimilate and collaborate with Christians on a voluntary basis. Like Las Casas, he includes black slavery as part of his colonial setup, on account of the Africans' greater propensity for hard labor.[27] His *Political Discourse* paints an almost idyllic picture of colonial relations: "The moor is a fine creature for agriculture, for they [*sic*] are accustomed to heat and labor; they get no remuneration beyond a free day a week, along with a small plot of land, which is so fertile that it feeds them during the remaining days of the week; if one could buy such peasants in Germany, what would it not be worth, and yet, what could they do there that would measure up to the Indies."[28] Although Becher does not mention Las Casas, the friar's indictment is implicit in the peaceful, agriculturally oriented German "model" settler.

For almost two hundred years, the 1597 translation remained the only available German edition of Las Casas's *Brevísima relación.* The next German translation, which appeared in 1790, exhibits a very different approach to the text: no introduction, no marginal notes accompany this faithful, moving, even dramatic recasting of Las Casas's pamphlet. A footnote to the first paragraph of this translation identifies "certain German merchants" as the Welsers: "As is known, it was the Welsers in Augsburg. They had advanced great sums of money to Charles V who in return pawned them this province."[29] The translator, D. W. Andreä, even attempts to reproduce Las Casas's wordplay by speaking about the "inhumanity of those beastly tyrants, the Germans" ["Unmenschlichkeit jener viehischen Tyrannen, der Deutschen," 152], although the pun *animales-alemanes* proves once again untranslatable. The responsibility for slave trade and the annihilation of native populations in Venezuela thus clearly rests with the German perpetrators, although the few comments do not emphasize a specific nation. The humanitarian concern that informs this translation becomes evident in those places where the translator renders Las Casas's "tan nefandos tiranos" with "diese vermaledeiten Barbaren" (150): barbarians, in eighteenth-century discourse, captures less the political aspects, than the moral dimension of the colonial enterprise; it puts German and other conquistadors claiming to belong to superior civilizations in their place.[30] Violent colonization is thus condemned as a general moral transgression, not attached to any specific "nation." The blindness to "German" colonial complicity is reproduced, albeit in a different way, in the two German reviews of the new Las Casas translation: while the reviewer in *Allgemeine deutsche Bibliothek* places the burden of responsibility completely on the Spaniards,[31] the *Allgemeine Literatur-Zeitung*—without mentioning German participation—laments Las Casas's exaggerations and lack of credibility, asking: "Why then do we need another translation of this often translated book, which makes a certainly not ignoble nation into monsters such as the earth has perhaps never borne?"[32] Finally, J. J. Engel's imaginative rendition of Las Casas's final thoughts, "Apotheosis of Las Casas; or, Sources of Peace of Mind" (1795),[33] only vaguely alludes to the "pitch-black names of those ruthless people, who killed a million innocents through sword, torture, and slavery within fifteen years," without naming either Germans or Spaniards.

The only eighteenth-century account of the Welser episode that mentions "German" perpetrators plays down the national at the expense of the individual. Paul von Stetten inserts in his factual report of the Welsers' financial dealings references to "Dalfinger's" and Federmann's "great cruelty," a judgment that is clearly derived from Las Casas's *Brevísima relación*.[34] The immorality of these "adventurers," their unwillingness to execute their masters' orders, their selfish greed is contrasted with the Welsers' wisdom and probity. The conquistadors' moral flaws not only caused their "well-deserved" demise (235), according to von Stetten, but jeopardized the Welsers' colonial enterprise forever: "Thus the Welsers lost a property that no German could ever or will ever be able to pride himself in owning" (239).[35]

The Welsers' failure to establish a viable South American colony met with increasing interest in post-Revolutionary Germany. Bartolomé de las Casas's popularity as critic of colonialism and its "tyrants" during the French Revolution and subsequent independence movements in Latin America, with which many Germans had sympathized, made it impossible to ignore his denunciation of German atrocities.[36] Nineteenth-century propagators and historians of colonialism, furthermore, felt the need to review and reevaluate the activities of these "honest" merchants — this time, however, in a decidedly national context. Now, the Augsburg merchants are identified with "Germany" and depicted as German representatives. The nationalist circles that advocate liberation from French imperialism as well as the formation of German colonies feel compelled to employ a variety of strategies to circumvent Las Casas's allegations in order to mitigate the Germans' share of guilt. Karl von Klöden (1855), for example, bases his sketchy and error-ridden account of the Welser colony predominantly on Las Casas, without identifying his source.[37] Yet while Klöden denounces the brutality of Ambrosius Alfinger and his expedition corps,[38] he praises as "good" conquistador Philipp von Hutten, who, in his account, becomes "one of us," "our knight." The opposition of good conquistadors (us) and bad conquistadors (them) forms the moral framework within which colonial activity is judged. Klöden never questions colonialism as such. On the contrary, he defends it as a means to establish order by preventing gangs of greedy, unruly pirates and adventurers from pillaging (435). In the course of his narration, the good conquistador, the good German who invites identification ("a German heart, of course, can sympathize more easily with another German's, with its sorrow, pain, anxiety, fear, hope and good fortunes, than with any stranger's," 442) eclipses the bad German, who is furthermore displaced by the even more evil Juan de Carvajal ("maybe there never was an eviler man," 440). In the end, "our Hutten" stands tall, as the glowing example of the German conquistador who is not motivated by greed and who treats the "natives" humanely.

A similar distinction between good and bad conquistadors appears in Karl Klunzinger's 1857 account of the Welser debacle, yet with less moralistic overtones.[39] Although Klunzinger declares Las Casas's allegations to be "exaggerations" (111), he still includes passages from the *Brevísima relación* as an appendix to his history of Germany's "share in the discovery of South America." Klunzinger's comments are characterized by the attempt to relativize Alfinger's cruelties in relation to those committed by Spanish conquistadors: "When according to Las Casas he would fall into the same category as Francisco Pizarro, Barthold and Richard von Treitschke call him the German Cortez; Adolph Seubert, moreover, lists him among his stars of Swabia" (65). The only truly cruel person, Klunzinger affirms, was Alfinger's Spanish military commander, Francisco de Castillo.

The accounts written during the heyday of German colonialism obfuscate or obliterate any German share in colonial guilt even more blatantly. Viktor Hantzsch, writing in 1895, considers the Welsers German prototypes, incarnations of "German industry and capital, German learning and entrepreneurial spirit"; their conquest becomes a truly national enterprise, "ein wahrhaft nationales Unternehmen."[40] While Hantzsch denounces atrocities committed by individuals, he attempts to contextualize these acts: they can be explained by circumstances. Bad characteristics of individuals are mitigated by recourse to a positive German national character: Federmann was not "bereft of crudeness . . . but full of German fighting spirit and *Wanderlust*" (33); Alfinger, "a brave soldier, a capable leader, a skilful administrator, a strict supervisor," although not "without a quick temper and cruelty" was loyal and true, "a genuine German soldier of the lansquenet times" (35). For Kurt Hassert, an ardent advocate of German colonialism and frequent contributor to the mouthpiece of the German Colonial Society, *Beiträge zur Kolonialpolitik und Kolonialwirtschaft,* the Welser enterprise has similar nationalistic overtones. While "national capital" [*vaterländisches Kapital*] and German enterprising spirit were, in the long run, unable to secure Germans a part in the "wonderlands" of the New World, Germans can look back with pride and nostalgia to the actions of "our German pioneers in Venezuela."[41] Konrad Haebler, finally, writing in 1903,[42] relies less on a distinction between good and bad conquistadors or "tough" but "goodly" Germans and cruel Spaniards than on one between bad conquistadors, such as Federmann (263), and good merchants, such as the Welser governors, paragons of "German enterprising spirit, German endurance, and German energy" (397). As he almost triumphantly states, Las Casas, in a chapter "dictated by burning hatred" (158), erred — not only when he attributed many atrocities to Alfinger and consorts, but when he calculated German profits from slavery: they were in fact much higher. The annihilation of the natives of Venezuela, he concludes, cannot be charged to the Welsers alone, "probably not even to them in the first place" (160). Haebler, although willing to engage in discussions about colonial abuses, locates his history of the Venezuelan colony squarely in the context of contemporary imperialism. German colonizers are different from other Europeans; indeed, the rare combination of martial energy and "protestant" entrepreneurial pragmatism exhibited by the Welser governors prefigures the modern Prussian imperialist.[43]

The issue of slavery, and particularly black slavery, which had resurfaced in late-eighteenth-century abolitionist discourse, is hardly touched upon in these revisions of colonial history. It was, of course, known that the Augsburg merchants, as well as the Brandenburg monarchs, had made their profits from slave trade. The Welsers had sold "hostile" Indians (*indios de guerra*) they had captured in "just wars" on the continent to planters on the islands. They had traded natives who had already been enslaved in intertribal wars for goods (*indios por rescate*), and transported black slaves from Africa to the Spanish colonies.[44] The Brandenburgers had bought blacks from slave hunters in their African outpost Gross-Friedrichsburg and sold them in St. Thomas. This dirty past became a dirty secret, which was only reluctantly unearthed and confronted by a few accounts later in the century.

Describing the trade in "black merchandise" that "unfortunately" constituted the foundation of the company, Richard Schück (1889) feels compelled to add that the Brandenburgers may have dealt with blacks more humanely than other nations, since they allowed infants to stay with their mothers (331). Hassert, who admits that the slave trade played a large part in the Welsers' project ("cannot be denied"), immediately dilutes his moral judgment by discrediting Las Casas, laying equal blame on all other colonial competitors, and finding fault with the "Indians" themselves; after all, they were not the "peaceful children of nature" that Las Casas had depicted, but "warring, in part cannibalistic savages, which, through incessant attacks and poisoned arrows, constituted a constant danger for the settlers" (299). Significantly, in the representation of one of the main Nazi propagators of colonial *Lebensraum*, Ernst Wilhelm Bohle, slavery or forced labor do not appear at all: the Welsers are just the recipients of an "honest family fief" [*ehrliches Familienlehen*] in Venezuela in return for their services; the Great Elector did not trade in slaves, but provided blacks with "protection" against slave traders, which caused many tribes to seek shelter in and around the German colony. Clearly, by 1941, the "animales alemanes" had metamorphosed into "kind white men who did not rob slaves and did much good to the natives."[45]

As this short history of the reception of the Welser episode makes clear, the Welsers' failure as colonizers and Las Casas's indictment of "German" colonialism had a major impact on later generations of Germans. In almost obsessive revisitings and reworkings, the violent and by no means glorious story of the Welsers' failed colonization of South America[46] was transformed into the foundational fiction of Germany's colonial origins, and of colonizing as a specifically German calling. In fact, the retelling of the Welser story helped to circumscribe German national identity by creating a national self as colonizer. The frustrations, self-doubts, and moral qualms — over having come too late and having done too little, and over Germans' complicity in colonial atrocities — were repressed in favor of a positive, affirmative, upbeat fantasy, which ended in an emphatic "no": no, Germany had not come too late — there was still territory to be had; no, Germans were not incompetent colonizers — on the contrary: their proverbial courage, industry, and organizational talent predestined them for that vocation; and no, Germans had no share in colonial guilt — their innocence in fact legitimized their claim to be given another chance. In other words, the "subtext" of failure was converted into, and contained by, an ultimately triumphalist fantasy. This fantasy hinged on a perpetual "what if": what if Germans had not failed in their first attempt at colonization? What if Germans were able to start anew? It filled the three hundred years since the Discovery and an imaginary future. In the words of the colonial revisionist Kurt Hassert, "How completely different the world would look today, if during those centuries that produced from modest beginnings the mighty naval powers of Western Europe, a powerful Germany had emerged, too, a Germany able to accommodate its population surplus in its own colonies rather than losing it as cultural fertilizer to others."[47] This perennial "what if" then proved a powerful stimulus for the imagination, the starting point for all colonial fantasies invented or reinvented by Germans between 1770 and 1870. Filling an absence, a void, these fantasies were compensatory fantasies, blueprints of a future reality. Even if a Neu-Deutschland had not materialized the first time around, it seemed, there was ample space for a New Germany — on paper.

2

A Conquest of the Intellect

Thus the eighteenth-century's spirit of enquiry has, as it were, discovered for us a new world in the New World, for the second time! — E. A. W. Zimmermann, Rückblick auf die neue Welt, *1809*[1]

Columbus, sailing through an unknown sea, and gathering directions from the stars with the recently invented astrolabe, searched for Asia by way of the West, according to a firm plan, not as an adventurer who entrusts his fate to chance. The success he obtained was a conquest of the intellect. — Alexander von Humboldt, Examen critique de l'histoire de la géographie du nouveau continent, *1837*[2]

The fantasy world of eighteenth-century Germans was nurtured by more than past colonial glory or mishap. Contemporary travels, contemporary explorations and investigations, captured the imagination of the German reading public just as much, if not more. Having emerged from the devastating effects of the Thirty Years War, the many states comprising the "Holy Roman Empire of the German Nation" were busily trying to consolidate their borders, rebuild their economies, explore, settle, and "colonize" their interiors. As roads and bridges were built to facilitate this process of reconstruction, and as commercial exchange between principalities increased, travel became a new way of experiencing and understanding the world. If the sixteenth century was the century of conquest and colonization, the eighteenth century was the "century of travels."[3] As one German observer put it: "No other era in world history has known more travelers than our century, indeed, traveling has become an epidemic."[4] As the aristocratic *grand tour* gave way to more bourgeois forms of cultural tourism, and as travel became more comfortable and affordable, the number of German travelers as well as the distances covered and the locations visited increased exponentially, to encompass eventually all of western Europe. The increasing "bourgeoisification" of travel also brought with it changes in motivation. Gradually, the *Bildungsreise* [educational tour] of young academics, artists, and writers, which had replaced the *Ge-lehrtenreise* [scholarly tour] of the Early Enlightenment, gave way to less aesthetically oriented, more pragmatic kinds of travels.[5] Toward the end of the century and particularly in the early 1800s, trips to the financial and political capitals of Europe, London, and Paris, would take precedence over the formerly popular tours to Italy or Sicily — at least for those interested in current affairs or commerce rather than ancient ruins.

The travel mania was accompanied by a travelogue mania. "More than ever, real travelogues have gone out of control," the same anonymous commentator who noted the traveling epidemic wrote, "they are legions [*eine unübersehbare Armee*]! Practically nobody in Germany takes a pleasure ride in the coach just for its own sake, or rides on horseback, or goes for a walk — no, north and south have to hear about it, have to read the worthy man's experiences and — what is worse — read his reflections on these experiences!"[6] The critic's open disdain for the low quality of this popular, populist genre may have veiled a more profound anxiety over loss of class privilege (pleasure rides for their own sake). It indicates the degree to which *Reiselust, Wanderlust,* the desire for adventure, movement, empirical experience was captivating increasingly larger segments of the German population. It also indicates a shift in literary tastes.

Although precise numbers vary, estimates suggest that while the general book production in Germany doubled between 1770 and 1800, travelogues alone increased by a factor of five.[7] As Thomas Grosser notes, by the end of the century "travel literature had become the most important medium of information on foreign countries."[8] Travel accounts had become so popular that even geographic compendia tended to appear under the rubric of "travelogue" in order to attract a wider public, while novels disguised themselves as "true travel relations." By 1784, German readers had become the primary consumers of travelogues in Europe.[9] In fact, while the number of travelers rose gradually, the number of armchair explorers participating vicariously in travels skyrocketed.

At the same time that the rising bourgeoisie "discovered" Europe and registered the regional, ethnic, class, and political differences within its boundaries,[10] individual explorers and scientists in the service of academic and/or economic interests pressed ahead in their discoveries abroad. The exploration of the — by now old — New World of South America and the "Eighteenth-Century's New World"[11] of the Pacific was principally undertaken by French and British officers and scholars, representatives of the new competitors in the colonial arena: Amédée François Frézier (Chile, Peru, and Brazil 1712–1714), Charles Marie de la Condamine (Ecuador, Peru, Brazil, 1736–1745), John Byron (Patagonia, 1740–1746), Lord Anson (1740–1744), and James Cook (1768–1779), to name just the most prominent. With the principal trade routes and port facilities known, interest in South America became now directed toward the continent's interiors. As the Spanish authorities reluctantly permitted entry into their colonies to — albeit few — foreign scientists, the exploration of interior regions, peoples, and resources replaced the former concern for mapping coastal outlines.[12] Dense jungles, steep mountain passes, and hidden natural riches became now a focus of real and imaginary pursuits.

While Germans fully shared in the European *Reisefieber,* only very few — compared to British or French explorers of the period — managed to travel beyond the boundaries of Europe. To be able to travel to Central and South America, they had to be independently wealthy (Humboldt), sponsored and financed by religious institutions such as the Jesuit order (Dobritzhofer, Nussbacher), or employed by foreign governments, such as the mining experts and/or natural scientists Haenke, von Nordenflycht, Helms, or Johann Reinhold and Georg Forster. Furthermore, in order to obtain a travel permit, it was necessary to procure the explicit support and protection from the colonial rulers, who had traditionally been loath to allow strangers into their territories or operations. If we are to judge by the travelogues published, the number of Germans who traveled to the New World in the eighteenth century — or who found something interesting to tell — was minuscule.[13]

Although comparatively few Germans actually participated in the expeditions to unknown territories, many took great interest in these exotic travels, as the large number of travelogues on the New World published in Germany indicates. Like other travel literature, writings on Latin America increased slowly in the first half of the eighteenth century, growing like an avalanche throughout the second. Whereas travel literature in general multiplied fivefold, German travelogues focusing on South America increased by a factor of eight: from about fifty titles in the years 1700 to 1750 to over four hundred between 1750 and 1800.[14] Most of these texts were not new accounts, nor were they originally written in German. Most were in fact translations from other European languages, pirate editions, or reprints of older texts that regained importance in contrast to or in conjunction with the more recent output. Nor were they all travelogues in the narrow sense, but summaries of, reflections on, or critiques of travelogues and the materials found therein. Indeed, travel accounts served as raw material for collected and "readers' digest" editions, geography texts, philosophical treatises, histories, novels, book reviews, and journalistic articles that swamped the book market after 1770.[15] "Voluminous" collections, such as the twenty-one-volume *General History of Travels by Sea and by Land* (*Allgemeine Historie der Reisen zu Wasser und zu Lande* [Leipzig, 1747–1774]), the thirty-five-volume *Collection of the Best and Most Recent Travelogues* (*Sammlung der besten und neuesten Reisebeschreibungen,* edited by J. F. Zückert [Berlin, 1777–1802]), or the thirty-one-volume *Collection of Curious New Travelogues from Foreign Languages* (*Magazin von merkwürdigen neuen Reisebeschreibungen aus fremden Sprachen* [Berlin, 1790–1810]) promised German readers not just "complete" information on travels around the globe, but "the best" and "the most recent." Histories, geographies, and philosophical "investigations" mapped, classified, and ordered this information; political articles actualized and complemented travel accounts; journals excerpted them; and book reviews commented on them. In their totality, these writings engaged all armchair travelers in a constant dialogue on and textualization of an ever more known and ever more accessible world, and an ever more mysterious or desirable "South America." If we add the titles of belletristic literature, of the South America fictions, Columbus epics, Robinsonades, and conquest plays to this list of travelogues and socio-economic-political commentaries, the continued infatuation with South America throughout the nineteenth century — despite a shift of attention to North America after 1776 — becomes even more striking.

To explain the meaning of this growing fascination in Germany with the colonized territories in the South/West — a fascination that literary scholars have hitherto ignored or played down[16] — it is important to analyze the nature of the texts in circulation: the shifts in authors, genre, subject matter, and geographic focus that occurred in the years between 1700 and 1830.

The first half of the eighteenth century constituted a transition between earlier myth-laden forms of encounter literature and later, more scientifically oriented texts. Reprints of older Spanish relations of the Discovery and conquest (Las Casas, Vespucci, Acuña) alternate with contemporary descriptions of travels by European explorers (Dampier,

Wafer, Frézier, Anson) or of exotic peoples (Lafitau, Vandiera, Orellana). Scientific accuracy coexists, even conflates with myth. Particularly noteworthy is the authors' continued preoccupation with mythical figures, such as Amazons, giants, and "headless men" (acéphales), as well as with mythical spaces (El Dorado), although the function of these myths seems to have changed. They no longer express the sense of wonder the first explorers felt upon taking in the new reality, but attest more to a preoccupation with normalcy and deviation typical of the rationalist eighteenth century (see part 2 of this book).

From about 1750 on, the nature of the travel literature changed profoundly.[17] Travel accounts became more diverse, more geared toward contemporary political developments, and more "scientific," that is, more focused on collecting information that could be integrated into global systems of knowledge. In addition to individual travel relations there were now multiple series or travelogue collections that combined all that was known about particular continents from the earliest times of discovery and exploration to the most recent. There were short journalistic pieces concentrating on the current state of a particular island or colony, as well as investigations into the history and "natural history" of entire peoples, usually written by Jesuits or Dominican missionaries who had spent many years among the "savages." Empirical observations of the flora, fauna, or tropical diseases specific to a region alternated with theories of origin and difference. Works for adults were complemented by books written specifically for a young audience. In short, there was a totalizing impulse to amass information, order it synchronically into geographies, diachronically into histories, and vertically into hierarchies of moral and cultural development, and make this structured information accessible to all strata and ages of the educated bourgeois public.[18]

As the century progressed, these three new trends in the literature on South America—toward diversification, actualization, and scientific globalization—became even more pronounced. Clearly, they were a function of the crisis the old colonial order was experiencing. The trend toward greater diversification of authors, topics, and regions marked the greater participation by more nations in the construction of new realities, or, possibly, the *desire* for greater participation. Diverse genres provided different means of approaching these distant realities. Short journalistic forms, for example, allowed for quick ways of "covering" an event, of inserting new developments into preexisting structures. Histories or philosophical treatises, on the other hand, created stable frameworks that organized firsthand observation into large-scale developmental models. Through representation of colonial scenarios and identificatory strategies (e.g., by inventing German protagonists), novels or plays anchored these perceptions in the imagination of their readers. The trend toward both actualization and historicization responded to a need to survey the colonial past in order to understand and legitimize the present. To read books of first encounters side by side with contemporary accounts not only permitted the readers to conceive of the history of the New World in terms of "colonial history," or rather, the inscription of Europeans into the New World, to the exclusion of "pre-Columbian" history; it also provided for a framework within which past performance could be criticized, change could be theorized, and the reading subject could insert himself as imaginary future agent. The trend toward the systematization of knowledge [*Verwissenschaftlichung*] and toward globalization, finally, allowed not just explorers, but armchair travelers to engage in conquest and exploration activity by establishing intellectual hegemony over elusive, resistant, even contradictory materials. Travelogues, the peoples and the territories they described, became common intellectual property, the raw material that was reworked, reshaped into European theories. "The Indian" became a European creation.

The trends in the book market were intimately connected with political developments in the colonies and in Europe: the deterioration of the colonial administration in the Spanish colonies and the attempts by the Spanish Crown to regain its control over them; the gradual opening of colonial boundaries to international trade due to economic pressures; the increasing competition and even warfare of European powers in the Caribbean region; a redefinition of the power and spheres of interests of church and state ("the Jesuit question"); and, last but not least, the emergence of abolitionism as a moral cause, which culminated in the slave revolution in Saint-Domingue and the establishment of the first free black nation.

The links between the dissolution of colonial control and political "actualization" in the South America literature are manifest, for example, in the cluster of texts dealing with the Jesuit question, their states (*reducciones*) in Paraguay and Peru before 1759, their wars against the Spanish and Portuguese Crowns, and their expulsion from South America and eventual prohibition (1773). Between 1756 and 1774, twenty-three book-length texts in German, written by Jesuits in exile and by government officials, attempted to engage their readers in the polemic involving the Jesuit order, the Catholic Church, and the Spanish state, a topic of particular interest to Germans, since German Jesuits had also been part of the colonizing efforts in Paraguay and Peru. By being intellectually involved in contemporary struggles and controversies, German readers could gain at least the illusion of direct participation.

This same intellectual-moral involvement centered on the revolutionary events in Saint-Domingue, which produced a plethora of writings on the pros and cons of the plantation system. Here, moral positions on slavery expressed in earlier overviews[19] and sympathetic accounts of the abolitionist debates in England clashed with reports by plantation owners of the atrocities committed by the black rebels. While German readers may have had fewer personal connections to these issues — although there had been a steady trickle of German immigrants to the Caribbean regions[20] — the question of revolutionary upheaval and change of the traditional order did bear immediately on their own situation in the revolutionary wars in Europe (see chapter 8). Indeed, the rebellion of the "slaves" on Caribbean islands could (and did) serve as a metaphor, and, in a way, as a war by proxy for Germans anticipating or fearing the rebellion of the "rabble" against their own feudal aristocracy at home.[21]

The renewed international competition for the Caribbean islands in the late eighteenth century is evident in a considerable increase in reports on the current political-economic situation of the French, British, and Dutch colonies there. Titles such as "Attempt at a Description and History of the Antillian Islands" or "Short Description of the Islands Recently Captured by the British Naval Power" abound, indicating an interest not only in the islands themselves, but in the fact that the colonial situation is in flux, and that colonies can change masters, depending on who is militarily stronger. To German (and probably not just to German) readers, "islands" had been synonymous with "colony" ever since Defoe's *Robinson Crusoe* had initiated an avalanche of *Robinsonades,* among them Schnabel's influential *Die Insel Felsenburg* (1731–1743), in which German colonists establish a model colony on a fictitious island. In the imagination of German readers, these fictions linked the memory of earlier German colonial attempts (the Great Elector's bid for a Caribbean island, see chapter 1) with the current European scramble. The many reprints of older travelogues side by side with recent historic-geographic-political island descriptions mark a new awareness of "colonial history," as a history of European battles over control of foreign territory, a history that is still in the making. It is a history in which Germans could become agents again, as J. F. E. Albrecht's fantasy play *Die Kolonie* of 1793 elaborates, presenting the history of a German family who build a peaceful colony ("neue Welt") on a formerly uninhabited island, thus establishing their place in the New World.

The peculiar voracity of Germans for travel literature raises a number of questions. What were the specifically German interests that fed the explosive growth of travelogues? How did Germans share in this literary "production" of South America? And did their contribution differ substantially from that of others?

Since most of the texts were translations of foreign sources, one might argue that there was no such thing as a specifically German preoccupation with South America. I suggest, however, that there was indeed a special role, function, or interest for Germans, which derived from their position as outsider looking in. Precisely because they were not involved in current colonizing activity and had no apparent interest at stake, German readers were freer to assume the distanced, "disinterested" voice of the critic who discusses issues "systematically" and "in principle."[22] Hence they compiled, edited, evaluated, and processed any information available on colonial activities. They examined the authenticity of reports and questioned their veracity.[23] They went back to the sources and compared them with newer documents. A critical awareness of the tendency to fictionalize and an endeavor to separate myth from fact characterized most of their comments. In the words of Johann Bernoulli, editor of one of the largest series of travelogues: "I oughtn't tattletale, but I can't help observing that with those paper eyewitnesses we can never be quite sure that their testimony does not rest on intuitive or symbolic remarks."[24] It was the self-imposed task of German critics to sift through and test the reports prepared by others.

As critical, disinterested, "objective" observers, German commentators delighted in the role of intellectual arbiter. It is noteworthy, for example, that the scientists and scholars in Göttingen and Leipzig who edited the twenty-one volumes of *Allgemeine Historie* not only amended the translations from Thomas Astley's *New General Collection of Voyages and Travels* (1745–1747) and Abbé Prévost's *Histoire générale des voyages* (Paris 1746–1791) but returned to the original texts for comparison, adding registers and commentary. The aim was to "capture all observations systematically and to understand them critically," to reproduce the sum of all knowledge and to pass it on to the general public.[25] There is a kind of imperial gesture, a sense that only those *not* directly involved can capture and sort the totality of lived reality "out there." The philological, totalizing classificatory impulse is evident in the writings of natural historians and philosophers of history, who integrate the experience of South American realities into global categories. Flaunting his erudition, Christoph Meiners, "ordentlicher Lehrer der Weltweisheit" [professor ordinarius of philosophy; literally, of secular wisdom] from Göttingen, lists no fewer than 396 works as sources for his philosophical history or philosophical anthropology, *Outline of the History of Mankind* (1786). As the title suggests, he had covered it all.

In most German commentators, the impulse to "objectify," "authenticate," and to process information was coupled with a moral impulse. Not directly involved in colonial activity at the time, they engaged in international comparisons, in pitting colonial competitors against each other, in weighing the atrocities committed by others against the probity of the colonial onlooker. Past German colonial experiments were rarely alluded to, and even then, uncritically. In an article on the disputes between Englishmen and Spaniards over the cutting of tropical woods in Honduras that appeared in the *Gelehrte Beyträge zu den Braunschweigischen Anzeigen* in 1764, for example, the author denounces the "injustice and cruelty" with which the Spaniards appropriated the riches of the New World, provoking the "envy and greed" of other nations. Referring to Bartolomé de las Casas's *Brevísima relación*, he relates in vivid detail the brutal killings, mutilations, and violations committed by Spanish conquistadors — without mentioning Las Casas's denunciation of German atrocities or any German participation in the conquest.

The "inhuman cruelties" committed by Spaniards, who exterminated "the innocent Caribs . . . almost completely," are also the topic of a series of articles on the West Indian Islands that appeared in the *Braunschweigische Anzeigen* of 1779. They, too, chastise the other European nations, the British, the French, and the Dutch, which "although they were repulsed by the cruelty of the Spaniards, considered it their right to take the Caribs' possessions and to subject them to their rule."[26] The narrative places the German settlers from Courland, who populated Tobago in the seventeenth century and who were driven out by the Dutch, alongside the "poor Indians." Both, the article implies, are victims of colonial aggression. As in previous centuries, the evocation of the Black Legend thus had political-ideological implications. The confrontation of cruel Spaniards — and now also greedy colonial competitors — with hard-working, victimized Germans reaffirmed the "political myth of German honesty and probity."[27] The German settlers are the natural allies of the colonized peoples; they are the "good" colonizers.

In their attempt to be "objective" and "moral," enlightened German commentators of the late eighteenth century tended to side demonstratively with the indigenous populations, whose unfair depiction by first explorers they lamented. A description of the Dutch colony of Surinam — of interest to German readers since "there is always a considerable number of our German compatriots who try their luck there" — sets out to dispel preconceived notions about Indian "savagery": "The natives of the country, who were denounced as wild and indomitable, are in fact not so, and would be even less so, if the Europeans had dealt with them I won't say more amicably, but more honestly, and had not insulted them in the crudest and most unspeakable ways. The Indians in all of Central America are as good in one place as they are prone to hospitality and sociability in others; but of course they are ready for revenge, like all wild peoples."[28] In commentaries such as this one, an attempt is made to correct misperceptions, understand the responses of the oppressed natives in a historical context, and establish alternative models of "polite," that is, civilized colonial interaction. The natives may indeed be cruel, vindictive, lazy — as the colonialists claim and as these commentators concede — but these traits are the result of inhuman treatment and are not inborn. In fact, the Galibis in Guyana are "humane, hospitable, and of sweet disposition";[29] the Caribs "courageous, brave, and crude, well-shapen and clean"; the Arawaks "kind-hearted and peaceful," "undoubtedly the better, sweeter, and more even-tempered race."[30] It is the Europeans whose inhuman treatment has made the "Indians" aggressive and vindictive. Yet among the Europeans, it is the Germans who have retained a morally superior position, because they have remained uncontaminated by colonialism. As Rainer Koch notes, the self-understanding of Germans as disinterested objective judges of the crimes of others led to a lack of critical self-reflection.[31]

Certainly, no evil designs lurked behind these revisionist writings. Their well-intentioned humanity, their struggle for objectivity, their rationality and sense of justice are apparent to today's readers, as are their blindnesses. Instead, a more complicated process is evident here. In the course of the engagement with foreign accounts from the perspective of the distant critical moral observer, readers were invited to share in the classification of the other, in the other's subsumption into, and subjection to, eurocentric categories and values. Hence they participated in the other's instrumentalization — for self-serving purposes. More often than not, the categorization of the other went hand in hand with a privileging of the self. This process is alluded to by Zimmermann, when he describes the effects of travelogues on voracious, sentimental German readers/consumers:

> Now one dwells with pleasure on the domestic bliss on the Pelew Islands or the moderation and loyalty of the negro; now one marvels at the riches of Aurengzeb or the Opokku. The reader's spirits flag at the accounts of the funerary sacrifice practiced by the Aborney, the scalping of the unfortunate prisoners, or the cannibalism of the Anziks. But they revive in the temperate zone; for here one sees how the human intellect marshals all resources toward the security or comfort of society, transforming the earth, changing dead fields into lush agricultural lands, reclaiming large areas from water, hemming the elements in, linking the remotest nations, transplanting the products of the New World into the Old; aye, altering the very climate.[32]

As readers of travelogues and accounts of South America, German *Hausväter* and *Hausmütter* are becoming active participants in this great civilizing enterprise: they approve, disapprove, suffer, rejoice with every step man takes toward greater control of nature and the natural universe. The victory of reason is near — and all the readers share in it. Travelogues, Zimmermann continues, "give us a measuring stick with which to measure the gradual progression of the deeper powers of human reason — the growth of the higher faculties."[33] In other words, travelogues became a vehicle for assessing the cultural distance between "them" and "us."

By providing readers with a measuring stick to assess their own superiority vis-à-vis other cultures, travelogues and other "scientific" writings engaged in what one might call intellectual colonialism: the gradual exploration and appropriation of hitherto undiscovered worlds into Eurocentric categories. Immanuel Kant recognizes and theorizes the affinity between knowledge acquisition and colonial appropriation when he writes toward the end of the analytic part of his *Critique of Pure Reason:*

> We have now not merely *explored the territory of pure understanding,* and carefully surveyed every part of it, but have also measured its extent, and

assigned to everything in it its rightful place. *This domain is an island, enclosed by nature itself within unalterable limits. It is the land of truth — enchanting name! — surrounded by a wide and stormy ocean, the native home of illusion,* where many a fog bank and many a swiftly melting iceberg give the deceptive appearance of farther shores, deluding the adventurous seafarer ever anew with empty hopes, and engaging him in enterprises which he can never abandon and yet is unable to carry to completion. Before we venture on this sea, to explore it in all directions and to obtain assurance whether there be any ground for such hopes, it will be well to begin by casting a glance upon the map of the land which we are about to leave, and to enquire, first, whether we cannot in any case be satisfied with what it contains, — are not, indeed, under compulsion to be satisfied, inasmuch *as there may be no other territory upon which we can settle;* and secondly, by what *title we possess even this domain,* and can consider ourselves as *secured against all opposing claims.*[34] (My emphasis)

Kant's narrative of exploring the island of truth and securing its possession against opposing claims defines the search for "truth" as a colonial takeover. Rather than being an "inhabitant" of the island, the knowledge-seeker is a seafarer who comes from afar. And rather than seeking to understand and "share" the island with others, "he" surveys, stakes out his claims, and takes possession of it, against competing claims, before he ventures forth to ever more distant shores. Even though Kant is speaking only about mental conquests and intellectual terrain, his choice of metaphor reveals the pervasiveness of the island fantasy in late eighteenth-century discourse and the extent to which theory has become complicitous with practical colonialism through discursive practices. As the German fascination with Robinson Crusoe makes clear, the quest for knowledge and the quest for material possession of this imaginary island are intimately linked in the colonial enterprise. While Kant only established a metaphorical connection between "Weltweisheit" and "Weltherrschaft," worldly wisdom and rule of the world, lesser, and more aggressive minds sought to make this connection real.

Colonizing Theory: Gender, Race, and the Search for a National Identity

Like sisters, the fields of knowledge move forward hand in hand. Navigation rested on astronomy; and astronomy was perfected by higher mathematics as well as optics and mechanics. The natural sciences, in the company of chemistry, finally, increased our knowledge of man and his preservation on extended travels; and natural history discovered and classified the innumerable products which have advanced our trade and industry well beyond that of earlier times. . . . We are no longer afraid of the greatest distances, nor of the equator which was so much feared in the past; and that is entirely the glorious work of serious knowledge. *Knowledge alone secures the merchant's, the trader's, the ship owner's capital.—E. A. W. von Zimmermann, introduction to* Taschenbuch der Reisen, *1802*

In mid-eighteenth century Germany, the nascent science of anthropology, or rather the sister arts of philosophy, natural history, and human anatomy, took a decisive turn.[1] Renewed, intense preoccupation with the Americas, triggered by Buffon's *Natural History* (1749; German edition 1755) and the slew of travelogues, histories, and personal accounts mentioned above, gave rise to theories of gender and race that would profoundly alter European and German self-perceptions. Supposedly natural differences between the sexes and between humans far away were renegotiated in the context of domestic ideological developments. While practically none of the theorists had ever visited the Americas, "America" served as imaginary testing ground for the development of constructs that assigned the white European/German male a position of power and authority over all kinds of feminized others, be they wives/children/servants, colonized women/feminized natives/colonized territory, or the "effeminate" aristocracy. Rather than marking a "crisis in male *imperial* identity," as British gender and race theories would do, these German theories point to a crisis in male *national* identity, or more specifically, a crisis in the self-perception of a demoralized, politically impotent bourgeoisie in search of affirmative models of collective identity.[2]

Colonial fantasies projected onto America reinforced the emergence of a masculinist bourgeois consciousness in opposition to aristocratic "decadence" and the emergence of a national consciousness in the face of territorial and cultural fragmentation.[3] While the former, as an incipient class consciousness, was intended to overcome the pervasive sense of political powerlessness [*Unmündigkeit*] shared by most middle class Germans, the latter responded to collective feelings of insignificance for want of national unity.[4] As fantasies of boundaries and mastery, of inclusion, exclusion, and hierarchization, the theories are veiled expressions of the longing for statehood, unity, and control over domestic territory that would determine much of Germany's history in the nineteenth century.

Significantly these fantastic projections in the guise of theory hinged on America and on Native Americans. It was the New World and not, for example, the Orient or Africa that triggered fantasies of national renewal through conquest, and control of territory through colonizing and ordering. This privileging of America may have been due to the sexual associations that the "conquest of America" elicited in its historically and geographically distant onlookers.[5] While, as McClintock affirms, India "was seldom imaged as a virgin land," and Africa contained no "veiled" secrets, America had been consistently represented as virgin territory, to be taken possession of and rendered fertile.[6] As Peter Hulme asserts: "Probably no single word has had to bear so heavy a weight in the construction of American mythology from the moment when, in Samuel Eliot Morison's immortal words, 'the New World gracefully yielded her virginity to the conquering Castilians.'"[7] The fact that the "new" continent's discovery could so easily be attributed to one man—Columbus—and one specific date—1492—and that the "conquest" and "domestication" were so massive and swift, and the returns so rich, may have contributed to anchoring sexual images and tropes in the European discourse on America. *La conquista* became male conquest par excellence.

Of course, the New World did not yield her virginity as gracefully as Morison claimed.[8] Conquest implies, dialectically, resistance. Hence "the inaugural scene of discovery is redolent not only of male megalomania and imperial aggression but also of male anxiety and paranoia."[9] Allegorical representations of America—from Philippe Galle's late-sixteenth-century engraving to the famous Tiepolo frescoes in Würzburg in the mid-seventeen hundreds—attest less to the desire of the conquerors than to the fear inspired by the unknown continent: the bare-breasted "savage" Indian queens in feather headdresses are armed with spears, bow, and arrows. Sitting proudly on ferocious animals, they are surrounded not just by a cornucopia of tropical produce, but by the vestiges of cannibalistic orgies.[10] Indeed, visions of loving embrace and blissful ecstasy are always placed in juxtaposition to and in constant tension with nightmares in which a savage, devouring, "phallic" femininity, in the form of impenetrable jungles, engulfing swamps and orifices, threatens to annihilate the innocent European colonist. Where he hoped to find an alluring mistress or a nurturing mother earth, he may well encounter cannibals, Amazons, or other monsters.[11] Not surprisingly, Vespucci, in Stradanus's depiction of the rediscovery of America, wears armor and sword under his floating gown—just in case.

By the mid–seventeen hundreds the gendered fantasies of the lure or threat of America associated with conquest had become an integral part of the European imaginary. The increased exploration of the New World's interiors, combined with the rationalist project of clearing up and civilizing a disorderly, diffuse, savage nature brought to the fore "the nature of the natives." In fact, "natives" had already lurked somewhere in the background, even as the allegorization of land as female body seemingly dispossessed and displaced them. The questions of who/what these "Indians" were; how they fitted into "global," that is, European categories; whether/how they could be domesticated, that is, instrumentalized, were thus closely linked to the project of conquest from its inception. The feminization of the territory and a racialization of its inhabitants went hand in hand; both served to justify domination and exploitation.

The eighteenth-century German theories that I discuss in the following chapters are informed by the expectations and fears generated by previous centuries of European writing about the New World. From the safe distance of the German province, and from the safe distance of the disinterested theorist, "natural philosophers" devise strategies for creating order and dispelling myths. By colonizing irrational fantasies and organizing them into seemingly rational structures, these theories not only define and contain a threatening or alluring "other"—but invent a self, which is male, white, and "German."

3

Gendering the "Conquest"

See yonder group, that scorn the vulgar crowd,
Absorb'd in thought, of conscious learning proud,
Who, rapt with foretaste of their glorious day,
Now seiz'd the pen, impatient of delay:
These shades shall late in Europe's clime arise,
And scan new worlds with philosophic eyes:
Immured at home, in rambling fancy brave,
Explore all lands beyond th'Atlantic wave;
Of laws for unknown realms invent new codes,
Write natural histories for their antipodes;
Tell how th'enfeebled powers of life decay,
Where falling suns defraud the western day:
Paint the dank, steril globe, accurst by fate,
Created, lost, or stolen from ocean late:
See vegetation, man, and bird, and beast,
Just by the distance' squares in size decreased:
. . .
There, with sure ken, th' inverted optics show
All nature lessening to the sage De Pau;
E'en now his head the cleric tonsures grace,
And all the abbé blossoms in his face;
His peerless pen shall raise with magic lore,
The long-lost pigmies on th' Atlantic shore;
Make niggard nature's noblest gifts decline
Th'indicial marks of bodies masculine.
—*Joel Barlow et al.*, The Anarchiad, *1786–1787*

Joel Barlow's *Anarchiad* pokes fun at the new breed of European *phi-losophes* who "scan new worlds with philosophic eyes." The specific target of his satire, the "sage De Pau," is the cause and center of the first major controversy about the New World, a debate that influenced all future colonial fantasies, not just in Germany, but throughout the Western world.

In 1768, the Dutch canon Cornelius de Pauw, protegé of Frederick II of Prussia, published his *Recherches philosophiques sur les Américains, ou Mémoires intéressants pour servir à l'Histoire de l'Espèce humaine* in Berlin.[1] This polemical two-volume treatise, which was immediately translated into German, generated a major intellectual controversy.[2] Within less than three years, a barrage of philosophical position papers, of refutations and defenses, appeared in the Prussian capital. The royal librarian and abbé Antoine Pernety rebutted de Pauw passionately before the Berlin Academy (1769) and before the general public (1770) in his *Dissertation sur l'Amérique et les Américains contre les Recherches philosophiques de Mr. de P***.* Three months later, de Pauw countered, no less cuttingly, with a *Défense des Recherches philosophiques sur les Américains* (1770). Within a year, Pernety had renewed his attack — this time with a two-volume in-depth examination of all pertinent issues — while, at about the same time, a third, anonymous philosopher, "Le Philosophe la Douceur" (presumably Zacharie de Pazzi de Bonneville), entered the polemic with a small pamphlet that, somewhat tongue-in-cheek, took issue with both parties. The various treatises were reworked and published over and over again, year after year, alone or in conjunction, while the press commented, elaborated, and took sides.[3]

The debate, which focused on the nature of the Amerindians — whether they were degenerate, weak, impotent, dumb, and thus inferior to the Europeans, as de Pauw maintained, or potent "rustic philosophers," equal if not superior to their European counterparts, as Pernety and Bonneville claimed — had a major impact on the discussion of difference, not just in Germany, but all over Europe and even beyond.[4] Although neither de Pauw nor Pernety nor, for that matter, Bonneville were Germans, in the minds of sympathizers and detractors alike their positions became identified with the locale of the debate, Berlin, or rather, with a specifically "Prussian" attempt at establishing spiritual hegemony over the New World.[5]

Significantly, neither de Pauw nor Pernety had much firsthand knowledge of America and its inhabitants. In fact, while Pernety could at least claim to have made some personal contacts with the indigenous peoples when he landed at Brazilian ports on his way to the Falkland Islands in 1763–1764, de Pauw had never even set foot on the American continent. Yet despite the many learned, even impassioned refutations based on personal observation, de Pauw emerged as the winner of the controversy. The public preferred his project — the supposedly systematic, "philosophical" search for "truth" — over Pernety's lengthy presentations of "evidence." It noted with relief that rather than adding one more eyewitness report to the hundreds already inundating the book market, de Pauw was out to create order from the chaos of contradictory information on the New World.[6] Furthermore, while they might disagree on single points, most "enlightened" readers enjoyed de Pauw's "amusing violence," his bold asides against cruel Spaniards, fanatic Jesuits, and their idealized depictions of "savages."[7] And they certainly shared his fascination with the supposed sexual "aberrations" of the natives.[8] As far as popular appeal was concerned, Pernety's pedantically erudite examinations could not compete with de Pauw's racy, at times shockingly "scabrous" (Gerbi) texts.

It is surprising to note de Pauw's appeal among the intellectuals of his time, particularly in Germany, England, and France. Not only was he asked by Diderot to compose an article on the Americas for the *Supplément* to the *Encyclopédie* (1776–1777), but after 1770, every philosopher, writer, or even natural scientist attempting to classify or describe the peoples of the New World felt compelled to engage in de Pauw's arguments, either explicitly or implicitly — from Raynal and Robertson to Herder, Wieland, Kant, Blumenbach, or Alexander von Humboldt, to name just the most prominent. As Antonello Gerbi has documented, there are echoes of the debate as late as 1821, in Hegel's dismissive remarks about the New World in his lectures on universal history.[9] Indeed, the two positions, de Pauw's and by implication Pernety's, acquired the status of paradigms in European colonial thinking. Curiously, de Pauw's radically derogatory attitude was considered the more enlightened, "progressive" one, as is indicated by the fact that he was made an honorary citizen of the new French Republic, alongside Klopstock and Schiller.

What made de Pauw's provocative, even offensive theories so attractive to western European, and particularly to German *philosophes?* Certainly not just the fact that they were couched in skeptic Enlightenment jargon and proposed, at least on the surface, a questioning of accepted beliefs. And certainly not because de Pauw's imaginary world approximated American "reality" any more closely than Pernety's — the falseness of most of his allegations and generalizations was obvious to anyone who had had a chance to travel in America. The attractiveness of de Pauw's system had deeper reasons. It has to be read in light of a pervasive European identity crisis. De Pauw selected already familiar observations and popular (mis)conceptions about otherness and constructed them into a seemingly coherent (American) reality that not only explained and atoned for the history of conquest but that provided the parameters for a new self-identity of the European male—that of "natural man" as "natural colonizer."

"Natural Men" and "Natural Man"

According to de Pauw, the Discovery and Conquest divided the world into two parts, into the Eastern and the Western hemispheres, into "Old World" and "New." This dichotomy—a reduction of the former four-part division of the cosmos—forms the basis for a series of further oppositions, and for their peculiarly alluring and threatening asymmetry. As he writes in the introduction to his *Recherches philosophiques:*

> No event in human history is more noteworthy than the Discovery of America. If one goes back from present times to those of the remotest past, no single event can be compared to this one; and it is no doubt a great and awful spectacle to see one half of the globe so much hated by nature that everything there is degenerate or monstrous.
>
> Which natural scientist of antiquity would have suspected that one and the same planet might have two such different hemispheres, one of which would be overcome, subjected, devoured by the other, as soon as it was discovered after centuries lost in darkness and the abyss of time?
>
> This surprising change [*révolution*], which transformed the face of the earth and the fortune of nations, happened very fast, because, for some unbelievable fatality, there existed no equilibrium between the attack and the defense. All power, and all injustice were on the side of the Europeans: the Americans had nothing but weakness; and therefore had to be destroyed, destroyed in one instant.
>
> Whether it was due to an unhappy connection of our destinies, or the necessary consequence of so many vices and shortcomings [*fautes*—translated into German as *Mängel*], this infamous and unjust conquest of the New World is certainly the greatest misfortune humanity has suffered.
>
> After the cruel victor had quickly murdered several million savages, he was visited by an epidemic disease, which by attacking at once the origins of life and the sources of procreation, soon became the scourge of the inhabited earth. Man, already weighed down with the burden of his exis-

tence, found, to top his misfortune, the germs of death in the arms of pleasure and in the bosom of delight: he believed that enraged nature herself had vowed his ruin. (iii–v)

In de Pauw's analysis, the Old World and the New are characterized by the opposition of strong versus weak, healthy versus diseased; what looked like an imbalance and injustice at first — the conquest, subjugation, and appropriation of the New World by the Old — is offset by "nature's revenge," syphilis, which the conquistadors supposedly contracted in the New World and which has wrought havoc on the Old.[10]

De Pauw clearly argues on two levels. While he overtly denounces the brutality of the conquistadors, he covertly blames the annihilation of the indigenous peoples on fate, or rather, on nature: because of their physical inferiority the "savages" *had* to be destroyed [*devoient donc être exterminés*]. Furthermore, on a moral plane, the natives' legacy, the deadly disease with which they contaminated the foreign intruders, far outweighs the harm these inflicted on them: in a curious twist, the conquerors become generic "man" who is not only weighed down by the burden of existence but punished for indulging in sensuous pleasures. So while de Pauw strongly condemns the destruction of the New World by the Old, he undercuts his verdict by suggesting that this "natural" process was inevitable, and that excessive punishment has already more than atoned for the infraction. The tropes, "les bras de plaisir," "le sein de la juissance," reproduce the *massacre* of the native warriors verbally, as they reduce the *sauvages* to their body parts, and feminize them, eliminating indigenous males altogether from the discourse. In de Pauw's American "reality," there remain only male conquerors and female savages, locked in deadly embrace.

The links between conquest and pleasure, pleasure and disease, disease and femininity, femininity and conquest suggested in these introductory remarks circumscribe de Pauw's whole philosophical project. In fact, all of his further "investigations" are explorations of, and variations on the same theme. His circular reasoning both prescribes the terms of the debate and frames the argument, setting up a trap from which Pernety and his other critics are unable to escape.

As de Pauw subsequently argues in his *Recherches,* the physical weakness of the "savages" — which caused their defeat — is a sign of degeneration produced by the American environment, the wet, swampy soils and moist airs of this continent that only recently emerged from the floods (1: 4–6, 23–28, 105). As proof for his theory of degeneracy, adopted from Buffon,[11] de Pauw claims that the humid, putrid habitat, this "venereal yeast" (1: 23), not only corrupted the natives, but also contaminates and weakens foreign settlers, plants, and animals, all of which lose their power to procreate after having been transplanted to the New World (1: 28). Weakness, degeneracy, corruption are, however, not just characteristics of the body; they affect the mind, the whole moral fabric as well. The natives are, as de Pauw says in one chapter devoted exclusively to the "génie abruti des Américains" (5: chap. 1), indigent and stupid (1: 122); they are not only physically impotent, but lack intellectual force, "genius" (1: 44). And their weakness makes them resort to the typical weapons of the weak: to lies, treachery, and wanton cruelty (1: 45).

De Pauw claims that in this and all other respects the natives are not only similar to, but identical to (and occasionally worse than) women (43). Linking women and American "savages" is, of course, not new.[12] What is new is de Pauw's attempt to provide a solid "scientific," that is, biological foundation for the analogy.[13] Significantly, he resorts to the theory of the four humors prevalent in antiquity, a theory that although on the wane among eighteenth-century scientists, continued to serve the general public as indicator of gender difference.[14] De Pauw revives these traditional conceptual principles — according to which both "the West" and women (the female "temperament") were distinguished from the East and men by their moist, cold humors — and translates them into geographic and physiological "fact" based on "evidence:" if Western nature "proves" its inferiority by its cold swampiness, the effeminacy and clammy, phlegmatic disposition of native men is conclusively proven by their lack of facial hair: "I know very well that in the attempt to explain why there is no hair on the body of the Americans, people have resorted to all kinds of subtleties which are not and never will be considered valid causes. . . . We, however, want to show that lack of hair stems from the moist constitution of their bodies, and that they are beardless for the same reasons that women in Europe and other parts of the world are beardless: their skin is bare because they have an extremely cold temperament" (1: 38).

De Pauw's systematic emasculation/femininization of the natives forms part of his strategy of "naturalizing" the conquest. Since neither sexual organs nor anatomy can explain the profound difference between European and American natives, and validate the supposed superiority of the former, the beard becomes *the* natural sign for "virility," that is, maturity, strength, wisdom, and potency. Beardlessness makes the natives "naturally" inferior to the bearded conquerors, a hierarchy which, according to de Pauw, they immediately recognized and accepted: "When these Americans saw for the first time the Spaniards with their long beards, they lost all courage: *for how could we resist, they cried, men who have hair in their faces and who are so strong that they lift up burdens we cannot even move?*" (3: 16)[15]

It is thus not the Spaniards' superior war technology, nor their conquering drive, cunning, or brutality, nor differences in cosmologies that brought about the defeat of the natives: the Indians were overwhelmed by the mere sight of "natural superiority": "The fashion which the Spaniards, and all Europeans in general, then had, namely to grow their beards, *would have alone sufficed to facilitate the conquest of America:* for the Indians could not stand the sight of bearded men, nor of dogs nor horses (3: 48–49, my emphasis).

The Conquest, in de Pauw's construct, is therefore not so much a natural takeover as a natural surrender: by law of nature, the weaker, the effeminate, the naturally inferior surrenders to the stronger, more virile, naturally superior. To affirm the native's emasculation is to assert the conqueror's superior masculinity, and vice versa.

"Natural surrender" also extends to the native women, albeit with different connotations. According to de Pauw, the Indian men's physical and spiritual impotence translated into lack of passion for the opposite sex (1: 42), with all its dire social and economic consequences: infertility, depopulation, a surplus of female offspring, and uncommonly high incidence of homosexuality (1: 63–69). No wonder then that Indians (of both sexes, as the German translation of the *Recherches* suggests . . .)[16] greeted the arrival of the Europeans with glee, since the potent conquistadors relieved the men of their burdensome marital duties, and provided diversion for their frustrated mates:

> Be it as it may, all narratives agree that the Indian women were exceedingly pleased at the arrival of the Europeans who—because of their sexual prowess, compared to that of the natives—resembled satyrs. If this strange paradox were not proven by a multiplicity of facts, one would not believe that they would have been able to surrender themselves willingly to the barbaric companions of the Pizarros and the Cortezes, who only marched over dead bodies, who had acquired the hearts of tigers and whose greedy hands were dripping with blood. Despite all the good reasons they had to hate those cruel people, the three hundred wives of the Inca Atabaliba [Atahualpa] who were taken prisoner with him at the battle of Caxamalca

[Cajamarca], threw themselves at the feet of the victor, and the morning thereafter more than five thousand American women came to the Spaniards' camp and *surrendered voluntarily,* while the unfortunate remains of their vanquished nation escaped more than 40 miles into the woods and deserts. (1: 69–70, my emphasis)

Not only did the women voluntarily surrender, but, according to de Pauw's duplicitous text, which relies on Vespucci and countless other prophets of "Malinchismo," they were more than willing to betray their men and "serve" the conquerors in whatever capacity they could: "Thus it is certain that the Spaniards found in them an unexpected eagerness and attachment: they served as interpreters and guides in all the expeditions that were undertaken against their fatherland and rendered great services to all the Conquerors who were the first to penetrate the islands and the main land" (1: 70).

In Vespucci's/de Pauw's fantasy, the conquerors' violent penetration of virgin territory — "terre ferme" associates *terra firma,* the continent, with "terre fermée," the closed land — is achieved by mutual consent. Or rather, the conquest is the result of an act of seduction: the native women, more in agreement with the Europeans' interests than the Europeans themselves ["plus portées pour les intérêts des Européens qu'ils ne l'étoient eux-mêmes," 1: 70], surrender their bodies/territory to the more potent male, while their denatured mates disappear into the wilderness. De Pauw's recourse to gender to mark the difference between Old World and New is thus not only a strategy to explain the lack of resistance among native men or the surrender of the women: it provides a vocabulary for the articulation of desire — not the desire of the self for the other, as in traditional conquest narratives, but the desire of the other for the self, the irresistibly virile European, that is, the real "natural man."

Natural Philosophers as Natural Colonizers

As de Pauw's account stresses over and over again, the New World is a place of disorder and deviancy. Not only are the native men hairless "like eunuchs" (1: 145), impotent, and prone to homosexuality, but their "irregularity" also extends to the size of their genitals (1:37)[17] and to the "fact" that they are lactiferous (1: 42). Not only do native women not suffer during childbirth, but they rarely menstruate, lactate excessively (1: 55), are frequently infertile, and sexually so voracious that they have to resort to "sex aids" to arouse their tepid husbands (1: 38). Indeed, in their sexual indeterminacy, that is, in their transgression of what de Pauw considers the boundaries of nature, native women and men coincide. "The more savage a people," de Pauw concludes, "the more the women resemble the men; & particularly in America, where men are beardless. . . . " And he adds: "The beautiful sex thus does not exist there" ["Il n'y a donc pas là de beau sexe," 3: 19–20].

"Disorder" is not limited to human nature; it extends to nature itself. The sexual indeterminacy of the humans corresponds to the indeterminacy of the American soil, its abundant swamps, its threatening bogs, in which boundaries are lost, human traces effaced, and men who venture into the wilderness are devoured and annihilated. Literally and metaphorically then, degenerate men and women occupied an ill-defined, untidy, disorderly, and potentially dangerous space "in be-tween" — until the conquistadors arrived on the scene to clean up. "Thus was the state of affairs in America when the Spaniards, to complete the country's misfortune, landed there: they greedily exploited the *disorder of the Indians* as legitimate pretext to destroy them" (1: 66, my emphasis).

In this configuration, the tasks of the conqueror and those of the colonizer are analogous, if not alike. Whereas the virile conquistador had reestablished a natural, that is, phallocentric order by destroying or dispersing the effeminate men and by putting mannish women in their "natural place,"[18] the colonizer, ever since, has been creating order out of chaos by drying up swamps, cutting down jungles, and "taming an unyielding earth" ["domter une terre ingrate," 1: 113].[19] The verbs with which de Pauw characterizes this domesticating endeavor, "éclaircir" [to clear up], "purger" [to purge], "diriger" [to direct], "saigner" [to bleed, to cure], "défricher" [to clear, 3: 13] belong to the material and literal as well as to the spiritual and figurative realm. Creating civilization is defined as both destructive, violent, and as constructive, healing. It implies the elimination, the cutting down of "wild growth" and the construction of a new "healthy" order by erecting clearly defined boundaries.

Despite his overt condemnation of the violence employed by the Spanish conquistadors, which places him squarely with other Enlightenment humanitarian thinkers, de Pauw is in complete agreement with the conquering/colonizing/ordering project itself.[20] In fact, he himself partakes of it: his own treatise is an attempt to cut through popular myths, through the monstrosities associated with the New World, and to contain or tame the monsters in order to reorganize America as an orderly, rational universe. After constructing precolonial American reality in terms of degeneracy, disorder, and disease, de Pauw goes on to refute or explain scientifically all those New World myths that have survived, even in the Age of Reason: the "blafards" or white negroes who are supposed to live in Darien are not a race of monsters, but a small group of diseased individuals (2: 5–46); the existence of the so-called Florida hermaphrodites is unconfirmed and unlikely — they are probably women with oversized genitals or men wearing women's clothes as an outward sign of their slave condition (2: 88–89);[21] the famous "acéphales" or headless men whom Lafitau still included among his peoples of the Americas (*Moeurs des sauvages amériquains*, 1724) are in fact humans deformed by the natives' "monstrous" habit of shaping their infants' heads or limbs (1: 152–153); and cannibals, although they once existed everywhere on the globe, are far fewer now and less ferocious than purported (1: 207–223).

In the context of his gendered model of natural conquest, two myths de Pauw attempts to dispel are of particular interest: the myth of the Patagon Giants and the Amazon myth — both of them transfers from Old World mythology.[22]

The story that South America's southern cone was populated by a race of giants dates back to its discovery by Magellan, whose men called the land "Patagonia" (= land of the big-footers) after supposedly spying a huge footprint in the soil.[23] Curiously, after having been laid to rest by Zedler and others, the myth of the Patagon Giants is revived in the eighteenth century, when Commodore John Byron reports having spotted, with his very own eyes, "200 giants at the coast of Tierra del Fuego" — as tall when seated as the commander, himself six feet in height, standing up.[24] Despite skepticism as to ulterior motives for these monstrous sightings[25] or doubts over the giants' anatomical probability,[26] the German scientific community around 1768/69 seems to agree that giants did indeed populate parts of the New World: if enlightened explorers of the eighteenth century had sighted them in the flesh, how could they *not* exist? According to the translator of Gabriel François Coyer's *Über die Riesen in Patagonien* (1769) "the number of testimonies assembled in this treatise amounts, in my opinion, to such evidence for the existence of a race of giants in Patagonia as could leave only the greatest skeptic still in doubt."[27] The greatest skeptic in the matter, however, is de Pauw.

Clearly, his theory of the decadence of the New World, his gendered model of colonial relations, and his belief in natural "order" oblige him to dismiss the existence of an inordinately strong, tall, manly indigenous people that, as many of his contemporaries would point out, associates the inhabitants of the New World historically with the old Germans, themselves giant men of arms (see chap. 5).[28] The passionate embrace of European conqueror and native maiden envisioned by de Pauw is metaphorically — and anatomically — impossible among such disproportionate partners, as Johann Christoph Erich von Springer's tongue-in-cheek account suggests:

> The kissing embrace of the Englishmen with respect to the giant women is fraught with similar difficulties. Unless we presuppose that the women sat on the floor — which, however, has not been reported — an Englishman desirous of kissing a giantess would have had to be catapulted up to her, and that motion would have had to be at least comparable to voltigating over the crest of a horse into a saddle, for a sixteen fist high horse would not be more than five feet high in the saddle. Yet we may want to relinquish this matter, for the sake of decency, and just assume that the women were sitting down during these caresses, while the Englishmen were standing up, or, possibly, sitting on horseback.[29]

In order to maintain the myth of the weakness and effeminacy of the South American natives and of their voluntary surrender to the stronger European male, de Pauw thus *must* dispel the myth of the Patagon Giants and any allusions to Patagon-German analogies: the New World giants are, he affirms, but figments of the mind of simple sailors (1: 281–326).

The other gender myth, the myth of the Amazons, is equally anathema to de Pauw's theories. The story of a state ruled by warrior women had been rekindled in the German imagination in the early eighteenth century with a reedition of Antonio de Orellana's *Relación* (*Die kriegerischen Frauen, oder: historische Beschreibung einer neu entdeckten Insel*, Berlin, 1736). The reprint of accounts by Orellana and other travelers, together with more historically oriented discussions of the feasibility of such gendered communities (e.g., Pierre Petit's *Traité historique sur les Amazones*, 1718; François Lafitau's *Moeurs des sauvages amériquains*, 1724, German tr. 1752; or Claude Marie Guyon's *L'Histoire des Amazones*, 1748, German tr. 1763) suggest a renewed interest in the connections between women, power, and transgression. Whereas Guyon considered a woman warrior state probable, based on his theory that only prejudice and education have kept women weak, de Pauw adamantly refuses to believe in the concept of a republic run entirely by "the most compliant sex."[30] In his mind, this is contrary to nature:

> Even if one had found a sufficiently large number of discontent women to form a whole republic, one would still not have more than a small part of a society able to survive on its own: the difficulty would reside in finding men stupid enough to allow themselves to be forced against their will to impregnate women who would chase them away as soon as the generative task was achieved. . . . In the imagination, this is as possible as Plato's Republic or as that of Thomas More; but if one wants to use some judgment and reflection, the whole edifice collapses, and all that remains are absurdities that revolt against, or destroy Nature. It is totally contradictory to assume that a woman would have a violent aversion against men and would still consent to become a mother; it would be monstrous if a mother smothered or abandoned her children, under pretext that these children aren't daughters. Is it so easy after this to assemble twenty or thirty thousand insane, murderous warrior women? The character of the most tender, the most compliant, and yes, if one wants, the least wicked sex, could it forget itself so much to commit regularly and by common agreement crimes that are only rarely committed by individuals moved by rage and despair? (1: 107–108)

In de Pauw's logic, motherhood and violence are incompatible. It is inconceivable that a true mother could kill children of a particular sex for social or political reasons. Women who do so are denatured monsters. In his eagerness to erect boundaries of normalcy, de Pauw (like Lafitau before him)[31] relates the myth of an independent women's republic back to known women's societies, religious orders (1: 113), thus containing the fantasy of female self-determination behind the walls of the convent.

All of de Pauw's investigations are characterized by his desire to reduce myths to natural causes or origins, and to domesticate them by including them in rational discourse. There are no gigantic wild men, no headless or one-breasted monsters; there is no alterity unaccounted for in the analysis and narrative of the "Prussian" *philosophe*. Everything strange or inexplicable that early travelers encoded in monstrous form is reduced to the familiar. Monstrosity is no longer that which is completely other; rather, it is defined as the deviation from the familiar — that is, the European — norm: olive-skinned men who are exceedingly small, such as the Eskimos ("avortons," 1: 259), beardless, long-haired men who behave like women (2: 92), and women who refuse to be wives and mothers — these are the *monstres* of the enlightened eighteenth century.

By conquering and domesticating the last vestiges of monstrosity, the philosopher-armchair conquistador incorporates and assimilates the unfamiliar. The fears and obsessions formerly exteriorized in monsters are reinternalized to become (again?) an integral part of his own culture. As icons of transgression, excess, or abnormality, cannibals, giants, Amazons, and headless men (or headless bodies) make their reentry into the European subconscious, whence they emerge to designate all that is threatening to the status quo.[32] As Antonello Gerbi, Peter Mason, and others have pointed out, the Europeanization of America thus goes hand in hand with an "Indianization" of the European imagination.[33]

The Dialectics of Conquest and the "Indian Disease"

The "Indianization of Europe," that is, the fear of contamination in the encounter with otherness, is at the core of the de Pauw-Pernety controversy. As de Pauw stresses the differences between Old World and New and Pernety the similarities, and as they attempt to emphasize their opposition to each other, they are engaged in what one might call a double dialectic: the surface debate about the true nature of the Americans is, at the same time, a probing into the identity of the European male in his relationship to his various biological, social, and political others. Since Pernety remains largely unaware of this double-layered project and multiple investment, he is unable to present a true challenge to de Pauw's seductive model of natural European superiority.

Despite attempts at presenting a more differentiated account of "the" Native American, Pernety remains essentially caught in the dialectics de Pauw has set up. The words with which Pernety characterizes his task echo de Pauw's Enlightenment project: to clear up the chaos ["débrouiller le chaos"], to disperse the clouds of prejudice ["dissiper les nuages du préjugé"]. His aim, however, namely to retain some of the "merveilleux" such as the Patagon Giants — places him in the anti-Enlightenment corner. De Pauw's construction of the New World as the negative in a series of binary oppositions continuously forces Pernety, who is out to prove that his New World is antithetical to de Pauw's, to adopt the positive pole. To contrast de Pauw's theory of degeneracy, Pernety must claim that nature has created its very "masterpieces" in the New World: the soils are fertile and bear abundant fruit (3: 35); the men are well built, tall, enduring, and healthy and live to an extremely old age (3: 46–48); their cultural level is in harmony with their physical needs (3: 95); their lack in so-called civilization is compensated by greater freedom and by a lack of those vices that accompany progress, such as ambition, vanity, and moral weakness (3: 95). In short, the New World is "paradise on earth" (3: 35). If de Pauw's theory of degeneracy required the absence of Patagon Giants, as Pernety suggested (3: 51), Pernety's depiction of the New World as somewhat larger than life clearly needed their presence.

The extent to which Pernety's counterevidence is also controlled by binary oppositions and gendered hierarchies becomes obvious when we turn to his analysis of the natives' "effeminate" beardlessness. As Pernety feels compelled to prove that the natives are in fact "real men," he insists that they do have facial hair — yet that they pluck it out for aesthetic reasons; and that they have secret knowledge on how to prevent beards from growing back (3: 120). De Pauw's association between beard and virility, between biological sign and cultural meaning is thus not questioned but reaffirmed.[34] Likewise, Pernety maintains that the native men are *not* indifferent to their wives, as de Pauw had claimed. On the contrary, since the Indians build their relationships on free choice, there is no need for "that blind furor we call love" ["cette fureur aveugle, que nous appellons amour"]. Instead, the natives treat their partners with friendship and a tenderness, which, "although alive and lively, never carries them away . . . to those excesses which love inspires in those who are possessed by it" (3: 82). In every sense, the Indians are not different from, but similar to the Europeans, only better: more genuine, more trusting, less corrupted and oppressed.

On the surface, the two positions fall into the traditional dichotomy of the "ignoble" versus the "noble savage," in which de Pauw assumes a Voltairean, Pernety a Rousseauean stance. Both clearly and repeatedly allude to this tradition: de Pauw when he refers to those who "pretended that . . . it is not the savages who are barbaric, but the civilized peoples" (3: 125), Pernety when he introduces his critique of de Pauw with a passionate indictment of the civilized world, "populated by men condemned to relentless work" ("habité par des hommes condamnés à un travail sans relâche," *Dissertation,* 3: 15). But beneath this purely academic exchange on distant peoples, questions on the relationship between sexuality and political power emerge that bear directly upon the situation in Europe.

In his article on de Pauw and Voltaire, Gisbert Beyerhaus called sexuality the "index fossil of [de Pauw's] folkloristic excavations" ("Leitfossil seiner folkloristischen Ausgrabungen," 476). Like other critics, he noted de Pauw's "almost Freudian" (Gerbi) obsession with "abnormal" sexual behavior, yet dismissed it, with no little embarrassment, as an indication of individual pathology, of interest only to the psychoanalyst, not the intellectual historian.[35] As I would argue, however, de Pauw did not voice an individual obsession — "aberrations" were an important focus in most late-eighteenth-century works of anthropology or natural history.[36] Instead, he gave expression to a social pathology that distinguished between sexuality, associated with chaos and disease, and "love," associated with order and "normalcy." This pathology is nothing other than the bourgeois morality that crystallized in late-eighteenth-century society in opposition to aristocratic "profligacy."

In his attempt to define the other in the New World as inferior to the European self, de Pauw resorts to a conflation of gender, geography, and morality. "Natives" and terrains of the New World are effeminate, treacherous, transgressive, in need of colonization (definition, demarcation, naming) by the male colonizer. By imposing a gender framework on the encounter between colonizer and colonized, and by grounding this gender structure in biology, de Pauw renders the violent appropriation of the New World natural and inevitable, if not desirable. However, the desire of taking possession is dampened by the association of sexual pleasure with fear of contamination: the conqueror risks contamination with syphilis; the colonizer may be infected with the disease of sloth in those infested swamps of otherness. He will degenerate and lose control, of himself and of his possessions, as happened to the Spaniards and Portuguese (3: 13). The remedy is either colonial abstention, which de Pauw sometimes advocates (1: vi) and sometimes rejects, or "love": man's exclusive libidinal fixation on one uncontaminated, untouched sexual object which he colonizes, that is, appropriates, names, and renders productive.

By introducing heterosexual love as the driving force behind colonization, particularly in his response (*Défense*) to Pernety's response (*Dissertation*), de Pauw is not celebrating sexual passion, as Beyerhaus suggests.[37] Love, to de Pauw, is a means of establishing order. This function of love becomes clearer when we compare his sexual-biological vision of conquest with Pernety's moral one. By remasculating the native men de Pauw had emasculated, Pernety attempts to cancel the biological determinacy of the conquest. It was not a natural surrender of power by the more effeminate to the more virile, he argues, but a betrayal among men, an immoral appropriation, in which the trusting natives were victimized by the Spaniards' (and their own wives') treachery, and in which all the responsibility rested with the Europeans. Syphilis is not an undeserved punishment for too much loving, as de Pauw had suggested, but part of a violent exchange between Old World and New.

The distinction between de Pauw's natural hierarchy based on difference overcome by love and Pernety's moral egalitarianism based on sameness achieved through negotiations comes to the fore in their lengthy exchange on male-female relations among the natives. De Pauw reiterates his main point that the natives are feeble in their passions and hence (pro)creativity. He rejects Pernety's conclusion that the natives' sobriety is related to the free association of men and women and liberal "divorce" practices: "He [Pernety] obviously talked about morality when the physical was at stake" (*Défense,* 3: 18). Passion for the other sex, de Pauw claims, is natural; it predates and is unaffected by social institutions like marriage and divorce. And since this "great principle of sociability is lacking or has been weakened in the minds of the savages, they fell all the more deeply into the dehumanization and disarray which entails all other possible disorders" (3: 19). And he exclaims: "How did he fail to see that love would have repaired all ills, and *that disorder is wherever love is not?*" (my emphasis). While in Pernety's idealized world love is an exchange among free individuals, in de Pauw's universe, love (= heterosexual passion) establishes gender order.

Love and order, love of order, love and work, love of work go hand in hand (3: 230).[38] As de Pauw's colonizing love eliminates (sexual) indeterminacy by excluding sexually indifferent or "devious" native men and domesticating sexually promiscuous native women, it (re)creates "natural order." One might say then that the matrimony between the Natural Man and the Natural Woman becomes the ultimate metaphor for the successful colonial encounter, and vice versa: the power relationship of colonizer to colonized becomes the model for a successful matrimony.

Clearly, de Pauw is not only speaking about the New World here — he is using the New to speak about the Old. Nor is he only providing a model for colonial relations within the family or among nations: in their indolence, their effeminacy, and their love of a carefree living, the degenerate "savages" are the carriers of a disease that might contaminate and corrupt individual European states at their very core — if it has not done so already.

The principal indicator of "irregularity,"[39] hair, provides the link between sexuality, power, and (social) disease within the familial and the political realm. In de Pauw's conceptual universe, hairlessness does not distinguish man from animal, as Blumenbach would argue,[40] or civilized man from wild man — it is above all a sexual characteristic. The presence or absence of a beard draws a sharp line between men and women and between true masculinity and true femininity. The beard becomes the "natural" indicator of one's place within the social hierarchy. In the words of the eighteenth-century cultural historian Karl Gottlob Schelle: "This beard . . . reveals to the women the intentions of nature; it teaches them humility, submission, and obedience."[41]

De Pauw's insistence on hair as a sign of natural supremacy suggests still another reading. From the seventeenth century onward, European male aristocrats were not only clean shaven, but wore increasingly bigger and more elaborate wigs, veritable lion's manes, depending on social status and wealth, while aristocratic women wore headdresses over two feet in height, decorated with feathers, flowers, and beads[42] — à l'américaine, as Pernety suggested when he wrote in defense of the natives' fashions: "In all our countries we see men and women enjoying the beauty of their finery, who wear plumes on their head like the savages and, since they have to dress, approximate as much as possible the taste of the Americans" (3: 118). In eighteenth-century high society, beards were considered *déclassé;* as Max von Böhn reminds us, only actors representing murderers or highwaymen were expected to wear a mustache.[43] While beardlessness and voluminous head hair were thus associated with class and power in the eyes of those who had class and power, in the eyes of the emerging bourgeois public they had a different connotation: they became the symbols of the leisure, excess, luxury, and effeminacy of the aristocracy. Wigs masqueraded power, while masking "degeneracy."

The links between hair, power, and disease were stressed by the fact that the wig had been introduced in the sixteenth and seventeenth centuries, simultaneous with the epidemic spread of syphilis, the "Indian disease" [indianische Krankheit], as it was also known.[44] Syphilis (or its treatment with mercury) led to loss of hair. Abundant hair suggested virility and vigor. Medical or cultural historians of the time such as Friedrich Nicolai thus associated the wig fashion with the sexual profligacy of the aristocracy, with their need to cover their balding, spotted heads with false hair to simulate health and strength in view of physical decline.[45] As another sign of social "disease" in the eyes of the critical public, aristocrats not only dressed and painted their faces like women — embodied in the fashion model of the *petit maître* — they also admitted powerful women into their ranks, as *maîtresses, salonnières,* and counselors.

By focusing on beardlessness as a sign of physical and moral degeneracy, de Pauw thus attacks not only the American Indians, but implicitly the European upper class, the aristocracy. The contamination of the conquerors by syphilitic natives alludes to a widespread "disease" among Europeans, particularly women, who are infested with aristocratic values and lifestyles. In the process of redefining virility as opposed to effeminacy, de Pauw proposes as the new natural man the bourgeois *Kraftmensch*[46] — one not modeled after the hairless savages of the New World, but one who carries his beard and natural hair as attributes of power, publicly, and who reestablishes the "natural" order everywhere.

Perneṭy's implicit political model is no less antiaristocratic than de Pauw's. He, too, attacks the "men dressed in gold and purple, whose indolence, comfortably stretched out on the divan, scoffs at the insults of the air [the inclemencies of the weather] under gold and blue wainscoting; and who open their eyes only to be dazzled by the splendor of the luxury that surrounds them, and who stretch out their hands only to reach for dainty dishes to arouse their muted appetites or to satisfy their sensuality, at the expense of the life and work of those men who moan under the burden of their cruel tyranny" (*Dissertation,* 16). Yet while de Pauw's alternative of a shift of power and control away from effeminate despots to new, "natural" rulers, can appear at once rational, logical, historical, and therefore realistic, Perneṭy's (and eventually "Le philosophe la Douceur's") Edenic vision of a free, nonhierarchical people roaming the wild can easily be relegated to the realm of the past, or the future — it has little to offer to contemporary Europeans.

Where then lies de Pauw's attractiveness for the Prussian monarch and for the Germans whose contact with the New World was largely intellectual? I propose that his peculiar association of the foreign with the familiar/familial, of the global with the domestic, and of love with possession, order, and control, carried a special appeal for Prussians eager to expand their boundaries and secure hegemony over conquered territories.[47] Throughout his forty-four-year reign, Frederick the Great was involved in intensive campaigns of internal colonization and aggressive wars of expansion, which, in his feud with Austria's Maria Theresia, had decidedly gendered overtones. As Frederick himself stated in his *Political Testament* of 1768, which appeared almost simultaneously with de Pauw's treatise, "The first hallmark of a prince should be to survive, the second, to expand."[48] While de Pauw's abject depiction of the New World may well have been designed to discourage Prussian colonizers from leaving their country,[49] his whole project can be read as an invitation to colonial activity on all fronts. Not only does he explicitly and repeatedly exempt Germans from any participation in, and guilt for, the conquest and subjugation of the New World (3: 151, 224), but he reiterates his conviction that man is made to tame, to domesticate the wild: unless this task is taken up, physical nature will degenerate and revert to its diseased chaotic state: "Nature has given man perfectibility to prevent the horrible disasters of which I have spoken, and which would undoubtedly befall us if our globe were only inhabited by savages. But one single civilized people can prevent all these evils; for one civilized people expands, establishes trading posts, sends colonies [*sic*], and constructs settlements" (3: 254).

One message to his Prussian readership is clear: if colonization can and should be done by one civilized people, by a nation not burdened with past colonial guilt, in which arts and sciences flourish (3: 157), by a people that fantasizes about its love for work and love for order, then the Prussians might be a perfect choice to play that role.

As Gerbi's study documents, de Pauw's colonialist legacy has been perfidious — worse, I believe, than Gerbi realized. Anticipating biological racism and theories of degeneracy by almost one hundred years, de Pauw established the binary frameworks within which colonizing nations would henceforth see their enterprise: as the natural superiority of the stronger and healthier over the weaker and "diseased"; as restrained, focused sexuality ("love") that establishes familial order, property rights, and clear-cut boundaries over an unclaimed, diffuse space; and as individual and national regeneration through the elimination of "degeneracy" and "degradation." By feminizing the other, and by stressing the threat of pollution through contact ("syphilis"), de

Pauw resexualized the conquest. He reinforced the peculiar tension between attraction and horror, temptation and restraint, that is symptomatic of the colonialist subjectivity and gave new impetus to the idea that the colonial "mission" is the mission of the steadfast male who, unperturbed by exotic lures, pursues his task of appropriating, ordering, and ruling.

4

Racializing the Colony

During my sojourn in Hesse-Cassel I observed many local negroes and was at leisure to dissect several male and also one female black body. — S. T. Sömmerring, On the Physical Difference between the Negro and the European, *1785*[1]

Who were these others that the European male set out to rule? This question preoccupied Enlightenment theorists from de Pauw onward. While gender had been the framework within which de Pauw and Pernety had classified, judged, and evaluated the "nature" of the inhabitants of the New World, "race" in its modern, biological definition became the overriding organizing principle, particularly after Cook's travels (1772–1775) had provided the missing link in his circumnavigation of the globe.[2] The discovery of the "copper-colored" peoples in the New World, "yellow- or brown-skinned" inhabitants on the Pacific Islands, and "black" aborigines on the Australian continent; the displacement of ever larger numbers of African slaves to the Americas and the subsequent debates on the morality (or economic profitability) of slave trade; the scientific and pseudoscientific preoccupation with the origins and genetic transferability of skin color and other bodily properties, and with the connection between physiognomy and character, created an environment in which differences, boundaries, norms, and deviations were discussed in ever more global, exclusive, and hierarchical terms. The preoccupation with gender did not disappear — on the contrary, race and gender became superimposed, so to speak, reinforcing each other to determine the position of each individual in the universal rosters created by natural history and comparative anthropology.[3] This is particularly the case for the South American Indians vis-à-vis both Europeans and Africans. The insistence on skin color, hair, and anatomy as *the* distinctive racial features, combined with deep resonances of the earlier gendered categories and descriptions, created for "redskins" — once again — the peculiarly ambiguous position of "in between." This time not in-between genders, but between continents ("between" Europe and Africa, Europe and Asia), colors (white and black, white and yellow), and symbolically charged directions (the North and the South, the East and the West). As a result, Indians were claimed both as "same" and "different." Or rather, they could be assimilated into fantasies of sameness, or rejected, ignored, displaced in fantasies of difference, depending on the epistemological and political interests of the viewer.[4]

From the de Pauw-Pernety controversy onward, and reinforced by a new, amended German edition of Buffon's *Histoire naturelle, Allgemeine Naturgeschichte* (1771–1774), and German translations of Linnaeus's *Systema Naturae* (1773–1776),[5] the discussion of difference revolved around three fundamental questions: What distinguishes one people from the next, or rather: where does difference reside? What is the cause of that difference? and What does this difference mean in a global context?[6] The varying answers to these questions are today generally recapitulated and identified by reference to "seminal" works by great thinkers: Kant's essay "Über die verschiedenen Racen der Menschen" ("On the Different Human Races," 1775); Blumenbach's *De generis humani varietate nativa* (*On the Natural Variety of Mankind,* 1775, 1781, 1795; 1798 in German); Herder's *Ideen zu einer Philosophie der Geschichte der Menschheit* (*Reflections on the Philosophy of the History of Mankind,* 1784); Kant's responses to Herder's *Ideen* in the *Allgemeine Literatur-Zeitung* and *Berlinische Monatsschrift* (1785–1786);[7] the physician Thomas Samuel von Sömmerring's lecture "Über die Verschiedenheit des Mohren vom Europäer" (1784);[8] his friend Georg Forster's short contribution "Noch etwas über die Menschenracen" (1786); and finally Kant's "Über den Gebrauch der teleologischen Prinzipien in der Philosophie" (1788) and *Anthropologie in pragmatischer Hinsicht* (*Anthropology from a Pragmatic Point of View,* 1798).[9] While these texts are undoubtedly representative of the various intellectual trends at the time, it is other works, which are today relatively ignored, that had a more profound impact on the political unconscious, perhaps because they presented their "facts" and conclusions in a style accessible to the general public, with illustrations and catchy titles: for example, Christian Ernst Wünsch's *Conversations on Man* (*Unterhaltungen über den Menschen,* with fourteen copper engravings, 1780 and 1796) or the many publications by the Göttingen professor of philosophy Christoph Meiners.[10] As the author of a short, often reprinted *Sketch of the History of Mankind* (*Grundriss der Geschichte der Menschheit,* 1785, 1786, 1793), and as the coeditor of and principal contributor to the *Göttingisches historisches Magazin*

(1782–1792) and its sequel *Neues Göttingisches historisches Magazin* (1792–1794), this "professor ordinarius of secular wisdom" (as the literal translation of his title, "Ordentlicher Professor der Weltweisheit," reads) provided his readers with philosophical speculation and biological theories that reaffirmed de Pauw's assessment of the Indians' special degeneracy in a world where everyone with a dark skin was not only "ugly" but inferior and hence destined to serve.[11] By selectively reproducing and recontextualizing earlier theories of physiological and cultural difference, and by indiscriminately using the anthropological terminology employed in the late-eighteenth-century discourse on human variations — *Rasse, Abart, Varietät, Gattung, Anartung, Entartung, Verartung* — Meiners, Wünsch, and others[12] created the pseudoscientific discourse on race that would gain such notoriety in the nineteenth century.[13] They codified a notion of racial difference that linked observations of the physical properties of specific peoples to conjectures about their intellectual, moral, and aesthetic value as compared to Europeans and, among Europeans, Germans. If we read the scientific-philosophical debate on the variations of the human species against, and in conjunction with, these popularizers, the subtle differences in the arguments, in ideological positioning, and in self-professed intentions acquire less significance than the commonalities in strategy, explanatory patterns, and conclusions.

Primitive Man and Primeval Man

Kant's 1775 essay "Von den verschiedenen Racen der Menschen" is considered the first theoretical milestone in the discussion of physical difference in Germany and the first time the term "Race" — adopted from the English language and from the animal kingdom — is introduced into German discourse on humans.[14] To Kant, the ability to reproduce with each other makes all humans one single species, irrespective of physical differences. "Abarten," genetically transmitted variations, constitute "Racen," which in turn are subdivided into "Spielarten," "Varietäten," and "Schläge," produced by "crossbreeding" and identified by the persistence and dominance of certain physical traits, such as hair color, hair consistency, or build.

Kant distinguishes between four races based on skin color: white (blond whites of northern Europe); black (Senegambian blacks from Central Africa); red-skinned (Huns, Mongols, or Calmucks in Asia and America); and olive-skinned (from India). All other races are "derivations" (432). The order of appearance not only indicates a hierarchy of importance — whites take precedence — but a natural historical order, since these races supposedly stem from one original race Kant defines as "Weisse von brünetter Farbe,"[15] brown-haired (dark-skinned?) whites who lived in the Mediterranean region but changed physical characteristics when they migrated to different environments.[16] Although they were starting from a common "stock" [Stamm] with a common genetic potential [Keime], humans were irreversibly transformed and subdivided into races by climate: the wet cold climate in northern Europe, the dry cold environment in Asia, the humid heat in Africa, and the dry heat in India.

In this racial-continental color scheme, the Indians of America, however, are assigned a special position. Since Indians occupy all imaginable climatic ranges, from dry cold to humid heat, explanations for physical difference based on climate clearly do not suffice to account for their common traits across the two Americas. Kant therefore employs a special explanatory strategy when he concludes that "the Americans" have not yet fully adjusted to their "new" continental environment:

> The Americans, finally, seem to be a not yet fully defined [eingeartet] Hunnic race. For in the extreme Northwest of America . . . , at the northern banks of the Hudson Bay, the inhabitants are quite similar to the Calmucks. Further south the features become more open and more prominent; yet the beardless chin, the uniformly black hair, the brown-red complexion, as well as the coldness and insensitivity of the temperament — all of which are remnants of the impact made by an extended stay in cold regions, as we will soon see — can be found from the extreme north of that continent to Staten Island. The extended stay of the forefathers of the Americans in Northeast Asia and adjacent Northwest America has brought to perfection the Calmuckian traits; the rapid expansion of their offspring southward on the continent, on the other hand, produced the American ones (433, my translation).

The Amerindians' special status as not yet "eingeartet" is obvious, he argues, if one considers the lack of body hair ("the suffocated growth of hair," 437) and their copper-red skin tone, both of which are products of cold weather, as is — he says in passing — their "natural predisposition," their cold, weak temperament, which "betrays a half-extinguished vitality" ["eine halb erloschene Lebenskraft," 438]. Clearly, de Pauw's theories of the Americans' clammy, hairless "decadence" form the background to Kant's racial distinctions. The implications of Kant's theory of the connection between racial character and environment — which he adapted, among others, from Montesquieu — are twofold within a colonialist context that includes the New World: first, hairless Indians lack vitality even to be useful slaves (see p. 438 footnote); and second, they are physiologically not yet at home in their new territory, hence cannot lay claim to the ground. Rationalist philosophy thus "proves" what conquerors had experienced all along: that the Indian was not man enough to defend his territories, territories to which he was not entitled in the first place.

It is, of course, problematic to give Kant's apolitical theories such a political interpretation. Kant did not go so far as to suggest that the Europeans were entitled to the Indians' land. But the continued insistence on the Indians' supposed weakness and uselessness in combination with a theory that makes them recent arrivals to the continent could indeed lend itself to a justification of colonial usurpation as the natural right of the stronger.[17]

The dissertation *On the Natural Variety of Mankind* (1775)[18] by the anthropologist Johann Friedrich Blumenbach has traditionally been understood as the antithesis to Kant's racial theories. Although Blumenbach shares Kant's monogenist position, he rejects as unscientific Kant's a priori categories and any attempt to classify humans into races by skin color, observed temperament, or supposed hairlessness:

> For on the first discovery of the Ethiopians, or the beardless inhabitants of America, it was much easier to pronounce them different species than to inquire into the structure of the human body, to consult the numerous anatomical authors and travellers, and carefully to weigh their good faith or carelessness, to compare parallel examples from the universal circuit of natural history, and then at last to come to an opinion, and investigate the causes of the variety. (98)

Variations in skin color or size "can never constitute a diversity of species," Blumenbach maintains, since they depend on a variety of exterior and interior influences (102–105, 113). Skulls are not indicative as long as many peoples customarily deform them (120); and hair grows on all peoples, even on Indians of the Americas, who, however, pluck it out (127). Infinite varieties take the place of "races," and these varieties are all related to one another by gradation. However, Blumenbach does conceive of four basic varieties, of which the Indo-European variety, once again, comes first:

The first and most important to us (which is also the primitive one) is that of Europe, Asia this side of the Ganges, and all the country situated to the north of the Amoor, together with that part of North America which is nearest both in position and character of the inhabitants. Though the men of these countries seem to differ very much amongst each other in form and colour, still when they are looked at as a whole they seem to agree in many things with ourselves. The second includes that part of Asia beyond the Ganges, and below the river Amoor, which looks towards the south, together with the islands and the greater part of those countries which are now called Australian. Men of dark colour, snub noses, with winking eyelids drawn outwards at the corners, scanty, and stiff hair. Africa makes up the third. There remains, finally for the fourth the rest of America, except so much of the North as was included in the first variety. (99)

The distinctions, it seems, are again based on skin color, hair, and physiognomy, only the boundaries around human varieties are re-drawn: the North American Indians now form part of the same human variety as the other peoples north of the Ganges, the Mediterranean, and the Amoor, and they differ in fundamental ways from the peoples in the south — South Americans, Africans, South Asians, and so forth.

In the second edition of his dissertation (1781), however, Blumen-bach introduces a five-part north-south-east-west division of mankind "as more consonant with nature" (p. 99 footnote). The new distinc-tions are not only informed by scientific observation but by aesthetics, and they contain conjectures about moral character:

The first of these and the largest [variety], which is also the primeval one, embraces the whole of Europe, including the Lapps, whom I cannot in any way separate from the rest of the Europeans, when their appearance and their language bear such testimony to their Finnish origin; and that west-ern part of Asia which lies towards us, this side of the Obi, the Caspian sea, mount Taurus and the Ganges; also northern Africa, and lastly, in Amer-ica, the Greenlanders and the Esquimaux, for I see in these people a won-derful difference from the other inhabitants of America; and unless I am altogether deceived, I think they must be derived from the Finns. All these nations regarded as a whole are *white in colour, and if compared with the rest, beautiful in form.*

The second variety comprises that of the rest of Asia, which lies beyond the Ganges, and the part lying beyond the Caspian Sea and the river Obi towards Nova Zembla. The inhabitants of this country are distinguished by being of brownish colour, more or less verging to the olive, straight face, narrow eye-lids, and scanty hair. This whole variety may be sub-divided into two races, northern and southern; of which one may embrace China, the Corea, the kingdoms of Tonkin, Pegu, Siam, and Ava, using rather monosyllabic languages and *distinguished for depravity and per-fidiousness of spirit and of manners;* and the other the nations of northern Asia, the Ostiaks, and the other Siberians, the Tunguses, the Mantchoos, the Tartars, the Calmucks, and the Japanese.

The third variety comprises what remains of Africa, besides that north-ern part which I have already mentioned. Black men, muscular, with prominent upper jaws, swelling lips, turned up nose, very black curly hair.

The fourth comprises the rest of America, whose inhabitants are distin-guished by their copper colour, their thin habit of body, and scanty hair.

Finally, the new southern world makes up the fifth, with which, unless I am mistaken, the Sunda, the Molucca, and the Philippine Islands should be reckoned; the men throughout being of a very deep brown colour, with broad nose, and thick hair. Those who inhabit the Pacific Archipelago are divided again by John Reinh[ard] Forster into two tribes. One made up of the Otaheitans, the New Zealanders, and the inhabitants of the Friendly Isles . . . etc. *men of elegant appearance and mild disposition;* whereas the others who inhabit New Caledonia, Tanna, and the New Hebrides, etc. *are blacker, more curly, and in disposition more distrustful and ferocious.* (100 footnote, emphasis mine)

Thus, although Blumenbach rejects the term "race" and the clear-cut boundaries between races that Kant had erected, his four or five varia-tions do revive the notion of substantial physiological-aesthetic-moral difference. Not surprisingly, in the third edition (1795) Blumenbach refers back to Kant when he begins his discussion of the native varieties of mankind by discussing skin color, "which although it sometimes deceives, still is a much more constant character, and more generally transmitted than others" (207).[19] "Hair" becomes the next indicator of "race," together with eye color, whereas "racial varieties of the face," as prefigured in the skull, form a complex third marker — complex be-cause of the difficulty of obtaining typical, undeformed skull speci-mens of the variations Blumenbach discusses. Nor is it surprising that Blumenbach's English translator in the nineteenth century returns to the Kantian term "race" to characterize Blumenbach's "varieties," since these differ from "races" only in the terminology.

Blumenbach also agrees with Kant on the primacy of the white race in terms of natural history, which he then extends to imply aesthetic superiority. In the third edition of *On the Natural Variety of Mankind* (1795), the "Caucasian" occupies first place both as the "primeval" and "the most handsome and becoming" variety (265). This variety "diverges in both directions into two, most remote and very different from each other; on the one side, namely, into the Ethiopian, and on the other into the Mongolian. The remaining two occupy the intermediate positions between that primeval one and these two extreme varieties; that is, the American between the Caucasian and Mongolian; the Malay between the same Caucasian and Ethiopian" (265).

In other words, the Americans, no longer part of the northern First World, now occupy a transitional space in the north-east-south, white-yellow-black division of the world, somewhere between the "most handsome" Europeans and one of the two "extremes," the "Mongolian" and the "Ethiopian."[20] Despite Blumenbach's repeated attempts to reaffirm the connectedness of all races by gradation and their common humanity, hierarchies of cultural development, of national-moral character and aesthetic properties keep reemerging as organizing principles in the texts. Whereas before, these principles were based on abstract conjectures about stages of civilization, they are now empirically legitimized by the "science" of craniology.[21] Difference is not only discernible on the surface, like color, but "more than skin deep."[22]

Apes and Humans: Anatomy Is Destiny

A divergence between intent and practice also characterizes the keynote address of anatomist Samuel Thomas von Sömmerring, "Über die körperliche Verschiedenheit des Mohren vom Europäer," held at the reopening of Mainz University in 1784.[23] In his study of the anatomical differences between "the Negro" and "the European," Sömmerring, a disciple of the Dutch anatomist Pieter Camper, had remarked on the similarities in the profile and jawline between Africans and apes. Implicitly attacked for racism by Blumenbach and others, who pointed out that selecting one trait like facial angles to suggest affinity meant ignoring all others that proved the contrary, Sömmerring felt the need to exonerate himself.[24] He insisted that his observation did not carry any value judgment: "The Negroes," he affirmed, "are true human beings, just like us" (xx). His protestations and Blumenbach's exhortations notwithstanding, the association of blacks with apes, and the idea of an "allegorical plan of creation" — from the orangutan upward to the Calmuck to the European to the classical Greek, or downward

"from the most beautiful European woman to the ugliest Caffer"[25] —
became a fixed element in late-eighteenth-century anthropological discourse and pictorial representations.[26] Sömmerring, albeit involun-
tarily, succeeded in establishing as natural fact the connection between
anatomical details and (clichéd) ideas of "racial character."

These ideas reappear, for example, in Herder's *Reflections on the
Philosophy of History of Mankind* (*Ideen zu einer Philosophie der
Geschichte der Menschheit*, 1784).[27] Like Blumenbach, Herder insisted
on human varieties derived from one original species of man. He rejected any division of humankind according to races based on region or
skin color or exclusive varieties (257–258). His *Ideen*, however, which
appeared concomitant with Sömmerring's article, partakes of the classificatory, evaluative impulse that had characterized the other contemporary natural histories. Like de Pauw, Kant, Sömmerring, and to an
extent Blumenbach, Herder attributes physical variation to climate.
Thus the Eskimos' supposed lack of sexual interest, their phlegm, and
passivity are caused by the cold climate of the regions they inhabit.
Whenever climate, however, does not suffice to explain physiological
or moral properties, Herder resorts to a putative innate "Nationalcharakter": the *Samojede*, "a kind of negro among the Northerners"
["gleichsam der Neger unter den Nordländern"] because "sensitive and
choleric" ["fein und hitzig"] must have brought this "national character" with him — it has not yet been dominated ["bemeistert," 213] by
climate.

Herder divides the globe into five climatic-geographic regions, which
also correspond to five basic varieties of mankind: the Arctic belt,
the Asian landmass ("Asiatischer Rücken"), the region of the beautifully formed peoples ("Erdstrich schöngebildeter Völker"), Africa, and
America. The farther away from the inclement climates of the North
and the closer to the temperate regions in the "middle," the more beautiful the shape, the more oval the face, the lighter the skin, and the
more harmonious the peoples' countenance. The milder Lapps live in a
milder region than the rough Eskimos (212). The peak of humanity is
to be found along the Mediterranean, where beautiful body and beautiful mind merge in matrimony to form the perfect man: "On the shores
of the Mediterranean Sea, human grace of body at last found a site
where it could marry the spirit and become manifest with all the charms
of earthly and heavenly beauty, not only to the eye but also the soul"
(225–226). Like Kant and Blumenbach, Herder mixes his observations
of difference with aesthetic judgments and conjectures about relative

position in cultural history. He does not indicate, for example, whether the marriage of physical and mental perfections refers to the current peoples along the Mediterranean coast or — as one is led to suspect — to some imaginary Greece, cradle of Western civilization. In any case, perfection is to be found in the temperate zones, in the middle between objectionable extremes. Herder's civilized, beautiful Mediterranean variety is as far removed from the northern bestial creatures (Calmucks and Mongols are characterized by their small, flat nose, their big protruding "animal" ears, bow legs and white, strong denture, "which, along with their entire facial structure, seems to characterize a predator among the humans," 215), as it is from the repulsive "barbarians" in the East ("The Japanese are almost invariably of poor stature, with bulging heads, small eyes, blunt noses, flat cheeks, crooked legs and almost no whiskers," 218) or the primitive tribes in the South ("the flat noses and thick lips of the common Negro," 231).

In his characterization of the Africans, Herder — who emphatically rejects slavery (262) — makes a clear attempt to disavow prejudice and present an "unbiased" picture (228). And indeed, the passages dealing with different African peoples exhibit an effort to differentiate. Since skin color is not the result of blood, brains, or semen, but of oils in the skin (that are being "cooked up" by sunshine, 234), "we all" have the potential to become "Negroes" (233), he states. However, racial prejudice and cultural arrogance reemerge when he tries to explain the Africans' difference from the Europeans by resorting to anatomy, that which lies under layers of skin.[28] Nature compensated these peoples for their lack of "nobler gifts" — capacity for intellectual and spiritual advancement — he claims, by endowing them with greater ability for sensual enjoyment.[29] The "drive of the senses" ["sinnlicher Trieb"] is one of the principal sources of pleasure for "these nations" (235); and the ability to enjoy the sensuous is located both in the Africans' "oily organization" and in their anatomy. Their flat nose, receding jaw line and forehead (and similarity to the ape's skull! 236),[30] and the "elasticity" of their body predestines Africans for the "thierisch-sinnlicher Genuss," for animalistic-sensuous pleasures. Not made for "finer spirituality," according to Herder, the African is thus locked into his anatomy: sensuous, strong, resistant, agile. If nature made him what he is, why should he be forced to leave his country, his station, his natural state? (236)

While Herder implicitly questions the perfectibility of the Africans, he proceeds very differently with the inhabitants of the last, admittedly

"most difficult continent" (239), America. Like Kant, he tries to come
to terms with the fact that Indians of similar physiognomy occupy a
wide variety of climatic zones and habitats. Like Kant and Blumenbach, he attempts to explain this phenomenon by reference to a state of
"transition" (241). In contrast to de Pauw and Kant, however, and
echoing Pernety's description of the noble savage, Herder characterizes
the "One Principal Character" (242) of the Amerindians as exhibiting
"healthy, contained strength, barbaric-proud desire for freedom and
for warfare that affects their public and domestic lives, education, government, business, and customs in times of war and peace" (242).
Herder does not dwell long on anatomy or skin color. When he does,
the descriptions of Indians are much more favorable than those of their
racial kin, the Mongols, Calmucks, and so forth. The Indians' national
character is not "natural," but was formed in the history of conquest
and colonization, in the battles for cultural survival and the processes
of adaptation, he affirms. Repeatedly, Herder blames the Spaniards for
having destroyed the Indians' culture and bent their spirit ("exhausted
by serfdom," 245). The Indians' savagery, passivity, and weakness are
responses to mistreatment, not innate (263–264), he argues, following
Montaigne's lead.[31] However, even if "we" ignore the decadence "they"
have suffered since the conquest and imagine them in their pristine pre-
Conquest state, the Indians, he suggests, occupy a culturally inferior
rank. In fact, their trusting kindness [*Gutherzigkeit*] and childlike innocence [*kindliche Unschuld*], the elementary nature of their institutions,
skills, and arts, provide Europeans with a mirror image of their own
history, their own cultural beginnings. Not surprisingly, some Indians
are like Germans, albeit at an earlier stage: "the inhabitants of Germany were Patagons only a few centuries ago, and are no longer so; the
inhabitants of future climates will not resemble us" (254).

Despite repeated attempts — by Blumenbach, Herder, and Forster —
to caution against facile hierarchical classifications and to suggest the
tentative, hypothetical nature of all observations of difference, the radical arbitrariness with which the world was divided into advanced and

In Herder's *Reflections* the different human varieties are not only
distinguished by their skin color and anatomy, but anatomy determines
their aptitude for history, that is, for development and change: while
anatomy limits the perfectibility of some (the Africans), it permits the
growth and development of others (the childlike Americans). It declares some as "different" and permanently locked into inferiority, others as "same" and hence able to grow.

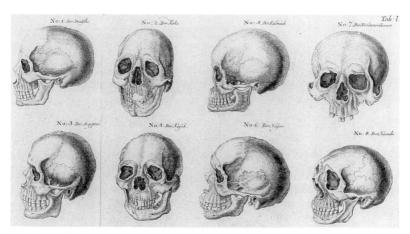

1. "Nationality Is Destiny: The German Skull." From Christian Wünsch, *Unterhaltungen über den Menschen,* vol. 1, 2nd ed. (1796). Courtesy of the John Carter Brown Library at Brown University.

primitive, beautiful and ugly, white and dark, moral and immoral, "masculine" and "feminine" peoples gained ground. By 1795, Blumenbach was able to invite his readers to choose among twelve different theories on the subdivision of mankind into human varieties (266). And by that time also, the term "race" had become generally accepted to denote physical and moral difference. In fact, Christian Ernst Wünsch, a professor at Frankfurt an der Oder, could then claim the preferability of the term "Menschenrassen" over "nation," "stock," "species," or "variety" since, he says, it stresses the biological connectedness of one people and their difference from another. "And a sense of denigration can surely not be evoked by the term, since the added title 'Mensch' lifts it up and ennobles it" (2–3). To thinkers like him, "Rasse" provides the biological underpinnings for a "national" cultural identity.

In the formation of the skull, *the* indicator of physical, mental, and moral superiority, race and ethnicity overlap. When Wünsch discusses the so-called human races, "or variations that noticeably differ from one another" (127), he resorts to eight skulls, among them "the German skull," as representative of European man. The German's "well-shaped jawline, beautifully curved temple, and beautifully formed forehead," which suggests "great mental capacities" (129) is contrasted with the "Kalmückenschädel" (133), the "Negerkopf" (134), the "skull of a North American," and the "head of a Carib," all of which are associated with animals and "bestial" properties (fig. 1).[32] In this scheme of com-

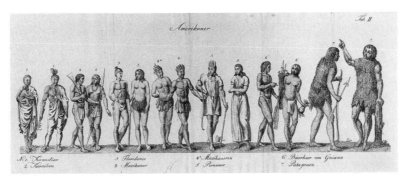

2. "Die Amerikaner: The Politics of Size." From Christian Wünsch, *Unterhaltungen über den Menschen,* vol. 1, 2nd ed. (1796). Courtesy of the John Carter Brown Library at Brown University.

parative anatomy, the German is farthest removed from the Calmuck and the African, who, in turn, are extreme opposites of each other. Since all the other heads, however, bear certain resemblances either to the German (Turk, Egyptian) or the Calmuck (Cossack, North American, Carib), it is the African who, Wünsch argues, remains "by himself," unrelated to any other, totally other. The "Negro," the (unrepresented) East Indian "pointed head" [*Spitzkopf*], the Mongol, and the Caucasian form the four cornerstones in Wünsch's racial-craniological square (139), in which Germans have reached the highest level of civilization, beauty, and morality.

In the discussions on "race" versus "variety," discursive commonalities seem to overtake differences in approach or conclusions. Whether they are monogenists who believe in one common origin of humankind (Kant, Herder, Sömmerring, Blumenbach) or polygenists who conceive of different human stocks that developed along parallel lines (Forster), whether they divide humankind into separate, distinct "races" or not-so-distinct "varieties," whether they take skin color or skull formation as the measure, all "anthropologists" in the 1790s seem to share the conviction that the white male is primeval "man," who possesses the most harmonious countenance and has therefore rightfully achieved cultural superiority (figs. 2 and 3). One's observation provides the basis for the other's hypothesis, and these hypotheses are recycled, restructured, and referred to over and over again, until they have acquired the status of significant "fact." This process of mutual, even circular reinforcement is, for example, obvious in Sömmerring's apologia, where he cites as one of the "proofs" for his hypothesis of the

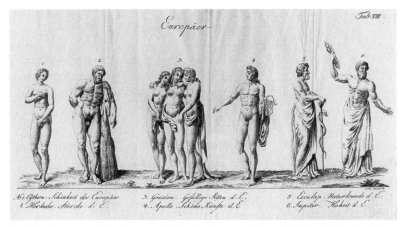

3. "Die Europäer: Embodiments of Classical Beauty." From Christian Wünsch, *Unterhaltungen über den Menschen*, vol. 1, 2nd ed. (1796). Courtesy of the John Carter Brown Library at Brown University.

anatomical difference of Europeans and Africans Herder's 1784 *Reflections*, in which Herder had quoted Sömmerring's own tract of 1784 as proof for his contentions. Likewise, Meiners will use "facts" from Sömmerring, Blumenbach, and Herder indiscriminately and selectively, irrespective of their scientific or philosophical disagreements with one another, in order to draw his racist "conclusions." While the works of individual thinkers, such as Herder's, are deeply inconsistent and contradictory, exhibiting both a tendency toward hierarchical classification and a desire for justice and cultural differentiation, an impersonal racist intertext emerges that "permits" mixing observations in natural history with aesthetic judgment, and aesthetics with conjectures about the course of cultural-political history.[33] The supremacy of the white European variety, evident in its advanced civilization — this intertext suggests — resides in physiology and anatomy, that is, in biology. In other words, biology explains "why a single continent, and certain peoples have almost always been the rulers, whereas all others have been the servants."[34]

This theory of the natural domination of the white race, proposed by Christoph Meiners in 1786, was reaffirmed in the face of serious political challenges in the 1790s, as the Haitian Revolution and the French Revolution broke up the "natural order" on both continents. The rebellion of African slaves on the Caribbean islands, their successful warfare against European armies, and the respective atrocities that were reported by black representatives and white plantation owners, threatened to undermine abstract categories of racial-moral superiority and required a reorientation of the European onlookers. Questions such as "What does difference reside in?" "Who is 'naturally' inferior, why, and to what effect?" "How can the natural order be reconciled with political order?" concerned even Germans, whose direct contacts with the plantation culture in the Caribbean and with the revolutionary wars there were relatively limited (see chapter 8). Germans felt compelled to contribute their share by discussing "dispassionately" and in "principle" the pros and cons of slavery, the legitimacy and morality of unrestricted rule over humans, and the implications of the slave rebellions for theories about racial difference[35] — partly, at least, because theories of "race," "slavery," and "colonialism" were intimately connected to self-perceptions and the search for a "German" ethnic identity within the European context. The changes in global race theories in the 1790s, and the renegotiation of the positions that "redskins," "blacks," and "whites" occupied in the mental frame of German anthropologists have to be read in the context of events in Saint-Domingue and of events across the border in France.

5

Patagons and Germans

Man himself, the inhabitant of this cold region of South America, exhibited two remarkable features: the cold more northerly interior shaped men into the sort of colossuses which resembled our German forebears who amazed Gaul and Rome . . . The adjacent southernmost part of the New World, Tierra del Fuego, a most desolate frozen island shattered into many pieces, had inhabitants corresponding to this habitat. All travelers called these Pesheräs a wretched, small, haggard, dirty, dull-witted sorry lot. Even such curiosity as is innate to many an animal species seemed to have been drained from them by indolence. They did not even desire to inspect the most remarkable edifice of human ingenuity, the European ship. — E. A. W. von Zimmermann, "The New World Revisited," 1809[1]

Haughty Britannia, thou, robbing from East and West
  Exquisite fragrant sprigs, that consume you in flames.
Glittering Phoenix! We, the industrious German bees,
  Gather from every mead honey, and know not for whom?
— J. G. Herder, "England and Germany," 1787[2]

The trends toward the systematization of the discourse on race and toward theories of insurmountable racial differences or racial-cultural affinities must be seen in relation to the revolutions both in Europe and its American colonies.[3] These events account for the confused responses by Germans whose humanitarian concern for slaves was now tested by the violent uprisings in the Caribbean (which also affected a few German plantation owners) and by the violent emancipation movement in the neighboring country (which affected all Germans across the Rhine). As sympathies with French and other revolutionaries subsided after 1790 and turned to conservative paternalist protectionism (of German territories, German governments, German conditions) or outright hatred toward any republican experiments, theories of race gained prominence that maintained or reaffirmed divisions rather than connections, and hierarchies rather than equality.

As the French imperialist threat to German territories increased, and as European nations engaged in colonial competition over the disintegrating colonies in the Caribbean, we can discern a tendency to conflate racial character with national character. Germans now inscribe themselves as "Germans" into global racial classifications where they appear in direct contrast to or peculiar affinity with "Negroes" or "Indians" on the one hand, and European nations on the other. In fact, one might speak of two interlocking, dynamic triangles: one of them corresponds to the *commerce triangulaire,* the Atlantic slave trade triangle Europe-Africa-America, that positions "the" German in relation to "the" African (slave) and "the" Indian;[4] the other pits Germans against the French and the British, as rivals and/or allies. Both triangles are dynamic insofar as shifts in the status of one group affect the image or self-image of the other. As the African descends from a position of "noble slave" (in the negrophile literature) to "brute beast" (in the reports of plantation owners), the abject Indian rises in stature. As slave trade and hence Africa lose their immediate interest as a colonial resource, South Americans gain in the eyes of potential masters or colonialists. The triangles also overlap: as German states are overrun by French revolutionary armies, (some) Germans discover their kinship with other "enslaved" or "colonized" peoples. They see themselves as the abject other—a situation they seek to revert by imagining others whom they can in turn colonize. Both Germans' self-perception and their perception of the "nature" of others are thus a function of positionality within a global order understood as "colonial."

Christoph Meiners, "the beloved philosopher of our fatherland," as Sömmerring had called him (somewhat tongue in cheek?),[5] becomes one of the principal revisionists of anthropological theory under the impact of the new colonial order, and a key witness to the shift toward a Germanification of colonial discourse in Germany.[6] His indebtedness to de Pauw and his anticipation of nineteenth-century biological theories make him a crucial link in the emergence of modern racism, and, particularly, modern *German* racism, since Germans as a separate identifiable subgroup figure prominently in his global categories.[7] What is more, by contrasting "true Germans" of superior blood with Wends, Slavs, Gypsies, Jews, and other "foreigners" [*Fremdlinge*], he prefigures ethnocentric ideologies that would gain ground in the latter half of the nineteenth century.[8]

The Black and the Red

In a series of articles in the *Göttingisches historisches Magazin* and *Neues Göttingisches historisches Magazin* that appeared in 1792, Meiners elaborates his theory of the basic opposition between "beautiful" and "ugly" peoples, the Caucasians and their multiple others.[9] Anthropology, it seems, has collapsed completely into aesthetics. Indicators of beauty are hair, skin color, and size, as the titles of his contributions suggest: "On the Growth of Hair or Beards among the Ugly and Dark-Skinned Peoples," "On Colors and Shades of Different Peoples," "On the Differences of Size of Different Peoples."[10] The fact that these "aesthetic" elaborations are preceded by a series of articles on slavery, which were written in 1790, immediately after the beginning of revolutionary uprisings in the French colony of Saint-Domingue, indicates the context in which Meiners's global physiognomy unfolds (on the context see also chapter 8).

As the titles of some of these earlier articles suggest, "On the Nature of the Americans," "On the Nature of African Negroes and the Subsequent Liberation or Containment of Blacks," "On the True Nature of the Slave-Trade and the Enslavement of Negroes in the West Indies," "nature"—human nature as evidenced in physical nature—forms the frame of reference for Meiners's race theories. Physiological details provide him with clues about cultural behavior. After emphatically pronouncing, on the first pages of "On the Nature of African Negroes," his support for the "growing enlightenment" ["wachsende Aufklärung"] and the emancipation of Jews and African slaves, Meiners retracts: the revolutionary fervor has gone too far in its demand for equality—an equality that is not just "impossible" but "unjust."[11] Some people are born inferior, Meiners maintains, and the rulers are now called upon to restore the privileges to those with inborn superiority. Meiners's list of naturally inferior races, classes, genders, and social groups links Africans with children, women, servants, criminals, and Jews. All these must not, and cannot, aspire to equality with their natural superiors, the white male Christian masters. In the subsequent seventy pages of the article, Meiners sets out to "prove" the natural inferiority of Africans and their "natural predisposition to slavery" (436) by resorting to the infamous analogy between blacks and animals. Sömmerring's observation as to the similarities of the jawline of apes and Africans serves him as positive evidence and starting point for a whole series of conjectures as to the Africans' inborn racial character.[12] Their supposed insensitivity to beatings and torture, their laziness, cowardice, lack of genius, tendency toward violence and treachery, their irritability, promiscuity, agility, and so forth, require that whites exert tight control over them. "All writers, even those who abhor unnecessary cruelty, concur that only starvation, strict surveillance, and beatings can get Negroes to work" (419), Meiners concludes. And since he never questions the right of Europeans to enslave Africans, he implicitly approves of such measures, although he overtly advocates "wisdom" and "kindness" (401) in their treatment.

Meiners's sources are a few, selected travelogues, "eyewitness reports" of Caribbean plantation owners, or anatomical studies that he exploits for his own purposes. Theories or observations that contradict his own apodictic statements are dismissed[13] on the grounds that positively described Africans cannot be "real Negroes"—they must be products of miscegenation with racially superior Arabs or Indians (441). Often, he resorts to circular reasoning to negotiate his point around opposing arguments. For example, moved by Blumenbach's caveat that one cannot deduce moral character from physical properties, Meiners seemingly dismantles, then rebuilds his own position: "I am not, by any means, adducing the verdicts of the common spirit of observation and of common sense concerning the significance of certain physical characteristics as evidence that the Negroes must be as limited in understanding and inferior in good nature as they are ugly; I merely bring it up so as to show that it is not altogether novel or unheard of to consider certain general and uniform formations or malformations of entire peoples not merely fortuitous and immaterial matters" (408). He then returns to his original position on natural inferiority, supporting it now not with observations of physical properties, but with conjectures about cultural differences: "But even if we had no idea that the Negroes are uglier in body and countenance than the Europeans, and that they have smaller skulls, a smaller and less pliant brain and coarser nerves than these, we would still be bound to conclude from their entire mode of living and acting that Negroes are significantly less sensitive and more irritable than whites" (409).

Although circular reasoning, frequent internal contradictions,[14] and incessant repetitions disqualify the text in the eyes of any critical reader, these stylistic strategies guarantee its pernicious impact on the general public—a public that has been exposed to racialist prejudices for centuries.[15] Under the guise of science, Meiners reintroduces and reaffirms

handed-down observations (often taken out of context), which he constructs into a system of mutually reinforcing racial stereotypes. With
rhetorical tricks he manipulates his readers into accepting this construction as truth. The many footnotes and the seeming openness to
debate lend scientific credibility and legitimacy to the enterprise, as
do references to Sömmerring, Blumenbach, and, implicitly, Kant and
Herder. The repetitions and causal/associative chains[16] that link one
physical property to all others — physical, moral, aesthetic, and intellectual alike — create an avalanche of determinacy or inevitability. Even
on the rhetorical plane, anatomy becomes destiny. Having been repeated over and over again, in one or another constellation, any conjecture turns imperceptibly into "fact." The initial observation of a similarity of jawlines between a human and a simian skull is used as the
foundation for a whole host of analogies with the animal world that
assign all Africans a position not just of inferiority but of natural service, as beasts of burden, to "humans," that is, white Europeans. The
purpose of Meiners's rhetorical tour de force is apparent in the questions and answers with which he closes his article:

> Before I continue, I ask those who know mankind and advocate justice
> [*Menschen-Kenner und Rechts-Lehrer*], whether they believe that such in-
> sensitive, excitable and phlegmatic, dumb and evil-minded people as the
> Negroes should be given such rights and such liberty, for their own good
> and that of others; that one could entice them with such goals to do good,
> and keep them under threat of punishment from doing bad; and that one
> could impose the same duties on them as on Europeans? I would be sur-
> prised if there was even one among my readers who would answer this
> question differently from the way in which all European nations who
> own slaves and who have slave legislation have answered it. (456, my
> translation)

Showered with such masses of "evidence," few readers were inclined to
disagree with Meiners or the European colonizers, for that matter.[17]
    A similar rhetorical appeal to the public's judgment opens the article
on the nature of the American Indians. Here, Meiners is even more
defensive and cautious. He does not want to create the impression that
he is out to manipulate his readers. The final decision about the truth of
his proposition is up to them, he concedes (103) — a proposition that,
again, claims to prove "natural" inferiority scientifically.[18]
    His first major point addresses the supposed physical uniformity of
all indigenous peoples (102). Any observable differences can be sub-

sumed into a unified "characteristic" picture of the American: he is small or medium-sized; has a "weak," "plump" body, "big shapeless" head, ears, or mouth, a "flat narrow" forehead, "small" eyes, high cheekbones, straight, "coarse" hair, no beard, and hands that are "either too small or too large" (109–114). Either way, he exceeds "normalcy," that is, European norms established by Meiners.

This exterior, Meiners proposes, matches and reveals the Americans' inner qualities. The characteristics he stresses correspond almost verbatim to those he claims to have discovered among Africans: a "bestial" insensitivity to pain that "almost" surpasses the insensitivity of European domestic animals or Negroes (114); a high irritability based on weakness that "almost surpasses that of sickly children and hysterical women among the white peoples" (117); a taciturn, melancholy, suicidal personality (116); the ability to imitate European customs without understanding them (118); a natural phlegm when it comes to working for Europeans (122); and so on. On the positive side, Meiners registers the Indians' agility, manual dexterity, physical endurance, sharpness of senses, and acuteness of memory. While Indians may not be able to serve as slaves because of their physical weakness, they might be useful as scouts or as artisans (130), he implies.

Meiners's argument culminates in a long discussion of the Indians' inborn "retardation" ["natürlicher Blödsinn"] that, in his view, accounts for all their other shortcomings and locks them into permanent childhood (137, 139, 140, 150, 151): "Apart from their indolence, lack of feeling, incorrigibility or imperfectibility of character, one encounters in the Americans all those phenomena that we, too, generally consider as signs of natural imbecility: childlike credulity, mendacity, obsequiousness, volatility, and moodiness, combined with an animal obstinacy and obduracy and an extraordinary gift for guile and dissimulation, which in turn are coupled with total absence of mind, lack of wisdom and deliberation" (145). The leitmotiv in this wholesale condemnation is the insistence on the Indians' evasive tactics: they refuse to be trained, used, and abused. They do not reveal their secrets; they do not obey; they dodge or withdraw. The ultimate sign of their "immense imbecility" is, Meiners affirms, that unlike Africans or southern Asians, they do not recognize the superiority of the Europeans (154).

As the two articles on Africans and Native Americans indicate, Meiners's characterizations of these colonized others are solely guided by considerations of their economic use value to Europeans. After having established the natural and permanent inferiority of both "races" vis-à-vis the European "race," and, implicitly, the right of the latter to subject the former, he focuses exclusively on supposed physical, mental, or moral characteristics that serve or impede colonial exploitation. The Africans' superior physical strength and resilience "predestine" them to menial work, while their resistance to forced labor and "insensitivity" to corporeal punishment require ever greater brutality to keep them at bay. The physical weakness of the Americans disqualifies them as slaves, but their peculiar hunting and tracking skills "predestine" them to serve whites in other capacities. Their resistance, Meiners suggests, has to be met not so much with brutal punishment — the Indians would just die from melancholy — but with greater cunning, for "all Europeans" know that "the more you are on your guard, the kinder and more willing the Americans are to serve you" (156).

After having reestablished the natural inferiority of the colonized and hence the Europeans' right to crush their rebellions, Meiners goes on to reaffirm the natural superiority of the colonizers, which by 1792 was somewhat shaky. Clearly, this reaffirmation is driven by the desire to regain control, if only in theory, and not just over European "possessions" abroad, but over cultural territory lost at home. His taxonomy provides Germans, threatened with French predominance, with the means to vindicate their "racial" superiority and with a framework for establishing a separate national-colonialist identity in the global race economy.

The Invention of the German Race

Whereas in 1790 Meiners had focused on the "nature" of racial others, now, in 1792, his energies shift toward the "nature" of the self. Where before he had tried to justify the enslavement and exploitation of Africans and Amerindians on the basis of their racial "inferiority," he now establishes the racial foundations for the "superiority" of "Germans" as the "fairest of them all" — a kind of "Snow White" syndrome.

In his 1790 articles on peoples of color Meiners had considered size, then strength, then skin color the principal markers of difference. Now it is hair that — more than anything else — separates the beautiful from the ugly. The lack of a beard is not just the principal deficiency of Native Americans, as de Pauw had claimed: it is the distinctive feature of *all* dark-skinned peoples (485). Beardlessness serves, again, as an indicator of sexual, physical, moral, and cultural shortcomings. As history has shown, Meiners recapitulates, the "smoothest," "weakest," and "most cowardly" of all peoples, the beardless Americans, could not withstand the manly bearded Europeans (502). And beards, he states, come with "better blood" (500).[19]

"Blood" is also the cause for variations in skin color ("On the Colors and Shades of Different Peoples," 627f). Like facial hair, skin color divides the world not only into fair and ugly peoples, but into hard-working and lazy (658), strong and weak, moral and immoral ones. Industry, strength, and morality are embodied by Europeans — yet not by all. Some Europeans are not up to standard either, Meiners suggests: "Lapps, Finns and some of their descendants, furthermore some herd-ers of Hun descent living between the Danube and the Dnjeper, finally Jews, Armenians, Turks, and Gypsies" (667). Even within Europe, skin color determines one's place in the natural hierarchy. And "the people with the whitest, most blooming and most delicate skin" are of Ger-manic stock, since "they live in Northern Germany, Denmark, Sweden, Norway, Holland, Great Britain and the adjacent islands" (668). Greek women may be superior to Slavic women, Meiners concedes, "but rarely or never do they attain, as to delicacy and whiteness of skin, the rosy cheeks of beautiful Englishwomen or German women and *Jung-frauen*" (668).

White is not only aesthetically or morally superior; it is also the alpha and the omega of human evolution. While the white and yellow skin colors are, in Meiners's natural history, the two original colors, it is the yellow color that must have branched out into red and black, be-cause of climatic influences. "The reason for my conjecture is that the yellow, red, and black peoples share all the essential elements of anat-omy, spiritual and moral gifts" (672). Meiners's afterthought, namely that the whites may also have descended from the yellow peoples, does not change the picture of us versus them, because the two have pro-gressed in different directions: the whites, as the vanguard of history, are moving ahead, while the yellow, black, and red peoples are stay-ing farther and farther behind. By 1792, racial types, even if they de-scended from the same stock, have become completely separate. As far as Meiners is concerned, the differences among the human species are irreversible.

Meiners's third article in this physiognomic sequence, "On the Dif-ference in the Size of Different Peoples," pushes the analogy between white, bearded, tall, civilized, and beautiful one step further: if "tall is beautiful," it is Germany that has produced the most beautiful men in all of Europe and the whole world (700). Yet not everyone living in

German-speaking countries are "Germans," according to Meiners's definition: "small" and "ugly" mountain dwellers in the German or Swiss Alps are probably not of German blood (701), nor are the Wends, Slavs, Jews, Gypsies, and other "strangers" [*Fremdlinge*, 702]. By basing his definition of Germanness on a few physical traits, Meiners establishes an exclusive, racialized national identity. Again, his argument is circular: tall, white, and bearded is a sign of physical and moral superiority; Germans are tall, whites, and bearded; ergo, Germans are superior to other Europeans, nay to all "ugly" peoples. All those who are neither tall, white, nor bearded are, by definition, not German.

As the next passage shows, however, Meiners is not thinking of his compatriots, but of the Old Germans, who, "strong like oak trees" and sustained by meat, milk, and beer, lived on the rich soils and under the blue skies of the fatherland, engaging in martial arts. "Spices" and artful concoctions were as foreign to them as corrupting luxuries, "lascivious books and plays" (703). Today's Germans, Meiners admits, are less tall and less strong. They have degenerated [*ausgeartet*], become smaller and weaker (707), because they indulge in culinary and sexual excesses and lack physical exercise. However, what they have lost in size, they can make up through military drill. If Germans practice martial arts, Meiners prophesies, and if they educate their minds, "they will become not only richer and more enlightened, but also more powerful and invincible than ever before" (710). In other words: even if a close look at the present indicates that Germans are not what their genetic makeup promised them to be, they can attain past superiority if they set their mind to it.

The three physical properties then—dense beards, white skin, and tall size—only function in combination. Together, they convey superiority. Yet while Germans naturally excel according to Meiners's racial hierarchy, they have to work hard to attain a position of supremacy in Europe, for there are others—the British, the Dutch, the Scandinavians—whose racial makeup makes them natural competitors for political power. Germans can only succeed if they do not indulge, if they control their urges for physical gratification and discipline their bodies.

Within the racialist framework, the restraint Meiners advocates relates also to cross-racial mixing. If "blood" is the cause of superiority and the marker of national identity, any mixing of bloods can only weaken the "national," that is, the militarized virile German body. Even though Meiners is convinced that white blood dominates in miscegenation and has already "improved" the genetic material of some races (in Bali, and in the Spanish colonies),[20] he propagates sexual abstention as a means of maintaining control. "Blood" thus becomes the primary and ultimate cause of difference: it creates racial "families," connected by blood ties, and excludes those of "different" blood lines; it separates brothers from others.

Germans and Their (Br)Others

Meiners's reductive, at times shrill theories of German natural superiority must be read against the despair and frustration felt by many German intellectuals in the 1790s over the fragmentation and weakness of "the German nation" in view of the French threat.[21] This threat is perceived as both cultural — the continued predominance of the French language and French cultural models among the elite — and military. In April 1792, as Meiners was composing his articles, the French National Assembly had declared war against Prussia's ally Austria. A Prussian offensive against the French revolutionary army in the summer of 1792 ended in Prussia's retreat and Austria's defeat. In October of that year General Custine and his "Latin hordes" crossed into German territories and conquered Mainz, beginning decades of on-and-off warfare, which culminated in Prussia's resounding defeat and occupation by Napoleon in 1806.[22] The sense of national victimization and "impotence" felt by many still reverberates 150 years later, when Rudolf Ibbeken writes about the Prussian defeat in terms of a rape.[23] The term "Vergewaltigung" suggests the gendered coordinates within which Prussians/Germans experienced this French assault on an imagined national body and the urgency of its "remasculinization." Germany must become a "man" — tall, strong, bearded — in order to rebuke the imperialist neighbor and assert its rightful place in the European family. Theories of Germanic macho superiority over effeminate Latin races are one way to turn the tables, if only in theory.

The boundaries between "self" and "other(s)" that Meiners erects in his two imaginary triangles provided disoriented Germans, unsure of *their* nature, with a "national intentionality" (Bernd Fischer). They established the parameters for the construction of a collective identity based on difference. As tall, bearded, white Europeans, Germans could feel "racially" superior to Africans and American Indians; as snow-white, hard-working, disciplined, manly *Germanen* they could claim superiority over external and internal others — over the French and British as well as the Jews and the Gypsies. Since this imagined identity

4. "Unequal Encounters: European and Patagon." From John Byron, *John Byrons, obersten Befehlshabers über ein Englisches Geschwader, Reise um die Welt, in den Jahren 1764 und 1765. Nebst einer genauen Beschreibung der Magellanischen Strasse, der Patagonischen Riesen, und der ganz neu-entdeckten Sieben Inseln in der Süd-See* (Frankfurt and Leipzig: Metzler, 1769). Courtesy of the John Carter Brown Library at Brown University.

emanated from a position of political and cultural insecurity, it was fraught with instability. Size, hair, or skin color proved to be ambiguous indicators of preeminence — not just in the European context, but also when it came to others overseas. If tallness and hairiness assigned cultural superiority, where would that leave bearded "giants" who, throughout the Middle Ages, had been considered to be fantastic embodiments of brute force and primitive dumbness? If whiteness conferred special status, why was it often associated with ghostliness, monstrosity, disease, or death? Once again, the Patagon Giants — those huge natives in South America who had already constituted a conceptual roadblock for de Pauw and Pernety — cropped up in anthropological discourse, destabilizing fixed categories and hierarchies. The fact that German anthropologists of the late eighteenth century continued to debate the existence of indigenous giants, "brothers" to the Old Germans, indicates both their acceptance of and discomfort with the categories established by Meiners (fig. 4).

Meiners, who is as fixated on difference and hierarchy as was de Pauw, does not deny the existence of extremely tall people in Patagonia. He takes great pains, however, to relativize their size: "It is as certain that there aren't such towering giants in Patagonia as some older travelers claim to have seen, as it is that the different tribes in Patagonia are of very different heights, and that even among the tallest of them, not all men are exceedingly tall" (723). However, the giants enable him to reiterate his point, namely that size alone does not convey superiority: "and this increase in physical size combined with a decrease in all other human qualities is a sure proof that physical size alone cannot create perfection, unless it is accompanied by strength, industry and other virtues of the mind and the heart" (723). Even if Patagons were like Germans in size, as he grudgingly admits, they do not belong in the same category as the latter, for they lacked the "virtues" that would have helped their civilizations to evolve.

The scientist Blumenbach doubts that Patagon Giants ever existed. Yet despite his skepticism, he dedicates three full pages in his 1795 edition of *On the Natural Variety* to this "race of men" whom he also likens to the Old Germans. While he disputes the claim that they were twice the size of Europeans — surely they were only six and a half feet tall! — he attributes their extraordinary height to not having intermarried with other races. Accounts by recent travelers indicate, Blumenbach writes, that the Patagon nomads must have started mingling with smaller peoples around them, which has brought them down to (European) size (253). Patagons and Germans, then, must have developed along similar lines; if Patagons have dwindled in size because of intermarriage, so have Germans.

In Wünsch's *Conversations* of 1796, the Patagon Giants are mentioned in conjunction with the "Arkansas" — tall, beautiful, blond, white-skinned Indians in North America — as the only two that "excel over all other peoples of that so-called New World" (135). Wünsch, too, feels compelled to relate them to "our forefathers, the old Germans, who outdid all other peoples with regard to size and strength" (144, tr. Arndt). Yet he plays down any association with contemporary Germans by exaggerating the savage character of contemporary Patagons: "They have very broad shoulders, big heads, large round visages, very wide white front teeth, long bristly hair, ponderous limbs, a dull copper tone of skin, and an almost giant-like aspect. . . . They don't wear ordinary clothes, merely a rough animal skin slung over their bodies." Constantly engaged in hunting or warfare, these barbar-

ians eat their meat raw (146), he reports with disgust. Indeed, un-
civilized brutes have nothing in common with today's civilized Germans who cook their meat.[24] According to E. A. W. von Zimmermann's
"The New World Revisited," finally, Patagon Giants "resembled our
German forebears" because of their inordinate size. In order to underscore the analogy between Patagons and Germans, he locates his "colossuses" in the quasi-imaginary "cold, more northerly interior" of
South America to distinguish them from the "dull-witted," "dirty,"
small-bodied peoples to the South. Size, intelligence, and cleanliness, it
seems, are reserved for peoples who, by definition, live "further north."
    As fantastic embodiments of sameness or difference, the Patagon
Giants thus mark the relative distance not just between Germans and
Indians but between contemporary Germans and Old Germans and
northern and southern peoples along a racial-ethnographic and a
historical-cultural divide: either the giant "Indians" were always different, extreme opposites of the white and beautiful races, or they were
"like us," our red brothers. Yet even if they were like us, they no longer
are: we have attained a higher level of civilization; they have either
degenerated or not evolved at all. As a mirror image from the past in
which Germans can reflect themselves, the Patagon Giants thus provide
the standard against which the evolution of Germans, their origin and
present (endangered) position, can be measured. Contemporary Germans, the discussion suggests, are lodged somewhere between their
primitive but powerful forebears and their depraved but civilized European neighbor(s), between brute strength and overrefined decadence.
    The instability of boundaries and hierarchies becomes even more
pronounced in the other dynamic power triangle that positions Germans against other Europeans and against others on German soil.
Here, Germans see themselves alternately as a nation conquered/colo-
nized by France and as a potential conqueror/colonizer — of its own
national territory and, eventually, of territories abroad. Although European relations are, strictly speaking, not "colonial," references to
colonial competition and a colonialist terminology suggest that colonialism forms an unconscious frame of reference even for European
power politics, a kind of scenario on which fantasies of national superiority or inferiority can be played out. In these imaginary power negotiations among Europeans, "racial" hierarchies are less significant than
alleged differences in "national character."
    The connection between national self-definition and definition of
others is already implicit in Herder's *Ideen* of 1784, where his lament

over the fate of the Indians contains a competitive aside against the present colonizers: "Why," he asks, "are the Spaniards the owners of this best of all territories," if they have not been able to cultivate it properly?[25] Meiners, in his 1791 essay on the degeneration of Europeans in the New World, unwittingly corroborates Herder's critique of the colonial practices of other Europeans. He reiterates his idea that all colonizers have become "more like Negroes and Indians" in the colonies, that is, "phlegmatic," "lazy," "cowardly," desirous of riches, of sensuous enjoyments and luxury.[26] In both cases, the missing third party is the "industrious German bee" who, in Herder's poem "England and Germany" of 1787 (see epigram), gathers honey and "knows not for whom."[27] Both Herder and Meiners explicitly or implicitly allude to "German industry" in contrast to the moral failings of other European colonizers, the "lazy" Spaniard and the "greedy" Englishman. Both thus suggest distinct national identities based on collective predispositions and prejudices.

As I indicated before, the context within which national difference is negotiated is, paradoxically, colonialist.[28] In their attempt to define the German nation historically, culturally, and politically and to determine its collective identity in opposition to others, German intellectuals such as Herder, Kant, or Fichte impose hegemonic, exclusive concepts of "national character" [*Nationalcharakter*], "national spirit" [*Nationalgeist*], or "nationalist feeling" [*Nationalgefühl*] on a heterogeneous, multicultural, and multilingual populace living within the borders of the long disintegrated Holy Roman Empire. The colonial liberation ideology, covertly directed at Germany's "colonizer" France and overtly at the colonizing powers England and Spain, is both liberating and expansive-hegemonic, that is, anticolonial *and* colonialist at once. In Bernd Fischer's words: "Herder's (and not just his) concepts of the nation are always characterized by both the myth of anticolonial self-liberation and self-determination and a decidedly colonialist politics toward the interior and toward the exterior."[29]

The connection between the definition of self and other on the basis of an essentialist national character on the one hand, and "colonial" competition on the other, becomes particularly pronounced in the 1790s and early 1800s. In his tenth collection of the *Briefe zu Beförderung der Humanität* (Letters for the Promotion of Humanity, 1793–1797), Herder launches his most extended critique of European colonialism to date. His tortured sentence seemingly implicates Germans as well: "About Spanish cruelties, British avarice, and the cold insolence of the Dutch — celebrated in heroic epics during the delirium of conquest — books have recently been written which do them so little honor that if there were a spirit of European community anywhere except in books, *we* would all have to be ashamed before most peoples of the earth of *our crimes against humanity.* Show me one country where Europeans arrived and did not become guilty of sinning against its unarmed, trusting people through restrictions, unjust wars, avarice, lies, oppression, diseases and harmful gifts, perhaps for centuries to come!" (my emphasis).[30] Yet the following sentences modify this wholesale condemnation of European complicity. Germans are implicated in colonialism/imperialism not just as perpetrators ("The old Prussians were annihilated; Lithuanians, Estonians, and Latvians under poorest conditions still curse, in their hearts, their oppressors, the Germans," 234), but also as victims (Christianity was imposed on them by force, 234). In fact, the letters immediately preceding and following Herder's colonialist invective emphasize the Germans' association not with the colonizers but with other colonized and oppressed peoples. In letter 113, in the enclosed poem "Der deutsche Nationalruhm" ["German National Glory"] and in letter 115, Herder reiterates their childlike innocence, their outsider position in Europe ("We Germans are the poor youth, the weak child," 222). If Patagons were the Germans of the New World, Germans now are the "Negroes," the Indians of the Old (225). If the first glory of a nation is innocence, the second, Herder says, is moderation:

The second glory is moderation.
The Hindus' and Peruvians' pain,
The rage of Blacks, the roasted Montezuma
Of Mexico, all call to heaven still
Begging to be avenged! —
Believe me, friend, no Zeus with his choir
Of gods will visit a people that,
Burdened with guilt, blood, and sins
and gold and diamonds, sits down to dine!
He joins instead the frugal meal
Of quiet Ethiopians and Germans.[31]

Political weakness thus translates into moral strength. Zeus will reward with his presence not the "greedy" English nor the "cruel" Spaniards but the "quiet Ethiopians and Germans." As a noncolonial (non)nation,

Germans have not heaped guilt on their heads. It is the old Spain and the "new Karthage," merchant England, that merit his particular scorn, and so would the "poor, guiltless Germans" (251), should they follow the British footsteps. Significantly, the reiteration of Germany's colonial innocence appears right next to a short characterization of Las Casas's indictment of "Spanish atrocities." Like other German observers of his time, Herder overlooks the cruelties committed by the "animales alemanes," the German animals, in the sixteenth century (see chapter 1), focusing instead on the moral depravity of the other European colonial powers.[32] By insisting on German industry and private virtues, by criticizing above all the crimes committed by others, Herder unwittingly creates a separate role for morally superior Germans whose lack of aggressive nationhood becomes a virtue in and of itself. While Herder may not have meant to single out Germans, his image of the poor but innocent German bystanders lends itself to exploitation by more ruthless and aggressive nationalists. The comparison of Germans with other Europeans creates a blank space into which Germans can inscribe their differing national character, which — since they already share the Europeans' physical superiority — predestines them to a great future. As if to compensate for the political role as victim of colonial aggression, Herder and others (Kant, Fichte, Kleist) thus transform the position of underdog into one of moral superiority and entitlement. Superimposed on Meiners's idea of German racial superiority, their concept of unappreciated national virtue creates a dangerous mix of self-pity and self-aggrandizement.

In Kant's *Anthropology from a Pragmatic Point of View* (*Anthropologie in pragmatischer Hinsicht*, 1798), finally, national character [*Volkscharakter*] and colonial interest intersect, and a predestination of Germans for the colony emerges. The British, Kant says, are driven by their mercantile spirit [*Handelsgeist*]; they are "unsociable" [*ungesellig*], in battle with the French for the rule of the world, a battle for survival or annihilation. The German, on the other hand, is honest, kind, and enterprising. Willing to subject himself to the will of the community, he is actually the better colonizer:

> And still he is a person of all lands and climates; he emigrates easily, and is not passionately fettered to his fatherland. But if he arrives in foreign lands as a colonist, he will soon form with his compatriots a sort of social club which, as a result of unity of language, and partially of religion, makes him part of a little clan, which under the higher authority of the government

distinguishes itself in a peaceful and moral way through industry, cleanliness, and thrift from the settlements of other nationalities. This is how even the English praise the Germans in North America.[33]

The European man who would best fulfill the fantasy of colonial cultivator is the peaceful, moral German. And the territory where he could best exercise his superior skills is the colonies that Spain, the brutal exploiter, will be forced to give up. It is a space which is already populated by his primitive "brothers" whom he can domesticate and educate, and/or by effeminate others who, although of different "blood," will profit vastly from the presence of these tall, bearded — and industrious! — whites.

P A R T   I I I

Colonial Families; or, Displacing the Colonizers

As for the reproach that as a German I chose for my subject a foreign hero and a foreign history, I scarcely find it necessary to answer it. The discovery of the New World, and the conquest of so mighty a realm as was Mexico, is important for all nations. Besides, we Europeans are so closely tied to one another by religion, by our customs, and by our system of government that we may regard each other in the aggregate as a single nation. And what is more, the conquest took place on behalf of a monarch who ruled Spaniards and Germans at the same time. —J. F. W. Zachariae, introduction to his epic poem, Cortes, 1766[1]

Although the purpose of the texts analyzed in the previous chapters was "scientific" or "philosophical" — to anchor theories of difference in empirical or textual evidence — the texts themselves are replete with colonial fantasies: fantasies of biological, moral, and cultural superiority, of natural attraction and surrender, blood brotherhood and enmity, ennobling love and debilitating disease. Fantastic configurations underlying the theories "explain" the historical power imbalances between Europeans and "natives," Germans and other Europeans, "true" Germans and those who are not. These fantasies are compensatory, insofar as they seem to cover up or compensate for a pervasive sense of lack: lack of national territory, unity, identity. They suggest "potency" in view of "impotence," significance in view of insignificance. They transform need — economic need and hence forced emigration — into a mission, a special German ability for colonizing, a colonial calling. Indeed, the foreign soil onto which these fantasies are projected becomes the testing ground for the development of a distinct sense of national self and national destiny.

While most of the fantasies I have identified so far were embedded in anthropological and philosophical theories as tropes (e.g., Herder's ennobling love, Kant's Island of Truth), illustrative anecdotes (the voluntary surrender of native women to Spanish conquistadors related by de Pauw), or subconscious structures (de Pauw's or Meiners's obsession with miscegenation and degeneration), the theories in turn generated fantastic colonial stories. They spawned allegorical master narratives in which the relationships between colonizer and colonized on the one hand, and among European nations on the other, were emplotted as family romance. Analogous to the theoretical race triangles discussed earlier, these two familial configurations — the "colonial family" and the "European family" — would overlap and interact, creating for Germans a doubly privileged position: both as "natural" master (*pater familias* or master of the colonial household) over weaker subjects (his native "children" or slaves), and as *primus inter pares* (the better youth, the more successful colonial rival) among the European nations.[2] As familial stories of courtship and marriage, procreation and child rearing, sibling rivalries and family feuds, these master narratives not just reconfirmed natural hierarchies but allowed for "natural" change over time within familial and generational frameworks.[3]

The use of familial metaphors to describe colonial relations is of course not new. In his *Brevísima relación,* Bartolomé de las Casas already alluded to familial imagery when he denounced the "countless unheard-of . . . cruelties, the violence and sinfulness" committed by the Spanish conquistadors against God, the king of Spain, and the innocent inhabitants of the New World,[4] and pleaded for kinder treatment. Quoting a letter from the bishop of Santa Marta, Las Casas wrote to the king: "I wish to say, great Caesar, that the means to remedy this land is for Your Majesty to remove from power these rascally stepfathers and to give the land a husband who will treat her with the reasonableness she deserves. And this must be done rapidly, for otherwise, the way she is being harassed and fatigued by these tyrants that have charge of her, I hold it a certainty that very soon she will die."[5]

The bishop's emotional plea to replace the "padrastros," the "rascally stepfathers" as the translator has it, not with a natural father but with a husband, anticipates the passage from colonial rape, pillaging, and neglect to colonial "love," the favorite metaphor in eighteenth-century colonial discourse: the love that establishes natural (gender) boundaries (de Pauw), improves the races (Meiners), that creates legitimacy and mutuality (Herder).

As Las Casas's terminology — father/stepfather — indicates, there is also another familial master fantasy at work. It implies that the indigenous populations at the times of conquest were in a state of infancy — "unverständige Kinder," as Hegel calls them,[6] that is, weak, innocent, trusting, but also ignorant and superstitious — a state that brutal, gold-greedy Spanish conquerors exploited for their own benefit. It postulates that a "good" colonizer should be like a father who will educate the natives, raise them to his level, and, eventually, release them into adulthood — in return for absolute obedience and complete assimilation into the "family."

Both familial fantasies, the deeroticized fantasy of an educational patriarchal father-child bond and the eroticized fantasy of a matrimonial union between European man and native woman/land are at the heart of the colonial romance so popular during the Enlightenment. These fantasies are not mutually exclusive, since women and children, as legal minors and in need of moral and intellectual "cultivation" and "domestication," easily substitute for one another as metaphoric representations of the colonial other. The two fantasies will therefore often appear side by side, or mutually subvert each other. They differ from the one contained in Las Casas's excerpt insofar as they (re)literalize the principle of attachment. The colonial family or matrimony they imagine is not just a metaphor for a special relationship between European colonist and American land, but the product of "real" encounters between conquerors and natives, colonizers and colonized, men and women — albeit in the realm of fiction.

The special attraction of these domestic fantasies for Enlightenment writers becomes evident if we remember both the paternalistic-didactic impulse and the sentimental-humanitarian sensibility prevalent during the last quarter of the eighteenth century. Added to this mentality is what I call an erotics of conquest, a desire for hands-on experience stimulated perhaps by the fantasies of miscegenation discussed in the previous chapter and the actual breakdown of the old colonial order. It is here that the insertion of the "German" male as the superior mind and superior body (Wünsch, Meiners), as untainted by colonial experience (Herder) and hence a potentially better "father-" or "husband-" colonizer (Kant) comes into the picture, or onto the scene. Significantly, all the literary texts discussed in this section are adaptations of English or French models into which German authors inscribe not just a particularly German perspective, but German protagonists as "new" and different colonial agents. The fantasies thus do not just reliteralize the principle of attachment: they literalize European rivalry over nuptile territory.

6

Fathers and Sons: Donnerstag and Freitag, Campe and Krusoe

You want to know what it was that drove me out into the world? — To tell the truth, the person who supplied the first impulse was an old acquaintance of us all, namely none other than Robinson Crusoe. At the tender age of eight I already resolved that I too would seek out an uninhabited island; and though I refrained from this last upon growing up, the word "America" remained for me, as for thousands of others, a kind of magic formula that was to open up for me the alien treasures of the globe. — Friedrich Gerstäcker, Selected Works, *n.d.[1]*

I asked my mother to give me a book as soon as possible. . . . She had been able to procure Campe's Robinson Crusoe *and handed it over to me. I fell upon it like one on the brink of starvation. Never had a book had such an effect on me. Every scene unfolded before me as if in a three-dimensional view, I was in transports of delight and envied the children in the tale such a preceptor; soon I grew so intimate with them as if they had been my siblings. . . . An entirely new world dawned on me. . . . I lived with Robinson, felt with him, he became my other self. . . . Save for the Bible, no book affected me so powerfully, none advanced my mind and broadened my horizon so significantly. — Karl Friedrich von Klöden,* The Self-Made Man: Autobiography, *1874*

Without a doubt, Daniel Defoe's *Robinson Crusoe,* published in 1719, is one of the most influential books of eighteenth-century Europe, both indicative *and* formative of the European mentality at a time of burgeoning exploration and colonial expansion. A colonial parable par excellence, *Robinson Crusoe* was quickly translated into all "major" European languages and cultures, where it has maintained a significant presence to this date.[2]

German readers appear to have been particularly fascinated by the story of the unruly son who, against the express advice of his father, goes to sea, falls captive, escapes, earns a fortune as a planter and slave trader in Brazil, and finally shipwrecks on a deserted island off the coast of Venezuela, where he establishes his own private colony, populated by domesticated animals and, eventually, by domesticated New World natives and reformed Old World slave traders.[3] Four translations of the book appeared in different German cities simultaneously in 1720; by 1782, one of these had already reached its fifteenth edition.[4] Innumerable rewrites, adaptations, sequels, and retranslations sprung up in the eighteenth and nineteenth centuries, creating a veritable literary avalanche and a new genre, the *Robinsonade*. More than any other text, *Robinson Crusoe* shaped the minds of German children, youths, and hence adults, from the eighteenth well into the twentieth century (fig. 5, Robinson's Family Tree).[5]

The figure of Robinson provided male and female writers in Germany with a space for identification and projection.[6] This identification, perhaps facilitated by Robinson Crusoe's alias Kreutznaer's German descent, was carried to its logical resolution when the naturalized Englishman Crusoe, son of German immigrants, acquired true "German" ethnic identities in subsequent decades ("eingedeutscht").[7] This German inscription into the British colonial adventure started with the 1722 novels entitled *Der teutsche Robinson* and *Der sächsische Robinson;* it continued with a Silesian (1723), a Thuringian (1734), a Polish-Prussian (1738), a Brandenburgian (1744), a Jewish (1756), a Leipziger (1757), and an "East-Friesian" (1755) Robinson. The Germanization of Robinson culminated in Campe's *Robinson der Jüngere: ein Lesebuch für Kinder* (literally, *Robinson the Younger: A Reader for Children*, 1779–1780), which, in a further rewrite, became the "new Robinson" whose trials and tribulations were clearly identified as "German" trials (*The New Robinson; or, Sea Voyages and Adventures of a German: An Entertaining and Instructive Story for the Common Man*, 1794). As paradigmatic adventurer and colonizer, Defoe's Robinson could apparently serve as foil for the projection of any national, regional, or personal interest.

Campe's immensely popular *Robinson the Younger* is a case in point.[8] Published in 1779 by the Hamburg publicist and Rousseau-inspired educator Joachim Heinrich Campe, it witnessed 24 German editions by 1831, and 117 by 1894, not to mention the innumerable translations, into "all European languages, even Russian, New Greek, Old Bohemian," and Latin, as the cover boasted. There were sequels and adaptations — for different audiences (school children and adults, bourgeois and farmers, boys and girls), different purposes ("specifically for those technologically inclined," 1797), different places (*Journey to Otaheiti and the South Sea Islands*, 1803), and different times ("revised according to the needs of our modern times," 1821). A veritable "Bible

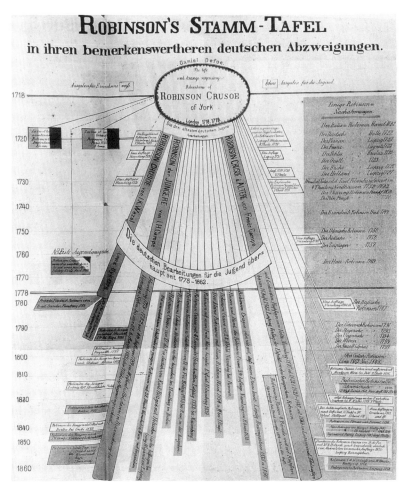

5. "Robinson's Extended Family: The Family Tree of German Robinsonades." From Johann Heinrich Campe, *Robinson der Jüngere. Ein Lesebuch für Kinder,* 63rd ed. (Braunschweig: Vieweg, 1862). Photograph by Biomedical Communications, Dartmouth College.

of the bourgeoisie" (Promies), *Robinson the Younger* and his extended literary family served as readings for all (literate) social classes and age groups, as a practical and moral guidebook for the whole Family of Germans in the years of national consolidation.[9]

In a programmatic introduction, the author himself identifies the purpose of his "Werkchen," his little opus, as he somewhat dismissively calls his two-volume, 360-page novel, in terms of the enlightened educational project initiated by Jean-Jacques Rousseau's *Emile* (1760): to

teach his young readers basic knowledge about domestic life by referring them back to nature and to physical reality; to educate them to be
God-fearing, virtuous citizens; to fortify them against the "epidemics of
the soul" [*Seelenseuche*] — passive, pining sentimentalism [*Empfind-
samkeit*] — by guiding them to productive practical activity [*Selbst-
thätigkeit*] and hands-on experience. And to achieve all this by creating
a literary figure whose adventures would entertain and stimulate the
youthful readers into complete identification ("as if he were Robinson
himself") and imitation (v–xi).

Campe also purports to pursue an ideological agenda quite different
from his intellectual forefather Rousseau, namely to create an awareness in his readers of the preferability of social life over life in isolation
("to make the manifold happiness of social life palatable"), by showing
how a man alone is helpless and unhappy, in dire need of a companion
and helpmate, that is, society (xi). As part of this socializing project,
Campe single-handedly creates a society through the literary form he
chooses, a society of interlocking families. The thirty-one chapters
of the book correspond to thirty-one evenings or installments, in which
a father — "Father Campe," author and father melting into one[10] —
tells the story of Robinson's escape from home and life on the island to
his extended family, as they are engaged in domestic activities (shell-
ing beans, weaving baskets, etc.). The father/educator-child/pupil
structure permeates the whole literary enterprise: it characterizes not
just the narrative situation but the plot itself (the relationship between
the father and Robinson; between Robinson and Freitag), creating in
turn a new extended family, the family of readers, whom the story tries
to mold into the national family (Father State and his enlightened citizens). In other words, the patriarchal father-child relationship that
governs both the subject matter and form of the novel encompasses the
readership and society at large in multiple and interlocking pedagogical
projects, in which teaching/reading generates "doing," and vice versa.

The self-professed educational goal has led literary historians to read
the novel solely within a national pedagogical tradition, as pedagocial
tract, didactic companion, or utopian program. The novel's connection
to the European expansionist, colonialist project was ignored.[11] The
question why Campe chose a Caribbean island as the setting rather
than an estate in the European countryside, why he fused Rousseau
with Defoe, leads us to the core of his pedagogical experiment, in which
education is metaphorically equated with colonization and colonization with education, the domestication of little savages. As Robinson

colonizes his Freitag on the island, creating the perfect colonial society, so Father Campe educates, colonizes, and colonializes[12] his young audience to prepare them for their role as future colonizers.

The Formation of the German Colonizer

Campe's version of *Robinson Crusoe* departs in significant ways from its English original, and it is here where we can speak of a German inscription into the colonial venture. The story Father Campe tells starts like a fairy tale: once upon a time, there were a father and a mother in Hamburg who had three sons. The oldest, who wanted to be a soldier, was killed in battle against the French; the second, who wanted to be a scholar, died of consumption; and only the youngest, "who for some reason was called Krusoe" (4–5), survives his passion to seek foreign lands. Driven away from home at age seventeen by irresistible longings, he returns, after spending nine years marooned on an island, as a mature, experienced, competent adult, ready to integrate into civilized society. Campe thus leaves no doubt as to which professional pursuits he considers useless, because unproductive: the military and the academic. The youngest son, although he has not "learned anything useful yet" (5) survives because his longings for distant lands can be channeled into productive pursuits and useful skills. Campe denounces not so much the desire to leave home, but a *Fernweh* bereft of the necessary mental (5) and physical (8) preparation. At the beginning of the novel Krusoe is a complete *tabula rasa, ein unbeschriebenes Blatt* [an uninscribed page]. His life as a castaway on the island serves as preparation for adult life, providing him with the kind of formation he needs to become a successful colonizer, a "real man," a formation his supposedly overindulgent parents and his premature departure from home had rendered impossible.

Unlike his literary predecessor Robinson Crusoe, Krusoe does not get involved in any African or Brazilian (ad)ventures — although the prospect of such ventures had tempted him into signing up for his voyage.[13] Instead, midway to the Guinea coast, he forsakes his search for "gold, ivory, and other things" (16) to head straight for the New World and a trip that ends in his shipwreck on a deserted island. Trade, slave trade, and plantation experience, so crucial in his literary model's material advancement, play no role in Krusoe's physical and moral development. Campe's focus is not on documenting material gain — in fact, unlike the British Robinson, the German Krusoe is not a "materialist" — but on presenting a convincing pedagogical experiment. Campe's protagonist is therefore not only younger, more inexperienced than Robinson the Older, but forced to create an existence from scratch, without the useful items Robinson was able to salvage from the wreck. The German Krusoe, a true self-made man, learns to achieve control over his mind (fear, despair, loneliness, 91), body (weakness, disease, 95), and environment by relying on his physical strength and ingenuity alone, without the start-up capital of tools, knowledge, or experience, and without paternal help. Part of Campe's educational project then is to show how "man" learns through observation and action, and how learning leads to domesticating his own nature (self-restraint) and nature around him. The island, suspended time, allows Krusoe to catch up with the education he has missed at home. As he struggles to secure first his livelihood, then the control over the island's resources, and eventually patriarchal rule over "his" colonial subjects, the readers, embodied by the narrator's children, learn alongside him to master all the skills necessary to become resourceful colonizers of their own environment. While Krusoe transforms the island into home, the children transform their home into Krusoe's island (56, 98, 124).

Although island and home merge into one, the island never loses its character as colony. Significantly, it is not so much an imaginary *locus amoenus* as a concrete utopia, the composite of all New World colonies appropriated by Europeans: not only is it "empty," that is, devoid of inhabitants who can lay claim to the territory, but it contains, in a nutshell, all natural products the New World "offered" to the old, from coconuts, potatoes, corn, cocoa beans, lemon and breadfruit trees, to gold, llamas, and guanacos. It is the Caribbean and Andean regions in one. This melange of resources provides Father Campe with pretexts for explaining natural sciences or displaying knowledge about the use of colonial raw materials. However, it also guides us to Campe's subliminal ideological agenda. As the island is transformed, in the narration, into the epitome of *the* New World colony, Krusoe turns into *the* explorer/colonizer par excellence, a German who not only discovers and takes over the island *now* (in the presence of the narration), but who is magically transported back to the beginnings of New World colonialism in the sixteenth century. As the father explains to his children, Krusoe's ignorance of the use value of the potato becomes understandable if we recall that "our Robinson" lived about two hundred years ago and that the potato was not introduced into Germany until the eighteenth century (61). As both a sixteenth-century and an eighteenth-century colonizer of an unclaimed rich island, the German protagonist "called Krusoe" is in direct competition with the Columbuses, Corteses, and Pizarros back then as well as with the British, French, and Dutch in the Caribbean now. His discovery, colonization, and conquest of "new" territory — in that order — can therefore be read as the fantasy of an alternative colonial project. In this context, the father's exhortation to the children not to judge other people (in this case Krusoe) prematurely, without having put themselves *in their place* and asked *if they would have done it better than they* (61), acquires added significance. After all, the novel invites the readers to put themselves in Krusoe's place, who puts himself in Robinson's place, who in turn had inserted himself into the Spanish colonial enterprise.

This project of multiple displacements also involves the forgotten German colonial history. As German colonizer of an island in the estuary of the Orinoco in the sixteenth century, Robinson Krusoe from Hamburg relives and replaces another "first": the conquest of Venezuela by the Welsers of Augsburg. The children's innocent question about Peru — "Isn't that the land where the Spaniards get all that gold and silver, which they extract from America every year, as you've told us?" (63) — recalls Federmann's belated arrival in "El Dorado," a few days after the Spaniards had claimed it for themselves (see chapter 1). A very different, nonviolent, rational colonization, Krusoe's romance with the Caribbean island thus replaces and obliterates the failed German conquest(s) in the past as well as the more recent colonial acquisitions by other European nations. As the fairy-tale beginning of the novel already suggested, Krusoe's quest for an island of *his own* and for a different colonial story rewrites German colonial history — past and future — as myth.

Colonial Encounters: German(s) and Indian(s)

The differences between Defoe's and Campe's novels and between the English and the German Krusoe are even more pronounced in the second volume of *Robinson the Younger*. The first volume had ended with Krusoe's sickness and quasi death — the second begins with his recovery. The caesura marks both his rebirth to faith ("as if reborn," 2: 3) and his restoration to colonial society on the island, his new home ("as if he had returned home after a long trip").[14] The first part, namely Krusoe's moral and physical education, strengthens him for the encounter with the "native" and prepares him for the establishment of colonial rule in the second. It is in the interaction between Krusoe and his colonial subjects "Freitag," "Donnerstag" (Thursday, Freitag's father), and eventually the Spanish and English castaways that the novel reveals its project as a distinctly German alternative.

Like his literary predecessor, Krusoe responds with terror when he encounters the footprint in the sand. Like Robinson, he is horrified at the thought of an imaginary other out there, ready to annihilate him. This imagined preencounter provides Father Campe with an opportunity to reiterate the main point of volume 1. As he tells his listeners, Krusoe need not have been afraid of those "wild, men-eating cannibals who, as you know, are supposed to have lived on the Caribbean Islands" (24), had he spent his early years working, exercising, and practicing virtue and restraint. Too much comfort breeds effeminacy ("weibisch"), that is weakness, love of luxury, and fear (24–25). Krusoe, born into a superior civilization, did not take proper advantage of its possibilities, did not become a "man," and therefore lost some of the competitive edge over the "savages." By training his body and fortifying his mind, and by combatting the savage within, he would have enabled himself (and will henceforth enable himself) to withstand the onslaughts of savagery.

Before Freitag actually appears, Father Campe thus uses the footprint to elaborate his pedagogical and anthropological theories. The fears of "savages," he assures, are unfounded. Although *die Wilden* are not quite human yet, they are "menschenähnlich," similar to humans. Their lack of humanity is attributable to a lack of (moral) education ("after all it's not their fault that they weren't better instructed and educated," 26), and the task of the civilized Europeans is to educate, that is, to "tame" them (27). His choice of words betrays his conviction that although the savages are perfectible, they can never be more than *gezähmte Wilde,* tamed savages. On first sight, Campe seems to be operating within an enlightened ideology, which postulates the basic equality of all humankind, although it differentiates between stages and hierarchies of civilization. Yet Krusoe's terror of cannibalism, his violent reactions to discovering the human remnants (vomit, unconsciousness), and Father Campe's smug comments ("May we thank our dear Lord for having allowed us to be born in a country where we live among virtuous, loving, helpful humans and don't have to worry about wild inhumans," 31) link his position to earlier (and later) less enlightened positions and suggest a much more profound division between "Menschen" and "Unmenschen" (33, 37) operative in the author's unconscious. This oscillation between an ideology of sameness and a profound fear of absolute alterity that can only be tamed into a semblance of sameness marks the whole second part of the novel.

In its complex negotiations of relationships (assimilation, integration, equality, sameness) the novel reveals its liberal "German" agenda. Defoe's Robinson had left no doubt as to the permanent inequality between himself and Friday.[15] At the first sight of Friday, he immediately thought of acquiring "a Servant, and perhaps a Companion, or Assistant" (158). Friday "corroborated" that interpretation by kneeling down and setting Crusoe's foot on his head as "a token of swearing to be my Slave forever" (159) — a phrase that would often be repeated in sentimental slave narratives (see chapter 8). In the course of the encounter, the "Fellow," the "Creature" metamorphosed into "my Savage" and finally "Friday," a person owned and named by the European, whom he recognized as his creator, the giver of his life: "he made all Signs to me of Subjection, Servitude, and Submission imaginable, to let me know, how he would serve me as long as he liv'd" (161). Friday's natural and permanent subservience was sealed by the name which Robinson bestowed on himself: "Master." This natural master-slave relationship was imbued with romantic overtones. First characterized as the "love" of the child for his father, it imperceptibly turned into a strong exclusive attachment: "I began really to love the Creature; and on his side, I believe he lov'd me more than it was possible for him ever to love any Thing before" (166). This development was already foreshadowed in the lovingly detailed description Robinson had given of Friday's physical appearance: "perfectly well made," "not too large," "well shap'd," "he had all the Sweetness and Softness of an European in his Countenance," "of a bright kind of a dun olive Colour, Nose small, . . . a very good Mouth, thin Lips, and his fine Teeth well set, and white as Ivory" (160). There was, in short, no contradiction between hierarchy and romance: as feminized other, Freitag could be the object of love *and* remain permanently inferior, a "natural slave."[16] Furthermore, as tool of Robinson's deliverance, he could disappear as soon as his task was completed.

Campe's *Unmensch,* in contrast to Defoe's, is on his way to becoming not only a *Mensch,* but a friend. Yet "natural" hierarchies get in the way of enlightened goals. The gradual transformation of Freitag from *Unmensch,* nonhuman, to *Untermensch,* subhuman, to Krusoe's *Untertan,* his subject, and finally Krusoe's *equal* is therefore acted out in a complicated set of pedagogical maneuvers. At their first encounter,

Freitag is as terrorized at the sight of Krusoe as Krusoe had been at the thought of the savage. The reason Father Campe gives for Freitag's terror is Krusoe's visible superiority: "whom [the savage] probably considered a superhuman being [ein übermenschliches Wesen], so that he did not know whether he should throw himself at his feet or flee" (38). As he later explains, it is the European's beard and his white skin color that signaled his superior status (58–59). The meeting of *Übermensch* and *Unmensch*, then, has different connotations than Defoe's master-servant encounter. By 1780, a sense of biological superiority has become firmly entrenched in the Europeans' mind.

By fleeing the cannibals and their abhorrent feast, Freitag shifts sides from "animal" to "human," an ascent that Krusoe, condescending "victor" and "hero" (37), confirms by raising him to his level: "Our hero, who was more interested in a friend than a slave, lifted him up kindly, and tried to convince him in any possible way of his good and loving intentions" (39). However, the rational project of uplifting the "savage" to the level of friend and "guest" [*Gastfreund,* 47][17] is undermined by Krusoe's fear of Freitag's otherness. Thus, despite egalitarian intentions, Krusoe feels compelled to play "king" with Freitag, using the word *cacique,* "which the savage Americans use to denominate their chiefs, as he fortunately remembered having heard" (47). Rather than integrating Freitag into the master-servant framework of his culture, Krusoe the anthropologist, deferring to native power relations, inscribes himself into the sociopolitical structures of the new world. By becoming Friday's *cacique,* he makes sure that Freitag understands the nature of the hierarchy, for the time being. Equality, the moral imperative by which Krusoe supposedly operates, cannot be realized in the interaction between the European and the Native American as long as the latter's subjection and assimilation are not complete. Krusoe, his professions to friendship notwithstanding, slips into the king or master role whenever the situation warrants. It is a role governed by political expediency, Campe suggests.

In order to pursue the utopian vision of a friendship among (un)equal men, Campe's Krusoe must avoid any hint of an erotic investment. In the father's dry words, Freitag "was a well-shaped young man, about twenty years old. His skin was dark brown and shiny, his hair black, but not woolly like that of the Moors, and long; his nose short, but not flat; his lips small, and his teeth white as ivory. In both ears he wore all kinds of shells and feathers, which he seemed to be no little proud of" (46). Father Campe's afterthought, "Actually, he was naked from head to toe" (46), indicates discomfort with the native's male physicality, a discomfort Krusoe controls by immediately covering his new friend with a homemade loin cloth before they sit down to eat together.

The relationship envisaged between Krusoe and Freitag is a "friendship" disguised as a ruler-subject relationship ("Robinson, with the dignity of a monarch, extended to him his hand in friendship," 47), or a ruler-subject relationship disguised as a friendship. The pedagogical enterprise both men are involved in affirms and reverses social and cultural stratification, as the narrator's ironic remarks suggest: "Robinson, the monarch, the absolute king and ruler of the whole island, master over life and death of all his subjects, carried out the task of a stable maid, right before Freitag's very eyes, milking, with his own noble hands, the llamas in the courtyard, in order to show his prime minister, who would henceforth carry out these duties, how to do it" (49). As in the ideology of enlightened absolutism, the king becomes "the first servant of his state"—without relinquishing the control and his position of absolute power. In fact, his royalty is natural (47, 48), which Freitag recognizes when he seats himself at Krusoe's feet, on the ground. Manifest in the European's physique and his superior knowledge, this "natural" asymmetry is not even shaken when Freitag (unlike Krusoe) is able to produce fire for their first meal together: on the contrary, to reaffirm Friday's ignorance, the father points out that Freitag had never heard of or seen the boiling of food (55).

The text oscillates between natural hierarchy/natural authority and voluntary condescension/voluntary self-restriction. Since Freitag's natural inferiority is likened to the ignorance of children (58), his growth and process of assimilation are also both "natural" and induced by education. As a "noble" savage, Campe suggests, Freitag is a human being and as such he can become a "man" like Krusoe (178), although the distance between his "minor skills" (making fire, building a boat, 76) and Krusoe's "major" organizational achievements and superior intelligence (101) will never allow him to overcome the gap completely. As Freitag associates with the colonizer and is coopted into his structures as "prime minister," he assumes a transitory position between *Unmensch* and *Mensch*. Krusoe's colonizing project is thus twofold: to assimilate the natives of superior intelligence and docility that can be integrated into the European power structure, and to exclude from the "family" those whose savagery is beyond remedy.

The Colony

Krusoe is well aware that his new status as colonial master creates for him the dangers of sloth and sensual excess (60). In order to maintain control over his colony of two, he has to develop a new master plan for himself, governed by hard work, moderation, and self-restraint (voluntary monthly "abstinence" from the society of Freitag, 61). As he teaches Freitag to speak German and instructs him in the Protestant faith (77), cultural domination and control become complete. The model German colonizer thus differs from his colonial competitors by not falling prey to the decadent excesses [*Ausartung*] that Spanish, French, or British plantation owners and slave masters on the "Sugar Islands" indulged in. Nor does he make the mistake of keeping his native assistant in permanent subservience. On the contrary: he uses Freitag's natural skills (familiarity with the terrain, physical agility, endurance) for his own purposes (defense of the colony, improvement of infrastructure, agriculture). Furthermore, rather than being an absentee landlord or a despotic colonial ruler, Krusoe works alongside his native workforce in order to maintain control over the product (fig. 6). Krusoe and Freitag are collaborators, allies. Together, they build a fortress as a protection against attacks by those who have not achieved their advanced moral stage, the cannibals.

Krusoe's official assumption of colonial rule, his retroactive "conquest," occurs when a European shipwreck finally provides him with the outer insignia of superiority and the means to defend his colonial property against both cannibals and European predators: uniforms, weapons, and tools. As he teaches Freitag how to eat with knife and fork, as he dresses in the clothes of the ship's commander, and as he fires his first shot, he becomes transformed, in the eyes of Freitag, into a godlike (123) ruler: "From this, and from everything Freitag had seen on the ship, he gained such a profound respect for the Europeans and especially his master that for many days, he was unable to return to the familiar friendly ways of interacting with him" (124). "He could not keep from admiring the invaluable invention of scissors and needle, and admitted over and over again that he and his countrymen, compared to the crafty Europeans, were but insignificant fellows" (131). Henceforth Krusoe is the "lieber Herr" (136) — both "dear master" and "dear Lord" — and Freitag his grateful, ever obedient servant. The arrival of the ship thus confirms (in Father Campe's narration) the cul-

6. "Krusoe and Freitag Playing House: Cannibalism Domesticated." From *Johann Heinrich Campe, Robinson der Jüngere. Ein Lesebuch für Kinder,* 63rd ed. (Braunschweig: Vieweg, 1862). Photograph by Biomedical Communications, Dartmouth College.

tural superiority of the colonizers and the lure of the superior civilization for the colonized.

Interested primarily in the formation of the model colonizer — a hardworking, orderly, modest, moral, God-fearing man who rules the natives with paternal kindness — Campe does not dwell much on the colony itself. The rescue of a group of Spanish slave-traders from the hands of the cannibals permits him to elaborate on Krusoe's organizational talents, his "enlightened absolutism" based on religious tolerance and a social contract (163). Krusoe is the benign patriarch, the *Landesvater,* as German rulers liked to see themselves. This paternalism also extends to his relationship to Freitag. While the rescue of Donnerstag, Freitag's father (who receives the name Thursday because he predates the latter), created a conflict between Freitag's loyalties to his biological father and to his new cultural father, this conflict is resolved in favor of the latter: both Donnerstag and Freitag decide to abandon their home in the New World and follow Krusoe to Hamburg; Donnerstag conveniently dies during the passage, so that Krusoe can fully assume the role of paternal friend, whereas Germany becomes Freitag's new *Vaterland*.

The move from the colony back to home also quells Krusoe's fears of Freitag's inherently savage nature. Friday, by foresaking the land of his savage fathers and adopting Germany as new fatherland, opts for complete assimilation, whereas the *Unmenschen*, the cannibals, have been exorcized, annihilated, or left behind on the South American mainland. The novel ends as fairy-tale-like as it began: as brother carpenters, Krusoe and Freitag live happily ever after in the free city of Hamburg, home of Father Campe and his family.

The "domestic" ending, the prodigal son's return into the fold of the family, his option for a modest carpenter's shop in which he, alongside his friend and companion Freitag, lives until ripe old age, suggests an anticolonial stance. Clearly, Krusoe was not in it for the money, nor was he keen on preserving his overseas possessions. His exclusive preoccupation with moral improvement over practical economic-colonial concerns is underscored when he loses, in another shipwreck, not only the few souvenirs, but the golden rock he had taken with him from the island. As the narrator-father speculates, maybe Providence wanted Krusoe to lose the gold nugget so as not to entice young people to follow his footsteps (202). Krusoe's "profit" from the colony, which he abandoned to the rule of others, is at best immaterial, spiritual. It has given him a sense of who he is and what he can do. The colony's legacy, then, is what Egon Menz has called its "irresistible moral": "practical knowledge, industry as repentance, and the conviction that no savage thing and no wild man can offer resistance where European intelligence and Divine Providence collaborate."[18]

To focus on the education of the colonizer does not necessarily entail an anticolonialist message. On the contrary, by deferring the actual conquest, Krusoe anchored colonialism in the imagination of his readers. In Father Campe's words: "Everybody talked about nothing but Robinson. Everybody wanted to see him, wanted to hear from his own mouth the story of his adventures! His father's house became like a public meeting place. There was no way around it: Robinson had to tell and tell, from morning to night" (204). Krusoe's story then is the true colonial legacy; it fires up the imagination and creates desire — a desire for adventure, a desire for the exotic, a desire for a utopian island, for a place where one can rule according to one's own dictates, free from paternal rule, where one can work with docile natives, or shoot those who refuse to give up their territories or savage ways. Not surprisingly, Campe's competitor Johann Carl Wezel, who had simultaneously produced a much more realistic Robinson adaptation, found few readers for his portrayal of failed colonization: nobody wanted to read about the pitfalls of private property and "real" colonialism with its injustice, egotism, envy, cheating, internal strife, brutality, and inequality (156–157).[19] By refusing to portray an actual colony but concentrating on the processes of colonization and the conquest of the mind(s) instead, Campe left room for imagining the self as conqueror.

Campe himself conceived of *Robinson the Younger*—his fiction come alive—as only the first step, the forerunner [*Vorläufer*] in a series of interlocking projects on European discovery and exploration: the story of the German colonizer *Robinson the Younger* (1779–1780) was followed by a book on the Spanish conquistadors themselves, entitled *The Discovery of America* (1780–1781) [*Die Entdeckung von Amerika*], and by a series of *Collections of Interesting and Thoroughly Useful Travelogues for Young People,* which Campe published in 1786–96, 1797–1802, and 1802–1813. Campe's colonial fiction thus not only antecedes, but anticipates real conquests. The close connection between the story of the fictional German colonizer Krusoe and the real Spanish conquistadors is not only chronological, but thematic.[20] Even in *The Discovery of America,* the education of the childlike natives, "poor ignorant people" (1: 54), constitutes the principal project—a project that the Spaniards, however, failed to accomplish. The personality and formation of the conqueror is again at the center of Campe's attention: the less educated, the less moral the conquistador. Columbus, a man endowed even as a child "with the best potential for all the greatest characteristics . . . was courageous and energetic, did not cherish sloth and effeminate laziness," but aspired to nothing more than to learn (1: 3). Cortés, of noble birth, possessed "unusual courage, an indefatigable endurance of all discomforts, a restless, hardpushing mind, and a burning desire to excel" (2: 19). Pizarro, "illegitimate son of a Spanish nobleman and a bad wench," although "noble at the bottom of his heart" (3: 180), failed to learn compassion and morality and therefore had to be chided. While Father Campe denounces the Spaniards' brutality—particularly Pizarro's propensity for massacres—he encourages his German children to emulate "good" Spaniards like Columbus or Cortés and to become, like them, "great men": "Noble and sublime spirits—take note, children!—are not deterred from their path toward a praiseworthy goal, not even by the greatest obstacles, as long as these are not totally unsurmountable!" (17). While this goal may be considered completely within the realm of metaphor — *per aspera ad astra* — the identification with expansionist colonialism is much more obvious in Campe's stories of "discoveries" than in Robinson's story.

Both Campe's *Robinson the Younger* and *The Discovery of America* are deeply duplicitous works. On the surface, they preach an enlightened bourgeois paternalism, a Protestant ethic, religious and cultural tolerance, and the perfectibility of *all* humans. They denounce materialism, violence, slavery, and colonialism as immoral, then and now.[21] Yet in their depiction of the Indians a profound ambiguity regarding the "savages' " true nature leads to a moral ambiguity about their treatment. The "pedagogical colonialism" Campe advocates only thinly disguises cultural annihilation. The rational, liberal development project of raising the "savage" to hitherto unknown levels of civilization by assimilating him completely into the "superior" culture has its own colonialist implications. Freitag's culture is ignored and/or replaced: his native language is repressed, his prior knowledge absorbed and instrumentalized, the connection with his people severed. In the transfer to Germany, he even loses his physical "difference." Whereas in the first encounter, Krusoe had carefully and approvingly registered Freitag's "non-African" Indian physiognomy, that marker of "difference" is erased when he gets to Hamburg. Supposedly, the Hamburgers do not note the "redskin" in their midst. Nor does Freitag raise the issue of racial difference or test the degree of their acceptance: completely fixated on his brother Krusoe, with whom he lives in celibate harmony, he never moves to populate Hamburg with little Calibans, as another literary predecessor had threatened to do. The total assimilation of Freitag thus marks not just the erasure of the "savage," his traditions, background, family, but the erasure of the individual, his conflicts, passions, and aspirations. Whereas Krusoe regained a sense of self and recuperated his past through the colonial adventure, "Freitag's" former identity is replaced by that of the colonized subject domesticated into the German family. While one might argue that Freitag, as "civilized savage," stands metonymically for any educational project, the confrontation between the education of Krusoe (becoming a man) and the education of Freitag (becoming assimilated) suggests otherwise.

The cultural, if not physical annihilation is divinely sanctioned, according to Campe. Since Indians are seen as both childlike (and hence "educable") and effeminate (i.e., prone to excess, cruelty, wantonness, sloth, and hence unfathomable and unreformable), the violence used by the conquistadors to "pacify" them may not have been so ill applied after all. In fact, according to the motto that there is nothing bad that does not have its good side ("God occasionally permits lesser evils to avoid greater ones," 2: 98), Father Campe develops a theory according to which the conquest and colonization of the peoples of the New World were ordained by God in order to end their brutal practice of human sacrifice and cannibalism. Cortés and Pizarro then are nothing but the tools of Providence, the executors of a predetermined outcome (3: 111). And in a dialectical twist, the conquistadors are also responsible for the liberation of the colonies: as Campe argues, by instituting a tyrannical regime, the early colonizers prepared the colonies for a greater freedom than Europe will ever experience: "Who can tell what all America may yet become once she will have completely shaken off the yoke of her European tyrants, and what she never would have become had she not borne this yoke for a time" (3: 99–100). Campe makes it therefore morally acceptable to sympathize with the conquerors, with those who excel by virtue of their courage and endurance, and whose cruelty is, after all, part of the divine plan. As the father tells his children: "We will forget a hundred times that our European compatriots were robbers and oppressors, and that the poor Americans were the innocent, besieged, and oppressed ones. And if we were to dish out victories, we would, without much scruple, dish them out to those men whom we have come to sympathize with. Don't worry, children. The causes of this are not evil. It is part of human nature to side with those who exhibit extraordinary courage and unusual effort" (1: 36–37).

As Campe himself recognizes, the moral Enlightenment model is thus subverted by a desire to identify with the victors of history. While the father takes great pains to teach his children to abhor the Spaniards' brutality toward the innocent natives, the narration of the heroic conquests itself enlists their sympathy with "our" conquistadors: "And now, children, won't you tell me what sentiment this narrative has stirred in you? Whom did you side with? Whom did you wish to win? Our brave Cortés or the Americans?" "Oh, the former!" "Oh fie! No, the latter." "Come, let's hear your reasons. You, Ferdinand, and you others who share his opinion, speak, just why do you take Cortés's part?" Ferdinand: "Because he did so well!" John: "And because he would have liked to keep peace if the savages had only wanted it." Diederich: "And because he is our fellow countryman." Kristel: "And because the story would probably have ended if Cortés had been defeated or even killed" (11: 36).

This development of empathy with the conqueror's story, this seduction by a "libido of conquest" (which is also, as "daughter" Kristel indicates, a libido of reading) is in evidence in the many sequels to Campe's novels that continue the dream of conquest and colony well into the nineteenth century — from Christoph Hildebrandt's brutally repressive *Robinson's Colony* (1810)[22] to *The Little Robinson* (1854) — and from the Caribbean island onto the South American continent (*The Patagonian Robinson*, Leipzig, 1854). There is hardly a colonizer, traveler, or colonial advocate in nineteenth-century Germany who does not proudly admit to having been lured into the colonial adventure by reading "Robinson" — from the economist-colonial theorist Wilhelm Roscher and the writer-adventurer Friedrich Gerstäcker (see epigram) to the infamous Carl Peters.[23]

Paradoxically, the libido of conquest, as it is presented in Campe's colonial *Bildungsroman,* has no sexual component. Colonial relations, as they are literalized in *Robinson the Younger,* are a form of "homosocial" male bonding, seemingly unaffected by desire. With the exception of the mother and one sister, both of whom play only a marginal role, there are no female protagonists in the novel. Unlike his literary predecessor Friday, Freitag displays no "feminine" charms — he and Krusoe are platonic brothers. In view of his young audience Campe's choice was probably conscious. However, the blatant lack of (hetero)sexual tensions and "the female" in this colonial "family" may have deeper causes. The formation of the young German colonizer is predicated, above all, upon learning self-restraint and manliness vis-à-vis alluring "effeminate" behavior. Unlike the British, the Spanish, or the French, he does not indulge in excesses; he craves neither material gains and luxury, nor sex and power. Unlike the cannibals, he does not devour human flesh or dance around fires. Instead, he is frugal, industrious, pious, Protestant. For him, the colony is a space of learning and regeneration, not a place for sensual enjoyment or material enrichment. He returns home a (new) "man" who has proven his natural superiority through physical stamina, moral conduct, and practical intelligence. In his contact with his native brother, whom he has molded after himself, he retains that control and restraint: he is just, fair, and aloof. In these and other qualities, the fictional Krusoe embodies the ideal colonizer as he was theorized by de Pauw and later by Meiners. Krusoe also anticipates the ideal German, as he appears in the racial/cultural theories of

Herder, Kant, and others. Campe's *Robinson the Younger* thus constitutes a stepping stone in the formation of a German self-image based on colonialist fantasy. Propelled by an immensely popular novel, this German self-image as "colonial man" could and did affect generations of readers at a moment of their greatest receptivity: during adolescence. Imperceptibly but all the more powerfully, *Robinson the Younger* helped propagate the myth of the benign, efficient, and restrained German colonizer, a myth that would permeate not just nineteenth-century, but also a good part of twentieth-century German literature.

7

Husbands and Wives: Colonialism Domesticated

Love, the fatal enemy to repose and innocence, love like mine, the inhabitants of these regions have never felt. The habit of desiring only what is permitted, conducts them quietly along the narrow path which their laws prescribe. But how cruel are those laws, to which youth, beauty, and love, are the sorrowful victims! How just and generous would it be to set them free!—Jean François Marmontel, The Incas, *1777*

If Robinson the younger had one major flaw, it was his lack of interest in (the other) sex, and hence in (pro)creating his own "family." For a mythical model of national regeneration, he lacked generative power, that ultimate proof of masculine potency. Whereas the older Robinson had managed to marry and produce children between adventures (although this was clearly a marginal occupation), his younger German version preferred the platonic company of his inseparable friend and assistant Freitag, with whom he lived "in peace, health, and useful employment" (205) to a venerable old age. Although *Robinson the Younger* engendered numerous literary offspring, the lack of possibilities for sequels induced many of Campe's imitators to marry Robinson off and to have him father a host of little adventurer-colonizers who could, in turn, sally forth and complete the tasks left undone by their progenitor. Robinson's marriage, however, remained an all-European affair, devoid of the erotic tension associated with the colonial adventure in the minds of most Europeans.

While Robinson Crusoe turned increasingly familial — Wyss's "Swiss Family Robinson" is a case in point — from the 1780s onward, another romance, which had hitherto led a comparatively subdued life, suddenly started to proliferate: the romance between conqueror and conquered. Unlike the former, this romance did not focus on the European family, but on a cross-racial and cross-cultural union. It replaced the erotics of pedagogy and a somewhat egalitarian model with heterosexual desire or an erotics of conquest — tempered, however, by ensuing domesticity. For the love story between European colonizer and native colonized that complemented the Robinson-Freitag story proposed not just brotherhood and integration or conquest and subjection, but a permanent love bond: the marriage of nations.

The heterosexual colonial romance, in which the European explorer-conqueror is cast as male, the Native American as female, had been in existence since the conquista. In fact, foundational "encounter" fictions — to extend Doris Sommer's phrase[1] — had cast the appropriation of America in stories of love and surrender throughout the colonial period. The difference between these earlier romances and those appearing in late-eighteenth-century Europe/Germany lay in their resolution: the earlier romances had tended to have tragic, the later ones happy endings. Thus, the early colonial master plot, familiar to us through the stories of John Smith and Pocahontas or Inkle and Yarico, was a tale of "shipwreck, hospitality, and ingratitude"[2] or, from the perspective of the American protagonists, rescue, love, and betrayal. The European colonizer, cast by a tempest against New World shores, was saved and sustained by a native woman, who became his natural wife. However, he abandoned her and (in the case of Inkle and Yarico) their child — even sold her into slavery — as soon as he had an opportunity to return to Europe and his former trading occupation.[3] The innumerable revisions and productions of this story of betrayal throughout the seventeenth and eighteenth centuries, in a variety of genres, attest to its central significance within the colonialist imagination.[4]

In all of these earlier conquest fantasies, the innocent, childlike American fell in love with the irresistible European and relinquished her "savage ways" in order to live with and serve the stranger faithfully. In Gellert's inimitable formulation:

With every rising day Yariko's art
with varied favors charms the stranger's heart,
and by each day's new tenderness shows best
what loyal heart may beat in savage breast![5] *(My emphasis)*

Clearly, the love-match fantasy exhibits an Early Enlightenment faith in the humanity of all races and sexes, and in human perfectibility; it expresses revulsion at the European's unwillingness to settle down and fulfill his new responsibility as protector of the natives and father to his newborn child. The ideological implications of this story are, however, also easily discernible. It rewrites the violent dispossession of the natives as the woman's voluntary surrender, thereby making it palatable

to European readers. Furthermore, as the Euro-American couple assumes center stage, it conveniently displaces the native man — not to
mention the European woman who is absent from the scene to begin
with. Thus while one might detect the stirrings of colonial guilt in the
moral outrage over the European's inability to reciprocate love and
form a permanent bond, it is also possible to interpret these earlier
versions of the colonial love story as symbolic representations of the
move from conquest and pillaging or trading to permanent colonial
settlements and long-term economic exploitation.[6] In any case, the initial infraction, the "destruction of the Indies," that is, the violent appropriation of territory and subjugation of its population, is repressed,
recast, substituted by a new infraction: the lack of commitment to the
conquered territory — a lack of commitment we had even observed in
Krusoe, the ideal colonizer.

This desire for a long-term commitment to or on foreign soil is apparent in the colonial romance that became the master fantasy of the latter
half of the eighteenth century and that will concern us now: the love
story of Cora and Alonzo at the center of Jean-François Marmontel's
sentimental novel *Les Incas, ou la Destruction de l'Empire du Pérou*
(*The Incas; or, The Destruction of the Empire of Peru*, 1777).[7] This
popular, widely imitated tale marks the beginning of a new phase in
colonialist discourse: a shift to "love" (rather than expediency, lust, or
violence) as that which unites the universal "family," and — paradoxically — a shift from raising and educating colonial elites (Freitag) to
settling down and "working the land."[8] Las Casas, whose work was
receiving belated attention among the West European public at the
time, serves as implicit point of reference. Not only does Marmontel
allude in his title to Las Casas's treatise on the destruction of the Indies
and to a tradition of moral outrage over Spanish atrocities, but the love
story of Cora and Alonzo is a literal elaboration on the matrimonial
metaphor contained in Las Casas's text: the land's need for a loving
husband rather than a "rascally stepfather."

In Marmontel's sentimental rewriting of the conquest, the two familial models for the relationship of conqueror-conquered — the educational paternalism of the father-child model and the erotic patriarchal-
ism of the conjugal model — make their concerted appearance: Alonzo
Molina, a "good conquistador," educated in Las Casas's humanitarian
tradition, goes to Peru to help the natives prepare against the Spanish
onslaught and to educate the Incas in modern warfare and Christian
thought. He falls in love with Cora, a "Virgin of the Sun," and seduces

her when a natural event, an earthquake, breaks down the walls of the temple in which Cora is kept. When Cora's pregnancy is discovered and the trial begins — according to Inca law any infraction of the vow of chastity is punished with the death of all her family members — Alonzo comes forward, and, admitting his responsibility, makes an eloquent and convincing plea for a new order, in which "natural" feelings and Christian forgiving, not revenge, reign supreme. Alonzo and Cora's subsequent marriage would be blissful and everlasting, were it not for Pizarro and his lot, the murderous, greedy "stepfathers" who conquer by force. Alonzo perishes on the battlefield, while Cora dies of grief on his grave, together with her newborn child.

The story shares with previous colonial romances the myth of the women's natural surrender, as well as the subsequent displacement of native men. For example, earlier in the novel, after another conveniently placed earthquake, Alonzo is rescued from the wrath of a "tribe of man-eaters" by their women, who, cognizant of his irresistibility, "devour him with their eyes" (1: 192):

> His auburn locks waving in long ringlets over the ivory of his captive shoulders, served as a foil to their enchanting white; and his shape, in which all the charms of elegance, grace, and majesty, were combined, completed every thing that was wanting to make a perfect model. In the court of Spain, in the midst of the most brilliant train of youth, Molina would have outshone all competitors. How much more rare and striking among those savages must have been the spectacle of such beauty? (1: 191)

The European male is the object of the eroticized gaze of the native women, who, rising above their savage men, establish the new Euro-American bond. Not only the cannibal "mothers" but also Cora, the "virgin" of the sun, fall for this natural conqueror of hearts, as her first thoughts upon setting eyes on him reveal:

> Happy would she have been had her timid eyes been never raised on Alonzo! One glance destroyed her; this imprudent glance presented to her view the most formidable enemy to her repose and her innocence. If he, by his grace and beauty had melted the hearts even of cannibals when thirsting for his blood, what must have been their influence on the breast of a virgin, simple, tender, ingenuous, and made for love! This sentiment, the germ of which nature had planted in her bosom, disclosed itself at once. (2: 6)

This encounter is the moment, however, when Marmontel's romance departs from previous models. Alonzo does not abandon, but stands by his woman and, once her condition is known, even accepts to exchange vows to remain with her until death. Despite the parallels to previous fantasies, Marmontel's colonial love story thus pushes the narrative of colonial desire one step further. Not only does "nature" rather than convention cooperate in, or even cause, the subjection of the woman/ land to the virtuous conqueror, thereby introducing an element of colonial determinism or natural law — but the conqueror accepts his charge, decides to stay, be fertile, and multiply, thus atoning for his past guilt. While the story of rape is, like in the de Pauw section quoted above (chapter 3), rewritten as one of "natural surrender," *any* past infraction or vestiges of guilt are once and for all expiated through the vows of marriage. By marrying Cora, Alonzo gives their union *ex post factum* legitimacy, divine sanction — and permanence.

This integration of conqueror and conquered into a new, permanent colonial order is underscored by Las Casas's role in the romance. The ailing Las Casas, venerated teacher and father figure throughout, becomes the child of the New World, when, in a much depicted scene (fig. 7) he is revitalized by mother's milk, offered to him from the breasts of Enriquillo's wife: "Approach, my wife, embrace my father; and let thy bosom compel his mouth to draw sustenance from it. . . . Adieu, my father, . . . I leave with you the partner of my soul; and I desire not to see her again till she shall have restored you to life and our love" (156).[9] It is the body of the native virgin in the case of Alonzo, and the body of the native mother in the case of Las Casas that become the vehicles for redemption and that provide "good" foreign conquerors with legitimate access to the new continent. Voluntary surrender to the stronger, the better, the more civilized European, and voluntary acceptance of the responsibility for the new continent's welfare combine in creating the new, mixed Colonial Family.

The degree to which the familial fantasy takes over and displaces stories of unrequited love and abandonment becomes even more pronounced in subsequent adaptations of Marmontel's and the other colonial romances mentioned earlier. It is a curious phenomenon, for example, that from the mid-1700s onward, writers in France, England, and Germany also revise the tragic conclusion of the Inkle and Yarico narrative to allow for a final reconciliation, with the result that, from 1780 onward, practically all Inkle-Yarico plays have happy endings.[10] In one particularly popular French version, Yarico is released from slavery, Inkle repents, and together, they rule over a Caribbean island.[11]

What then are the ideological implications of this shift from tragic to

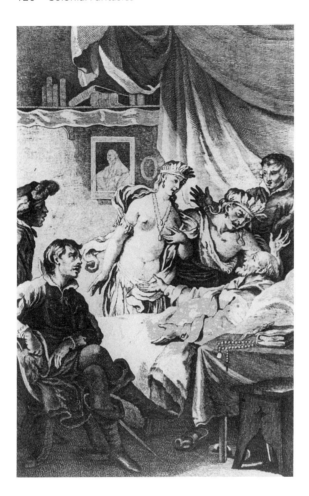

7. "Enriquillo's Wife Nurturing Las Casas: Europe Rejuvenated." From Jean-François Marmontel, *Les Incas, ou la Destruction de l'Empire du Pérou* (1777). Photograph by Biomedical Communications, Dartmouth College.

happy ending, from concubinage to marriage, and from fleeting encounters to permanent commitments? Why did this shift occur around 1780, and what is its significance within a colonialist mind frame? To what extent does it complement or undermine the other developmental master fantasy, the story of Friday's and Krusoe's formation? And what, if any, is the particular investment of German authors who were so eager to rewrite both the Inkle-Yarico and the Cora-Alonzo stories to allow for alternate models of colonial interaction and more enduring colonial relations?

A closer look at one of the most influential late-eighteenth-century adaptations of Marmontel's love plot, August von Kotzebue's *Die Sonnen-Jungfrau* (*The Virgin of the Sun*, 1789) and its sequel *Die Spa-*

nier in Peru, oder: Rollas Tod (translated alternately as "Pizarro" or as "The Spaniards in Peru; or, Rolla's Death," 1794–1795)[12] may help us find answers to these questions. Again, we are dealing with texts that must have hit a nerve in prerevolutionary Europe, particularly in Germany, if we are to judge by their popularity.[13] Although disdained, even ridiculed by highbrow critics, Kotzebue's two plays were immediately translated into all major European languages. They were copied by hacks who tried to cash in on his success (e.g., Friedrich Ludwig Schröder, *Ataliba, Father of His People,* 1794, or Julius Graf von Soden's *Franzesko Pizarro; or, The Vow in the Sun Temple,* 1815), converted to operas, ballets, and *Singspiele,* and performed for seasons on end at the most famous European theaters — in Weimar, Berlin, at the Burgtheater in Vienna, at Drury Lane and Covent Garden.[14] The *Sonnen-Jungfrau,* for example, appeared 160 times in the repertory of German theaters until 1829. What is more: not only were the two plays translated into English and published in England, Ireland, and the United States, but their English adaptation by the playwright Sheridan was eventually retranslated into German and performed over and over again on the continent. It is therefore safe to assume that no other single playwright, indeed, no other single writer with the exception of Campe, influenced German thought on colonialism more than Kotzebue, who molded and reflected the attitudes of his dedicated, enthusiastic audience: the German bourgeoisie.[15] His popularity as a playwright was such that in Weimar, under Goethe's very own direction, his plays were performed over four hundred times, while Goethe's own productions scored a low 153.[16]

Like Campe, Kotzebue exploited an immensely popular literary model to inscribe his own "German" version into the existing colonial fantasy. Unlike Campe, however, he resorted not to the didactic model of storytelling and dialogue, but to another highly effective medium to carry his message: staged drama. Although the protagonists of the plays are non-Germans, the mere fact that German-speaking actors were impersonating conquistadors and colonizers day after day on stage, in the presence of an enthusiastically applauding German-speaking public, increased the sense of spectatorship, moral arbitration, and actual participation in the colonial drama that had unfolded and continued to unfold across the ocean — and under their very own eyes. If analyzed not just against the backdrop of Marmontel's story but in conjunction with another comedy by Kotzebue, *Die Indianer in England* (1789), the two conquista plays reveal their colonialist investment and their particularly "German" perspective on the conquest and colonization of South America, and on colonialism in general.

Natural Conquests

The plot of *The Virgin of the Sun* deviates but slightly from its French model. Like Marmontel's protagonist, Kotzebue's Alonzo is a "noble" Spaniard who rejects the bloody practices of Pizarro and his soldiers and opts for educating the natives instead. At a service in the temple, Alonzo sees and falls in love with Cora, a "noble" Peruvian virgin dedicated to the service of the sun god. The intervention of nature — an earthquake that breaks down the walls of the sun temple — facilitates the meeting of the two lovers, who consummate their marriage in all innocence in the wilderness adjacent to the temple gardens. When Cora's pregnancy and thus their crime against religion and state become evident, Cora and Alonzo are condemned to death by the priests. Up to that point, the play reproduces the Alonzo-Cora episode in *Les Incas* to the letter. However, in its resolution it departs from its model significantly. The two lovers are saved from execution not because of an impassioned speech by Alonzo on "love and nature" (which in Marmontel's narrative had moved the Inca and his people to adopt the new religion of reason, 2: 118). They are saved, literally in the last moment, by Rolla, a native warrior who, consumed by unrequited love for Cora, organizes a popular uprising and forces the Inca to pardon the two lovers. Neither the humane Inca Ataliba nor his shaken highpriest are able to counter the law of the land, despite their conviction of its inhumanity. Nor are Alonzo or Cora willing to fight for the supremacy of natural feelings over convention: they comply, self-sacrificially, hoping to be reunited in death (Alonzo: "I have deserved death, and submit to it willingly," 88). It is Rolla the unloved rebel, the revolutionary, who brings about change. His passion for Cora translates into the action that leads to a final reconciliation — yet only after he, enticed by Cora, willingly relinquishes his weapons and subjects himself to the paternal authority of the Inca. In the end, love has defeated hatred, forgiveness the desire for revenge, and natural morality social convention — through a series of multiple self-sacrifices and acts of self-subjection. A new pact seals the reconciliation between noble Spaniards and noble Peruvians, who together create a utopian community governed by love of family, love of virtue — and love of paternal authority, the internalized Law of the Fathers (241). Alonzo, Cora, and their unborn child form the holy trinity of a new, integrated society that blends the European and the South American in harmonious, productive (= fertile) patriarchal union: "Long live the Inca!" (96).

The second play, *The Spaniards in Peru*, written five years later in the midst of Revolutionary Wars and the Haitian slave uprising, resumes the drama of the military conquest that the first "domestic conquest" had eluded: it leads the audience back to the camp of Pizarro, who, in his attempt to subject the Peruvians once and for all, does not shy away from "human sacrifice." He plots to attack the Indians when they are peacefully gathered in prayer. Alonzo, torn between his loyalty toward king and fatherland and his love for the new virgin territory turned motherland, chooses to side with the Peruvians in their struggle against foreign invaders. Although Pizarro's men lose this battle, due, again, to Rolla's superhuman efforts, they capture Alonzo, the renegade. Pizarro plans to avenge Alonzo's "betrayal" by torturing and executing him, but the valiant Rolla prevents him from doing so. In order to prove his undying love for Cora, Rolla saves not only his friend and "brother" Alonzo but, at the sacrifice of his own life, Alonzo's infant son who had been dropped in the woods by the panicking Cora and picked up by Pizarro's soldiers. Thus, while the bloody usurper Pizarro is defeated and the heroic Indian leader Rolla is killed, the Euro-American family can live happily ever after.

The overt message of both plays, conveyed with humanitarian pathos, is clear: love supersedes war. Particularly in the second, the old Las Casas is given ample opportunity to denounce the bestiality of the Spaniards' treatment of the Indians, a bestiality that is underscored by Pizarro's rape of and disdainfully exploitative relationship with his mistress, Elvira. In the spontaneous, loving, and fertile union of Alonzo and Cora, Europe and South America, Kotzebue proposes a more peaceful alternative to the "rape" of the land by greedy conquistadors. In a probably unconscious mixing of gender and metaphor, Kotzebue transforms what appeared to be an act of aggression into an act of love. Alonzo's conquest of Cora, which was at first interpreted as a desecration of the temple, a hostile act, is in truth — Kotzebue suggests — a kind of holy communion; what was seen as a metaphoric "stab in the back of his Peruvian brothers" ("Dolchstoss in den Rücken seiner Peruanischen Brüder," 128), is presented literally as loving "penetration" of their sister, as copulation based on mutual attraction.

The initial infraction or crime, namely the European's takeover of the native body ("murderer of virtue," 190; "seducer," 191), becomes the cause for and *movens* of a multiracial, multinational reconciliation that is expressed through the image of the "restoration of the family." Cora's and Alonzo's trial with its happy resolution brings to the fore Cora's biological family and Rolla's unknown father, reuniting and integrating all into a larger unit, the family of the state (with Father Ataliba at the helm) and the family of nations (Rolla: "I have a father living — a father who loves me, whose heart will sympathize with mine. Yes, I am reconciled to the world!" 69). Significantly, however, the two native families are flawed: the high priest's illicit love for a virgin of the sun had produced a son out of wedlock, Rolla, whose identity had to be hidden. The priest's belated acknowledgment of paternity does not wipe out the "stain" on Rolla's birth: Rolla can never transcend "illegitimacy." Likewise, Cora's family is problematic. When they hear of her "crime" (224), her father and brother first forsake her before they can begrudgingly "forgive" her. Too steeped in traditional religion, or too "passionate" (= archaic) in their adherence to honor, the play suggests, they are reluctant to make the leap toward a New-Testamentarian European reconciliation based on love and forgiveness. Cora's option for Alonzo as "new family" then is not just predetermined by nature, but legitimized by the demise or moral insufficiency of the families she leaves behind.

The egalitarian overtones of this seductive familial model should not deceive us. Despite the titles *The Virgin of the Sun* and *The Spaniards in Peru; or, Rolla's Death,* the drama focuses neither on the Peruvian virgin, nor on the Spanish aggressors, nor on the heroic Peruvian warrior, but on the plight of the noble European colonizer caught between two cultures. As "villain" and "hero" respectively, Pizarro and Rolla are basically one-dimensional characters. They pursue one and the same goal. Both are fighting for control of the territory, one as its conqueror, the other as its defender. Both fail: the power-hungry Pizarro unwittingly prepares his own death; Rolla sacrifices his life. Not surprisingly, Pizarro and Rolla meet and separate as "equals" in the play, unable to attain the object of their desire. The good European colonist Alonzo, on the other hand, is given more complexity. He has to make moral choices; he is able to elevate the "enemy" to the status of brother, friend, lover; he conquers and civilizes not by force, but by much subtler, "natural" means. Cora surrenders to Alonzo, not to Rolla, because he is the better man — not a warrior, but a cultivated cultivator of lands. As his friend Don Juan describes him to the audience: "Don Alonzo Molina quitted the savage followers of Pizarro, because he abhorred their barbarities, because he loved in every Indian a brother — that was a noble principle! — I will go, he said, among these kind-hearted people, and by cultivating their minds, and instructing them in the arts of civilized life, become their friend and teacher. — Objects worthy of my friend!" (*The Virgin of the Sun,* 15).[17] In *The Spaniards in Peru,* Alonzo's civilizing educational project is even more clearly stated. Asked by Elvira how he would defend his "treason" before Las Casas, Alonzo responds:

> What I would tell him? I would lead him by the hand through the fields of Quito; look, how everything flourishes and flowers! How here the plow works through uncultivated fields and there the seeds are growing to bring rich harvests: this is my work! Look, how contentment smiles on every cheek, because justice and mildness eliminated barbarian law: this is my work! Look, how here and there many a one lifts up his gaze in adoration of the one and only true God! This is my work, I'd say. And Las Casas would take me in his arms and a tear of mild wistfulness would fall on me and bless me.[18]

The attractive image of the European benefactor only thinly disguises the cultural hierarchy at the heart of Kotzebue's colonial romance. Despite the plays' appeals to the brotherhood of all men, the Europeans' patronizing, condescending discourse reveals the difference between brother and brother, man and woman, and the right of the one over the body and mind of the other. Hitherto "barren" fields will be cultivated and made fertile by the more fertile mind, heathen ignorance and superstitions will cede to the one and only true Christian religion. Hitherto savage hordes will be taught to cohabit in peaceful communities by the loving European colonizer. Clearly, Kotzebue promotes a "humane" type of rule that is neither characterized by usurpation and pillage like Pizarro's nor by tribal warfare and archaic ritual like Rolla's. It is, however, a colonial rule, exercized by a European over South Americans and justified by his perceptions of their supposedly inferior culture.

By recasting the conquest in the mold of a love match, with Europe as man and South America as woman, Kotzebue legitimates hierarchy and colonial subjection as natural. Yet if we recall both Rousseau's theories of the so-called natural relations between the sexes, which Kotzebue espouses, and the real conditions of wives in late-eighteenth-century Germany, we can understand the ideological implications of this marriage between two cultures. Love is the glue that cements a relationship of inequality, between the "master of the house" and his legally and economically disenfranchised subject. Love covers up for violence; unlike conquest, a term that contains and preserves the power contest, "love" masks rather than characterizes colonial relations.

The Demise of the Noble Savage

Race does not seem to be an issue in Kotzebue's idealized encounter. As Virgin of the Sun and daughter of an Inca nobleman, Cora is the European's "equal" — (en)lightened by the light of the sun and the elevated social status that denotes "class." In addition, she has an attraction that her European class-mates, steeped in repressive conventions, no longer possess: she follows her feelings with spontaneity and innocence. Kotzebue's vision of the spontaneous sexuality reigning among unspoilt "natural women" comes close to the utopia of a sexually free society elaborated by Diderot (*Supplement to Bougainville's Travels*) and others. Her "innocent" surrender to the man she loves and to his culture serves as a device to obliterate any cultural and ethnic identity and difference she might have had. Before the drama even started, *she* has become *his*.

In the relationship between Alonzo and his competitor Rolla a different eclipsing or obliteration takes place. As I indicated before, the character of the rival-brother Rolla is Kotzebue's invention. By introducing and then killing off this noble savage, Kotzebue literally re-enacts the exclusion of the native male from the colonial romance. As Alonzo's only rival to the Virgin (territory), Rolla must die so that the Euro-American family, Alonzo, Cora, and their child, can live happily ever after. His displacement and death, in fact, are foreshadowed and "legitimized" in the very first act of *The Virgin of the Sun*, even before Alonzo appears on the scene. Rolla, the formerly proud warrior, wounded in treacherous civil wars among the natives, has withdrawn into a hidden cave, defeated by his unrequited love for Cora. Surrounded by dense bushes and "wild" thicket (*Wildnis*) and accessible only by a "Schlangenpfad," a winding "snake" path, the cave becomes a feminized space, the locale for a return to origins — in Rolla's case a return to the jungle, to savage ways, to uncontrolled passions. Forgetful of his duties to the fatherland as warrior and warlord (113), his existence as caveman permits him to indulge in the "wild burning flame" inside him. He has no family that can turn passion to love, no community into which to integrate.

As the allusion to the snake suggests, this thicket is also a potential paradise—the space where Alonzo met the Virgin of the Sun in all natural innocence and produced the family of the future. As the sun sets over Rolla, transforming the thicket into a dark place of death (night/death, 121), it rises for Alonzo to witness marriage and rebirth. The dual valence of *Wildnis* as space of both atavistic savagery/descent into chaos ("savage thicket," 123, which equals Rolla's passion) and promise/cultivation, procreation ("tender thicket," 123, which equals Alonzo's love) anticipates the change from an apparent symmetry and equality among the two men to underlying asymmetry and hierarchy. Rolla's regression to the cave, to pining over unfulfilled love, to resignation and passivity, feminizes him. Alonzo's entry of the thicket, on the other hand, made him a "man," a father. Cora's embracing of the "father" Alonzo over the "orphan" Rolla, her "first act" that antecedes the first act of the drama, confirms this asymmetry, an asymmetry that existed from the start, before the start.

Before Rolla can be removed, or rather, remove himself from the scene, he is elevated to the role of "brother" (158). In its insistence on the brotherhood between Europeans and natives and the equal value of their monotheic religions, the play repeatedly expresses a liberal position that supersedes even Campe's. Yet Rolla becomes a brother only by the restraint of his own desires and the self-sacrificial, selfless support he is willing to extend to the Euro-American couple. The native warrior can assert his humanity only as a warrior, not as a cultivator, and only in war, not in peace—therefore not permanently. In a curious rewrite of native rebellions in the New World, Kotzebue has Rolla's revolution motivated by private, apolitical concerns. The "freedom" the revolt has written on its banners is the freedom Rolla demands for the two lovers, the freedom to marry and to colonize. The people do not need freedom from tyrants, since at their helm they have two or three kind fathers who reign in unison: the benign Inca Ataliba, "father to his people," the enlightened high priest (Rolla's father), and Alonzo, "savior" of the Inca, educator of the people, and father of Cora's son—in short, a triumvirate of local elite, reformed clergy, and foreign colonizer/colonists. Rolla's function in the play is subservient to the needs of the new family. As emblem of atavistic passions ("a storm chases me—a stream carries me away!" 234), of violence as political means (205,

"My sword shall cut your chains," 287), of revolution and war, he has to cede to the new order characterized by domesticity, paternalism, cultivation of the land, and peace. "Virtue" and "reason" triumph (240) over vice and superstitions, as the morally superior European triumphs over his New World brother.

The Politics of Marriage

Although the familial metaphor universalizes, decontextualizes, and sentimentalizes colonial relations, these colonial relations form the backdrop and sometimes the antithesis to the colonial fantasy. The connection between colonial interest and colonial practice, and the politics of rewriting come even more to the fore in Kotzebue's comedy *Die Indianer in England* (literally, "The Indians in England"; translated as "The East Indian," since some of the protagonists come from India), which appeared in February 1789, slightly before *The Virgin of the Sun*. Here, the scenery has been transferred to England, to the home of the colonizers and the house of "John Smith," in an allusion to another colonial fantasy. Despite the "domestic" setting, all players are directly involved in the colonial drama overseas. On the one hand, there is the family of the colonizers: the father and bankrupt merchant John Smith (who has apparently badly administered the gains he made from the colonies); his "good" son Robert, a kind-hearted, overly generous ship's captain and West Indies trader (who will forge the new bonds with the colonized); his "bad" son Samuel, the greedy tax collector (who inhibits "free trade" and therefore has to be removed from the "scene"); and the virtuous Liddy, Smith's compliant daughter and pawn in the colonial enterprise. On the other, there is the family of the colonized: not the *Indianer* of the Occident, as the ambiguous title might suggest, but East Indian subjects from Mysore (one of the Indian territories Britain has been intermittently at war with):[19] Kaberdar, an Indian "nabob" and his daughter Gurli ("girlie"?), who have sought refuge in Smith's house from the bloody "civil wars" in India. Like *The Virgin of the Sun,* the play proposes a cross-racial, cross-cultural "colonial marriage" as (re)solution — two marriages in fact, since Gurli marries John Smith's son Robert, and Liddy, Kaberdar's long-lost son Fazir. Race plays no role in this fusion of colonizer and colonial elite either. As Kaberdar's description of Gurli suggests ("She is my daughter, a good girl, a child of nature, her dowry being a thousand pound sterling," 275–276), the motivation for the union is purely financial. The

Indian gold serves to fill the coffers of the impoverished colonizers. The Indian family's noble origins ("formerly ruler over thousands," 216) increase its attraction for the British merchant class. The "children's" naturalness guarantees complete supremacy of the more educated, more dynamic, and more "manly" Europeans. Gurli, the unspoilt child of nature, follows only her impulses and speaks in the third person like Friday, as does her brother, Fazir, who like Rolla is overwhelmed by his feelings and needs a firm hand.

Kotzebue suggests that the new contract between progressive British merchants moving freely between the East and West Indies and wealthy colonial elites embodied in the double marriage has two enemies. In England, enemy number one is the customs inspector Samuel, whose restrictive, inquisitive personality threatens to come in the way of "free trade" — the free-moving captain-merchant who is willing to take risks (that is, marry a woman whom he does not know). In India, it is the "bad natives," Kaberdar's evil brothers (one cross-eyed and long-nosed, the other pumpkin-headed! 244) who resented his collaboration with the British colonizers and toppled him in a revolution. While Kaberdar's flight from the colony might signal a temporary retreat from colonialism, the "marriage" between colonizer and colonial elite in fact seals a new kind of "subsidiary alliance," one built not just on mutual love, but on mutual benefit. By marrying the first-born son of the nabob, Liddy (and through her, her family) acquires access to his wealth. By marrying the nabob's daughter, Robert acquires access to wealth and the land's resources. And, through their father, both provide imperial "protection" for the new colonial marriage — a new "common-wealth" in every sense of the word. Kotzebue's fantasy can thus be interpreted as a generic colonial fantasy that fictionalizes the transition from trading (e.g., the East India Company) to "permanent" revenue settlement and that represents violent territorial appropriation in terms of a familial transaction.

Read with and against *The Indians in England*, Kotzebue's *Lust-Spiel* about the Spaniards in Peru discloses its neocolonialist impetus, the desire to partake of the conquest of virgin territory and to put colonialism on a new, more permanent base by including local elites into the "family." Rather than staying in England, so to speak, the colonizers return to the colonized territory where they establish a new and more effective kind of rule.

The questions remain as to why these seductive familial fantasies became so prominent toward the end of the eighteenth century, and what role they reserved for their German spectators. It has been argued that conciliatory romances such as the ones by Kotzebue followed a Pietism-inspired sentimentalist impulse that affected much of late eighteenth-century popular literature: as avid consumers of popular plays or novels, the public craved happy endings.[20] While this argument has merit, it does not account for the timing, this resurfacing of the matrimonial metaphor in the 1790s. Nor does this explanation help us to assess the meaning of the metaphor within its historical context. In order to understand the popularity of colonial romances with happy endings, we should look at what needs these symbolic representations fulfilled within the sociopsychological structures of European/German readers. As Helen Callaway has convincingly argued, "[I]mperial culture exercised its power not so much through physical coercion, which was relatively minimal though always a threat, but through its cognitive dimension; its comprehensive symbolic order which constituted permissible thinking and action and prevented other worlds from emerging."[21]

The emergence of a fantasy of virtuous conquest and colony as a sacred, indissoluble bond, in which the conqueror abandons his mother country to stay with his new bride is, I would argue, intimately linked to two historical developments: on the one hand, to the revolution and subsequent independence of the British colonies in North America, and on the other, to the threat of dissolution of the Spanish colonial empire in South America and the gradual opening up of hitherto closed areas to other imperial contenders.[22]

Although they take place in different countries, Kotzebue's romance as well as the numerous rewritings of the Inkle-Yarico plot provide a model for the successful maintenance of European hegemony, a "revolution" with a happy ending. As settler, cultivator, and "husband," the foreign intruder affirms his control over the local elite and his rights over the land, even as he breaks his ties with the mother country. As Egon Menz has proposed for the North American scene, the victory of the British colonists over the British motherland was seen by the former as an entitlement to the land: by avenging the natives against the "conquerors," the victorious colonists assumed the "natives'" place, becoming their heirs, their "grandchildren."[23] From 1776 onward, the European colonists were "the Americans," whereas the original Americans had become "the Indians," a race "doomed to go under." Kotzebue charts a similar process for South America, when he proposes that Alonzo "go native" by marrying into the colonial elite and assuming his place as heir to their land/daughter. The fateful conflation of land with woman, which had formed part of the European imaginary since the Discovery, lends credence to such an interpretation. Clearly, the progress from intruder to lawful owner of the land, from "rapist" to loving "husband," is the sustaining myth in all of the marriage romances discussed.

In addition to providing a legitimate release for colonial desire, the matrimonial fantasy suggests the possibility of permanent colonial control at a time when insubordination and revolts in the colonies — for example, the Tupac Amaru uprising in Peru, 1780–1781, the *comunero* revolt in the New Granada, 1781, and the repeated slave rebellions on Caribbean islands from the mid-1700s onward — have become an ever present threat to European rule. In contrast to the educational father-child model, according to which the child would eventually be released into independence by a natural transfer of power, matrimony, in its eighteenth-century ideological status at least, implies permanent inequality and bondage. The promise of "eternal love" stabilizes and veils the actual power relationship among the conjugal partners. While this marriage channels sexual drives into legitimate "commerce," the genealogical and the generative claims remain firmly in European hands. Nor does the model provide for any resistance to heterosexual libidinal determinism. Cora clearly recognizes Alonzo's "invincible attraction," his unquestioned superiority and rights to her over any native competitors, who, as we have seen, are displaced by the advent of the European.

The marriage romance, then, constructs a controlled three-step process of colonial takeover: first, as bride, the other is familiarized — she becomes part of the same species; second, as wife, the other is taken possession of, assimilated into the family and subjected to European patriarchal control; and third, as "land," the other becomes depopulated, dehumanized, an empty space that yearns to be filled, a blank spot on the map that demands inscription by its new occupant and master. Whatever was "savage" or "threatening" in the New World, that is, whatever resisted domination, is thus tamed, integrated, domesticated. The native woman is thus the emblem of both distance and familiarity: foreign territory that has been appropriated and transformed into "home" through ownership and cultivation.[24]

The attractiveness of this foundational fiction to colonial and protocolonial nations is obvious. To the former, because it veils their own implication, the violence, the immorality, the injustice at the bottom of colonial expansion. Hence the texts' insistence on "civil wars" among

Indians that warrant the benign interference of European "protectors." To the latter, the foundational fiction provides a "window of opportunity," an inroad into the symbolic order of colonialism. Alonzo, the virtuous conqueror who, in contrast to eighteenth-century Spaniards, has not rejected Las Casas but learned from him, can become the object of identification, the model colonist, for any European nation in search of its "place in the sun." The indictment of Spain and the idea of a "conquest by virtue" (*The Incas*, 157) propagated by Marmontel's and Kotzebue's texts would appeal to those bent on not repeating the mistakes of the past, those, in Marmontel's words, who want to "conquer without oppression" (150) and to rule benignly, fatherly. Thus Herder can dream in 1784 of a time when, in his words, the European "genius," will espouse "the generative power of this young bride" America, and create "from her womb beautiful offspring"[25] under better, more humane colonial conditions — after the demise of the Spaniards.

Kotzebue's texts also prefigure who might join the new colonial family. Like Campe, he does not rely on his readers'/viewers' identification alone, but inserts a German into the colonialist scenario — not so much as agent than as matrix, as progenitress: like Robinson Crusoe, Mistress Smith, the mother of the young colonizers in *The Indians in England*, is of German descent. In other words, the two happy colonial couples are the offspring of a British-German-Indian coproduction. Although Mistress Smith's old-fashioned insistence on lineage and "French" manners make her an object of derision in the play, her role in the colonial family is vindicated by the mere existence of her "children" and their bright prospects. While the German mother fails to adapt to the more egalitarian familial interaction of the new generation and has not yet learned the more liberal-bourgeois English forms of commerce, her offspring has already secured for themselves a place in the colonial family of the future. German colonial aspirants can thus participate in Kotzebue's colonial scenario in two ways: by putting themselves in Alonzo's shoes and playing his role, or by discovering ancient colonial connections, blood lines that — as Seubert's poem of 1887 suggests — establish "natural" rights to foreign soils.

These plays may have held still other attractions for their German audience. The new "colonial" order, embodied in the loving relationship between conqueror and conquered, strong and weak, may have served to assuage fears of cataclysmic change and underscored the conviction — expressed over and over again — that German conditions did not warrant revolutionary overthrow. Surely the familial closeness between ruler and ruled, benign *Landesvater* and obedient *Landeskinder,* precluded an upsetting of the old order, as long as the authority was grounded in "love." By the same token, the reciprocity implicit in the concept of matrimonial "love" sent a clear warning: Germans would not stand by their "man," their ruler, in a moment of crisis, if he did not observe his part of the marriage contract and protect the land against unlawful usurpers.

The Indians in England was first performed in February of 1789. At the time of the *Virgin of the Sun*'s inaugural production, December 1789, the repercussions of the most recent earth-shattering event — the French Revolution — had not yet reached Riga, Latvia, where Kotzebue staged his play of colonial harmony. *The Spaniards in Peru* already betrays some concern over chaos and warfare threatening the newly constituted colonial family, which is not surprising, if we consider the circumstances surrounding its date of appearance, 1796. It is not until much later that the fantasy of peaceful familial coexistence collapses completely. In 1807, Heinrich von Kleist writes another, belated takeoff on Marmontel's Cora-Alonzo story, *The Earthquake in Chile* (published in 1810). In this cruel tale of deception, misjudgment, and anarchy, the political seismographer Kleist registers not just one earthquake, the great earthquake of 1647, but three or more "natural catastrophes": the earthquake of Lisbon of 1755 that shattered Europeans' belief in Divine Providence; the earthquake of 1789 that broke with the old political order; and the Haitian revolution that initiated a process of rebellions which would finally lead to the independence of all South American colonies.[26] These multiple, superimposed cataclysms threaten the survival of the "colonial family" — both literally and figuratively — and expose the hypocrisy of the familial political model. The couple in Kleist's version of the Marmontel story is no longer constituted in the natural bond between European conqueror and native princess. In fact, the two protagonists are both white, and they are of different social classes. The union between the Spanish upstart Jerónimo and Doña Josepha, the daughter of a colonial nobleman, member of the *criollo* elite, is facilitated again by an earthquake, which breaks open the prison into which Jerónimo, as Josepha's seducer, had been flung. Yet the union must fail, for neither the old aristocratic order nor the new, revolutionary (dis)order have room for a marriage across classes and nations. Kleist's Euro-American family, which survived the old order thanks to "natural" intervention, perishes under the onslaught of the revolutionary mob. While Kleist may have lamented the demise of the colonial family and the traditional colonial order, his depiction of the blindness and brutality of the old colonial elite and the violence governing colonial relations exposes the familial model for what it is: wishful thinking.

Betrothal and Divorce; or, Revolution in the House

Every German ought to rejoice in the knowledge — corroborated by Tacitus — that the fate of the servants among his brave forebears was incomparably milder and by far not as inhumane and contrary to nature as among the proud world conquerors, who considered themselves civilized and our forebears, barbarians. — *Heinrich August Ottokar Reichard*, On the Legal Conditions of Negro Slaves in the West Indies, *1779*[1]

Therefore, dear muse, oh let,
let him retain that quill,
good spirits will prevail,
and vanquish tyranny,
which they, I know not why,
endured so patiently!
Who fears you, Sansculotte!
not us, Parisian Hottentot!
We'll defy your song of blood!
Prussia's alive, and God is God!
— *Johann Wilhelm Ludwig Gleim, "An Herrn von Archenholz, den 31. Dez. 1793"*[2]

On the night of August 22, 1791, the slaves of the northern plains of Saint-Domingue rose against their masters. The rebellion caught on fast. Within two weeks, the number of rebels rose to ten thousand. By the end of the year, 100,000 slaves were involved in what turned out to be a "terrifying three-sided civil war."[3] As all recent historians agree, it was not only a battle between the races, but a class war, between *grands blancs* and *petits blancs*, *petits blancs* and mulattoes, mulattoes and free blacks (*affranchis*), black or mulatto slaves and their white or mulatto masters, who in turn enlisted the help of black soldiers.[4] And it was an international colonial war, since it involved not only the French, English, and Spanish eager to secure or expand their colonial possessions, but Scottish, Swiss, and German mercenaries in their service.[5]

The bloody fighting lasted thirteen years. Napoleon's attempts to reinstate slavery in 1802, after it had been abolished in 1793, were unsuccessful. The French troops were defeated by the combined revolutionary forces and by yellow fever. The revolution ended in 1804 with Haiti's declaration of independence from France and with General Dessalines's coronation as "Emperor Jean-Jacques I." Significantly, the first victory for black emancipation and the first step toward universal decolonization implied, at the same time, the restoration of monarchy.[6] Yet Dessalines did not remain in power long. He was assassinated in 1806 by *affranchis,* free propertied mulattoes who resented his supposed partiality with the masses of former black slaves. In the words of Haitian historian Patrick Bellegarde-Smith: "The alliance of slaves and *affranchis* that had led to independence was wrecked by unresolved class-based conflicts. . . . These conflicts had their genesis in colonialism and have not been transcended; they continue to affect the course of social, economic, and political development in Haiti even today" (45).

The German public took considerable interest in the events in Saint-Domingue from their very inception. Press reports about "current conditions" on the island alternated with excerpted translations of often conflicting eyewitness accounts, with critical commentary and with reprints of important documents such as proclamations, speeches, and correspondence by the major protagonists of the revolution, Toussaint l'Ouverture and Jean-Jacques Dessalines.[7] This interest was owing less to the presence of German soldiers on Haitian soil than to the symbolic significance of the rebellion of slaves against their masters. Unlike the Spartacus uprisings in Roman antiquity, which had served as abstract point of reference for advocates of emancipation until 1792, this slave rebellion was neither as distant in time nor as distant in space as one might have wished. As a consequence, "St. Domingo" became an ambiguous signifier whose meaning shifted with every change in the political scenario. As literal enactment of the liberation of "slaves" from their "despots"—images by which German bourgeois intellectuals in their first enthusiastic endorsement had defined the French Revolution[8]—"St. Domingo" alluded not only to the Saint-Domingue uprisings, but allowed for implicit references to the French Revolution as well as to actual and potential revolutionary struggles at home. Within a symbolic discourse of "slaves breaking their chains," "St. Domingo" thus marked the speakers' position on colonial independence wars of any kind, on any challenges to order outside and inside their own borders. In the imagination of German eyewitness reporters, the French "slaves" fighting aristocratic "tyranny" were superimposed on the image of the Haitian slaves rebelling against colonial exploitation. After 1793, fear of bloodthirsty Jacobins and radicalized masses led to associations between revolutionary hordes and savage "cannibals." *Sansculotte* rhymed with *Hottentot,* not only in the poem by Gleim quoted as epigram, but in the mind of German readers, for whom Hottentots were the proverbial black other.[9] In fact, representations of scenes from either battlefield borrowed stock images, even whole constellations from the other, so that the symbolic topographies overlapped despite geographic and cultural distances.[10] What is more, the horror stories from one scenario tended to "reconfirm" those from another, fomenting an undercurrent of race and class anxieties. Thus, when the liberal Hamburg journal *Minerva* presented its readers in January 1792 with an account of the Saint-Domingue uprisings, the sober, seemingly disinterested assessment of the causes for revolt with which the article started gives way to a detailed "painting of the horrors" perpetrated by "die Neger": "The Negroes carried the body of a child on a spike as their banner. Not just evil masters and their families were doomed to die, but even the most kindhearted ones. 'I have done you nothing but favors,' one colonist said to his slave who threatened to kill him. 'True,' the latter responded, 'but I had to swear to kill you.' Another plantation owner, who had made it a point to treat his slaves with humanity and kindness, was tied between two boards and slowly sawed in two."[11]

This account is echoed in narratives of the September 1792 massacres in Paris, published in *Minerva* half a year later, where the generic collective of "die Neger" metamorphoses into "der Pöbel," the merciless rabble that rapes women, dismembers men, and puts children's bodies on spikes in a revolutionary frenzy.[12] Wherever there are bloodthirsty "tigers," there is "Africa," in Saint-Domingue as well as in Jacobin France.[13]

In all these instances, revolutionary disorder is associated with race and class; it is acted out within, or against a familial context. Violence is perpetrated *by* "black monsters" [*"schwarze Ungeheuer"*] — the slaves of the colonies as well as the slaves of Paris, whose blackness is both external and internal, inborn and acquired, a mark of poverty and a sign of moral degradation. Violence is perpetrated *against* all "innocents" embodied by the white family: against the fatherly king and against fatherly benign masters, their pure women, helpless infants, and weak old relatives (fig. 8). It is as if the "cannibals," exorcized in

8. "Revolution in the House: The Demise of the Colonial Family." German antirevolutionary pamphlet of 1804. Courtesy of Dr. Marcel Chatillon, Paris.

the Robinson narratives, had suddenly returned, in the form of "black" revolutionaries and female furies.

Whenever reports want to stress the particularly revolting nature of an event, they depict women as the main perpetrators of violence, as emblems of revolutionary excess. The proverbial women turned hyenas who tear off men's limbs and engage in acts of cannibalism are as much a threat in Paris as they are in Saint-Domingue, if we are to believe Dubroca's account of the "cannibal war" (456), which appeared in *Minerva* in 1805.[14] Speaking about the execution of Belois, one of Dessaline's allies, Dubroca writes: "His wife shared his fate, a wild animal in human form that always dripped with blood and found a particular pleasure in mutilating the unhappy prisoners and tearing their entrails out." And he continues with general observations about black women's tendency toward excessive violence: "In fact the negro and mulatto women took an active and direct part in the crimes and horrors of any kind which made the accidents of this colony so particularly horrendous. Always and everywhere they could be seen at the most horrible scenes; and perhaps their hands killed more whites than the hands of the blacks; indeed, to them are attributed premeditated barbarities and cruelties that are more appalling than those the wild soldiers of this army have been reproached for" (121).

While commentaries and assessments may try to weigh the evidence and provide political or economic explanations for historical processes, the figures of speech and metonymic representations reveal their paranoid unconscious by establishing very different semantic links: between *Neger,* beasts, monsters, women, cannibals, and the masses, who, unfettered, released from their cages, freed of their chains, in a "bestial frenzy" will start an all-out attack against those institutions that guarantee patriarchal law and order: the family, the monarchic state, and last but not least, the colonial system, that is, both the plantation culture and the international colonial power structure.

The threat to established order abroad and at home and the subtle maneuvers of positioning vis-à-vis all forms of emancipation also underlie the literary representations of the Haitian Revolution that appeared in German-speaking countries at the time of the two revolutions: Friedrich Döhner's *Des Aufruhrs schreckliche Folge; oder, Die Neger* [The Terrible Consequences of the Rebellion; or, The Negroes], a play that appeared in Vienna in 1792;[15] Johann Gottfried Herder's *Negeridyllen* [Negro Idylls] published in 1796;[16] August von Kotzebue's sentimental drama *Die Negersklaven* [The Negro Slaves] (1796);[17] Heinrich von Kleist's novella *Die Verlobung in St. Domingo* [published in English as *The Betrothal in Santo Domingo*] (1811);[18] Theodor Körner's takeoff on Kleist, his play *Toni* (1812);[19] and Caroline Auguste Fischer's short story *William der Neger,* which was published in five installments in *Zeitung für die elegante Welt* from May 19 to May 24, 1817.[20] All of these texts — even those whose obvious purpose is abolitionist and whose topic only marginally touches on the revolutionary events in the Caribbean — renegotiate the relationships between race, class, and gender within a colonial context. Or rather, they rewrite the colonial love stories as they are turned, literally, upside down by the revolutionary conflicts. Where submissive women turn into man-eating hyenas, the family, clearly, is in deep trouble.

Unnatural Encounters

As indicated in the last chapter, at the beginning of the 1780s the story of Inkle and Yarico had gravitated toward ever more happy endings. Compassion for the betrayed slave, strong abolitionist sentiments, and an underlying crisis of authority made this shift toward a conciliatory romance attractive to European, and particularly German, writers. In the process of rewriting that colonial romance, Yarico's identity as the Native American, whom the seventeenth-century European castaway had encountered on South American shores, became more and more blurred. In the minds of her European defenders, she was "Negro and Indian" at once, epitome of the woman of color in bondage, the dark continent that had been exploited and oppressed by the white conqueror and that demanded redress.[21]

The irresistibility of this fantasy of belated redress and reconciliation is obvious even in nonfictional eyewitness accounts or personal travel narratives such as Colonel Gabriel Stedman's popular *Narrative of a Five Years Expedition against the Revolted Negroes of Surinam* (1790).[22] Stedman's sketches on slavery and the flora and fauna of Surinam are structured around a "true" romance, namely his short-lived liaison with the mulatto slave Joanna, which he consciously conceives as a "Counter part of Incle & Yarico" (599). In a curious confusion of life and letters, Stedman proposes to free his beloved slave Joanna and their son and marry her, rather than selling her into slavery as the literary character Inkle had done. While Stedman's well-intentioned attempt to make belated amends for Inkle's act of treachery fails because of the strict slave laws and his limited financial means, it reiterates and confirms the merger, by the end of the century, of two colonial fantasies in the imaginary space of the "Caribbean": the fantasy of a natural, spontaneous sexual attraction of the white man to the (colored) native woman ("natural conquest"), and the fantasy of a long-term union between Europe and America, colonizer and colonized ("marriage"). In this merger of two master narratives, the abolitionist *littérature négrophile* of the 1770s, which had tended to repress the desire for miscegenation, gets transformed, radicalized, by the literature of natural conquest.[23] By the same token, the conquest and marriage fantasies change with the insertion of the black or mulatto slave as "significant other." The marriage fantasy becomes more pronouncedly erotic and even more pronouncedly hierarchical, since the grateful "slave" will look up eternally to her beloved "master" who bought her freedom — or who promised to do so. In Stedman's words: "From this Instant the Beauteous Maid was mine, nor had I ever after cause to repent it as shall be seen more particularly in the Sequel — Now pale envy do thy utmost, while I shall continue to Glory in this Action, as much as this virtuous Slave did pride in making me her choice" (101).

Whatever their implicit intentions, the reality of race relations in the Caribbean, and the first wars of decolonization with their supposedly "terrible consequences" for all involved, shattered these and other master fantasies of love and reconciliation across the racial, class, and national divide.[24]

Döhner's play *The Terrible Consequences of the Rebellion; or, The Negroes* appeared in 1792, shortly after the news of the first massive slave uprisings had reached Europe. Set in revolutionary Saint-Domingue, it focuses on a mixed couple: Marie, the daughter of the cruel, treacherous French plantation owner Tirleton, and Omar, Tirleton's noble slave. Marie and Omar have fallen in love and aspire to a life of peace and happiness. While they join hands in marriage shortly before the final showdown, their lives are shattered by the conflicting loyalties to their respective families who are engaged in deadly battle.[25] Bound by vows to each other and by "blood ties" or "nature" to their kin, their union is doomed: Omar is executed for defending his father against white aggression; Marie stabs herself to death.

Within the framework of a Romeo and Juliet drama, the play elaborates the confluence of the two colonial fantasies named above. References to the conquest, or rather, to Kotzebue's *Virgin of the Sun*, abound: the slaves use "quipos" for communication, just like the Incas; Omar, "son of the Sun" (8), and Marie, "daughter of the Sun," take an oath before the sun (34) never to separate; Omar attempts to discourage his brothers from committing violence by referring to the failed resistance against Spanish conquerors in Mexico and Peru (17). By the same token, the play reenacts the desire for cross-racial union, yet with a significant difference: it is not the white European who desires to legitimize his attraction to the native or black woman, as the colonial romance had it, but the white woman of the planter class, whose love for the black slave causes her to transgress the boundaries of her race and station.

Despite its daring revision of traditional plots, Döhner's play sends mixed messages to its audience.[26] While the marriage (63, 79) between Marie and Omar is depicted as the morally superior solution, a utopia informed by enlightened eighteenth-century humanitarian assimilationism comparable to Kotzebue's *Virgin of the Sun*,[27] it is also a sign for the Revolution, in which "natural" gender roles and traditional hierarchies are upset: in which, in other words, the transgressive behavior of women and slaves causes the final catastrophe. After introducing a revolutionary transformation of relations between blacks and whites, slaves and masters, Döhner's play thus offers a conservative resolution: the transgressive couple is eliminated/eliminates itself; the criminal plantation owner is punished with popular contempt; and a gentler paternalistic colonial order reminiscent of earlier, less erotic fantasies emerges.[28] Not surprisingly, it is the German planter Fleri who embodies the perfect fatherly colonizer. As Omar tells his black brothers: "It is not the white color that outrages you — our forefathers at one time deemed it the color of the gods — but the harsh, cruel treatment which *some of them* mete out to the likes of us. Not all of them do, to be sure; is there among you a slave of the honest Fleri, the German planter? Not one! Yet he [the ringleader] leads you astray and incites you to wholesale slaughter and universal destruction" (32, my emphasis).[29] The instigator of the black rebellion is, in fact, a disgruntled white. If there were only German planters like Fleri, there would not be a revolution: "Our master is our father! — If all colonists were like you, noble man, either the rebellion would not have happened, inasmuch as I think of it as a consequence of dreadful treatment — or foreign powers would have found it very difficult, if not impossible, to incite satisfied people to rebellion."[30]

In Döhner's regressive colonial universe, the natural colonial order is no longer the conjugal one, but the parental one — regressive, since the other is infantilized, stripped of eros and power. The natural fathers with their insistence on blood ties, that is, race, and their violent demands for their children's total allegiance must be replaced, he suggests, not by an interracial "marriage," nor by a Robinsonian "brotherhood," but by the colonial "family" of the plantation household in which benign white planter-fathers watch over their loyal slave-children just as the good European colonial power watches over its obedient colonies.

The text also establishes a semantic connection to the French Revolution, another rebellion of the masses. As the (also) benevolent governor remarks about the blacks, who were misguided by a resentful white idealogue: "Indeed, liberty means to blindfold the rabble, to plunge the dagger into the heart of the country; it masks private design and egotism; their horrid roar will turn to amazement and terror when the blindfold falls and the victims find themselves in the abyss whither they have been flung."[31]

It is indeed the global "colonial" order that is at stake in this uprising of the "slaves." While repeated references allude approvingly to British abolitionism, it is the abolition of slave *trade*, not the abolition of slavery or colonial rule, that Döhner's play advocates. The enlightened colonial family of plantation owners and plantation slaves will not need new workforce from Africa, since it will generate its own laborers right at home. A paternalist plantation system based on "family" allegiances and firm but gentle rule will, Döhner suggests, avoid the terrible consequences of open rebellion: the destruction of the international colonial family and death of its weakest (but economically most productive) members.

"Negro Idylls"

The violence and abuse at the heart of the plantation family surfaces in two texts that appeared almost simultaneously and concomitant with the revolutionary wars on German soil, Johann Gottfried Herder's *Negro Idylls* (1797) and Kotzebue's tragedy *The Negro Slaves* (1796). Neither addresses the Haitian Revolution directly—their purpose seems to be a more universal moral appeal—yet both exhibit basic symbolic patterns that unwittingly reinforce the paternalist, colonialist message of Döhner's play.

Both texts are based on a short story entitled "Zimeo" that appeared in Johann Ernst Kolb's *Erzählungen von den Sitten und Schiksalen [sic] der Negersklaven* [Narratives of the Customs and Fates of the Negro Slaves] (Bern, 1789). Subtitled "A Touching Reading for Kind-Hearted Men" ["*Eine rührende Lektür Menschen guter Art*"], this Swiss collection assembles excerpts from works by European authors containing factual information on the slave trade and the conditions of slaves in the Caribbean, reprints of newspaper articles, and "true" stories, all of which seem to be rewritten or edited by Kolb to form an almost continuous narrative in which abuses of bad European slaveholders alternate with the generosity of good slaveholders and the plight of—a few— extraordinarily noble slaves. The editor's role as "nonpartisan" collector of evidence and opinion (afterword, 288), his stated purpose of moving Europeans to ameliorate the suffering "even among slaves" (ibid.), is undercut, however, by his very preface. In a short overview of the history of slavery, Kolb emphasizes that Africans engaged in slave trade "long before the Portuguese," and that all negroes are "born slaves to their despots" (v). They themselves treat each other cruelly, worse than animals (v), he affirms, a fact that "all travelers" agree on. His subsequent characterization of Africans remains within the paradigm established by contemporary natural histories:[32] they are devious, secretive, rebellious (xi); they love song, dance, and glitter, and tend towards melancholy and suicide (xiii); their women procreate with ease, unaffected by Eve's curse, just like the orangutangs (xvii); they have an instinctive knowledge of herbal medicines as means of self-preservation, just like animals (xix); and their revolting practice of devouring human flesh associates them with ravenous beasts (xx). The picture of the "depravity" [*Sittenverderbniss*] of "all blacks" that Kolb paints serves to highlight the few exceptions to the rule, the "expressions of gratefulness, magnanimity, and nobility of soul that occasionally break forth, here and there" among extraordinary individuals (xxi). The stories are thus set up to affirm handed-down prejudices, rather than to challenge preconceived notions.

The tale of "Zimeo," written by a certain Georg Filmer, relates such an exceptional event in Jamaica. The first-person narrator, a Quaker, witnesses a slave uprising from the house of his friend Paul Wilmouth, a planter from Philadelphia, who, unlike the other slave owners, treats his slaves like a father and releases them into freedom after ten years (7). The leader of the rebellion is the fugitive slave Zimeo alias John, an "Apollo"-like African prince, who seeks revenge for having lost his natural wife (Elavoe, alias Marianne) and father-in-law (Matomba, alias Franz) when the three were sold to British and Spanish slave owners, respectively. The slave uprising is thus represented not as a politically motivated act but as an act of personal revenge. Little does Zimeo know that the kindly, sensible [*empfindsam,* 15] narrator has already bought Marianne and Franz from their cruel Spanish master and brought them to Wilmouth's plantation. When Zimeo approaches the plantation and spares Wilmouth's and his family's lives at the request of their grateful slaves, the black family is thus miraculously reunited. Together, Zimeo, Elavoe, and Matomba take leave from their hosts to retire to the free slave community in the mountains, where the narrator will visit them "once peace has been made between their compatriots and our colony" (37). Significantly, Elavoe and Matomba keep their English slave names as a token of gratitude to their former master. The uprising is over as soon as its cause — personal distress — has been eliminated; kindness breeds perpetual gratefulness and a permanent voluntary submission, albeit only symbolically.

The story establishes the typical abolitionist dichotomy between bad slave owners and their paternalist alternative. Through the insertion of the narrator, however, whose national identity is kept ambiguous (German/Swiss name? Quaker from Philadelphia? Trader, not plantation owner?), it creates a third position, that of the participant witness and critical-moral commentator, who, by purchasing and manumitting the two mistreated slaves, intervenes benevolently in the story, making the final reunion of the black nuclear family possible.

The relationship between this compassionate moral "I" and the "we" of the colonizers is at the center of Herder's *Negro Idylls* (letter 114 of his *Letters on the Promotion of Humanity*). Integrated into his scathing critique of European colonialism and cultural arrogance, four of these five "idylls" rewrite, in verse form, tales from Kolb's anthology: "Die Frucht am Baume" ("Grausamkeit der Christen gegen ihre Sklaven," 59–63); "Die Brüder" ("Quaschi," 42–47); "Zimeo" ("Zimeo," 6–37); and "Der Geburtstag" ("Der Quaker Miflin und sein Neger," 54–58). "Zimeo" reproduces its original almost verbatim, insofar as its protagonists speak the lines provided by the narrative. However, there are significant differences between Herder's verse rendition and Kolb's original. Herder's Zimeo is not the leader of a rebellion, but remains "unstained by blood," as the text insists on repeatedly (242, 243). He descends from the mountains to appease his brothers, rather than incite them to rebel. The story of his captivity also differs from the Swiss original: Zimeo does not marry Elavoe (here Elavo) on board the slave ship in an act of passionate desperation, before his god Orissa,[33] but is already married to her from the start. Herder's Zimeo is thus morally cleansed, a "demigod," "born to rule," not to serve (243). Herder de-politicizes his protagonist(s) in order to stress their moral superiority (246) and the atrocious effect of the slave trade on black families. He also isolates him from the African community. Right from the start, Zimeo is different. The image of fear and wanton destruction ("The cattle plains were full of fear / Screams of the fugitives, pursued by blacks") depicted in the first two stanzas is suddenly interrupted by the entrance of this one exceptional individual:

Then a man stepped before us, not stained by blood,
And kindness spoke from his demeanor
Which instantly changed from rage to sadness, scorn to sorrow. (242–243)[34]

His first words are a plea for compassion for the suffering individual — himself ("turn your hearts to poor Zimeo") — and an attempt to distance himself from his "brothers" ("he is not stained with blood"). Like Friday, he speaks of himself in the third person before he can shift to the I, the I of the moral, apolitical individual who comes down from the mountains to bring peace. While the text does focus on one extraordinary African who relates the story of his captivity to elicit compassion among his audience, it creates a rift between the superior protagonist and all those blacks who rebelled against their masters, reminiscent of the good savage-bad savage split of the South America narratives.

Zimeo's interlocutors are an anonymous "we" into which the narrator has integrated himself. Except for one moment when Zimeo professes that henceforth he "shall love two whites" (244), the poem provides no clue as to who these "we" are and how many of them there are. Are they all whites? A small group? A family? As one is led to believe by the narrative, the "we" is an abstract category, that encompasses all "true humans" [wahre Menschen], that is, those who act humanely. They form an island of morality in a sea of violence — yet it remains an island of slave owners. As the black family composed of Zimeo, his wife, son, and father-in-law depart, the white slaveholding plantation household is left intact — even the freed slaves "kissed our knees and swore never to leave us" (243). Violence is thus not seen as germane to the master-slave relationship and the colonial situation. It is that which *others* — some depraved individuals — perpetrate, not *we*. Furthermore, the violence of a "few" whites is canceled out by the violence of the black mob.

Kotzebue's play *Die Negersklaven,* also an elaboration of Kolb's story,[35] professes a similar ideology to Herder's. Although he changes the nationality of his protagonists, invents a dramatic ending, and banishes the political-revolutionary background almost completely (198), the solution he proposes remains squarely within the "colonial family" model envisaged by Herder or Döhner. Like Döhner, Kotzebue reintroduces erotic tension, focusing on the desire of a white European for a black slave. But this time it is the thoroughly evil British planter John who covets his beautiful and virtuous African slave, here called Ada (this episode had been mentioned by Zimeo in Kolb's narrative, but not elaborated on). Ada, however, refuses John's advances since she still mourns the violent separation from her husband "Zameo." When, by miraculous coincidence, Ada, Zameo, and his father are all reunited on the plantation, John resorts to threats and brutal force to make Ada his. In order to avoid ignominy for her husband and loss of virtue on her own part, Ada entices Zameo to kill her, which he does before killing himself.

The basic conflict between whites and blacks is again depoliticized, acted out as a moral conflict between two opposing familial-colonial paradigms (that do, however, have wider political implications, for example, the implicit references to Lessing's Enlightenment drama *Emilia Galotti*).[36] On the one hand, we have the white planter family of the despotic John and his younger brother, William, an abolitionist sympathizer who has inherited their deceased father's paternal kindness toward the slaves. On the other, the black slave family of Ada, her husband, and her father-in-law, who in their insistence on propriety and virtue are prototypical members of the eighteenth-century European bourgeoisie. The absence of mothers in both families and the exclusively male lineage indicates that these families are not so much representations of biological units as political metaphors. While the white family is characterized by ideological divisions and competition among "brothers," the black slave family, broken apart by geography and the *code noir* (the list of rules organizing master-slave relations, enacted in 1685), is characterized by its desire to cohabit harmoniously and honorably. Slavery, that is, absolute rule of whites over blacks, has caused the rifts in both families. It brings out the worst in immoral whites; it physically destroys morally superior blacks. Yet while Kotzebue overtly advocates the abolition of slavery by presenting a moving picture of the slaves' sufferings, he indirectly endorses it: *freed* slaves, he argues, in consonance with Herder,[37] will make even better, because voluntary, workers. Benign paternal rule will help avoid rebellion, tying the black children even closer to their white fathers; it will internalize slavery, creating "slaves without chains"[38]: "your slave, with pleasure" (228). Well aware of the needs of his public and in tune with this positive "master" fantasy, Kotzebue provides an alternate ending for his bourgeois tragedy: before Zameo can kill Ada to preserve her virtue, William, the good brother, purchases their freedom. The black family can live happily ever after, as voluntary slaves to their white superfather. As Zameo says to William: "You set me free, and I am your slave forever; with my arms tied I could have run away, but you cast my heart in fetters — I shall never leave you!" (229)[39]

Ada reaffirms that bond when she compares her relationship to her husband with that to her master: "Love is mightier than freedom!" (240). The love that unites slaves and masters is, however, not erotic or sexual — sexual desire leads to violence, as John's example had shown — but, as in Döhner's play and Herder's poem, it is familial. It is the love of children for parents, of childlike women for their fatherly protectors and husbands.

The implicit racism and classism of Kotzebue's thinly disguised family idyll and its "universal" applicability — for colonial, social, and gender relations — surface in a remark made by a freed black, that class of blacks that German intellectuals of the 1790s particularly sympathized with: "The Negro needs so little to be happy. Give him a bagpipe and glass full of unadulterated rum, and he will work for weeks, without complaints. That your good father knew well" (32).[40] He "knew it well," one might surmise, since he was familiar with the popular belief, expressed by Herder, Kolb, and others, that Africans are by nature simple, pleasure-loving, unfit for higher aspirations (see chapter 4). The question thus is not how to abolish slavery, but how to avoid a rebellion and secure, at the same time, the willingness of the slaves to serve forever, "without complaints," bound to their master by love, gratitude, and obedience.

Like Döhner but less explicitly, Kotzebue hints at who might be the ideal master. In an exchange on slavery, the two British brothers criticize all current colonial powers:

> John: Are you saying that the other nations are doing better than we English? William: No, I am sorry to say! The Spaniard makes the negroes into companions of his sloth; the Portuguese misuses them for his excesses, the Dutchman as victims of his avarice. The Frenchman bends them under heavy labor and often denies them their merest needs; but at least he laughs with them at times, which makes their misery more bearable. The Briton never smiles or condescends to their level. (23)[41]

And the German? the German spectator is led to ask. The answer is implied by way of elimination. Unlike the others, the German planter would take care of his slaves like a father, just as the enlightened *Landesvater* treats his happy *Landeskinder,* thus avoiding the ferment of revolutionary thought that has been spilling over the borders. His plantation would "distinguish itself in a peaceful and moral way through industry, cleanliness, and thrift from the settlements of other nationalities," to repeat Kant's characterization of the German colonizer (see chapter 5).

Betrothals and Divorces

If in the final decade of the eighteenth century Kotzebue and Herder could still believe in the feasibility of a reconciliation between white colonizers and black slaves, the dream of a familial plantation idyll was certainly over by 1811. By the time Kleist wrote his *Betrothal in Santo Domingo,* Haiti had gained its independence and survived a violent civil war, while the Spanish colonies on the continent were threatening to break away from their colonial mother, or rather, father country. Prussia, on the other hand, defeated and "colonized" by France in 1806, was starting to organize its resistance to French imperialism. No wonder then that colonial, familial, racial, and gender questions would resurface and intersect in the works of German writers around 1810, albeit with very different connotations.[42]

Since it is impossible to do justice to Kleist's complex novella and to all its ramifications in the narrow context of my investigation, I will focus only on those aspects that make it part of the colonial romance and the "familial" discourse at the turn of the century. Kleist's story recapitulates the familiar white-black love story, yet subjects it to even greater revolutionary strain: escaping with the family of his uncle from a part of the island already under black control, the young Swiss mercenary Gustav chances upon a plantation taken over by the mulatto Babekan and her light-skinned daughter, Toni. Toni, in the past, has lured many a white man into the trap of the house, where he would be killed by Congo Hoango, Babekan's unrelenting spouse. This time, however, Toni falls in love, surrenders to Gustav, and vows to protect him. Their "betrothal" is terminated when Gustav, distrustful of Toni's attachment to him and of her "yellow" skin color, shoots first her, and then himself. The envisaged marriage between two cultures and two races — propelled by the revolution — ends in violence and dissolution.

In the first paragraph of his *Betrothal*, Kleist shatters the paternalistic fantasy of harmonious familial conviviality between whites and blacks on the colonial plantation. Monsieur Guillaume de Villeneuve, clearly one of the "good" planters, had not only rewarded his slave Congo Hoango "with innumerable favours and kindnesses" but he freed him, "gave him house and home, . . . even appointed him as manager of his considerable estate, . . . [and] even made him a legatee under his will," adopting him as a kind of son. And yet Congo does not assume the position of grateful child:

> Remembering only the tyranny that had snatched him from his native land, [he] blew his master's brains out, . . . set fire to the house in which Madame de Villeneuve had taken refuge with her three children and all the other white people in the settlement, laid waste the whole plantation to which the heirs, who lived in Port-au-Prince, could have made claim, and when every single building on the estate had been razed to the ground he assembled an armed band of negroes and began scouring the whole neigh-

bourhood, to help his blood-brothers in their struggle against the whites.
(231–232)[43]

The narrator's abhorrence at this blatant lack of "gratitude" is evident through rhetorical devices that top off the story of "betrayal" ("not only"—"even"—"even"—"moreover"—"crowning"—"and yet"). Clearly the fantasy of familial master-slave relations comes to a screeching halt when Congo blows his master's brains out. The colonial family of white planter-parents and black slave-children no longer provides an ideological smokescreen for the continuation of slavery. The black family of Congo Hoango and his associates have already occupied the master's house while the white family—like the slaves of old—have become the fugitives in the wilderness.[44] Nor is there hope for the fantasy of an erotic union across race boundaries. The marriage between white and black, although physically consummated, remains an unfulfillable proposition, a verbal "betrothal." The "unnatural" conditions surrounding the lovers highlight the unnaturalness of Toni's surrender or of Gustav's proposition: Did Gustav take advantage of Toni, did he seduce her out of fear of death? Or was it a consensual relationship born out of "true love"? How can "true love" develop in an instant, among unequal partners? How can a relationship be consensual if there is a clear power imbalance—this time in favor of Toni, who holds Gustav captive? By integrating his love plot into a political situation of extreme violence, Kleist questions the colonial fantasies of natural surrender and blissful slave-master relations. Instead of the "natural" hierarchical familial relations between whites and blacks that Döhner and Kotzebue had proposed, his story concludes with a pragmatic "man-made" contract among equals: the black leader Congo Hoango is forced to grant free passage to the Stroemlis, the white colonizers, in return for their promise to spare Congo's sons whom they hold captive. For Kleist, the problematic engagement between blacks and whites can only end in a complete "divorce."

Kleist's skepticism also extends to the role of the moral third in this revolutionary spectacle.[45] The fantasies of a marriage between blacks and whites, or of kind familial relations between slaves and masters are blown to pieces by a complex revolutionary reality that the European participant observer Gustav is unable, or unwilling, to decipher. Blinded by reductive racialist categories derived from contemporary anthropological discourse that neatly separates white (= good) from black (= evil), and steeped in the colonial romance in which people act on moral impulses as individuals, not on historical experience as collectives, Gustav cannot assess the meaning of Toni's "yellow" color, nor the depth of Babekan's rage. Thus, in a crucial passage, namely when Toni asks him "how it was that the whites had come to incur such hatred in this place," Gustav, "a little disconcerted," replies "that the cause lay in the *general relationship* which as masters of the island they had had with the blacks" (241).[46] He is unwilling to name this "general relationship" and analyze its impact on Toni, Babekan, and himself. Instead, he justifies slavery by referring to its long practice and—again without analysis—immediately proceeds to a characterization of the slaves' resistance as "mad lust for freedom . . . which has seized all these plantations [and] has driven the negroes and creoles to break the chains that oppressed them, and to take their revenge on the whites for much reprehensible ill-treatment they have had to suffer at the hands of *some of us,* who do our race no credit" (my emphasis, 241).[47] Although Gustav uses all the liberal catchwords associated with revolution such as "breaking chains" and "oppression," his selectively moral reading of history and his unreflected support of the status quo are obvious. "After a short pause" he switches to the story of the black slave woman who, "overturning . . . all human and divine order" (242), took revenge on her white master by infecting him with yellow fever. Convinced that "no tyranny the whites had ever practised could justify a treachery of such abominable vileness,"[48] that is, morally outraged at an individual response and the revenge of the woman to boot, the planter is unable to recognize or name the generic violence perpetrated against this woman and against all other slaves. His willingness to make love to a woman whom he had tried to rape earlier, hoping that she will save him now, and Gustav's sympathies for this "wretched" man when the woman returns abuse with abuse, indicate to what extent Gustav partakes of the "marriage as redress" ideology the encounter literature had propagated. In fact, one might argue that he himself falls into the same pattern when he promises to marry Toni after having seduced her in order to secure her collaboration in his liberation. Clearly, Gustav's perceptions are channeled by reductionist models and selfish interests. Even when he asks questions about personal histories, he fails to understand the answers. For example, when Babekan tells the story of her abandonment by her wealthy white "husband," Gustav, "smiling at Toni," simply responds: "Why, in that case you are a nobly born and rich girl" (240).[49] Babekan's attempt to break through his naive conclusions by emphasizing that Toni's father formally repudiated paternity and that her white master Monsieur Villeneuve whipped her for getting pregnant, thereby permanently disabling her, garners no response. Gustav is unable to read history(ies) and his own fateful involvement in it (them). To assume that despite these historical experiences a light-skinned Babekan would act kindly toward a white stranger during a slave revolt is utterly naive. To assume that he, a Swiss officer in the French army, remains an outsider to the conflict between blacks and whites, is reckless. Kleist leaves no doubt that in a revolution there is no moral third.

While Kleist exposes and denounces the naïveté of this position rather than sharing it,[50] Theodor Körner, in his dramatization of Kleist's story, returns to the moralistic marriage fantasy, which becomes in his revision an overt fantasy of patriarchal control. Where Kleist makes miscegenation — the confusion of race, gender, and class — the central metaphor, Körner abandons all indeterminacies in favor of clear white-black, male-female, superior-inferior binaries. Toni not only decides that she is "white," but Gustav accepts her pledge of whiteness and believes in her (61).[51] In fact, Körner acts out the fantasy of the Strömlis, "the monumental lie" with which Kleist's story had closed.[52]

It is Toni, the white native, who is made to express her preference for the "superior" Europeans and her moral objections to the revolution on the well-trodden ground that one planter's crimes do not justify a *levée en masse*:

For what one cruel wretch committed here,
Why wreak revenge upon the entire people?
Because they are not black like your black brethren;
Because the Sun endowed them more benignly
And makes the color of their milder day
Glow brightly from their whitened countenance?[53]

Körner also places into her mouth the fantasy of women's greater proneness for revolution and greater depravity when it comes to taking revenge:

Male warriors bloody wrath I may forgive,
Not so a woman's sanguinary plot,
Which God has execrated as the foulest crime.[54]

Consequently, Toni is allowed to abandon the world of mothers,[55] the colony, which is represented as the world of instinct, violent disorder, ruses, poison, and witchcraft, and enter the pantheon of white fathers as Gustav's dutiful wife. Before she can enter this world of fathers, however, Toni must prove her worth by killing her black stepfather, Congo Hoango ("O God! — my mother! — my own mother / Forces the dagger into this pure hand!" 15) and metaphorically burying her mother ("With this pain, she's burying her mother," 66).

Körner transforms Kleist's colonial drama of miscegenation into a drama of gender misallegiances with very different territorial implications: Toni's rejection of the mother territory, as a land of revolutions, treachery, and subversive battles for freedom,[56] and her option for the *Vaterland* and for the role of submissive "angel" in Gustav's household imply a counterrevolutionary message directed against mother France and an integrative patriotic message directed at Prussia. Thanks to Toni's shift of allegiances and Gustav's faith in her excellence, the risky "betrothal in Santo Domingo" can end in a safe paternalistic marriage in Berlin, where Toni's repressed otherness will remind her of her duty to be eternally thankful. As in Gleim's poem, mentioned in the introduction, slaves and tyrants, colonized and colonizers, exchange places: in Körner's fantasy, the Prussian territory, colonized by French hordes (themselves former "slaves") has to be restored to its rightful white masters who will reestablish over it their paternal/conjugal rule.

The neat separation of localities and races, the internal connection between various revolutions, and the return to a paternalistic solution are also at the center of Caroline Auguste Fischer's little known story "William der Neger." As in Döhner's play, the initial revolutionary racial configuration ends in regressive paternalism. As in Kotzebue's, the realms of black and white end up being clearly divided. And as in Körner's, the revolutionary scenario is Europe, while the New World uprisings provide only a distant echo. Unlike either of her predecessors, however, Fischer's fantasy envisages both a reform of paternalism and successful decolonization.

Again, her story relies on the black-white love plot. William, a young ex-slave, is educated in the house of the enlightened Sir Robert, "a declared enemy of the vicious slave trade" (34), who wants to prepare him to become a leader in the colonial liberation wars. William falls in love with Molly, a young artist, but their engagement is broken off when William recognizes insurmountable obstacles to their union: his internalized feelings of racial inferiority toward the "divine white woman" (35); the recognition that Molly, although she had passionately responded to his first advances, does not truly love him and can never be happy with him in her racist environment; and the recognition that this union will keep him from his task, to work toward the emancipation of the slaves. While William goes off to South America to join the revolution, marries a black woman, and has a son, Molly marries Sir Robert and bears him two children. The "divorce" between black and white would be complete if it were not for William, who sends his son to be raised and educated by Sir Robert and Molly while William completes his revolutionary mission.

Like Döhner, Fischer imagines a relationship between black and white in which the woman is white and the African is intellectually superior. Unlike Döhner, she does not "punish" this revolutionary transgression of traditional race, gender, and class boundaries by killing off the transgressors. Instead, she opts for a separation in friendship. While she does not produce the revolution in male-female relations one might expect and instead opts for a return to the all-white patriarchal marriage, the parallels between William and Molly are such that one could read William as the revolutionary other of Molly. He acts out the desires for radical change that Molly does not, and cannot realize. In Caroline Auguste Fischer's tale, "St. Domingo" becomes the distant utopia where revolutions are carried out successfully, whereas Europe, which flirted with revolution for a short while, has returned to the old, patriarchal, familial order, completing the neat separation of topographies, classes, and races. The retreat of the whites back to Europe (Körner) is thus counterbalanced by the exodus of the black to America (Fischer). In Fischer's conscious rewriting of the slave trade triangle, Europe becomes the place that educates the black leader for the revolution in the colonies. Clearly, Simon Bolívar looms large.[57]

The trajectory described by the six texts in question follows the shifting attitudes in Germany toward the French Revolution and toward emancipatory movements in general. The onset of a bloody revolution in which "slaves" not only break their "chains" but "murder whites," in the formulation of Kleist's narrator, brings the colonial romance to an abrupt end. Instead of providing fantasies of assimilation, appropriation, and domestication of the other, the new texts, written under the shock of the revolutions, show the terrible consequences of too much colonial engagement. Whereas the earlier works conjure up images of enlightened paternalism to counter the lure/threat of revolutionary transgression, the later works, written in the wake of French imperialism and occupation, mark a retreat to patriarchal traditions, away from "revolutionary" race and gender confusions. In Kleist's *Betrothal,* those who fused and were confused are only joined in death and, symbolically, in the safe soil of Switzerland. In Körner's *Toni,* the heroine cannot marry, all in white, until after she has cut her ties to her black mother-country and opted for her white fatherland. In Fischer's "William der Neger," written during the Restoration period, Molly and William, after a short interlude of shared passions, take different paths. He leaves to liberate his black brothers across the ocean; she returns into the safe arms of her white father substitute.

In the process of this retreat from colonial encounters, that which is other — the Native American, the African, the female, and implicitly the rebellious lower classes — gets killed, repressed, left behind, or coopted, domesticated, and whitened. Toni leaves her revolutionary past, her black witch-mother, to become the angel in Gustav's house; Molly, "the divine white woman," successfully exorcizes the memory of William the Negro and his colonial struggle to live happily ever after in her affluent all-white surroundings. Despite the supposed spontaneous attraction of the races for one another, all texts conclude with a fear of and retreat from contact. And yet it seems to me that Fischer, at least, was not quite satisfied with this fantasy of racial purity and neat segregation that obfuscates its internal violence. For in the figure of William's black son, whom William bequeathes to Molly and Sir Robert as his legacy at the very end of the story, Fischer introduces a new element of confusion into the European family and with it a new need to take position in the ongoing struggle for emancipation.

Virgin Islands, Teuton Conquerors

I procured Campe's Discovery of America; *I read it with great interest and not without profit of various kinds; moreover, my imagination was very well able to picture the sun-glistening landscapes of those islands, which had hitherto existed in a state of virginal concealment.—Karl Friedrich von Klöden,* The Self-Made Man: Autobiography, *1874[1]*

The world is not apportioned quite:
Still many an earthly tract
Bides conquest like an eager bride:
The strong she will select.
There's many an isle yet waits and lures
From palm and plantain grove:
The seawind blusters, breaker roars,
Up, joyous Teutons, rove!
—Felix Dahn, "Song of the Germans beyond the Seas," 1886[2]

The violent processes of decolonization in the Americas from 1790 to 1820 produced in Germany fantasies of disengagement and separation. The metaphoric divorce was anticipated in Freitag's abandonment of cannibalism in favor of "civilized" behavior and his native island in favor of an assimilated existence as an artisan in Hamburg. It continued with Toni's option for whiteness and the world of the German fathers. It culminated in Molly's retreat from revolutionary change to the safe haven of enlightened patriarchy in Europe. In a way, literature illustrated the imminent separation of the colonial family and of spheres of interest, a separation that was brought about by a series of wars of independence, in both North and South America.

The retreat of Europeans from the New World also found its "philosophical" explanation. In his *Lectures on the Philosophy of History*, which he delivered in Berlin in the years 1822–1831, Friedrich Hegel resorts to theories provided generations earlier by Buffon and de Pauw to confirm the New World's newness, its lack of history or historical consciousness, and hence its lack of interest to the Old.[3] The New World's "physical immaturity," he claims, is evident in the vastness of its shallow rivers that have not yet had time to "dig their own bed"; its cultural immaturity is a consequence of the physical and intellectual weakness of its natives who were unable to resist the attack of conquerors; its political immaturity has led to chaos and revolution in the southern part of the hemisphere and to a lack of nationhood in the North. Hegel concludes with the statement that America, as the land of the future, is not yet "ready" [*fertig*] — neither as far as its "elements" are concerned, nor with respect to its "political integration." As the land of the future, he says, it does not concern "us" here at all: "Als Land der Zukunft geht es uns überhaupt hier nichts an" (220). In other words: America to the Americans, Europe to the Europeans!

Hegel's representation, however, undermines the simple confrontation of Old World as the world of history, and New World as the world of nonhistory. On the one hand, the New World is in its childhood stage; its political structures do *not yet* exist. On the other, America is the continent of the *no more:* the Aztec and Inca Empires were destroyed; their highly developed civilizations collapsed. This destruction, according to Hegel, was predetermined because "nature" had to cede to the "intellect," "natural culture" to European civilization: she had to perish "sowie der Geist sich ihr näherte" (200). Throughout, Hegel uses the passive voice to underscore the weakness of the natural culture ("she" in German) and its preordained surrender to the stronger *Geist* ("he"): the New World "was discovered"; the Indians "were treated brutally," they "were annihilated," they "were displaced." By excluding Europeans as agents and by framing the process in a gendered terminology (to which the German language lends itself easily), Hegel reproduces the natural determinism of this process of violent appropriation even syntactically: the weaker cultures *had to* go under. He also revives, once again, the fantasy of the natural surrender of the effeminate South to the virile European conquistadors elaborated by de Pauw and propagated by the numerous South America romances in the wake of Marmontel. Thus while Hegel turns his back on the contemporary struggles of the Latin Americans — to the philosopher of history, a preconscious "people without history" is of no concern — he keeps the gendered fantasy of conquest alive. Furthermore, by reiterating de Pauw's assertion that the Indians were sexually feeble (supposedly, they had to be called to their "marital duties" by the priest's bell, 202), he supports the right of the stronger, more potent competitor to replace the weaker in the possession and cultivation of what appears to be "unclaimed" territory. Despite his recommendation to leave America alone, Hegel's philosophy of history thus contains the colonialist fantasy of the New World's natural subjection and hence the germ for a renewed interest in processes of colonial appropriation.

Not surprisingly, the fantasies of the natural rights of the strongest over virgin territories, which had been domesticated in the fantasy of blissful marital relations at the end of the eighteenth century, make their concerted reappearance in the 1830s. Crucial in this process of rediscovering South America as virgin territory open to new explorers, even German ones, are a series of personal and literary discoveries facilitated by the decline of the Spanish colonial empire and new access to old materials: the voyages to Central and South America of Alexander von Humboldt and the subsequent publication of his travelogues; the discovery and publication of Las Casas's transcript of Columbus's log and other important colonial documents by Martín Fernández de Navarrete (vol. 1 of *Colección de los viajes y descubrimientos que hicieron por mar los españoles desde fines del siglo XV,* Madrid, 1825–1837; German edition 1826–1890);[4] and last but not least, Washington Irving's imaginative re-creation of Columbus's life and those of his companions (*History of the Life and Voyages of Christopher Columbus,* 1827; German editions 1828–1831),[5] based in part on Navarrete's collection.[6] In light of Columbus's own first impressions, finally available in print, Humboldt's explorations and writings take on new meaning. Irving's imaginative yet historically "true" re-creation of Columbus's life in turn brings to life the personal triumph and tragedy of the Discoverer for a generation raised on Campe's more didactic account of the Discovery. Indeed, Irving's Columbus biography serves not just as a reference to writers — scholarly as well as creative ones — but as a catalyst. It facilitates the imaginary merger of two inspiring explorers, Christopher Columbus and Alexander von Humboldt, and the rapid Germanization of the fantasies of discovery, exploration, and colonization. The conflation of the two historical figures in fictionalized renditions of their explorations accelerates the process of mental reengagement with the colony after decades of practical and imaginary disengagement.

9

The German Columbus

Boldly, with confidence high, Columbus went cleaving the main,
Gazing with rapturous eye aloft to the stars of the night.
Yet to physical vision alone he opened the portals of ocean,
Treasure he found, but alas! mere transient terrestrial gold.
Lo! see a second explorer — now course through Okeanos' realm —
Humboldt! 'Twas you who unlocked the world to the eye of the mind.
Treasure you brought to light from the deepest shaft of cognition
Wherewith to slake the sacred thirst of enquiring man.
Souls you did not redeem from the blaze of unquenchable fire,
Minds, though, you did set free from the bond of delusion and myth.
— Friedrich Christoph Förster, dedication to Alexander von Humboldt, in
Christoph Columbus, the Discoverer of the New World, *1842*[1]

The Prussian count Alexander von Humboldt, a geologist by training
and a naturalist by predilection, traveled to Central and South America
from 1799 to 1804. He spent most of his remaining years (he died in
1859) in Paris and Berlin, where he processed the immense amounts of
information on geography, flora, fauna, peoples, and their past that he
had collected in the New World. His publications, from *Ansichten der
Natur* (*Aspects of Nature*, 1807) and *Voyage aux régions équinoctiales
du Nouveau Continent, fait en 1799–1804* (*Personal Narrative of
Travels to the Equinoctial Regions of the New Continent,* 1807–1839)
to *Kosmos. Entwurf einer physischen Weltbeschreibung* (*Cosmos: A
Sketch of a Physical Description of the Universe,* 1845–1862), provide
a romantic vision of the new continent, its sublime, rugged mountains,
dense jungles, and vast plains. As Mary Louise Pratt has noted, Humboldt "reinvented" America as "nature in motion," as a place of energy
and abundance, as a "living organism," with "man" — European man
to be sure — as discoverer and explorer of hitherto hidden natural beau-
ties and riches.[2] The "erasure of the human" (125) which Pratt observes
in Humboldt's South America accounts, thus does not include all men,
but "only" the South American native. He neither populates nor owns

the territories that the European explorer, the "imperial I/eye" sees, as it were, for the "first" time.

While Humboldt occasionally takes into account the inhabitants of the New World, particularly the creole elites,[3] the image of European man entering, exploring, and classifying "empty" territories and their treasures prevails. De Pauw's fantasies and Buffon's and de Pauw's theories reverberate in Humboldt's texts, even if he does not quote them directly. Humboldt counters the tradition of denigration of the New World's physical nature by idealizing nature. Yet his characterization of the natives as feeble and degenerate indicates his indebtedness to that very same tradition.[4] Although Antonello Gerbi, in the pages dedicated to Humboldt, is quick to point out that Humboldt's emphasis is "quite different" from de Pauw's, for the thesis of the natives' decadence "serves mainly to reaffirm his [Humboldt's] belief in the substantial natural identity of all men, at both ends of the scale of civilization" (414), Humboldt's observations serve to confirm what the public had been told or wanted to hear all along: that conquests are natural events, and that they are nonviolent as long as the weaker, recognizing his weakness, cedes. I am less concerned here with Humboldt's explicit intentions, or with the contradictions in his own writings than with the impact his utterances (this time legitimated by his position as "objective" scientist and as eyewitness observer) would have on an audience reared on the fantasy of natural conquest and natural right of the stronger. In fact, the antithesis between empiricist and theorizer, evolutionist and antievolutionist, idealizer and denigrator of the New World's physical nature, which has been evoked to distinguish Humboldt from de Pauw and Hegel, dissolves when we look at the complementary fantasies that inform the position of all three: the fantasy of the "impotence" of the nature of the New World, which extends to its inhabitants, a fantasy that both Hegel and de Pauw espoused, and the fantasy of the potent European penetrating virgin forests and terrains implicit in Humboldt's exuberant descriptions.

Gerbi's commentary on Humboldt, written one hundred years later, illustrates the continuing power this imaginary scenario held over its European audience. In Humboldt's descriptions "the enthusiasm of the first discoverers seems to come alive again," Gerbi notes.[5] He credits Humboldt for having achieved "the peaceful conquest and intellectual annexation to its own world, the only Cosmos, of the regions which until then had been hardly more than an object of curiosity, amazement, or derision." In his characterization of Humboldt's style, Gerbi evokes a quasi-erotic encounter. On the one hand there is the explorer: as he "moves toward this conquest his mind is open and excited, touched with that slight euphoria that still today comes over any of us leaving behind the problems and the unnumbered ancestral voices of our civilization"; on the other, there is the anthropomorphized landscape of "low thick woods," "vast rivers," and "soaring white peaks," whose "crude rationality" and "naive perfection" he discovers "for the first time," and which he appropriates peacefully, adoringly. In the encounter with unspoilt nature, the weary European becomes reinvigorated; he "feels reborn." Clearly, Humboldt's prose revived in his readers the subject-position of the eroticized, ecstatic conquistador which was repressed (yet present) in the didactic Krusoe narrative and the domestic(ated) Cora-Alonzo fantasies.

Although the radical liberal Humboldt chose to live mostly in Paris and publish most of his works in French first, his work acquired special significance in the more conservative German context. In the German imagination, Humboldt metamorphosed into a German Columbus, an explorer who by conquering South America intellectually took on the legacy of the conquista, changed its nature, and opened up the continent for renewed exploration and colonization. One of the most popular Humboldt biographies in the nineteenth century, Hermann Klencke's *Alexander von Humboldt. Ein biographisches Denkmal* (1851),[6] for example, serves the avowed purpose of reserving Humboldt for Germany:

> Take the case of England and France, those arbiters of European civilization: Is not every member of these nations able to name their national heroes in the sciences or the arts with the same familiarity and pride as their commanders and statesmen? Is he not elated over their works, believing himself entitled to a share in the glory which the hero of scholarship has shed on his nation? What about us Germans then, who boast a Humboldt, a man the French envy us for and try to claim as one of *their* classics because he has spent a long time in Paris and written many of his works in French — should we not give proof of our maturity as a nation [*Volksmündigkeit*] by seeking to come as close as possible to him in spirit and pay him the esteem due to him by our insight into his life as a scholar and scientist? (12)

Humboldt, "this scientific Columbus of modern times" (47), this "discoverer of a new scientific and real world" (92), is to Klencke not just the "successor," the *Nachfolger* of the first Columbus, but he surpasses his model, as he surpasses all models, all geniuses or heroes of history. As the epigraph to this chapter suggests, Columbus only discovered a physical new world and gained material riches, whereas Humboldt opened up an intellectual universe with potentially much greater, spiritual rewards — rewards that Germans will be able to reap, too. As these and later texts propose, the identification with Humboldt the explorer will lead the German nation to adulthood, to national maturity.

Whereas Klencke's first edition proposed to popularize Humboldt in Germany and bring his achievements home to all Germans, the seventh, amended edition of 1876, published long after Humboldt's (and Klencke's) death and after the foundation of the German Empire, is even more explicit in its repeated attempt to claim a unique, incomparable hero, not just a second Columbus, but a better first:

> Discoverers are to be found in all nations; but in which epoch of history did any man move like him, *like our Alexander von Humboldt,* through air and sea and land, over mountain peaks and into mines? *He is the only one....* The heroes of mankind have achieved extraordinary things — and Humboldt? Where is the man who could match his titanic energy? There is no one, not a single one! ... Can Aristotle be compared to him? The former encompassed the culture of his people — the latter the culture of six thousand years of world history! Like the great Prussian King, *Alexander von Humboldt* merits the epithet: *'the unique.'*[7]

Klencke's panegyric biography establishes a sequence of discoveries and discoverers which peaks with Humboldt's second ("scientific") Discovery. In addition, he introduces another genealogy, one that moves from learning to desiring, and from fantasy to practical action. Joachim Heinrich Campe, Robinson's intellectual father, is supposed to have planted the seed of *Wanderlust* and *Forscherlust* in the young Humboldt when he briefly served as tutor to the five-year-old in the castle of Tegel: "[H]e, who edited the *Robinson* and enriched the children's world with fantastic images of bold discoveries and new worlds — wouldn't this man, as first educator of the brothers Humboldt, have left his imprint on the minds and imagination of his young wards and laid the groundwork, particularly in Alexander, for the latter's powerful *drive for voyages of discovery* to overseas territories?" (18). Klencke's term *Entdeckungsreisen* — voyages of discovery, rather than *Forschungsreisen,* voyages of exploration — aligns Humboldt more with the community of bold discoverers who laid claim to new territory than with that of scientific explorers. Humboldt thus becomes the "father" of a new generation of explorer-discoverers who are inspired by his works and lectures (147) to stake out new intellectual and territorial property.

Humboldt's scientific legacy, Klencke affirms, is above all a profitable legacy ("ein hoch verzinsbares Erbgut," 157) to the German people. To his mind, Humboldt's nationalist intentions are clearly spelled out in the fact that *Kosmos,* his scientific *summum,* was written in German, for Germans. Humboldt's Columbian legacy of material and scientific discovery and conquest thus becomes a national endowment bestowed on future generations of Germans, to be used and augmented. "He is the one," a pamphlet of 1886, published by the German Colonial Society, reads, "who directs the men who have dedicated themselves with great earnestness to the new colonial and global-economic endeavors of the German Reich, to pay tribute to geographic and scientific exploration and to pay highest attention to the medical investigations of hygienic conditions in tropical and subtropical territories, and to the experiences of practicing cultivators in distant lands." "German Science," in other words, did not just point the way to "energetic actions in colonial matters," but must continuously "stand by them."[8] To late-nineteenth-century German colonialists, Humboldt was a "predecessor."

Humboldt's own fascination with the Discoverer and his tendency to stylize himself as a second Columbus facilitated the conflation of Humboldt with Columbus, and Columbus's assimilation into German culture as a quasi-German cultural icon. The identification with the great model is implicit in Humboldt's hymnic characterization of the "century of Columbus" that began with Columbus and extends into the present and future, and that began as an individual undertaking and ended as an international, collective enterprise:

> If the character of a century is "the manifestation of the human spirit at a given time," then the century of Columbus, by unexpectedly extending the sphere of our knowledge, has imparted a new momentum to future centuries. It is the nature of discoveries that touch upon the collective interests of society that they enlarge both the circle of conquests and the terrain left to conquer. Feeble souls believe that in each epoch humanity has reached the high point of progress. They forget that — given the intimate interconnection of all truths — the more one advances, the larger the territory appears that is still to be covered, limited by a horizon that incessantly recedes.[9]

Like Columbus's Discovery, Humboldt's discoveries opened up a new continent for enterprising colonizers. If Humboldt was a second Co-

9. "The Second Columbuses: Washington, Humboldt, Franklin." Frontispiece of Friedrich Christoph Förster, *Christoph Columbus, der Entdecker der neuen Welt. Ein Volksbuch zur Belehrung und Unterhaltung bearbeitet nach den besten Originalquellen* (Leipzig: Teubner, 1842). Photograph by Biomedical Communications, Dartmouth College.

lumbus, then the nineteenth century would become the century to reap the benefits from the second Discovery. As a "German," Humboldt had inscribed not just himself but Germany in the international pursuit of new territories; his successes had obliterated Germany's past failures and paved the way for future glory.

The infatuation with the Columbus-Humboldt connection and the conflation of the two heroes in the nineteenth-century German imagination are manifest in a series of texts that celebrate Columbus's achievements in the light of Humboldt's. Indeed, the Columbus-Humboldt dyad, or rather, the second Discovery, becomes *the* favorite topic of nineteenth-century popular epic and drama (fig. 9).[10] If fantasies of loving encounters, surrender, marriage, or cultural assimilation characterized the late eighteenth century, the nineteenth is, again, the arena for fantasies of heroic (con)quests, in which Columbus, or Columbus-like figures, discover, explore, and take possession of new continents. What distinguishes these fantasies from prior ones is the "euromyth" (Pratt) of empty spaces, or rather, emptied spaces: where there had once been virgins of the sun, with whom the European engaged in a contractual relationship, there is now just virgin territory. The libidinal investment is thus no longer directed at humans — not even allegorically — but at their land. Furthermore, where German competitors before had to prove their moral superiority over others — particularly "cruel Spaniards" — the Teutonic hero now confronts savage nature all by himself.

10

The Second Discovery

Sail on, captain courageous! What if the witlings deride you,
What if the mate at the rudder let go limp his hand on the wheel,
On, ever westward press on — there must *the coast-line appear,*
Bright and distinct as it lies shining ahead in your mind.
Trust in the guiding god and ply the quiescent ocean:
Were there no coast yet, it would presently rise from the brine,
For in eternal alliance is Nature *with* Genius:
That which the latter has pledged, the former is sure to fulfill.
— Friedrich Schiller, "Columbus," from Poems, *1776–1799*[1]

In nineteenth-century German literature, the lone Discoverer looms large. He is the epitome of the courageous individual, the visionary genius who — as in Friedrich Schiller's distich — has imagined the coast of the New World, which, Venus-like, has to emerge from the ocean because he willed her to. In the image of a second creation, the fertile male mind brings forth female territory, which is, by definition, his. German Columbus dramas thus anticipate what would become an obsession in German cultural discourse of the late nineteenth century: how to shed the association with the world of ideas and enter the world of *Realpolitik;* how to reach political maturity as a nation and join the ranks of the European colonial powers; that is, how to achieve control of its own territory by expanding into new lands. A "German" Columbus, the many Columbus dramas suggest, would show the way.

The connection between lone discoverer and virgin land to which he is entitled by virtue of his mental effort is at the center of all German Columbus dramas: from the Romantic dramatic poem "Columbus" by August Klingemann (1811),[2] whose prelude is headed by the above stanza from Schiller, to Karl Werder's and Friedrich Rückert's Columbus plays in the 1840s,[3] written under the impact of Alexander von Humboldt's publications, or the plays composed for the four-hundredth anniversary of the Discovery in 1892.[4] As Klingemann's Columbus ruminates on the day of the Discovery, the New World is "the sure property of my spirit, for her discoverer is her second creator" (250).

All plays share more or less the same plot line: they spend much time on the frustrating negotiations between Columbus and the Spanish Crown; they reproduce the tensions on board before the discovery of land and the encounter with the New World "natives"; and they link the destruction of the Indies to Columbus's own demise. While they all argue for a conflation of invention and ownership, thought and action, fantasies and their realization, they differ in their characterization of the protagonist and in the basic political dilemma he is facing. In fact, over the course of the century, we can observe a metamorphosis of the Columbus figure: from Romantic visionary to scientist in the service of the state to colonialist activist; and from misunderstood genius to guilt-laden foreigner to hero vindicated by history. As the embodiment of the will to action, Columbus can serve as foil for the projection of a variety of dreams; he can become the vehicle for the creation of a new "German" identity and mission. If read as enactments of national desires the Columbus plays reveal their wish-fulfilling function within the nineteenth-century German imaginary.

A Second Chance

Klingemann's 1811 play anticipates the unconscious structures of practically all German Columbus plays in the nineteenth century. It stands at the threshold between eighteenth-century matrimonial fantasies and nineteenth-century fantasies of the lone conqueror, between paternal-conjugal models of colonial relations and dreams of "rebirths" and new beginnings. As theater director in Braunschweig and prolific author of popular plays, Klingemann was attuned to the needs of his audience.[5] His play is symptomatic of the neocolonial interest generated in a non-Spanish public. It faithfully registers the changes the colonial romance underwent as the desire for colonial possession became stirred up in the wake of the breakup of the Spanish colonial empire. The cry "westward, ever westward," moreover, is not just guided by a colonialist imagination — it also anticipates the Prussian drive for the expansion of the German national territory.

While the play, in its diction and plot, bears similarities to Kotzebue's South America dramas and other forerunners — cannibals are pitted against noble Indians who collaborate with benign whites; good conquerors are pitted against treacherous ones; and a love plot recalls the possibility of a permanent cross-Atlantic union — it departs in significant ways from eighteenth-century fantasies. It shifts the attention away from the encounter, focusing instead on the personality of the explorer as "foreigner" and misunderstood genius, who is innocent of any moral wrongdoings. The extinction of the native populations which the Discoverer unwittingly caused is explained away by recourse to internal strife among the Indians and "natural selection." Most importantly, the author provides Columbus with a second chance to undo, or redo, what the Spaniards had done wrong the first time.

Throughout the play, Columbus remains the outsider, the exceptional genius — the "foreigner" (*Fremdling*, 311; *fremder Abenteurer*, 312); the Genoese (305, 307, 328), as he is called by his detractors; the "savior," the "God" as he is hailed by his admirers. Literally alone, he stands between both camps ("Here I stand among you, a single man," 254) — the enraged, fratricidal "Indians" and the enraged, fratricidal Spaniards — only to appease both sides, since he is with God (244). Not relying on anyone ("I place trust in myself and in Nature, which has not lied to anyone yet," 247) — he creates, he wills his new world, and the New World complies.

Columbus is not only different; he is superior to all. The natural, unbridgeable inequality between him and the other Europeans and between him and the Americans is manifest from the very start. The New World instinctively recognizes Columbus's superiority. "She" offers herself to him in the person of Malwida, Guacanagari's virginal daughter, who, at first sight of him, immediately "knows" (274) that "he is the sun god," for "his eye is luminous with sun flares" (275). This natural superiority does not allow for an uplifting matrimonial union, as in the Cora and Alonzo fantasies; it produces the natural demise of all those who are "inferior." Malwida dies in Columbus's arms when she tries to protect him from Hatuei, her jealous native suitor. She dies "a Christian," whereas Hatuei, in his impotent rage against Spanish intruders, can never quite transcend the "savage" — perishing, significantly, poisoned by his own arrow. Departing from the Marmontel-Kotzebue tradition, the matrimony between conqueror/explorer and native princess seems no longer conceivable. Columbus does not fall in love with the native princess, nor can she ever attain his godlike heights. He remains the object of her veneration, accepting her sacrifice, just as he accepts the sacrifice of his "comrades in arms" ("You are a god, I cannot attain thee!" 388).

Columbus is not just a godlike creator (321) but a Christ figure; he is

God the father and son in one. As a born-again Christ, he is the misunderstood, unappreciated sacrificial "savior" (408–409) who suffers for the sins commited by others. His mere presence inspires "Christian" harmony among the natives who beg him to remain as their protector, to guide and to christianize them. Whereas everyone around him is motivated by selfishness and brutality, Columbus alone remains innocent. When the Spanish traitors try him for supposed treason and enchain him, he accepts this punishment as just atonement for the guilt he has unwittingly incurred: the guilt of having caused the destruction of the Indies by having turned over the new territories to Spanish greed and cruelty (396). Unlike his sacred model, he is not crucified in the end. The play does not end with Columbus's death, but with his release from the chains he had been cast in by Bobadilla. As the action comes to a close, he is given another chance to save the (new) world, through renewed action:

"The curse of the dying man still resounds in my ear!
Oh, will I be strong enough to avert it
From these countries?"
(Making a resolution)
"Well then, so be it!
With daring will I now begin my task.
And if posterity were to judge this historical moment,
May it judge my self, *and not my fate!"*[6]

Cleansed of any historical guilt, the text suggests, Columbus can redo the colonization, avoiding the moral pitfalls the second time around. As a born-again Columbus, the discoverer can become the object of identification for Germans who are just "like" him — honest, moral, paternal, disciplined, tenacious, courageous, hard-working, and intelligent — and who deserve to be given a second chance, too.

To focus on Columbus's national difference and extraordinary moral acumen, to depict him as a father figure who treats his young Spanish supporters and the childlike natives with kindness and severity, and to create a happy ending by giving him the opportunity to undo the mistakes made during the first round of colonization is, I would argue, a fantasy created for a "postcolonial" German public ready for a more humane repetition of the colonialist endeavor. By referring implicitly to Las Casas and explicitly to Abbé Raynal (407), Klingemann has integrated into his text the moral outrage over the atrocities committed by Spaniards. In that sense, his play is heir to eighteenth-century humanitarianism and to the role of moral arbiter Germans assumed throughout the Enlightenment. But the play's message is not anticolonial. As Klingemann sympathizes with the natives whose paradisiac life was disrupted by the European invaders, he also defends the global christianizing/colonizing mission. Malwida "naturally" abhors the bloodthirsty, Old-Testamentarian ways of her Indian suitor; she is irresistibly drawn toward the Christ-bearer Christopher Columbus, as are the most "enlightened" of her fellow Indians, the noncannibalistic kind, to be sure. Their natural surrender to the stronger ends in a kind of pre-Darwinian natural selection. In order for Columbus's "pacifying mission" to be accomplished, it seems, the new generation of Indians must die: both Hatuei, the unrepentant savage, and Malwida, the convert, perish by their own hands. As Columbus prepares for his second, more successful colonization, he has unwittingly (and therefore guiltlessly) deterritorialized any competitors for the virgin territory which he only possesses, fittingly, in or through her death (368).

All subsequent Columbus dramas exhibit the same basic structure: the lone stranger and visionary thinker creates in his mind a New World, which becomes his object, his property. Having to share it with the Spaniards, he is forced to watch (or reluctantly participate in) its destruction. Although unappreciated, even accused of crimes, the discoverer receives a belated vindication when he is absolved of any crimes. Either he himself or his successors and heirs can now legally take over the land, which has been emptied of its original rulers and of bad, that is, Spanish colonizers. By staging the Discovery as the quest of the foreigner with superior physical, intellectual, and moral properties whose superiority is gratefully acknowledged by the "savages" and whose apotheosis and reward do not come until much later, Klingemann's play reveals its investment in the German nationalist project. The drama reinforces idealized German self-perceptions and unacknowledged desires: the self-construction of the innocent bystander and honest broker, of the disinterested explorer and humane father figure, and the desire for recognition, power, moral clearance, and a second chance at conquest. As such, the play shares in the creation of a cultural unconscious, of a repertory from which politicians, colonial-national propagandists, and other playwrights could, and did, draw their supporting images and arguments well into the twentieth century.

From Thought to Action

If Klingemann's Columbus was a Romantic visionary who dreamt up the New World before he took possession of her, the protagonist of subsequent Columbus dramas is depicted as the scientist who deducts her existence from his calculations. As both foreign explorer in the service of the Spanish kings and viceroy of newly conquered territories, he has to negotiate the thin line between disinterested science and interested public policy, scientific exploration and colonial appropriation, thought and action. Indeed, the conflict between scientist and state is the thematic focus of several plays written after 1836, after both Irving's Columbus biography and Humboldt's *Examen critique* had appeared in German.[7] While Irving's text is raided for historical detail, Humboldt clearly serves as inspiration and personal model for the Columbus figure, as the many cross-textual references suggest. In the plays written before the failed Revolution of 1848, visionary and scholar merge, as Columbus's dream is now based on solid scientific foundations.[8] Their resolution, furthermore, suggests as a next step the opening up and international exploitation of new territories.

It is perhaps not surprising that the two texts in which Columbus emerges as scrupled scientist-explorer in the service of powerful kings were written by German professors in the Prussian capital Berlin, the professor of literature Karl Werder (*Columbus,* 1842) and the professor of oriental linguistics Friedrich Rückert (*Cristofero Colombo; or, The Discovery of the New World,* 1845). What distinguishes the two plays is not their literary merit—both are lengthy dramatized history, Rückert's clumsy opus was never performed—but their struggle over the question of the relationship between "Geist" and "Macht," knowledge and its instrumentalization. In other words, how does Columbus the scientist square with the mission of empire? And how can science have it both ways: serve the state and remain pure?

Propelled by similar concerns, the two plays provide comparable resolutions. Werder's Columbus, a lone, driven "stranger" (53, 61, 140), professes his vision that science can conquer the world peacefully. During his first encounter with Pérez, the abbot of La Rábida, Columbus explains Portugal's rise to power through intellectual rather than military conquests: "Yes, and not with weapons or political cunning, but through the arts of peace; through the wisdom of an academy, through the spirit of exploration of a monarch who knew how to wrest kingdoms from superstition and doubt. Who took on the ocean as his opponent, declaring war on it over his jewel, India."[9] Pérez's response echoes Humboldt's text: "We live in a momentous era. The mission of knowledge becomes but wider with every advance. Our horizon, as it expands, moves ever farther into the distance" (5). Columbus characterizes himself as a divinely inspired "inventor" (9) in search of royal sponsors. Before he can convince the abbot of the validity of his project, he has to undergo a series of intellectual tests in which he proves that he is no longer in the throes of medieval superstitions or irrational belief in magic forces. The main problem Columbus faces, however, is how to convert this knowledge into action. The scientist-explorer needs a state to back him up.

In the second of the play's two parts, entitled "Columbus's Death," the drama explores the consequences of the collusion of knowledge with power. Columbus, in search of collaborators, has aroused the desire for gold, the devil of greed [*Habsuchtsteufel,* 106], which forces him to engage in immoral actions such as slave trade to satisfy the greed of others.[10] Demanding positions of privilege for himself as "Admiral of the Ocean Sea" and "Viceroy," entitled to one-tenth of the income of the New World, he has directed popular envy and rage at himself. By making a kind of Faustian deal, he has become tainted. However Las Casas, who is given much prominence in the play as moral arbiter, provides him with a moral "out": Columbus's sufferings, his enchainment, have ultimately cleared him of any guilt. He becomes the martyr (222) to the cause, who has expiated his guilt and that of others.

Werder takes great pains to save the scientific project from reproach. Columbus and the king are portrayed as unequal competitors. While Columbus charges the king with envy for his intellectual superiority, the king charges him with arrogance and an exaggerated sense of self. "The rule is the ruler's" (220), Fernando says at Columbus's deathbed. "You dared to go with us. What's yours, have it! Keep it with all your might, and use it at your discretion — the glory, the world's memory, the open future — they're all yours. That was granted to you by God. To us, He granted the crown — and with it the power even over your actions. As long as you breathe under our sceptre, our hand rests on you, our subject" (221). The battle over the supremacy of the scientist or the head of state ends with the resignation of the former, although, when it comes to posterity, the lone "genius" prevails (226).

The play focuses exclusively on Columbus's plight and on the politics in the "metropolis." The natives are literally removed from the scene: while the first part ends with the scream "Land! Land! Land! Land!"

and Columbus's comment that the thought has now become reality and his glory gained permanence (81), the second part begins after the colony has long been established and most Indians are already assimilated, killed, or displaced. Indians only appear in the reports of the colonists, as victims, collaborators, or resisters — objects, not agents. The already familiar dual image of "the Indian" is embodied by Anacaona, queen of Xaragua, who is naturally inclined toward "peaceful" Christianity and collaboration with the Spaniards, and her husband Caonabo, the fierce "Carib" who fights the intruders. It is not until the third scene of act 2 that Caonabo enters the stage — tied and speechless. And it is not until the third scene in act 4 that Anacaona makes her belated and literally short-lived appearance: immediately after Las Casas persuades her to accept suffering as her fate and to become a nun, she is killed by Ovando before Las Casas's very eyes, as all her nobles are massacred. Henceforth, Las Casas will bear witness to the destruction of the Indies (201) and to "Spanish atrocities" (208). Columbus, in turn, dies like Christ ("It is fulfilled," 224), "crucified" by the interests of the state. His very last words reemphasize his intellectual-material legacy: he opened up the whole world so that it "belongs" to all of Christianity — "nothing is locked any more" (224). His sacrifice vindicates him, the mission is accomplished. Despite Werder's scruples as to the fateful collusion between intellectual and state, the outcome apparently sanctions the means.

Rückert's *Cristofero Colombo* (written in 1845, possibly after Rückert had seen the performance of Werder's play in 1842) reiterates the supposedly unwitting complicity between science and empire and the scientist's ultimate vindication. It appears as if he felt the need to pave the way for an even smoother transition from "science" to "conquest," theory to practice. Colombo, who sees himself the equal of kings (291), is introduced as *Gelehrter* [scholar] and "Italian," the two words that encapsulate his "essence" (294). Yet when he talks about his long-cherished project, the exploration of the earth's West, and of the "empty spaces" that fascinate him, the desire for empire [*Weltherrschaft*] reveals itself in his diction, which, again, closely follows Humboldt's model (and bears some affinity to Goethe's Faust):

Whatever I was able to rake in of arts, of sciences,
Seemed to endow me with some arcane energy for hidden goals.
Of the fine arts I learned, above all, how to wield the pen
With artistry, thereafter mastered the picture script of drawing, painting;

I practiced and refined my writing so as to choose the finest strokes
To fashion a diploma for myself as admiral of the seas.
For the future I also planned the composing of letters in lofty style,
Reporting when the conquest of the world would be achieved.
In drawing and painting, though, my hand was solely ruled
By the urge to put on record, to map, each undiscovered land;
And more than filled-in land, I treasured vacant space,
Where, with so much discovered, more yet remained to be. (303, my
emphasis)[11]

Colombo's unwavering faith in science,[12] in the empirical reality of his dream, is undercut by the "golden ball" of the pomegranate he uses to explain to the abbot the shape of the earth and the logic in positing a New World. The pomegranate in Colombo's hand symbolizes not only the "globe, held by God's hand" — and hence Colombo's desire to imitate the Maker — but also alludes to the apple of Eden, to forbidden knowledge and fateful temptation. As the abbot muses, "What may he be thinking about, thus holding the apple? The round globe, or golden mountains?" (296).

On the one hand, then, the lofty project: to add to the Old World its new, better half, in order to rejuvenate it (329); to improve the New World by having it dominated by the intellect; to lead it away from the "darkness" of nature to the "light" of civilization, as Colombo puts it. On the other hand, the consequences of that process: the moral contamination of the conquerors and the destruction of the inhabitants of that New World. In his denunciation of Colombo's share in white man's guilt ("How come my hands created evil, when my mind seemed to be called to create good?")[13] Rückert is much more unrelenting than Werder. His Columbus becomes a tool of destruction (598); he started what others completed (632). In his drama, the division of powers between scientist and statesman, thought and action, is even less clear-cut than in Werder's. Yet while he does not shy away from laying the blame for the destruction of the New World also on its Discoverer, he builds into his drama the by now conventional historical-cultural determinism that ends up exonerating all Europeans. Before the first encounter with the inhabitants of the New World takes place, a chorus of native "spirits" presages the demise of the innocent "children of nature" at the onslaught of civilization (423). The arrival of the Spanish ships is greeted by the cacique with immediate recognition of inferiority: "Aren't they the flower of creation, and we its dark leaves?"[14]

And in true de Pauwian fashion, he remarks upon the ugliness of the Indians' "midnight colors" and their "unmanly" lack of facial hair.[15] Colombo, in turn, feels moved to dismiss the "first attempts at art by these pitiful minors" ["ersten Kunstversuche kümmerlich Unmündiger"] and to trap the gullible "children" like birds by offering them bells. As Hegel stated, the New World has to go under. Whereas she had to cede to Europe's superior civilization according to eighteenth-century theories, she now has to give way to superior science.

Like Klingemann, Rückert resorts to familiar gender fantasies to explain the power imbalance between Europe and the New World. It is, again, the native women, who instinctively recognize the superiority of the newcomers and are made to serve as mediators, facilitators of the takeover. While the men, with the exception of Guacanagari's tribesmen who are not "Caribs," resist the strangers and die in bloody battles, Anacaona suggests natural surrender, as "land and sea surrender to the sky": "These strangers from another world are called to rule" (525, 557).[16] Her daughter Higuamota, like Malwida and all her sisters before her, chooses a Spaniard over her fellow natives, since — as Anacaona "knows" — "white men respect their women more" (563), whereas the men "here" are not interested in female beauty (564). In opposition to eighteenth-century models, however, the native women of nineteenth-century Columbus dramas as well as the native men must die before the marriage is consummated. The fantasy of a second Discovery and natural ownership of the land requires the removal of any native from the scene.

Like Werder, Rückert denounces the greed and violence of the Spanish conquistadors on moral grounds. Yet simultaneously he keeps the fantasy of natural attraction and subjection alive. The eternal feminine on both continents, he suggests, encourages conquests. It is only fitting that (dead) women, in a gesture of reconciliation, also bring about Colombo's apotheosis. In a final dream vision, Queen Isabella and Queen Anacaona both appear to the dying Discoverer to absolve him. As both affirm, he has "borne his chains" and thereby expiated his guilt. The queens' last two speeches provide a glimpse into the decolonized "future" — which is the present of the playwright:

Isabella: *Above destruction's horrors raise*
             Your eyes serene and free!
             Into a golden future gaze
             And see your destiny!

> *In the new country's blood-soaked earth*
> *Old Europe finds a fresh rebirth.*
> *The savage tribes decay*
> *And your* pimentos, *both,*
> *That never care repay;*
> *Here's room for better growth:*
> *Beneath America's blithe skies,*
> *Behold, free states arise!*

Anacaona: *Let it not disconcert your ease*
> *What you have heard from her!*
> *I am the tribal queen of these*
> *Now being ruined here;*
> *Thus the unmourned* pimento *died*
> *As civilization it defied.*
> *But mark: of the* pimento's *race*
> *A root is burgeoning again*
> *And filling its old place;*
> *And in Colombia*
> *Your name will shine afar.*[17]

In other words: the destruction of the Indies has permitted Europe to rejuvenate itself in the Americas. The withering and dying of "savage tribes"/branches (*Stämme* implies both) provided *space* for new growth, the growth of colonies that eventually freed themselves from Europe. It is not entirely clear whether Rückert includes in this vision the free states of Latin America, which, by 1845, are already involved in fierce neocolonialist struggles, or whether he is shifting his gaze to the "Free World" to the north. Anacaona's words reiterate her position that the "Pimentobaum," the indigenous growth, had to die unlamented since it refused to be civilized.[18] Despite professions to the contrary, Rückert thus places guilt not with the conquerors, but with those natives who resisted European cultural dominance. The new growth that will sprout from the roots of the old tree will understand the significance of the European contribution, (s)he suggests, and will give Colombo his belated due.

Despite ideological differences or changes in character and plot, all subsequent Columbus fantasies written before Germany's colonial period share Werder's and Rückert's desire to clear Columbus of guilt by pointing (like Campe had done sixty-five years earlier!) to Latin America's decolonized future three hundred years later.[19] In all of them, an innocent Columbus becomes the victim of Spanish power- and profit-driven merchants and courtiers. And in all, the mediation of a woman provides him with absolution, or with the possibility to repeat and complete the Discovery and Conquest. As he says on his deathbed in Hermann Theodor von Schmid's drama of 1857, "[T]hen I shall be pure again! Whole . . . absolved! My name will not be accursed in mankind's memory!" And before his inner eye the New World emerges in new paradisiac splendor: " . . . the lands I discovered . . . (*lapsing into a visionary state*) What is this? . . . Where am I? . . . What balmy fragrance. . . . O spicy breezes of Hispaniola. . . . These are lands such as the world has not beheld! What cities . . . what realms. . . . They do not execrate me . . . they bless me. . . . The happiness I sought has taken root . . . is burgeoning! Freedom has risen from the chains. . . . (*recumbent*) What of the clouds? Pierce them . . . westward! westward! . . . Land! . . . Land!"[20]

The "clouds" that momentarily obscured his vision and that suggest the conquest's moral turpitude are quickly brushed aside to make room for a second sally west. In Schmid's play, the natives are not killed on stage — they have already disappeared from the cast, a cast that is now exclusively European. The desired land is a pristine paradise, not because it has never been discovered, but because its native cultures have been replaced by colonies which now blossom in "freedom." Its virginity restored, paradise can be appropriated once again, by new, purified Columbuses. As Schmid and others suggest, paradise can be regained by a new generation of conquistadors.

Germany's India

Of all nineteenth-century German Columbus dramas, Karl Kösting's *Columbus: A Historical Drama* (1863) reveals most clearly Germany's specific investment in the Columbus myth.[21] Written in the wake of the formation of the German Tariff Union (Deutscher Zollverein, 1854), the foundation of the German National Society (Deutscher National-verein, 1859), and of the German Reform Society (Deutscher Reform-verein, 1862), all of which pursued German unification in one way or another, Kösting's *Columbus* explicitly addresses the processes of German identification with the Italian explorer-conqueror that the earlier plays had only hinted at. Kösting also highlights aspects that were downplayed in previous colonial fantasies: both the libidinal investment in the colonial adventure and the fear of direct physical contact with natives. Columbus's true desires, he reiterates, are territorial, not sexual.

In his highly suggestive "Prolog," Kösting establishes a fanciful connection between Columbus's search for "India" and Germany's quest for an India of its own. The "spirit of the stage" suggests to the budding poet to take his subject matter from history in order to help create a future from a glorious past and overcome the "sick" present state Germany finds itself in. Geniuses from the past should, he admonishes, be reborn on stage, to be given to the world a second time (xi). This makes the poet wonder about his secret attraction to Columbus, and Germany's special affinity with the Discoverer:

What drew me irresistibly to hold
Columbus in a mystic sympathy,
So that I gladly proffered him my soul
To be imbibed so long and ardently?

My German people, nation future-bent,
Without a present, owning but itself,
It walks, a suppliant, mid the nations' wealth,
Disparaged, slighted, suing for consent
To hatch the world it carries in its soul,
Belong unto itself and to its offspring whole —
In this great martyr's suffering see your own!

Seeking your India — a free Germany —
Undaunted sail the seas of time afar,
The ageless spring of mankind's liberty
Will crown your voyage — an America.[22]

According to Kösting, Columbus and Germany share the vision that allows them to struggle and suffer, despite rejection and antagonism, until they can "hatch" the world both carry within their heads. Like Columbus, Germany will discover its "India," its "America" — which are not geographical sites, but states of innocence and freedom to be reached by sailing through the ocean of time. If the German Genius wills this America, Kösting affirms, Nature must comply.

While Kösting claims to use Columbus's quest metaphorically, not as a call for the discovery and colonization of actual colonies, the analogy between discovery and the creation of an empire on the one hand, and self-discovery and the creation of a unified national territory on the other, sustains the fantasy of nation building as colonization that we encountered earlier. It is noteworthy that Kösting represents these and other "generative" processes as birthing. Columbus conceived of the new territories, and delivered them to the world; likewise, Germany will conceive of its free and unified state, and deliver. The "poem" created by the playwright-midwife is, in itself, a brain-child; like a water fountain, it is the product of the marriage between wellspring and light (xii), creative energy and reason. Even Columbus partakes of this proliferation of familial-organicist imagery, when he "suckles" the poet's soul.[23]

The appropriation of birthing imagery for the male creative process is certainly not new. The Romantic poets frequently used birth metaphors to underscore the supposed spontaneity or "organic" nature of their artistic production. What makes Kösting's play so original and revelatory of subconscious processes is the superimposition of conflicting sexual imagery in a decidedly colonialist context: maternal birthing metaphors and images of benign paternity are at odds with images of sexual desire for "virginal" objects; expressions of sexual desire, in turn, must cede to images of male competition and male bonding. Kösting is up front about the libidinal investment in conquest. In his *Columbus,* the colonialist venture is a natural urge, a sexual drive. He depicts the relationships between rulers and people and between nations as sexual relations. Yet it is not physical gratification his conquerors are after. After representing colonialism as heterosexual impulse, Kösting eliminates all feminized others, replacing them with male genealogies and homosocial relations. Underneath the sexualized or gendered tropes lurks the singleminded pursuit of power and riches. In the end, the copulation and birthing processes produce not an "other," but a more successful replica of the self.

From the onset of his colonial drama, gendered images have to explain power relationships among individuals and nations and degrees of violence in their interaction. Columbus — victim of Spanish arrogance — is "pregnant" with a world "that begs to be born" (16). To the haughty bishop Fonseca who opposes Columbus's project, the Spanish "state, exhausted and bruised by rough war embraces," needs a doctor (3). After the wars against the rapist Moors, Kösting implies (in a complete reversal of historical events), "she" requires rest, recovery, no new encounters. Both Columbus and Spain are feminized to signal their current state of impotence.

The picture is reversed when the actual Discovery begins: now the Spanish discoverers are masculinized, whereas the New World beckons with feminine charms. When Columbus's men revolt on board, he tempts them on by referring to India, "where each of your moans will be rewarded by a woman's kiss and each drop of sweat by a grain of gold" (57). Back in Spain, he describes how San Salvador, "a beautiful page in front of the king's door," appeared to "our happy impatience, which, in amorous unease swept ever ahead, tenderly lured on by balmy airs" (71). Columbus couches the attraction of land and riches in the language of sexual gratification. He relates how he and his "comrades" were driven by "painfully sweet longing" (71), until one evening the sun set over a "mountain altar." The "marriage" of the scent of flowers, the song of nightingales, and the murmur of springs produced sweet intoxication and a complete sense of bliss (72). Indeed, the voyage of discovery, in Columbus's report to the kings, becomes a "Brautfahrt" ["a wedding voyage"] of love-starved conquerors.

While the conquerors are urged on by erotic visions and sexual needs, which highlights their irrepressible masculinity, their forward thrust, the islanders are described as innocent children of Mother Nature, without desires or needs of their own. As the New World's children, they just inhabit the soil, they cannot own it. Hence the land and its "chaste fate" are to be entrusted to Spanish hands. The infantilization of the natives is the pretext for their disempowerment: natural law dictates that as children, not "real men," they cannot take care of the land and render it productive.

Columbus's report to the kings abounds with references to unheard-of sensory pleasures that clearly appeal to an erotics of conquest. Ojeda alludes to the other, the fearful side of conquest when he calls India the "beautiful whore, with whom I fell in love and who takes revenge on us whites — who ravaged and seduced her — by poisoning us" (101). "India" is thus virgin or whore, depending on the projected needs of her ravagers. Yet, she is also "the child," the brain-child of Columbus. Columbus alludes to himself repeatedly as "father" to this new progeny, an epithet that is taken up whenever the "protection" of the new colony is discussed.[24] Pérez, as Columbus's mentor, is India's godfather (78); Spain, supposedly, her mother. In fact, Spain's lack of care of this new child makes her, in the eyes of colonial critics, a "child murderess" (95). The oscillation between erotic-conjugal and protective-paternal images, between lover and father, indicates the ambiguous status of the colonial project in the German imaginary, the need to reconcile colonial desire with moral qualms about such desire, and to cover the former with references to the latter.

This ambiguity is acted out on the body of Caona, the biological daughter of the cacique Caonabo and the metaphoric daughter of "India," the land, and hence embodiment of and heiress to the New World. She is desired and attacked by Fonseca, Ojeda, and Bobadilla, the "bad conquistadors," and protected by her adoptive father, Columbus, the good Discoverer (117, 122); yet she escapes them all by wilting away and dying in a Spanish prison. As in all previous Columbus dramas, this embodiment of and heir to the New World causes her own destruction and that of her culture. When she chooses to accompany her "white father" (135) to Spain to share his prison, her "brown father," cursing Columbus and all he stands for, commits suicide — significantly — with Columbus's dagger. As Kösting proposes, Caona, like Freitag, Toni, and all other "natives" before her, freely chooses the European "father." Caonabo-Caliban, in turn, underscores his double self-emasculation. As he curses his white rival in paternity, he eliminates himself with the other's "instrument." Again, the natives self-destruct to make room for the better father or the stronger sons.

The paternal is imbued with erotic rivalry. Indeed, Columbus's relationship to his Indian "daughter" is far from fatherly. Columbus and Caona are continually shown to be in passionate embrace (117, 132). Dying in prison, Caona becomes "Columbus's angel" (139). His obituary to the "brown child" turns into a panegyric to femininity and to the powers of women to heal what men injure. As Columbus says to Pérez:

You have but seen life's rose,
I smelled her scent. For woman,
O, Pérez, is life's scent, the shadow
Of life's heated day, the golden whiff
That, soft and warm, like evening's red
Hovers around man's tortured self.
We men can but inflict wounds,
Their tender task is healing.[25]

As the conflation of metaphors suggested from the very start, Columbus's obsession with his "child" India-Caona is purely figurative, an expression of colonial desire, natural attraction, and a natural power disequilibrium. In fact, Columbus's "love" is an end in itself, part of the colonizer's subjectivity, directed at possession and control. Caona's timely death in the arms of her white father symbolically wipes out the children and heirs of India — there is no chance for a marriage of cultures — leaving room for another paternity and for a new genealogy that the previous Columbus plays had hinted at, but never acted out: Columbus's reconciliation with and legacy to his "adopted son" Ojeda. The young conquistador returns to Columbus's deathbed to tell his dying mentor how he continued and completed the work of the older. While Columbus was arguing with the Spanish Crown over the new islands, he, Ojeda, discovered the true object of Columbus's longing, a continent rich in pearls, gold, and silver. Columbus's parting words literally confirm the transfer of power and legitimacy from father to son. He blesses "this India, *my son*" ["dies Indien, meinen Sohn"], whom he bequeaths to mankind as a heroic successor who will take on "his father's battle" (151). In Kösting's imaginary universe (and not just in his), the shift from daughter to son, and from native land to European conqueror, defines Columbus's legacy to future generations: with all the "innocent children" gone, the second conquest of virgin territory can in truth begin. Columbus, in Pérez's last words, is a "victor," model for any heroic discoverer after him:

In men's hearts
His memory will live, the name Columbus,
Will honor everyone who, as he did,
Uncovered a new land to human mind
And blazed a trail to freedom's temples.
The time will come, you warrant, when a people, free,
The baneful murk of hierarchies cast off,
As thankful pilgrims will turn back to you
And yours, garland your likenesses,
And celebrate your feast exultantly,
Ye benefactors of mankind!

Pérez's last words also extend this legacy to Germans, for

Poets will sing of your heroic deeds,
Nations awakening will hark in hope
And proudly sense your pulses' beat in theirs![26] *(My emphasis)*

The "manch erwachend Volk" [many a nation awakening] is a clear allusion to Germany, which, in 1863, seems well on its way to political unification, although not to freedom from hierarchy and convention ("Dem finstern Bann des Formelzwangs entwachsen"). By making the conqueror of foreign territories the harbinger of "freedom," Kösting establishes dangerous links between national liberation and unification, national unification and expansion, expansion and natural selection. If Columbus's adopted son, the brutal Ojeda, can "legally" inherit the empty lands of the New World that his "father" bequeathed him in his last will, so can others.

11

Colonial Fantasies Revisited

All great and successful developments first go — one might say — through a state of the unconscious, or, what's often the same, of enthusiasm. — Friedrich Fabri, Five Years of German Colonial Politics, *1889*

Since the times when Charles V bequeathed today's Venezuela to the Welsers, we Germans have been attracted to those blessed and paradisiac regions, which can be subsumed under the name "Tropical South America," with particular might. — Vice Consul C. Herb, "The Prospects of New Enterprises in Tropical South America," 1902–1903

One of the later Columbus plays, Karl Weickum's *Dramatic Painting, in Five Acts, from the History of the Discovery of America,* which appeared in 1873 and in a second edition for the celebration of the four-hundredth anniversary of the Discovery, fulfills the fantasy hinted at in all the plays that preceded German unification. In it a German, Martino Behaim, son of Martin Behaim the map maker, participates in the Discovery of the New World, which, as he says, he will announce to "Emperor and Empire" (76) upon his return to Germany. As a unified nation, Germany can finally become an equal partner in the colonial endeavor, Weickum's play suggests. Like its predecessors, it also contains other moments of wish fulfillment. Rather than ending with Columbus's death, it ends with the opening of the "great gate to the West" (104). As Columbus proclaims, he has paved the way for throngs of peoples to move to the New World and to make use of its rich lands, which beg to be occupied and cultivated by anybody who has the strength and ability to colonize.

The shift to German protagonists as the voices and agents of future colonization gives rise to the displacement of Columbus.[1] The process of identification underlying the earlier plays has served its consoling and inspirational purpose: Columbus as the misunderstood, lone visionary; as the moral kindly father; as the scientist interested in knowledge and theory, not in acquisition of wealth; as a man who found his

glory late and who was not vindicated until the nineteenth century —
this Columbus had been just like the German nation, underrated, misunderstood, at best a late bloomer. Now, however, unified Germany is
fit to emulate him. Columbus has passed on his legacy to a new race of
discoverers, of German Behaims, who appreciate his contribution more
than the ungrateful Spaniards, who, after all, flung him into prison: "It
is up to you, sons of the fatherland, to pick this fruit from the tree!" the
educator G. A. Riecke admonishes his male youth.[2] Indeed, his mission
as trailblazer for world traffic accomplished, Columbus can be filed
away as a man of his times, as a Catholic bound by the religious superstitions of the Middle Ages, a romantic dreamer, a representative of
backward Spain.[3] The German Empire, Columbus's successor and heir,
does not need to rely on him anymore. It is on its own, ready to discover
its own "German India,"[4] not on paper, but in practice.

Colonial Fantasies and the Colonial Movement

The shift of focus to an aggressive expansionism legitimized by past
abstention characterizes the German colonial movement of the 1870s
and 80s. The foundation of the Empire in 1871 not only crowns the
unifying nationalist effort, it also marks the beginning of concerted
colonialist activity on many fronts. Up to 1871, advocates of colonial
ventures had had to contend with the absence of a central government
and hence with a lack of official enthusiasm for state-sponsored ventures. Most of the suggestions for colonial action had concentrated on
demanding official protection for the massive flow of emigrants, particularly to North and South America, as a consequence of shifts in the
rural economy.[5] Now, the presence of a strong national leadership in
Berlin provided at least the preconditions, if not the will, for catching
up with the European neighbors in the matter of territorial expansion.
In the words of the colonial advocate Eugen von Philippovich: "Only
the political power based on full nationhood, which only a unified
Germany can provide, permitted us to satisfy our long-held wish."[6]

As Woodruff Smith points out, the new German government was at
first reluctant to engage in colonial ventures outside its borders, despite
increasing popular support for the "colonial idea." Private colonial
societies such as the Westdeutscher Verein für Kolonisation und Export
(1880), the Kolonialverein (1882), and the Gesellschaft für deutsche
Kolonisation (1884), which later merged with the Kolonialverein to
form the German Colonial Society (Deutsche Kolonialgesellschaft) in

1887, therefore took on the task of spreading colonialist propaganda and forcing the government's hand by collecting capital, sending out emissaries, and purchasing territories, that is, by creating *faits accomplis*. The newly gained territories would then be put under imperial protection, to ward off competition from England. In 1884, Bismarck placed areas that the tobacco merchant Lüderitz had acquired in Southwest Africa "under the protection" of the German Empire. That same year, the government declared Togo and Cameroon German protectorates. In 1885, it ratified East African land purchases the adventurer Carl Peters had negotiated. Between 1883 and 1888, it proceeded to acquire colonies in the Pacific (Samoa, New Guinea, Kiaochow). By 1888, the Empire had thus accumulated territories several times the size of Germany, at first reluctantly, later more and more enthusiastically.

Throughout the debates about the need or drive for colonies and Germany's "colonial mission," the myths and fantasies analyzed in previous chapters played a major role. They formed the cultural residue from which colonialists could fabricate their arguments, or to which they would resort in their appeals for support. The impact these fantasies had had on the German subconscious was recognized by colonial propagandists such as von Philippovich, who in 1887 called on Germans to prove their superiority as men of action, after centuries of dreaming:

> Now it will become evident whether the Germans in the aggregate can also be practical minded, or whether the enthusiasm that has seized thousands of mature men is merely the afterglow of the jubilant ardor kindled in our young minds by Red Indian tales and the fairytale splendor of life in the tropics. I won't deny my own belief that this element of longing reverie about distant lands full of mind-boggling gorgeousness played a part in all this — considering that many a fine action, after all, has flown from turbid drives.[7]

All of the colonialist literature alluded to or bandied about colonial fantasies, whether it advocated traditional agricultural "settlement colonies" (mostly in South America) or trade and plantation colonies (in the tropical regions of Africa and the Pacific).[8] The fantasies were kept alive in the face of evidence to the contrary. While settlers in South America, for example, complained that there was no more "virgin territory" available or that the so-called virgin soil was much less fertile than they had been led to believe,[9] propagandists of large-scale colonial expansion such as A. Geffcken or A. Fick[10] continued to refer to the metaphor to stoke colonialist sentiment. The world is not partitioned yet, Geffcken argued, "there is still on foreign continents ten times as much unused land as the German nation could cultivate" (71). In a similar vein, Fick polemicized: "Isn't it banal by now to warm up the old wife's tale of a partitioned world, at a time when a Heinrich Barth, a Livingstone, Stanley, Robert Flegel, Nachtigal, Rohlfs, Buchner, Schweinfurt and others have shown a whole continent to be most promising territory for colonization; at a time when we know but the coasts and rivers of South America and when Central America is in the hands of half-European half-barbarians and Asia, the Indian archipelago, finally, promises plentiful scope for the civilizing mission of European culture-nations [*Kulturvölker*]?" The map Fick drew for his audience shows in white "vast territories still completely in the hands of savages or half-barbarians, that is, undistributed lands" (78). These undistributed territories, he insisted, were waiting to be seized by the best colonizers, the "conquerors of Strassburg and Paris" (80), the Germans. "Is it our fault that our race is more enterprising in all its endeavors, better able to overcome all difficulties, richer in successes?" another contributor to the *Koloniale Beiträge* asked, rhetorically (1:436).[11] In these propagandistic writings, the collectivity of Germans appears, more often than not, as an individual body: either as "the state," "the fatherland," "the nation," or as "the" German — equipped with distinctive national and "racial" characteristics, qualifications, and physical-sexual needs. The nation as a whole has become a youthful edition of Columbus.

The sexualization of conquest and the identification of collective players on the colonial stage — the German nation, the foreign competitors, the colonies — is particularly apparent in a review of the third edition of Wilhelm Roscher's popular *Kolonien, Kolonialpolitik und Auswanderung* [Colonies, Colonial Politics, and Emigration] of 1848, which appeared, revised and amended by Robert Jannasch, in 1884. The reviewer, the anthropogeographer Friedrich Ratzel, calls colonization "a driving and creative force." He distinguishes between Roscher's academic, theoretical, and somewhat passive definition of colonialism and Jannasch's energizing, active understanding of the concept:

> It is significant that one can tell at once that the two Roscher sections were conceived in a quiet German university town, whereas the section by Jannasch took shape nowhere but in the capital of the new Reich, in the most intimate contact with the *central organs of our nation's life, in the warmth,*

but also the dust, of their live functioning. There we found ourselves in the lecture hall . . . here we breathe the air of action. . . . Jannasch demands an answer in deeds, not words. "This economic hurricane has swept away many legitimate wishes and hopes; a new world has taken shape, dominated and guided in its development by new interests; a new society has been formed whose mission it is to make the newly created economic condition serve the purposes of a new social order yet to be created!" . . . He points to the effect of this boom on the birth rate and, in short order, on emigration and colonization. Where with Roscher we still conceived of the rate of emigration in the main as a phenomenon of the *nation's body at rest,* Jannasch calls upon us to remember above all that it, along with colonizing activity, must also be looked upon as a positive symptom of the *release of individual as well as collective energies* and should be treated and utilized as such.[12] (My emphasis)

The colonizing nation, a body "full of vital energy," is ready for action on "new territories of production and consumption" (21). Virgin territories become the recipients of an overflow of force, a surplus of strength [*Kraftüberschuss*] that is both material and immaterial: surplus of population, surplus of capital, and surplus of intellectual energy [*Überproduktion an geistiger Arbeitskraft*].[13] In their advocacy of forceful colonial acquisition, Fick, Fabri, Peters, or Hübbe-Schleiden transform observable geographic-economic phenomena — sharp increases in the German population in the 1870s and 80s, increased unemployment due to the financial crash of 1873, and increased emigration, on the one hand; advanced industrialization and capital accumulation on the other — into an irresistible natural force, a vital urge to spill over into other territories. So far, the waves of emigrants, undirected, had poured mostly into the United States, where they had integrated with other waves of immigrants. Now, colonialists argue, they must be redirected to South America, so that German settlement colonies may be established that would maintain close ties to their mother country.

The "natives" [*Eingeborene*], defined as the Amerindian population or as native-born *criollos* respectively, can either be ignored, since they (supposedly) do not cultivate the land and therefore have no title to it (or, as some argue, are racially inferior and therefore naturally subject to German settlers), or they may be "assimilated," that is, absorbed by the culturally higher "race."[14] Once "purified," these colonies of German-speaking settlers, using German products and trading exclusively with Germany, will, by nature, seek the imperial protection of the "motherland," thereby strengthening both its own and the mother-land's economic well-being. Or, in somewhat different terms: new colonial outlets for the overpopulation and overproduction in German intellectual and industrial areas will rejuvenate and invigorate the "fatherland" rather than sapping its strength (as traditional emigration to the United States did).[15]

The metaphors that characterize this intercourse among nations are, again, both sexual and familial.[16] As in the fantasies that predated colonialism, sexual fantasies are tempered by familial ones. Wilhelm Roscher justifies colonialism in terms of a procreating and parenting instinct which he locates in the nation at large: "Just as the individual, for the all-round development of his intellectual faculties, needs to live the life of a father or a mother, so entire nations, too, need to experience procreation on the large scale, i.e., found colonies."[17]

The Prussian historian Heinrich von Treitschke, one of the most rabid defenders of imperialism, is even more outspoken in his association of colonialism with natural urges, and sexuality with a "will to power." In his lectures on politics, delivered at Berlin University in 1893–1894, he argued that it was the natural prerogative of large, powerful states to colonize small, weak ones: "All great nations in the fullness of their strength have desired to set their mark upon barbarian lands. All over the globe to-day we see the peoples of Europe creating a mighty aristocracy of the white races. Those who take no share in this great rivalry will play a pitiable part in times to come. The colonizing impulse has become a vital question for a great nation."[18] This colonizing impulse, which is a sign of national maturity and virility, will prove extremely fertile: "When once the trained resources of labour and capital of a civilized nation are poured forth upon the virgin soil of a savage country and there [are] allied with Nature, the three great forces of production co-operate so effectively that colonies progress with incredible rapidity."[19] The Intellect, which had, in conjunction with Nature, "delivered" the New World in the Columbus dramas, reappears in the colonialist propaganda literature as the new productive forces of labor and capital. The "child" these forces produce on uncultivated ("savage") soil is the "daughter colony."

While the metaphors that appear in these and other programmatic statements betray their indebtedness to the conjugal and paternal fantasies of the past century, the revival of a more aggressive Columbian myth in the nineteenth has clearly left its mark. The once so popular

fantasy of the marriage between Europe and America reverts to predatory rape fantasies as soon as the consolidated nation can direct its
attention outward. The new Germany, "the young giant," unable to
restrain his excess of strength, must overflow into foreign territory or
take it by force, if there is resistance.[20] Little attempt is made to hide the
brutality of the takeover: the conquering state is entitled to follow "his"
impulse to dominate; the conquered is not asked for love, consent, or
even complicity. In the general battle for subsistence carried out by the
European rival nations ("Kampf ums Dasein"), as post-Darwinian discourse has it, the wishes of the desired objects are irrelevant, or rather,
they are nonexistent. The metaphoric conflation of colonial relations
with gender relations and the representation of the conquest as a loving
encounter so popular from 1770 to 1830 are thus replaced by another
set of legitimizing biologistic fantasies: the natural urge to procreate,
the "natural impulse" to take possession of "virgin" territory, and the
"battle for survival" all species and nations supposedly engage in. In
either fantasy, the focus is on the male state, whether he fights with his
rivals over territories or whether he plants his seeds in virgin soil. And
both only thinly veil the true motives for colonial expansion: the drive
for appropriation and exploitation of land and resources for profit.

The other familial fantasy, the fantasy of nonerotic paternal-
pedagogic or protective relations between colonizer and colonized embodied in the Krusoe-Freitag brotherhood and kept alive in some of the
Columbus dramas, is also rewritten in this late-nineteenth-century
colonialist environment. Wilhelm Roscher, in his quote mentioned
above, introduces a parent-child relationship not between a "civilized"
European father figure and a "childlike savage," but between "mother-"
or "fatherland" and "daughter colony." Similarly, Treitschke speaks of
"newborn States" and "the parent State and its children" in the context
of colonial expansion and takeover.[21] The "family" imagined in these
fantasies is thus no longer a family across national or racial divides, as in
Campe's *Robinson* or even Kösting's *Columbus*. On the contrary, the
"daughter colonies," which seek the protection of their motherland, are
purely German daughters, product of an encounter between virile state
and unclaimed territory. Hence these daughters preserve their linguistic
and cultural traditions and their biological ties to their parent for the
rest of their lives.[22] The motherland, in turn — if she is not an uncaring
"stepmother" — takes her helpless offspring under her maternal wings
and protects them from the rapacious designs of other nations.[23] Again,
violent imagery is tempered by recourse to (ambiguous) familial mod-

els, one natural urge—to take possession—by another—to mother/to parent. Recourse to gender stereotypes serves, as it did before, to justify *and* camouflage concrete economic and imperial interests, such as the need for raw materials or markets.

The partiality of most German colonialists for South America, despite the large acquisitions in Africa, and the persistence of emigrationist colonialism as *the* model for colonial relations—a phenomenon that Woodruff Smith noted with puzzlement[24]—can be explained by the more benign familial associations South America conjured up in the German imagination. This was the place where familial and erotic fantasies could be recast and acted out, where a German Columbus could still find his "India." Dead or docile "natives" would not come in the way of German settlers or the German nation's desire to "procreate" and "mother."

The situation was somewhat different in African or East Asian colonies, where German settlers would succumb to the harsh climatic conditions and where a native population had not been displaced or "tamed," that is, where the nation could not father purely German daughter colonies. In order to propagate and legitimate the establishment of trading colonies or plantation colonies in which a large native labor force would be subject to a few German colonial administrators, colonialists alluded to another aspect of the parental fantasy: the pedagogical model so popular among eighteenth-century philosophers and educators (Herder, Campe, Meiners). In the uncultivated "dark continent," they argued, humans constitute the main exploitable asset. Africans, although they have superior physical strength and are an ideal workforce, are culturally inferior and lazy. Hence they need to be "educated"—educated to work. "Erziehung zur Arbeit," as the process of forced labor was euphemistically called, would be the task of Germans who, by creating loyal, punctual, obedient workers, fulfilled their cultural mission. As Friedrich Fabri suggested, not without regret: "Modern culture has advanced beyond a mere system of exploitation; it calls on colonially active states and nations to recognize it as their task to lift up subject peoples to a higher cultural level."[25] To educate Africans to work, if necessary by force, was a "national pedagogical task" [*eine nationale Erziehungsarbeit*]. By learning to work, Africans would become loyal colonial subjects, eternally grateful to their great white masters. As proof of such civilizing influence, the *Deutsche Kolonialzeitung* reports an incident from Germany's colonial history: When the Brandenburg colony in Africa, Gross-Friedrichsburg, where "everybody had lived in happy industry," collapsed (see chapter 1), the African chief Jean Cunny "refused to surrender the fortress to the Dutch." "He did not want to accept surrender and did not sway in his loyalty. . . . Long after the Prussian flag had disappeared from African soil, travelers could still find traces of the Brandenburgian foundation in the way of life, in the *spirit of order and industry* of the descendants of the Negroes who had been *educated by the Brandenburgian settlers*" (my emphasis).[26]

The idea of a special mission of Germans to educate is taken to a higher pitch by Hübbe-Schleiden in an article entitled "German World Hegemony," written after Bismarck's resignation in 1890, when imperialist propaganda became even more unabashed. Not world trade, not sea power are the goal of the German nation, he maintains, but "the solution of the most difficult, farthest reaching, and, at the same time, economically most rewarding cultural question: the cultivation of natural peoples and natural territories."[27] Only Germans, with their great "organizational talent, patience, and daring" can achieve such a goal. And only cultural tasks of that magnitude that have a lasting impact on mankind can lead a people to world hegemony.

Like Treitschke, Hübbe-Schleiden only carried one of the favorite colonial fantasies of his day to its logical extreme. While Treitschke elaborated on the irrepressible natural impulse of the mature, virile German state to take possession of virgin territories, Hübbe-Schleiden deduced from the "right" of the supposedly culturally stronger to educate weaker civilizations a German right to world hegemony. Both fantasies contain reverberations of earlier, more benign familial models—the conjugal and the pedagogical fantasies of the late eighteenth century—to which they allude in order to render the claims more acceptable and more natural. Both barely hide their own aggressiveness and their profound fear of others: of Native Americans and European colonists laying claim to colonial territories; of African laborers rebelling against their German masters. The slave uprisings in the French Caribbean at the beginning of the century, which also form part of Germany's cultural memory, are reminders that the "domestication" of blacks is not to be taken for granted. The independence movements in the Spanish and British colonies suggest that colonies, like children, "outgrow tutelage."[28] The shrillness and insistence with which images of masculinity, hegemony, superiority, and supremacy are being evoked have their roots in feelings of "national insecurity": the fears shared by many nineteenth-century Germans that they inhabit a nation rendered effeminate, impotent by colonization, a nation that has to prove its maturity in a series of virile (= martial) acts. While official discourse would not admit to these fears, eliding them with bombastic claims instead, the fantasies themselves reveal their phobic undercurrent: They show how the "family" — whether the national family, the European family, or the cross-Atlantic family — was in the end not to be trusted.

How well the subconscious registered the multiple levels of such "familial" interaction is apparent in the name chosen for the society for German settlements in South America, founded in 1885 by the Kolonialverein: "Herman." The name not only associates "Germanos," the old Germans, with the familial "hermano," brother; it also conjures up the legacy of another German, "Hermann der Cherusker," Arminius, chieftain of the Cherusci tribe. The message of peaceful brotherhood with the Romance-language-speaking host countries in South America embodied in "hermano" is thus subtly undercut by what could be considered an insider joke — the implicit reference to the Germanic chieftain who had united the Germanic tribes and defeated the Roman legions in the battle of Teutoburg Forest in 9 A.D. No *hermano* to Romans, "Herman the German" forced his enemies to relinquish all imperial possessions beyond the Rhine, preserving "this side" for exclusive German colonization. Ironically, he became the symbol of German national liberation and unification after German armies had defeated, once again, another set of "Roman hordes" — Napoleon's troops — in the Wars of Liberation.

While it is not known why the German colonialists chose to call their colonial society Herman, the choice of such an ambivalent name, which combines allusions to Germanic traditions of reconquest with fraternal overtures, exemplifies the main points I have been trying to make throughout this study: how gendered/familial fantasies of colonial relations had populated the German imaginary even in precolonial times; how fantasies of marriage or brotherhood had contained unacknowledged desires for rulership and control over resources; and how these "colonial" fantasies had participated in the German nation-building process, becoming a driving force for "colonizing" action. The presence of these fantasies even in political discourse, and at a time when colonial practice could have shattered visions of blissful togetherness or German superiority, indicates the strong hold they must have had over the imagination of generations of Germans reared on Robinson, Cora and Alonzo, and Columbus stories.

The colonial fantasies did not only persist during Germany's brief colonial period; they outlasted it. Even after the nation had lost its colonial possessions in 1919, the myth of Germans' exceptional ability to establish a *Heimat* abroad, in paternal alliance with grateful "natives," was alive and well. "All [Negroes] say it quite openly," Walter Schatz claims in 1939, "that they long to have German rule back."[29] Like no other people, the Germans are predestined to colonize, the Nazi mythmakers maintain, and "the colonies are waiting."[30] In order to sustain the dream of colonial power — the colonies that were "robbed" by the allies will have to be returned to their rightful owner — Nazi apologists resort to eighteenth-century paternal fantasies: "Just as children piously and full of trust surrender themselves to the protection of their father, venerating him and yet feeling close to him as his children, so our natives approach, free and easy, the *Führer*. . . . They cannot be incited nor persuaded that they had had it bad under German administration."[31] Where once the *Landesvater* embodied the paternal "colonizer," colonizer and father now merge in the "Führer." And the Führer-Vater is called upon to save his children from those "rascally stepfathers," who, once again, have kept Germans from proving that they can do it better. . . .

Epilogue: Vitzliputzli's Revenge

At ease and by no means without grace she sat at his feet, and as he casually stroked her red velvet back (as the gentlemen would probably express it) with a gentle hand, he fancied himself to be Christopher Columbus, with the continent he discovered nestling against him in the shape of a delicate woman.
— *Gottfried Keller,* Die Berlocken[1]

To my enemy's own homeland,
Which goes by the name of Europe,
Will I flee to take my refuge
And begin a new career there.
— *Heinrich Heine, "Vitzliputzli"*[2]

Between 1770 and 1870 the German imaginary evolved, or revolved — from paternalist developmental to conjugal assimilationist fantasies in the late eighteenth century to fantasies of disengagement in the early nineteenth century and, finally, renewed engagement in the nineteenth. These fantasies emerged alongside developments in the Spanish, British, and French colonies in Latin America and the Caribbean — their struggle for independence and neo-colonialist or imperialist attempts to reconquer old or secure new territories. They were fueled as well by developments inside Germany: by liberal models of a benign, protective father state that would naturally release its children from tutelage once they had grown up; by growing nationalist resistance against French military and cultural imperialism, accompanied by a drive for national unification; and, eventually, by the militantly competitive assertion of difference and strength vis-à-vis all of Germany's European neighbors. By the time national unification was achieved, the myth of Germans as superior colonizers and of Germany's moral entitlement to its virgin island had become firmly entrenched in the popular imagination by way of positive identificatory figures such as Columbus, Humboldt, and "German" conquistadors — the Welsers, the Great Elector, the Bechers and Nettelbecks of the past. These myths were so powerful that they eclipsed colonial realities, as many of the colonial narratives, written by actual colonizers on the spot, attest.[3] While the discourse of colonial advocates in the 1880s and 90s eventually dropped all moral pretenses and revealed its predatory, hegemonic impulse to any discerning reader, colonial novels and tales, from Frieda von Bülow to Hans Grimm, continued to maintain that "German chivalry, German diligence, German labor, the German sense of justice, German honesty, and German education" predestined Germans to rule over racially and culturally "inferior," yet eternally grateful and loyal peoples.[4] The colonial legend even survived Germany's loss of colonies and Germany's total loss of moral capital during the Nazi years. As Joachim Warmbold sums up in 1988, "The effectiveness of colonial propaganda is demonstrated not least in that the myth of the 'noblest white colonial and cultural power' that 'won the sympathy of the natives by means of its just and socially caring policies' continues to live on unbroken until today."[5]

Yet can one posit a historical determinism that necessarily led from one stage of fantasizing to the next and that *had* to end in Nazi expansionism or racist extermination policies? Was there a teleological progression from nation without state to *Volk ohne Raum,* people without space?[6] Was there no resistance to mythmaking, no critique? In fact, there was considerable opposition to colonialism in Germany — first in the form of moral outrage over Spanish colonialist practices and slavery, then more on economic and ideological grounds: the colonies, it was quickly discovered, would not produce sufficient revenues and would cost the state more than they earned. There was also opposition to the nationalist anti-French and anti-British rhetoric among more cosmopolitan or internationalist sectors of the population, the progressive bourgeoisie, and the socialist working class. However, moral exhortations, an idealistic internationalism, or bookkeeping arguments could not stem the enthusiasm, the tide of libidinal energy tales of conquest and heroic encounters generated in the public, particularly among the young. Young men were swept away by colonialist desire, the desire for the exotic, for testing their strength and skills in a foreign environment. While critics of colonialism seriously argued against colonizing, they were, for the most part, unable to perceive the gut attraction posed by "conquest" and hence were unable to weaken its appeal.

It is perhaps not surprising that the most discerning critics of popular colonial fantasies were themselves writers — writers who lived on the margins of German society and whose integrity and sense of artistry kept them from buying into facile models. In my discussion of Kleist's *Betrothal in Santo Domingo,* I have already indicated how his play with narrative perspective and conflicting linguistic codes betrays his unease with the racist position of his protagonist Gustav. Kleist's novella questions, almost from the start, any possibility of realizing the "colonial marriage." A more radical debunking of colonial myths — and specifically the Columbus/conquest myth — took place in two later works: the epic poem "Vitzliputzli" by the Jewish exile Heinrich Heine, written in the late 1840s in Paris and published in 1852 in his poetry cycle *Romanzero,*[7] and the story "Die Berlocken" [The Watch Chain Ornaments] by the Swiss writer Gottfried Keller, which forms part of a sequence of thematically interlocking frame narratives entitled *Das Sinngedicht* (The Epigram, 1881). Possibly, openly neocolonialist and imperialist activities such as the Mexican-American war, in which Mexico lost almost half of its northern territories to the United States (1845–1848), or the sharpening of the nationalist conquest/national unification discourse after 1848 helped in creating a particularly critical consciousness in observers who were, in more than one sense, at the margins of this discourse.

Both Heine and Keller deconstruct the tradition by confronting the tropes and narratives that make up the colonial fantasies of eighteenth- and nineteenth-century German culture with counternarratives that challenge or expose their lies. Throughout his oeuvre Heine refers to political events in Latin America in connection with events on the European continent. He associates the fate of the natives in the New World with that of the Moors and Jews in fifteenth-century Spain, with German peasants suffering under feudal lords and Indian Brahmins lamenting the destruction of their world by British colonizers.[8] Colonial independence wars on the American continent conjure up memories of revolutions back home.[9] Heine thus refuses to juxtapose "us" with "them" and to buy into hierarchies, be they racial or cultural. He depicts processes of colonization not euphemistically as "natural surrender" or "marriage of cultures," but as acts of cannibalism on the part of powerful regimes, as they incorporate and assimilate territories and peoples — "here" and "there."

In his epic poem, "Vitzliputzli," written in the years of his decline when the ailing poet, confined to the "mattress grave," became increasingly preoccupied with questions of conquest,[10] Heine attacks the familial colonial fantasies on three levels that correspond to three historical moments. The *Präludium* is a mock "first encounter" with America in which the poet, a latter-day Columbus, "reinvents" the New World by relating it to concepts and experiences of the Old. Heine also pays homage to another reinventor, Alexander von Humboldt, when he stresses the New World's pristine beauty, but unlike Humboldt, he locates the New World's youth and beauty in memory and the imagination, not in its historical present.[11]

This is America indeed!
This is a new world, really new!
Not today's land, which already
Withers, Europeanized.[12]

Even in the supposedly pristine territory evoked by Heine's allusion to that trope ("the day Columbus / Plucked it sparkling from the ocean"), colonial history, that is, destruction and transformation, has already left its mark. The "new soil," "new flowers," and "new perfumes" that had so enchanted the conquistadors of old have already been imported, incorporated into the Old World. History has inscribed itself literally in the body of the monkey, who, at the sight of the foreign intruder, makes the sign of the cross and displays his hairless backside that bears the tricolor black-red-and-gold. The Catholic Church and German national myths have both left their mark on the body of the animal, which thus becomes a kind of "animal alemán," in Las Casas's sense. The shift from territory to woman to monkey echoes and mocks traditional gendered analogies in European accounts of the New World.[13] In the mutual gaze of the monkey and the poetic "I," the poet both reconstructs and erases the difference between Old World and New so that the two mirror, refract, "ape" each other, thereby exploding the "old"–"new" opposition. The present New World, with its violent clashes and aborted revolutions is no different from the Old; the Old is no less "savage" than the New.

The second part of "Vitzliputzli" spells out the betrayal, greed, and destruction implicit in the colonial experience by re-creating the next step in colonial appropriation: Cortés's conquest of Mexico. Here, the central trope is not mutual refraction but mutual incorporation: While the Spanish conquistadors incorporate more and more foreign territory, Aztec warriors literally incorporate Spanish conquistadors. Instead of a holy alliance, a marriage of Europe and South America that earlier writers had fantasized about, Heine exposes conquest and colonization as an unholy communion, in which one cannibalizes and thereby transforms the other. No moral or educational superiority justifies the Conquest, nor is it sanctioned by loving consent. Instead, Heine uncovers the roots of colonialism in betrayal, greed, and violence, in the colonizers' subjection and victimization of the other, and in the emergence of new, "cannibalized" cultural forms.

Heine's critique of the seductive, euphemizing colonial discourse of his forbears and contemporaries is carried even further in the third part of "Vitzliputzli," Vitzliputzli's revenge. Whereas the second part was characterized by a constant shifting of scenario and perspective, from the Spanish to the Mexican and back to the Spanish, now the poet assumes the voice of the vanquished: the dethroned Mexican war-god Huitzilopochtli, whose Germanized name, Vitzliputzli, already made Campe's children laugh, swears that he will in turn "discover" the Old World to haunt the colonizers.[14] Again, Heine proves to be a true historian, a "prophet looking backward," for Vitzliputzli's prophesy, placed into the sixteenth century, has already become reality in the three hundred years since the Conquest: by 1851, colonialism has haunted the colonizers; it has drained their resources, created dependencies, and fomented revolutionary backlashes. Heine is also a seismograph of the present, who registers even the minutest sociopolitical "movement": for the cannibalistic orgy and Vitzliputzli's return, which serve as central metaphors for colonial incorporation and corruption, do not only address past colonialism and the older familial fantasies of peaceful coexistence, but also anticipate and undermine future competitions for a place in the sun. In place of the Columbian myth of a clean slate, a *tabula rasa,* Heine presents images that anticipate the dirty entanglements of international corporatism. By assuming the perspective of the colonized, and ending the poem with Vitzliputzli's anguished prophesy, Heine underscores the plight of cultures that have been violently subjected. However, by lending his voice to a bloody war-god, who, through priests and ritual, had repressed his own people, Heine extends his "colonial suspicion" to include any form of domination and control.

Keller's colonial counterfantasy "Die Berlocken," published one generation later, takes the discussion away from the realm of politics to uncover the gender structure of colonial fantasies and the libidinal economy at work in representations of colonial encounters. The story, told by a female narrator named Lucie, in fact responds to a previous narrative entitled "Don Correa," told by a male narrator, which sums up all previous colonial "male fantasies," from the fantasy of paternal education to fantasies of interracial marriage, in which the "dark, or rather light-brown" natural woman remains the colonizer's loving and voluntary slave/wife.

The protagonist of the male fantasy, the Portuguese admiral, governor of Rio de Janeiro, and viceroy of Angola, Don Salvador Correa de Sa Benavides, is discoverer, conquistador, and colonial ruler in one. His involvement with colonialism in Africa and the New World, furthermore, associates him with the transatlantic slave trade — a trajectory he literally undertakes when he travels from Portugal to Brazil, from Brazil to Africa, and back to Portugal. The story consists of two parts, divided according to the dual image of the dark continent woman, so prominent in eighteenth- and nineteenth-century literature: the whore and the virgin, the demon and the saint, the cunning trickster and the "natural woman." Tainted by his disastrous marriage to a Portuguese noblewoman, a witchlike *Machtweib* whom he has beheaded for her sins, Don Correa falls in love with an African slave, whom he eventually marries. Like Freitag before her, Zambo, baptized Maria, is worthy to be elevated to Correa's cultural heights, because although a slave, she has noble features (a distant relative of the Queen of Sheba, as the text ironically describes her), light-brown skin, and flowing hair, "not as woolly as that of negroes" (285). As an unspoilt "natural" woman, a docile "child," obedient slave, and exotic object of desire (312) she is the ideal object of conquest in every sense: "Just see, said the women, how well she knows how to obey her kind master. Indeed, his highness has made quite a conquest" (292). What elevates her above her predecessor, the power-conscious, manipulative European woman — whose head had to be cut off! — is not just her complete subjection to her master/creator ("I am now all yours, and can't be otherwise, like the sea," 313),[15] but the "freedom" with which she accepts his taking possession of her (314). In his "male fantasy" aptly entitled "Don Correa,"[16] all the trappings of the heterosexual love match between European conqueror and dark continent make their concerted reappearance — from the light-skinned noble native (Freitag/Joanna/Cora, etc.) to the devouring savage (the phallic witch/the rebellious cannibals) and from the paternal planter to the seductive conqueror — as the critical Lucie immediately recognizes.

Her counterfantasy, entitled "Die Berlocken," highlights the erotic underpinnings of the conquest fantasy and the political implications of a challenge to the *ancien régime* among the sexes. A young military during the reign of Marie Antoinette, Thibaut de Vallormes, is given a golden watch without a chain or adornments as a present from the dauphine. He is told to "conquer" the missing parts in due course, a cryptic remark he understands to mean that he has to conquer women's hearts to obtain "trophies" that he can then attach to the watch to demonstrate his prowess. In due course, he becomes a true lady-killer who conquers and accumulates many fetishistic tokens of his successes — until, when fighting in the Wars of Independence in North America, he supposedly falls in love with an Indian maiden. As the French soldiers, "eager to satisfy their curiosity and desire for the ideal natural state' (328),[17] lure the "savage red-skins," Thibaut crosses the river in the other direction, "irresistibly drawn" toward Quoneschi, the red "child of nature" (328). The "natural woman" is to be his ultimate conquest: "How surprised would philosophical Paris be," he muses, "to see him return to the salons with this embodiment of nature and authenticity in his arms" (329).[18] When he proposes marriage, Quoneschi indicates that she wants the *Berlocken,* the bundle of trophies hanging from Thibaut's watch chain. Thibaut, convinced that this gift seals the marriage pact, gives her the tokens of his conquests — which, the following day and to Thibaut's horror, appear dangling from the nosegear of Quoneschi's fiancé, the brave warrior Thunder Bear.

In a complete reversal of the conquest myth, the European conqueror does not encounter empty virgin territory, but territory that is already taken. Compared to the dancing, powerful Indian in his war gear, whom the female narrator describes in all his colorful glory ("imagine a composite of gloriously grown huge limbs of the most saturated copper red, painted from head to toe with yellow and blue stripes, on each breast are drawn two huge hands with fingers spread, just to give you a taste of what is still to come," 334),[19] the European pale-faces provide but a poor spectacle. They are tolerated "guests," not owners of the new territory. Just like Columbus before him, Thibaut, with European cultural arrogance, had thought he had "understood" the language and gestures of the child of nature. Fancying himself a latter-day Columbus, he had been sure of his rights over this woman who sat in her proper place, at his feet: she was the continent *he* discovered. Yet in Keller's ironic counterfantasy, this continent outwits its "natural" master, depriving him of the outward signs of his conquering prowess, the dangling *Berlocken.*

Despite their difference in tone, Heine and Keller share the urge to dismantle the myths of conquest. From the perspective of the outsider — the suffering Jewish exile, the "woman" — they tell stories that undercut the tradition of colonial master fantasies and challenge the emerging colonial order. And yet their voices were not heard, their attacks on colonialism not understood. Speaking with the voice of reason, of irony, the two authors (and others like them) were politically marginalized or drowned out by the tide of popular writings that appealed not to reason and compassion, but to psychological needs: the need to feel superior, in control, and the desire for gratification. Writings that were easily accessible, sentimental, and that provided a heroic self-image for individual and nation. Writings that found familial language — the language of love, marriage, and family — for familiar motivations: greed for profit and power. As *counter*narratives, furthermore, both Heine's and Keller's texts were bound up with the German national project, even as they sought to undermine it. There was no escaping hegemonic discourse, since it prescribed the parameters within which opposition could be articulated. Heine's and Keller's texts are therefore doubly significant for us today: they are proof that resistance to hegemonic discourses was, and continues to be, possible. And they are living proof to the — admittedly pessimistic — conclusion that "great literature" is ultimately no safeguard or panacea against self-serving fantasies.

Notes

Unless otherwise noted, all translations from the German are by Walter Arndt, and all translations from Spanish or French are mine.

Preface

1 "Thematics and Historical Evidence," in *The Return of Thematic Criticism,* ed. Werner Sollors (Cambridge, Mass.: Harvard University Press, 1993), 131.

Introduction

1 "Lächelt nicht über den Phantasten, der im Reiche der Erscheinungen dieselbe Revoluzion erwartet, die im Gebiete des Geistes statt gefunden. Der Gedanke geht der That voraus, wie der Blitz dem Donner. Der deutsche Donner ist freylich auch ein Deutscher und ist nicht sehr gelenkig und kommt etwas langsam herangerollt; aber kommen wird er, und wenn Ihr es einst krachen hört, wie es noch niemals in der Weltgeschichte gekracht hat, so wisst, der deutsche Donner hat endlich sein Ziel erreicht. Bey diesem Geräusche werden die Adler aus der Luft todt niederfallen, und die Löwen in der fernsten Wüste Afrikas werden die Schwänze einkneifen und sich in ihren königlichen Höhlen verkriechen. Es wird ein Stück aufgeführt werden in Deutschland, wogegen die französische Revoluzion nur wie eine harmlose Idylle erscheinen möchte." Tr. Ritchie Robertson from Heinrich Heine, *Selected Prose* (London: Penguin, 1993), 292–293.

2 Mary Evelyn Townsend, *The Origins of Modern German Colonialism, 1871–1885* (New York: Columbia University Press, 1921), 22.

3 Gustav Adolf Rein, "Das Problem der europäischen Expansion," *Europa und Übersee, Gesammelte Aufsätze* (Göttingen: Musterschmidt, 1961), 54.

4 Focusing almost exclusively on England, Robert Young, in *Colonial Desire: Hybridity in Theory, Culture and Race* (London: Routledge, 1995), sets his accents somewhat differently. To him, "colonial desire" is a "covert but insistent obsession with transgressive, inter-racial sex, hybridity and miscegenation" (xii), whereas the German fantasies suggest that colonial desire extends less to interracial sex than to the possession of land.

5 Klaus Theweleit, *Male Fantasies,* tr. Stephen Conway (Minneapolis: University of Minnesota Press, 1987).

6 Recent studies of the imaginary focus almost exclusively on England, or on an

unspecific "Europe" — which generally translates into England and the western tip of the continent. See Peter Hulme's *Colonial Encounters: Europe and the Native Caribbean, 1492–1797* (New York: Routledge, 1989); Robert Young, *Colonial Desire* (1995); Anne McClintock, *Imperial Leather: Race, Gender and Sexuality in the Colonial Contest* (New York: Routledge, 1995); or Margo Hendricks and Patricia Parker, eds., *Women, "Race," and Writing in the Early Modern Period* (New York: Routledge, 1994). Mary Louise Pratt's *Imperial Eyes: Travel Writing and Transculturation* (New York: Routledge, 1992) has a wider geographic range, yet analyzes the representational practices of travel writers, rather than "imaginary" encounters.

7   "Post-Colonial Theory and German Studies," unpublished talk delivered at the German Studies Association meeting in Chicago, 1995. As Lennox reports, there are various recent publications or projects in preparation that attempt to address this lack: Gisela Brinker-Gabler's anthology *The Question of the Other(s)* (Binghamton: State University of New York Press, 1995); Arlene Teraoka's *East, West, and Other*; Nina Berman's *Orientalismus, Kolonialismus und Moderne. Zum Bild des Orients in der deutschen Kultur um 1900*; Sara Lennox et al., eds., *The Imperialist Imagination* (the last three titles are forthcoming).

8   Jacques Le Goff, "Mentalities: A history of ambiguities," in *Constructing the Past: Essays in Historical Methodology*, ed. J. Le Goff and Pierre Nora (Cambridge: Cambridge University Press, 1985), 169. Young's *Colonial Desire* and McClintock's *Imperial Leather* have taken a similar approach; both use psychoanalytic terminology to analyze the sociopolitical imaginary.

9   Louis Althusser, "Marxism and Humanism," in *For Marx*, tr. Ben Brewster (London: Verso, 1979), 233.

10   Edward Said, *Orientalism* (New York: Random House, 1979), 8.

11   Homi Bhabha, "The Other Question: The Stereotype and Colonial Discourse," *Screen* 24, no. 6 (Nov./Dec. 1983): 24.

12   David Trotter, "Colonial Subjects," *Critical Quarterly* 32, no. 3 (1990): 3–37, quote from 10.

13   Ibid, 4. Bhabha, "The Other Question," 19.

14   Bhabha, "The Other Question," 25.

15   See Robert Young, *White Mythologies: Writing, History, and the West* (London: Routledge, 1990), 154. Bhabha acknowledges that much, it seems, in footnote 1 to his essay "Difference, Discrimination and the Discourse of Colonialism," in *The Politics of Theory*, ed. Francis Barker et al. (Colchester: University of Essex Press, 1983), 210.

16   This absence was noted by Nancy Armstrong, "The Occidental Alice," *Differences: A Journal of Feminist Cultural Studies* 2, no. 2 (1990): 4. In "Orientalism Reconsidered," in *Europe and Its Others*, ed. Francis Barker et al. (Colchester: University of Essex Press, 1985), Said speaks of Orientalism in terms of "similar issues raised by the experiences of feminism or women's studies, black or ethnic studies, socialist and anti-imperialist studies" (15), of a "praxis of the same sort, albeit in different territories, as male gender dominance, or patriarchy, in metro-

politan societies." The usefulness of a gender analysis in the "same territories," however, eludes him. As for Said and Bhabha, gender is also of little interest for Hulme, although the fantasies he studies organize the colonial encounter along gender lines. See, for example, his essay "Polytropic Man: Tropes of Sexuality and Mobility in Early Colonial Discourse," in *Europe and Its Others,* ed. Barker et al., 19, where the focus shifts quickly from sexuality to mobility.

17   Most cultural critics locate the advent of biological racism in post-Darwinian times: see Kwame Anthony Appiah, "Race," in *Critical Terms of Literary Study,* ed. Frank Lentricchia and Thomas McLaughlin (Chicago: University of Chicago Press, 1990), 276; or Martin Barker, "Biology and the New Racism," in *Anatomy of Racism,* ed. David Theo Goldberg (Minneapolis: University of Minnesota Press, 1990), 18–37. More familiar with the German context, George Mosse is one of the few to stress the eighteenth-century foundations of modern racism in his *Toward the Final Solution: A History of European Racism* (New York: Fertig, 1978), 1–50. The most recent exploration of race and gender in a colonialist context, Anne McClintock's *Imperial Leather,* leaves no doubt about the conflation of the two concepts, but she concentrates her analysis on late Victorian England.

18   For the analogy between race and gender in the scientific discourse of the nineteenth century see Nancy Leys Stepan, "Race and Gender: The Role of Analogy in Science," in *Anatomy of Racism,* ed. Goldberg, 39. On woman as the embodiment of "savagery" that has to be tamed and colonized, see Sigrid Weigel, "Die nahe Fremde — das Territorium des 'Weiblichen.' Zum Verhältnis von 'Wilden' und 'Frauen' im Diskurs der Aufklärung," in *Die andere Welt. Studien zum Exotismus,* ed. Thomas Koebner and Gerhart Pickerodt (Frankfurt am Main: Athenäum, 1987), 171–199.

19   Franz Kratter, *Die Sclavin in Surinam* (Frankfurt am Main: Esslinger, 1804).

20   See Said, *Orientalism,* 19.

21   Since I concentrate on fantasies, not on science, my take is different from Sheldon Pollock's, who, however, also noted the German *Sonderweg*—as it related to Indology—due to the absence of colonies. He posits an abstract "morphology of domination" over and beyond colonialism, whereas I see colonial fantasies as preparatory to colonialist activity and intimately connected with the colonialism of other European powers, which German writers and readers participated in vicariously. See Sheldon Pollock, "Deep Orientalism? Notes on Sanskrit and Power Beyond the Raj," in *Orientalism and the Postcolonial Predicament: Perspectives on South Asia,* ed. Carol A. Breckenridge and Peter van der Veer (Philadelphia: University of Pennsylvania Press, 1993), 76–133.

22   Heinrich Simonsfeld, *Die Deutschen als Colonisatoren in der Geschichte* (Hamburg: Richter, 1885), 49. For a discussion of this repression of a brutal tradition, see, for example, Helmut Bley, "Unerledigte Kolonialgeschichte," in *Deutscher Kolonialismus. Materialien zur Hundertjahrfeier 1984,* ed. Entwicklungspolitische Korrespondenz (Hamburg: Gesellschaft für entwicklungspolitische Bildungsarbeit, 1983), 9–16. On the continuity of the German "Kolo-

niallegende" see Detlef Bald, Peter Heller, et al., *Die Liebe zum Imperium. Deutschlands dunkle Vergangenheit in Afrika. Zur Legende und Wirklichkeit von Tanzanias deutscher Kolonialvergangenheit* (Übersee-Museum Bremen, 1978), 195–203. It can, of course, be argued that similar mechanisms are operative in the official self-representations of other imperialist nations, particularly the United States, who share the Germans' sense of mission.

23   Edward Said, *Culture and Imperialism* (New York: Knopf, 1993), 9. The debate between economic or political explanations of the colonialism/imperialism distinction to which Said alludes forms the point of departure in most contemporary analyses: when exactly colonialism turned into imperialism; what exactly the distinctions between the two ideologies and practices were; whether modern monopoly capitalist imperialism can at all be compared to earlier imperialist expansions, etc. See, for example, Wolfgang J. Mommsen, *Theories of Imperialism*, tr. P. S. Falla (1980; rpt. Chicago: University of Chicago Press, 1982), or Eric Stokes, "Late Nineteenth-Century Colonial Expansion and the Attack on the Theory of Economic Imperialism: A Case of Mistaken Identity, *Historical Journal* 12 (1969): 285–301.

24   For the struggle between an emigrationist or settlement ideology and an economic ideology in German colonialism before "imperialism" see Woodruff Smith, *The German Colonial Empire* (Chapel Hill: University of North Carolina Press, 1978), 19. Referring to Lenin's five criteria of imperialism (*Imperialism: The Highest Stage of Capitalism*), the East German historian Horst Drechsler (*Let Us Die Fighting: The Struggle of the Herero and Nama against German Imperialism, 1884–1915*, tr. B. Zöllner [London: Zed Press, 1980]) locates the onset of imperialism in 1898 (3). He, however, is analyzing economic-political realities, not ideologies. Helmut Böhme ("Thesen zur Beurteilung der gesellschaftlichen, wirtschaftlichen und politischen Ursachen des deutschen Imperialism," in *Der moderne Imperialismus,* ed. W. Mommsen [Stuttgart: Kohlhammer, 1971]), on the other hand, analyzes German imperialism purely in terms of its ideological function, as *Ablenkungsmaneuver,* "as the attempt, purely in the service of agricultural-feudal interests, to maintain the social status quo despite industrialization by generating and manipulating imperial claims," 54.

25   Smith, *The German Colonial Empire,* 15ff, 18.

26   Gustav Siebenmann, "Das Lateinamerikabild der Deutschen. Quellen, Raster, Wandlungen," *colloquium helveticum* (Bern: P. Lang, 1980) 7: 57–82, quote from 67. The use of "Amerika" to denote the United States is, of course, equally sloppy.

27   I have consciously incorporated these and other ideologically charged terms — not in order to repeat the act of appropriating difference into sameness, but to highlight the positioning that went on in the minds of eighteenth-century Europeans, as they redesignated the other as "savage" or their world as "new." On the terminology see Anthony Pagden, *European Encounters with the New World: From Renaissance to Romanticism* (New Haven: Yale University Press, 1993), 14. As Hegel remarked in his lectures on "Reason in History" [Die

Vernunft in der Geschichte], delivered in 1815, the division of the universe into Old World and New was "essential": "this world is not just relatively, but completely new [*überhaupt neu*], if we look at it in all its specific physical as well as political being [*Beschaffenheit*]." In *Die Vernunft in der Geschichte*, 5th ed., ed. Johannes Hoffmeister (Hamburg: Meiner, 1957), 199.

28 One of the principal German colonialists, Friedrich Fabri, advocated colonial settlements in South America over those in Africa (*Bedarf Deutschland der Colonien? Eine politsch-ökonomische Betrachtung* [Gotha: Perthes, 1879]), and was still advocating them ten years later in his *Fünf Jahre deutscher Kolonialpolitik. Rück- und Ausblicke* (Gotha: Perthes, 1889), 137. Carl Peters, the infamous East Africa "explorer," complains in his memoir that the attention of his newly founded "Gesellschaft für deutsche Kolonisation" (1884) quickly shifted to South America, as soon as he, an advocate of purchases in Africa, turned his back (*Die Gründung von Deutsch-Ostafrika* [Berlin: Schwetschke, 1905], 46).

29 See Pagden, *European Encounters with the New World*, 11, whose reference is, however, more generally European. As Yolanda Julia Broyles has shown, this fascination for the exploitability of the South American continent did not translate into greater interest in its culture — on the contrary: for most, South America remained just a space for projections. See Broyles, *The German Response to Latin American Literature* (Heidelberg: Winter, 1981), chap. 1.

30 On the Germans' predilection for South America fantasies over African ones, see Joachim Warmbold, *Germania in Africa: Germany's Colonial Literature* (New York: Peter Lang, 1989), 20–25.

31 Frank McLynn, *Hearts of Darkness: The European Exploration of Africa* (New York: Carroll and Graf, 1992), chap. 3.

32 *Taschenbuch der Reisen*, ed. E. A. W. von Zimmermann, 8, no. 1: 18–19.

33 The feminization of South America, rather than America as a whole, is most pronounced after 1776, when the northern colonies declared their "independence." See, for example, William Robertson's comparison between northern and southern Indians in his *History of America* (Alston, England: Walton, 1800), 4: 210–212.

34 See Sander Gilman, "The Figure of the Black in German Aesthetic Theory," *Eighteenth-Century Studies* 8 (1975): 373–391; Sander Gilman, *On Blackness without Blacks: Essays on the Image of the Black in Germany* (Boston: Hall, 1982); Andreas Mielke, *Laokoon und die Hottentotten. Oder über die Grenzen von Reisebeschreibung und Satire* (Baden-Baden: Koerner, 1993). Also Warmbold, *Germania in Africa*, 25.

35 As George Mosse has convincingly argued, popular literature provides a much better access to the German (or any other national) mind than great works of art. See "Was die Deutschen wirklich lasen. Marlitt, May, Ganghofer," in *Popularität und Trivialität*, 4th Wisconsin Workshop, ed. Reinhold Grimm and Jost Hermand (Frankfurt am Main: Athenäum, 1974): 101–120.

36 Quoted by Eda Sagarra, *An Introduction to Nineteenth-Century Germany* (Harlow: Longman, 1980), 173.

Part I   Armchair Conquistadors

1   "Wohlan dann, dapffere Teutschen, machet, dass man in der Mapp neben neu
Spanien, neu Frankreich, neu Engelland, auch ins künfftige neu Teutschland
finde. Es fehlet euch so wenig an Verstand und Resolution solche Sachen zu
thun als anderen Nationen, ja ihr habet alles dieses, was darzu vonnöthen ist,
ihr seyd Soldaten und Bauren, wachtsam und arbeitsam, fleissig und unver-
drossen, ihr könt auff einmahl viele gute Sachen thun, durch ein exemplarisches
Leben und gute Ordnung die Indianer zu Freunden und civilen Menschen, ja
vielleicht gar zu Christen machen."

2   See the Las Casas-Sepúlveda debate in Spain in 1545 and its European repercussions, Lewis Hanke, *All Mankind Is One: A Study of the Disputation between Bartolomé de las Casas and Juan Ginés de Sepúlveda in 1550 on the
Intellectual and Religious Capacity of the American Indians* (De Kalb: Northern Illinois University Press, 1974) and Juan Friede and Benjamin Keen, eds.,
Bartolomé de las Casas in History (De Kalb: Northern Illinois University Press,
1971).

3   See, for example, Urs Bitterli, "Die Überseebewohner im europäischen Bewusstsein der Aufklärungszeit," in *Fürst, Bürger, Mensch: Untersuchungen zu
politischen und soziokulturellen Wandlungsprozessen im vorrevolutionären
Europa*, ed. Friedrich Engel-Janosi et al. (München: Oldenbourg, 1975), 186–
214. The mutual transformation of cultures, the "transculturation" has been
studied above all by Latin Americanists. See for example Angel Rama, *Transculturación narrativa en America Latina* (Mexico: Siglo Veintiuno, 1982), or,
for a discussion of the various approaches to transculturation, Silvia Spitta,
Between Two Waters: Narratives of Transculturation in Latin America (Houston: Rice University Press, 1995).

1   Germans and the "Conquest"

1   "And how shall those countless souls be compensated that are burning in hell
because of the greed and inhumanity of those bestial German tyrants." (My
translation cannot reproduce the pun *animales/alemanes*.)

2   *Ambrosius kämpfte dort mit Schwabenkraft,
War er sich gleich des Zieles nicht bewusst,
Für Deutschlands Sache — ein vergess'ner Held.
Doch wo er pflanzte seiner Lanze Schaft,
Wo ausgeblutet seine tapfre Brust,
Erwuchs ein Recht uns an die neue Welt.*

3   The literature on German participation in the conquest is abundant, although
either outdated or politically biased: German texts up to 1945 are for the most
part colonialist and apologetic, partaking of the colonial legend; texts written
by non-Germans before and during the Nazi period, or by East German authors during the fifties and sixties stress the atrocities committed by German
imperialists. Only recently have there been a few isolated attempts in both East

and West Germany to assess the German role more objectively. Konrad Haebler, *Die überseeischen Unternehmungen der Welser und ihrer Gesellschafter* (Leipzig: C. L. Hirschfeld, 1903); Kurt Hassert, "Die Welserzüge in Venezuela. Das erste deutsche überseeische Kolonial-Unternehmen im 16. Jahrhundert," *Beiträge zur Kolonialpolitik und Kolonialwirtschaft*, ed. Deutsche Kolonialgesellschaft (Berlin: Süsserott, 1901–1902), 3: 297–317; Kurt Hassert, "Johann Joachim Becher, ein Vorkämpfer deutscher Kolonialpolitik im 17. Jahrhundert," in *Koloniale Rundschau. Zeitschrift für Weltwirtschaft und Kolonialpolitik* (Berlin, 1918), 148–264; Karl Klunzinger, *Der Antheil der Deutschen an der Entdeckung von Südamerika* (Stuttgart: Sonnewald, 1857); Viktor Hantzsch, *Deutsche Reisende des sechzehnten Jahrhunderts*, Leipziger Studien auf dem Gebiet der Geschichte 1, no. 4 (Leipzig: Duncker & Humblot, 1895); E. Jacobi, "Ein bayrisches Kolonialunternehmen im 17. Jahrhundert," *Beiträge zur Kolonialpolitik und Kolonialwirtschaft* (Berlin: Süsserott, 1903), 5: 184–192; Jules Humbert, *L'Occupation allemande du Vénézuela au XVIe siècle* (Bordeaux: Féret & Fils Editeurs, 1905); Germán Arciniegas, *Los Alemanes en la conquista de América* (Buenos Aires: Losada, 1941); Juan Friede, *Los Welser en la conquista de Venezuela* (Caracas and Madrid: Ed. Edime, 1961); Heinrich Volberg, *Deutsche Kolonialbestrebungen in Südamerika nach dem Dreissigjährigen Kriege. Insbesondere die Bemühungen von Johann Joachim Becher* (Köln: Böhlau, 1977); Siegfried Huber, *Entdecker und Eroberer: Deutsche Konquistadoren in Südamerika mit zeitgenössischen Erlebnisberichten und Dokumenten* (Olten: Walter, 1966); Gaby Weber, *'Krauts' erobern die Welt. Der deutsche Imperialismus in Südamerika* (Hamburg: Libertäre Assoziation, 1982). On Germans in Dutch service see J. P. l'Honoré Naber, ed., *Reisebeschreibungen von deutschen Beamten und Kriegsleuten im Dienst der niederländischen West- und Ostindischen Kompagnien 1602–1797*, 3 vols. (Haag: Nijhoff, 1930); or Hermann Kellenbenz, "Deutsche Plantagenbesitzer und Kaufleute in Surinam vom Ende des 18. bis zur Mitte des 19. Jahrhunderts," *Jahrbuch für Geschichte von Staat, Wirtschaft und Gesellschaft Lateinamerikas* 3 (1966): 141–163.

4   Hantzsch, *Deutsche Reisende*, 1.

5   See Volberg, *Deutsche Kolonialbestrebungen*, 23ff.

6   Richard Schück, *Brandenburg-Preussens Kolonialpolitik unter dem Grossen Kurfürsten und seinen Nachfolgern (1647–1721)* (Leipzig: Grunow, 1889), 1: 193, 207, 231, 234, 245, 309. Hermann Kellenbenz, "Die Brandenburger auf St. Thomas," in *Jahrbuch für Geschichte von Staat, Wirtschaft und Gesellschaft Lateinamerikas* 2 (1965): 196–217. Inspired by Dutch merchants, the Great Elector got involved in African ventures: an expedition to the west coast of Africa led to the founding of an African Trade Association which, under the leadership of Benjamin Raule, sent two frigates to the Gold Coast. In 1683, the Prussian expedition completed the construction of a fort, Gross-Friedrichsburg, and in 1687 another settlement in Arguin, both primarily dedicated to facilitating slave trade. The two "colonies" collapsed because of financial trouble and fierce competition from the Dutch. They were sold for 7,200

ducats and 12 blacks to the Dutch West Indies Company under Friedrich Wilhelm I in 1720. See also Richard Lesser's "patriotic" article "Die Kolonialpolitik des Grossen Kurfürsten," in *Deutsche Kolonialzeitung* 1 (1884): 196–200. Lesser, linking the Great Elector to more recent colonial ventures, only speaks about "other trade purposes," but does not mention the slave trade.

7   See Volberg, *Deutsche Kolonialbestrebungen,* 63–92, and 123ff, esp. 135–136. E. Jacobi, "Ein bayrisches Kolonialunternehmen," 200–224. See Hassert's tendentious essay "Johann Joachim Becher," in *Koloniale Rundschau.*

8   See Heinrich Simonsfeld, *Die Deutschen als Colonisatoren in der Geschichte* (Hamburg: Richter, 1885). Simonsfeld's overview of Germany's colonial past evokes as heydey of German colonialism the late Middle Ages, particularly the activities of the Hansa and the Deutscher Ritterorden. Germany failed to engage in modern colonialism, he argues, because nationalist movements and then the Reformation and religious wars fragmented the Reich and directed the attention inward (36–39). His essay is a plea for renewed colonial efforts — colonization understood as conquest-Germanization-civilization — under state sponsorship and "protection." For a more factual account see Werner Conze, "Einheit und Vielfalt in der deutschen Geschichte," in *Ploetz. Deutsche Geschichte, Epochen und Daten,* ed. Werner Conze and Volker Hentschel, 2nd ed. (Freiburg: Ploetz, 1979), 9–15.

9   Volberg, *Deutsche Kolonialbestrebungen,* 35. Volberg also notes the opposition, the doubts, and lack of interest among the general public in colonial ventures during the late seventeenth century (173). My point here is less rooted in any official, practical interest in colonizing than in fantasies of island colonies, as they became so popular in the wake of Defoe's *Robinson Crusoe* and Schnabel's *Die Insel Felsenburg.*

10   My account relies mostly on Juan Friede's exhaustive study, *Los Welser en la conquista de Venezuela,* which I supplement with information and commentary from Haebler, *Die überseeischen Unternehmungen.* To use the modern term "German" in this prenational context is somewhat anachronistic. The Welsers' "Germanness" became an issue in the nineteenth century.

11   Friede, *Los Welser,* 46ff: emigration by subjects of other nations in the Holy Roman Empire was off and on permitted, but official privileges to colonize and trade were not.

12   Ten percent for the first three years, then increasing by 2 percent every year until, by the eighth year, the metal tax would amount to 20 percent = one-fifth (see Haebler, *Die überseeischen Unternehmungen,* 162).

13   See Friede, *Los Welser,* 19–25, esp. 24, and 221–222.

14   The identity of Alfinger is not conclusively established; according to Haebler, Ambrosius Alfinger is identical with Ambrosius Ehinger; Friede (*Los Welser,* 166ff) asserts separate identities.

15   As Haebler points out, the colony was profitable for the Welsers insofar as they made much money from the slave trade; it became profitable for the Spaniards as soon as the settlers concentrated on exploiting the true riches of the land, the soils and climate, for agriculture. But that had not been the interest of the

German merchants bent on quick results (*Die überseeischen Unternehmungen,* 358–366). The moral question forms the red thread through Friede's monumental study (see his conclusions, *Los Welser,* 564). I am not referring to his "acquittal" of the Welsers as "men of their times," *gentes de su época,* but to the outcome of the court hearings (see Haebler, *Die überseeischen Unternehmungen,* 392ff).

16 See Nikolaus Federmann's *Indianische Historia. Eine schöne kurzweilige Historia Nicolaus Federmanns des Jüngern von Ulm erster raise . . .* (Hagenau: Bund, 1557).

17 Schiller's poem "Die Theilung der Welt" did not refer to colonialism at all, but to the fate of the artist, for whom only immaterial, otherworldly rewards are still available. The famous line "Was thun! spricht Zeus, die Welt ist weggegeben" or some similar formulation was, however, frequently used in colonialist circles. See, for example, Wilhelm Georg Roscher, *Kolonien, Kolonialpolitik und Auswanderung,* 2nd ed. (Leipzig: Winter, 1856), 342: "When the new world was partitioned, our nation of poets and thinkers came too late"; or Carl Peters, "Aufruf zur Gründung der 'Gesellschaft für deutsche Kolonisation,'" March 28, 1884, quoted in *Das koloniale Deutschtum. Ein Volkslesebuch,* ed. E. G. Jacob (Bayreuth: Gauverlag Bayrische Ostmark, 1939), 8. An article by a certain Dr. A. Fick in the *Deutsche Kolonialzeitung* of 1884 bears the appropriate title: "Ist die Welt vergeben?" [Has the World Been Divided Up?], to which the program of the *Kolonialzeitung* responds, defiantly: "[D]enn noch ist die Welt nicht vergeben" — "for so far, the world has not yet been divided up!"

18 According to Hantzsch, a colonialist sympathizer, competition with the Spaniards and Portuguese caused the failure of the German enterprise (Hantzsch, *Deutsche Reisende,* 10).

19 See D. J. U. Hübbe-Schleiden, *Deutsche Colonisation. Eine Replik auf das Referat des Herrn Dr. Friedrich Kapp über Colonisation und Auswanderung* (Hamburg: Friederichsen, 1881); Friedrich Fabri, *Fünf Jahre Deutscher Kolonialpolitik. Rück- und Ausblicke* (Gotha: Perthes, 1889); Heinrich Simonsfeld, *Die Deutschen als Colonisatoren.*

20 Quoted after Bartolomé de las Casas, *The Devastation of the Indies: A Brief Account* (New York: Seabury Press, 1974), 111ff. The translation by Herma Briffault is, however, quite imprecise, at times wrong. One example for many: "han asolado, destruido y despoblado estos demonios encarnados más de cuatrocientas leguas" is translated as "they ravaged, incarnadined, and depopulated these dominions," instead of: "these incarnate devils ravaged, destroyed, and depopulated more than four hundred leguas" (112).

21 The Welsers were Catholics, yet as capitalists interested in profits, they "observed a suspicious neutrality in the European religious battles" (Friede, *Los Welser,* 23), which added to the general hostility toward them. Alfinger and Federmann supposedly sympathized with Lutheranism, which explains in part the bishop's ire.

22 Friede, *Los Welser,* 4–18, 573. Normally, the "black legend" (*la leyenda negra*)

is invoked to denounce Spanish cruelties, particularly in the seventeenth and eighteenth centuries.

23   Hanke (*All Mankind Is One*) has identified three peak moments in the European Las Casas reception: his popularity reached a first climax at the end of the sixteenth century, a second during the French Enlightenment, and a third during the Independence movement. Since I am concerned with the German context, the accents are set differently.

24   The quotations are from: Bartolomé de las Casas, *Newe Welt. Warhafftige Anzeigung der Hispanier grewlichen, abschewlichen vnd vnmenschlichen Tyranney, von jhnen inn den indianischen Ländern, so gegen Nidergang der Sonnen gelegen, vnd die Newe Welt genennet wird, begangen* . . . (Frankfurt am Main: n.p., 1797; my translation). See also the motto, which stresses Spain's unique responsibility. The German translation is a translation of Jacques de Miggrode's French translation, which also had an anti-Spanish propagandist purpose. See Benjamin Keen, "Introduction: Approaches to Las Casas, 1535–1970," in *Las Casas in History*, ed. Juan Friede and Benjamin Keen (De Kalb: De Pauw University Press, 1976), 8. As Keen asserts (11), de Bry's Latin version "rejected the notion of a unique Spanish wickedness or cruelty." The German version, however, does make that claim.

25   For example, "*su* infelicidad y ferocidad," which clearly refers back to the "tiranos animales o alemanes" in the previous paragraph, is translated as "I will now stop writing about *these* acts of tyranny" ["Ich wil nun von der verfluchten Tyranney zu schreiben auffhören"]. As a consequence, the "sie" of the slave traders in the following sentence, which in the Spanish text refers, again, to the Welsers, remains without referent in the German version; "tyranny" is thus depersonalized.

26   For a discussion of Becher's importance see Volberg, *Deutsche Kolonialbestrebungen*, 47ff., especially 95.

27   Hassert, "Johann Joachim Becher," 257, somewhat sheepishly, alludes to the "general" practice of slave trade in the seventeenth century to whitewash Becher; his reference to J. Nettelbeck, "der berühmte Verteidiger Kolbergs," who for years worked as captain of a slave ship, has the same function.

28   "Ein Mohr ist eine edle Creatur zum Landbau, denn sie sind der Hitze gewohnt und der Arbeit, sie haben weiter keine Besoldung als einen Tag in der Woche frey, sammt einem kleinen stücklein Lands, welches so fruchtbar, dass es sie die übrige Tage der Wochen durch ernehren kan; wann man solche Bauern in Teutschland kaufen könte, was wäre es nicht wehrt, und dennoch, was würden sie da thun können, das gegen Indien zu rechnen wäre?" (Quoted in Volberg, *Deutsche Kolonialbestrebungen*, 135).

29   "Es waren bekanntlich die Welser in Augsburg. Sie hatten Karln dem Fünften grosse Summen vorgeschossen; deswegen verpfändete er ihnen diese Provinz." (*Die Verheerung Westindiens. Beschrieben von Bischof Bartholomäus de las Casas*, tr. D. W. Andreä [Berlin: Himburg, 1790], 143).

30   See Keen, "Approaches to Las Casas," 23f. Pagden, *European Encounters with the New World*, 13f. Karl-Ludwig Löhndorf, *Marmontels Incas, Untersuch-*

ungen zu ihrer Stellung in der Literatur der Aufklärung, ihrer Aufnahme und Nachwirkung (Ph.D. diss., Bonn, 1980), 61, notes that Las Casas's *Brevísima relación* was used in western Europe throughout the late eighteenth century to support enlightened demands for tolerance and to polemicize against obscurantism, religious fanaticism, and the Inquisition.

31   *Allgemeine deutsche Bibliothek* (Berlin, 1791), 105: 173–175.

32   (Jena, 1792), 1: 38 (my translation). See also Herder's short treatment of Las Casas in the context of European colonialism and German supposed innocence (chapter 5).

33   "Entzückung des Las Casas; oder, Quellen der Seelenruhe," *Die Horen* 1/2, no. 3 (1795): 70 (my translation).

34   Paul von Stetten, *Bartolme Welser. Lebensbeschreibung zur Erweckung und Unterhaltung bürgerlicher Tugend* (Augsburg, n.p., 1778–1782), 228 (further references are cited directly in the text; my translation). There may be others, but this is the only text I have discovered to contain references to the Germans.

35   An exception to the rule is Theophil Ehrmann's "El Dorado" in *Allgemeine geographische Ephemeriden* (Weimar: Landes-Industrie-Comptoir, 1808), 136–165, who insists on the German contribution to both discovery of the land and destruction of the South American native population. But his is already a postrevolutionary nineteenth-century focus.

36   See Karl Wilhelm Körner, introduction to *La independencia de la América española y la diplomacia alemana* (Buenos Aires: Universidad de Buenos Aires, 1968), esp. 33–36 and fn. 1.

37   Karl Friedrich von Klöden, "Die Welser in Augsburg als Besitzer von Venezuela und die von ihnen veranlassten Expeditionen der Deutschen dahin," in *Zeitschrift für Allgemeine Erdkunde* (Berlin, 1855), 433–455. All quotations in the text refer to this edition (my translations).

38   "The Germans now moved to the neighboring land of the Alcolades, from whom they extorted much gold with unimaginable cruelty and whose houses they burnt; indeed they devastated the whole blood-soaked land from Tamaleque to the river Lebriria and even to the province of Sta. Marta, with fire and sword, leaving bloody footprints everywhere" (438).

39   Karl Klunzinger, *Der Antheil der Deutschen;* references in the text are taken from this edition.

40   *Deutsche Reisende*, 17.

41   Kurt Hassert, "Die Welserzüge in Venezuela," 299.

42   Konrad Haebler, *Die überseeischen Unternehmungen.*

43   The evaluation of that colonial enterprise in terms of national differences between colonizers continues. In Germán Arciniegas's 1941 diatribe against Germans, *Los Alemanes en la conquista de America*, Ehinger and Federmann, "two diabolical forces" (84 in the English edition, published in 1943), become the inventors of the chain gang and of concentration camps for Native Americans (90, 108); Spanish "colonizers" excelled over German "intruders" because they had a "more rural understanding of life" (103) and were less governed by "sterile ambition" (164), etc.

44 Friede, *Los Welser,* 543–565, Friede, "Das Venezuelageschaft," 171–172. Friede points out that it was not the Welser company that dealt in Indian slaves, but the conquistadors in their services and the settlers (555). This fine distinction, however, seems irrelevant when it comes to perceptions. The Welsers were the "Germans" at the colonial front and, as such, responsible for all actions.

45 Ernst Wilhelm Bohle, chief of foreign affairs of the NSDAP (National Socialist Party), state secretary of the Foreign Office, foreword to Hans Ernst Pfeiffer, *Unsere schönen alten Kolonien* (Berlin: Weller, 1941), 1, 4.

46 Paul Kayser relates an anecdote that demonstrates how profoundly the failed colonial ventures affected German self-perceptions. After acquiring the first German protectorates in West Africa in 1884, the Emperor William I is supposed to have said: "Only now can I look the Great Elector's monument straight in the face" (introduction to *Brandenburg-Preussens Kolonialpolitik,* viii).

47 Kurt Hassert, "Johann Joachim Becher," 264.

2 A Conquest of the Intellect

1 "So hat denn der Forschungsgeist des achtzehnten Jahrhunderts in der Neuen Welt für uns gleichsam zum zweiten Male eine neue Welt entdeckt!" (my translation).

2 "Colomb, en parcourant une mer inconnue, en demandant la direction de sa route aux astres par l'emploi de l'astrolabe récemment inventé cherchait l'Asie par la voie de l'ouest, d'après un plan arrêté, non en aventurier qui se fie au hasard. Le succès qu'il obtint était *une conquête de la réflexion.*"

3 See, for example, the contributions in *Reise und soziale Realität am Ende des 18. Jahrhunderts,* ed. Wolfgang Griep and Hans-Wolf Jäger (Heidelberg: Winter, 1983); *Reisen im 18. Jahrhundert. Neue Untersuchungen,* ed. Wolfgang Griep and Hans-Wolf Jäger (Heidelberg: Winter, 1986); and Hans-Wolf Jäger, ed., *Europäisches Reisen im Zeitalter der Aufklärung* (Heidelberg: Winter, 1992). More theoretical overviews are provided in Wolfgang Griep, "Reiseliteratur im späten 18. Jahrhundert," in *Hansers Sozialgeschichte der Literatur,* ed. Rolf Grimminger (München: Hanser, 1980), 3: 739–764; William E. Stewart, *Die Reisebeschreibung und ihre Theorie im Deutschland des 18. Jahrhunderts* (Bonn: Bouvier, 1978); Ralph-Rainer Wuthenow, *Die erfahrene Welt. Europäische Reiseliteratur im Zeitalter der Aufklärung* (Frankfurt am Main: Insel, 1980); and Klaus Laermann, Hans Joachim Piechotta, Uwe Japp, Ralph-Rainer Wuthenow, et al., *Reise und Utopie. Zur Literatur der Spätaufklärung* (Frankfurt am Main: Suhrkamp, 1976). More recent studies also take women's travels into account: Annegret Pelz, *Reisen durch die eigene Fremde. Reiseliteratur von Frauen als autogeographische Schriften* (Köln: Böhlau, 1993).

4 By an unnamed writer, "Über die vielen Reisebeschreibungen in unseren Tagen," *Berlinische Monatsschrift* 4 (1787): 319–331, quote from 325.

5 For the various shifts in German travel literature in the eighteenth century, in terms of travelers, aesthetics of the travelogue, aim, and readership, see William E. Stewart, *Die Reisebeschreibung und ihre Theorie.*

6   See fn. 4.

7   W. Griep, "Reiseliteratur im späten 18. Jahrhundert," 739.

8   Thomas Grosser, "Der mediengeschichtliche Funktionswandel der Reiseliteratur in den Berichten deutscher Reisender aus dem Frankreich des 18. Jahrhunderts," in Jäger, ed., *Europäisches Reisen,* 275, 276.

9   W. E. Stewart, *Die Reisebeschreibung und ihre Theorie,* 189.

10   For a discussion of internal "others" see, for example, the contributions of Dieter Richter, "Das Bild der Neapolitaner in der Reiseliteratur des achtzehnten und neunzehnten Jahrhunderts," in Jäger, ed., *Europäisches Reisen* (1992), or Alfred Opitz, "Durch die Wüste, Lichter tragend. . . . Sozialgeschichte und literarischer Stil in den Reiseberichten über die Iberia um 1800," in Griep and Jäger, eds., *Reise und soziale Realität* (1983).

11   Alan Frost, "The Pacific Ocean — The Eighteenth Century's 'New World,' " in *Captain James Cook: Image and Impact,* ed. Walter Veit (Melbourne: Hawthorn Press, 1979).

12   See Pratt, *Imperial Eyes:* chap. 2.

13   The numbers of Germans in South America were, of course, larger than the amount of their literary output. See, for example, Kellenbenz, "Deutsche Plantagenbesitzer," 141–163.

14   These numbers are the result of my own investigation. I compiled a bibliography of approximately 950 works on South America, from 1700 to 1900, which encompasses mostly book-length texts but also a few longer articles in journals. It also includes geographic compendia with a substantial portion on the South American continent, anthropological treatises that focus on the "Indian" as one of the three, four, or five "races" of the earth, or travels to the Pacific if they included lengthy stops along the South American coast and descriptions of its landscape or population. Except for the de Pauw-Pernety debate that was carried out in Prussia, in French, it does not include French works, although, to be sure, the educated elite spoke and read French with ease, and as a matter of routine. As a review in the *Jenaische Zeitung* of the French translation of Edmund Burke's *An Account of the European Settlements in America* said: "In French, it's of more general use!" [*gemeinnütziger auf Französisch*] 99, no. 11 (Dec. 1767): 826. If I had added French titles, the numbers would have, of course, been even higher — but I wanted to concentrate on texts that were accessible to all literate groups in Germany. The bibliography is available upon request.

15   On the phenomenon of philosophic recycling as "theoretical or conjectural history" (Adam Smith) see also Pagden, *European Encounters,* 84–87.

16   Baginsky notes a shift in interest from South to North America because of increased emigration to the new continent and because of a pronounced interest in the struggle for independence of the North American colonies: Paul Ben Baginsky, *German Works Relating to America, 1493–1800* (New York: N.Y. Public Library, 1942), viii. As my own investigations indicate, this perceived shift may have had more to do with the interests of North American collectors who donated books to the Public Library, than with the reality of the German book market.

17 See Pratt, *Imperial Eyes*, 9.

18 See William E. Stewart, *Die Reisebeschreibung und ihre Theorie*, 188–193.

19 Heinrich August Ottokar Reichard, *Über den gesetzlichen Zustand der Ne-gersklaven in Westindien* (Leipzig: Weygand, 1779); Matthias Christian Spren-gel, *Vom Ursprung des Negerhandels. Ein Arbeitsprogramm* (Halle: Hendel, 1779).

20 See, for example, Kellenbenz, "Deutsche Plantagenbesitzer und Kaufleute," 141–163.

21 For a detailed analysis of this issue see my article "Crossing the Boundaries: The French Revolution in the German Imagination," in *Representing Revolu-tion: Essays on Reflections of the French Revolution in Literature, Historiogra-phy, and Art,* ed. James Heffernan (Hanover, N.H.: University Press of New England, 1992).

22 See Rainer Koch, "Liberalismus, Konservativismus und das Problem der Ne-gersklaverei. Ein Beitrag zur Geschichte des politischen Denkens in Deutsch-land in der ersten Hälfte des 19. Jahrhunderts," *Historische Zeitschrift* 222 (1976): 533.

23 See, for example, Eobald Toeze's foreword to *Des Admirals, Lord Ansons Reise um die Welt in den Jahren 1740, 41, 42, 43, 44,* tr. Eobald Toeze (Leipzig: Vandenhoek, 1749), xxiii; or the review of Dobritzhofer's *Geschichte der Abi-poner* in *Allgemeine Literatur-Zeitung* 1, no. 84 (April 1785), where stylistic awkwardnesses are attributed to the author's "honesty and reliability."

24 "Ich sollte nicht aus der Schule schwatzen; allein ich muss doch anführen, dass man bey den papiernen Augenzeugen nie ganz sicher ist, ob ihr Zeugniss auf in-tuitiven oder symbolischen Bemerkungen beruhet." *Johann Bernoullis Samm-lung kurzer Reisebeschreibungen und anderer zur Erweiterung der Länder-und Menschenkenntniss dienender Nachrichten* (Berlin: Richter, 1782–1783), 1: 339 (my translation).

25 Peter Boerner, "Die grossen Reisesammlungen des 18. Jahrhunderts," in *Reiseberichte als Quellen europäischer Kulturgeschichte.* Wolfenbüttler For-schungen (Wolfenbüttel: Herzog-August-Bibliothek, 1982), 21: 65–72.

26 *Braunschweigische Anzeigen,* nos. 30–33 (April 1779), 235.

27 See Dietrich Briesemeister, " 'allerhand iniurien Schmehkarten pasquill vnd an-dere schandlose ehrenrürige Schriften zun Model.' Die antispanischen Flug-schriften in Deutschland zwischen 1580 und 1635," *Wolfenbüttler Beiträge* 4 (1981): 180.

28 *Braunschweigische Anzeigen,* nos. 27–28 (1770): 209 (my translation).

29 *Braunschweigische Anzeigen* (1778): 288.

30 *Taschenbuch der Reisen, oder unterhaltende Darstellung der Entdeckungen des 18ten Jahrhunderts, in Rücksicht der Länder-, Menschen- und Producten-kunde. Für jede Klasse von Lesern,* ed. E. A. W. von Zimmermann (Leipzig: Fleischer, 1803), 2: 19, 26.

31 Rainer Koch, "Liberalismus, Konservatismus . . . ," 533.

32 "Bald verweilt man mit Wohlbehagen bei der häuslichen Glückseligkeit auf den Pelew-Inseln, oder bei der Mässigkeit und Treue des Negers; bald bewundert

man die Reichthümer des Aurengzebs oder des Opokku. Die Gefühle werden niedergedrückt bei der Erzählung von dem Todtenopfer des Aborney, von dem Skalpieren der unglücklichen Gefangenen, oder von der Anthropophagie der Anziker. Aber in der gemässigten Zone richten sie sich wiederum auf. Denn hier sieht man wie der Geist des Menschen alles zur Sicherheit und Bequemlichkeit der Societät aufbietet; wie er die Erde umbildet, todte Felder in reiche Fluren verwandelt, grosse Länder dem Wasser abgewinnt; die Elemente einzwängt; die entlegensten Nationen miteinander verbindet; die Produkte der neuen Welt in die alte verpflanzt; ja das Klima selbst verändert." Von Zimmermann, *Taschenbuch der Reisen* (1802), 1: 2, 3.

33 Ibid., 4.

34 *Immanuel Kant's Critique of Pure Reason*, tr. Norman Kemp Smith (London: Macmillan, 1973), 257.

Part II   Colonizing Theory

An earlier, shorter version of chapter 3, entitled "Dialectics and Colonialism: The Underside of the Enlightenment," appeared in *Impure Reason: Dialectic of Enlightenment in Germany*, ed. W. Daniel Wilson and Robert C. Holub (Detroit: Wayne State University Press, 1993), 301–321. All translations from the French in this chapter are mine.

1   The "philosophers," anatomists, and natural historians under scrutiny in this section can also be considered the first anthropologists, since they focused on the study of man and on the study of cultural difference.

2   Anne McClintock, *Imperial Leather*, 27. Since the bulk of this chapter was written (and appeared) long before McClintock's excellent study of European/British imperialism came on the market, in my revisions I have used her work to test my theories against and to explore German "difference." The term "bourgeoisie" is, of course, an anachronism. Neither bourgeoisie nor "middle class" serves to characterize the small class of civil servants, merchants, and professionals that comprised the German middle sector at the time.

3   See, for example, J. G. Herder, *Briefe zur Beförderung der Humanität* (Berlin: Aufbau, 1971), letter 6, 1:27: "everything in it [the fatherland] is divided."

4   "National" in this prenational context implies tendencies, the formation of a national "vision."

5   See Annette Kolodny, *The Lay of the Land: Metaphor as Experience and History in American Life and Letters* (Chapel Hill: University of North Carolina Press, 1975), or McClintock, *Imperial Leather*. In his paper on Mercator's Atlas of 1595, José Rabasa makes a similar observation: Old World and New World are already organized on the map according to gendered binary oppositions. See "Allegories of the 'Atlas,'" in *Europe and Its Others*, ed. Francis Barker, Peter Hulme, et al. (Colchester: University of Essex Press, 1985), 1: 4. See also Peter Hulme, "Polytropic Man: Tropes of Sexuality and Mobility in Early Colonial Discourse," in *Europe and Its Others*, 17–32.

6   McClintock, *Imperial Leather*, 31.

7   Hulme, *Colonial Encounters,* 158.
8   See one of the earliest accounts of rape in Michele Cuneo's "Letter on the Second Voyage," 28 October 1495, in *Journals and Other Documents in the Life and Voyages of Christopher Columbus,* tr. and ed. S. E. Morison (New York: Heritage Press, 1963), 212.
9   McClintock, *Imperial Leather,* 26.
10 See Hugh Honour, *The European Vision of America* (Cleveland: Cleveland Museum of Art, 1975), 85–95; or pp. 84ff in his *The New Golden Land: European Images of America from the Discoveries to the Present Time* (London: Allen Lane, 1976).
11 For a discussion of this dual image of femininity, as it translates to dual representations of explorations, see Sigrid Weigel, "Die nahe Fremde — das Territorium des 'Weiblichen.'" The meaning of Amazons and monsters in colonial discourse is discussed by Peter Mason, *Deconstructing America: Representations of the Other* (London: Routledge, 1990). Recently, McClintock has also theorized this "gender ambivalence," *Imperial Leather,* 25–28.

3   Gendering the "Conquest"

1   Born in 1739 in Amsterdam and educated by Jesuits (whom he learned to hate), de Pauw, canon at Xanten, went to Berlin on a diplomatic mission and was asked by Frederick II to stay on as his private reader and intellectual companion in 1767–1768 and, again, in 1775. Although Frederick II wanted to keep him in Prussia for good, de Pauw decided to return to Xanten, where he died in 1799. See Henry Ward Church, "Corneille de Pauw, and the Controversy over His 'Recherches Philosophiques sur les Américains,'" *PMLA* 51, no. 1 (March 1936): 178–206; and Gisbert Beyerhaus, "Abbé de Pauw und Friedrich der Grosse, eine Abrechnung mit Voltaire," *Historische Zeitschrift* 134 (1926): 465–493.
2   I have limited myself to the main protagonists of the debate itself. Page numbers in parentheses in the text refer to the first editions of these works (for a complete list see the bibliography).
3   See, for example, the reviews in the *Hallische Neue Gelehrte Zeitungen* 39 (May 15, 1769): 308–310; *Göttingische Anzeigen von gelehrten Sachen* 1 (1769): 1369–1372; 2 (1771): 997–998; 1035–1038; 1046–1048; 1067–1071; 1087; *Der teutsche Merkur* 4, no. 2 (Nov. 1773): 178–191; 5, no. 3 (March 1774): 259–286; 6, no. 1 (April 1774): 57–75; 7, no. 2 (August 1774): 228–251.
4   It generated many rebuttals in the United States and Latin America. See Antonello Gerbi, *The Dispute of the New World: The History of a Polemic, 1750–1900* (1955), rev. and enl. ed. (Pittsburgh: University of Pittsburgh Press, 1973); Hugh Honour, *The New Golden Land;* Manfred Tietz, "Amerika vor der spanischen Öffentlichkeit des 18. Jahrhunderts. Zwei Repliken auf de Pauw und Raynal: die 'Reflexiones imparciales' von Juan Nuix y Perpiñá und die 'México conquistada' von Juan de Escoiquiz," in *Iberoamérica. Historia-*

sociedad-literatura. Homenaje a Gustav Siebenmann, ed. José Manuel López de Abiada and Titus Heydenreich (München: Fink, 1983), 2: 989–1016.

5   See Carli, who, in his *Lettere americane* attacked de Pauw for writing "from the depths of a German province" and for thinking that "everything outside Breslau is barbaric and savage" (Gerbi, *The Dispute of the New World,* 237).

6   See, for example, the review in the *Hallische Neue Gelehrte Zeitungen,* cited in note 3, which considers de Pauw's text the answer for all those looking for "something that would be more than a travelogue, something that would reconcile contradictions, refute lies, and examine reports in order to provide a reliable knowledge of that continent." Likewise, Immanuel Kant praised Pauw's intellectual effort, "even if nine-tenths of his material is unsupported or incorrect" ("Reflexionen zur Anthropologie," in *Gesammelte Schriften,* Akademie Ausgabe, ed. E. Cassirer [Berlin: Reimer, 1913], 15: 389). See also Church's — more recent — assessment: "Yet for all its lack of purity and conciseness, de Pauw's style is quite readable and entertaining, being saved largely by its amusing violence" (Church, "Corneille de Pauw," 184).

7   Church, "Corneille de Pauw."

8   Gerbi, *The Dispute of the New World,* 52; Honour, *The New Golden Land,* 131.

9   Gerbi, *The Dispute of the New World,* 417ff.

10   For an assessment of the much-debated issue of syphilis see Alfred W. Crosby, "The Early History of Syphilis, a Reappraisal," in *The Columbian Exchange: Biological and Cultural Consequences of 1492* (Westport, Ct.: Greenwood Press, 1972), 122–164.

11   Buffon's theory of degeneracy had related to the flora and fauna exclusively; de Pauw extends it to include humans. See Gerbi, *The Dispute of the New World,* 3–31. Buffon was retranslated into German after de Pauw had given his theories new publicity: *Herrn von Buffons allgemeine Naturgeschichte. Eine freye mit einigen Zusätzen vermehrte Übersetzung nach der neuesten französischen Ausgabe von 1769,* 7 vols., tr. Heinrich Wilhelm Martini (Berlin: Pauli, 1771–1774). This translation also contains a new appendix on humans: "Zur Beschreibung der unterschiedenen Arten von Menschen."

12   See, for example, Margarita Zamora, *Reading Columbus* (Berkeley: University of California Press, 1993), 152–179.

13   In his introduction, de Pauw alludes to this "naturalist" approach when he compares his interest in "aberrations in human nature" with the naturalist's fascination with, for example, procreation among bisexual snails [*Zeugungsart der Schnecken*].

14   For a discussion of the history of humoral theories see Londa Schiebinger, *The Mind Has No Sex? Women in the Origins of Modern Science* (Cambridge, Mass.: Harvard University Press, 1989), 161–187.

15   "Quand ces Américains virent pour la première fois des Espagnols à longue barbe, ils perdirent dès-lors le courage: *car comment pourrions-nous résister, s'écrierent-ils, à des hommes qui ont des cheveux dans le visage, & qui sont si robustes qu'ils soulèvent des fardeaux que nous ne saurions seulement remuer?*"

The next sentence, paradoxically, takes back the claim that the savages were visually overwhelmed — but de Pauw "punishes" them verbally for this oversight: "Les Péruviens parurent le moins épouvantés à la vue des Espagnols: ils crurent même qu'ils étoient lâches & efféminés, *mais ils se détrompèrent bientôt.*"

16   In the German translation "Les Indiennes" become "die Indianer" — to the German readers the delight of both Indian men and women at the arrival of the Spaniards must have been obvious. . . .

17   De Pauw repeatedly points to the smallness of the natives' penises (metaphorically alluded to as 'instrument') while he only once mentions their allegedly oversized testicles.

18   A similar process is described by Bernadette Bucher in her analysis of early iconography relating to the New World, *Icon and Conquest: A Structural Analysis of the Illustrations of de Bry's Great Voyages,* tr. Basia Miller Gulati (Chicago: University of Chicago Press, 1981).

19   "Ingrate" has, of course, many meanings — from thankless to unproductive, barren. I tried to combine various meanings, because the anthropomorphic underpinnings in de Pauw's discourse are evident.

20   Tietz, "Amerika vor der spanischen Öffentlichkeit," 991–993.

21   For a recent discussion of "berdaches" and their cultural significance in European and American cultures see Richard Trexler, *Sex and Conquest: Gendered Violence, Political Order, and the European Conquest of the Americas* (Ithaca: Cornell University Press, 1995).

22   On myth transfer see Rudolf Wittkower, "Marvels of the East, a Study in the History of Monsters," *Journal of the Warburg and Courtauld Institutes* 4 (1942): 159–197; Peter Mason, *Deconstructing America;* and Sigrid Brauner's "Cannibals, Witches, and Evil Wives in the 'Civilizing Process,'" in *"Neue Welt"/"Dritte Welt". Interkulturelle Beziehungen Deutschlands zu Lateinamerika und der Karibik,* ed. Sigrid Bauschinger and Susan Cocalis (Tübingen: Francke, 1994), 1–28.

23   Antonio Pigafetta, *Allgemeine Geschichte der Reisen nach den Südländern,* quoted in the introduction to John Byron, *John Byrons, obersten Befehlshabers über ein Englisches Geschwader, Reise um die Welt, in den Jahren 1764 und 1765. Nebst einer genauen Beschreibung der Magellanischen Strasse, der Patagonischen Riesen, und der ganz neu-entdeckten Sieben Inseln in der Süd-See* (Frankfurt and Leipzig: Metzler, 1769). Also Johann Heinrich Zedler, *Grosses vollständiges Universal-Lexikon, 1732–1763* (1740; rpt. Halle: Akademische Drucks- und Verlagsanstalt Graz, 1961), 26: 1275.

24   Zedler's account of 1740 reduces the Patagons to almost normalcy: they are "Pentagones," five ells = 7½ feet tall. "As far as their bodies are concerned, they should not be taken for monsters; in view of their savage demeanor, however, they may well pass for monsters." John Byron (see note 23) returns them to their monstrous height. See also the report in *Braunschweigische Anzeigen* 58 (July 29, 1767): 460.

25   See the exchange between Dr. Matti [Maty] and M. de la Condamine, related in

Braunschweigische Anzeigen 73 (Sept. 10, 1766), where de la Condamine attributes the revival of the Patagon Giant myth to a British ruse: they used it as a pretext to send ships to South America where they wanted to establish a colonial stronghold (590–591).

26 Johann Christoph Erich von Springer, *Physikalische Untersuchung, ob auch Patagonische Riesen möglich, und die Erzählungen davon wahr sind* (Leipzig: Hilscher, 1769).

27 *Über die Riesen in Patagonien. Ein Sendschreiben an den Herrn Doctor Maty, Sekretär der königlichen Societät in London, von dem Herrn Abt Coyer, Mitglied derselben Gesellschaft,* tr. Samuel William Turner (Danzig: Wedel, 1769), 115. For a more ironic reference to Patagonian Giants see C. M. Wieland, "Über die vornehmliche Abnahme des menschlichen Geschlechts," in *Sämmtliche Werke* (Leipzig: Göschen, 1821), 31: 237–238.

28 E. A. W. von Zimmermann, *Geographische Geschichte des Menschen und der allgemein verbreiteten vierfüssigen Thiere* (Leipzig: Weygand, 1778–1783).

29 Springer, *Physikalische Untersuchung*, 47.

30 Claude Marie Guyon claims to have personally seen the "strange, or newer Amazons" in America (*Geschichte derer Amazonen,* tr. Johann Georg Krünitz [Berlin: Rüdiger, 1763], 201), which leads him to speculate on whether New World Amazon republics are, in fact, colonies of the Old's (207). See also Abby Wettan Kleinbaum, *The War against the Amazons* (New York: McGraw-Hill, 1983), 140ff.

31 *Moeurs des Sauvages*, 1: 171–172.

32 See, for example, my article "Crossing the Boundaries: The French Revolution in the German Literary Imagination," in *Representing Revolution: Essays on Reflections of the French Revolution in Literature, Historiography, and Art,* ed. James Heffernan (Hanover, N.H.: University Press of New England, 1992), 213–236.

33 Peter Mason, *Deconstructing America*, 60.

34 Ten years later, Johann Friedrich Blumenbach would come down squarely on Pernety's side, citing as evidence all those who did discover bearded Amerindian peoples. Yet by that time, the supposed "beardlessness" of the natives or the "scantiness" of their beards had become not only an established "fact" but a culturally meaningful observation. "Einige zerstreute Bemerkungen über die Fähigkeiten und Sitten der Wilden, von Prof. Blumenbach," *Göttingisches Magazin* 6, no. 6 (1781): 409–425.

35 In addition to Beyerhaus, Church, and Gerbi (see notes 1 and 4), see Honour, who spoke of the "salacious tidbits on sexual malpractice," *The New Golden Land*, 131.

36 See, for example, the appendix in Buffon's *Allgemeine Naturgeschichte:* "Zur Beschreibung der unterschiedenen Arten von Menschen"; Blumenbach's *On the Natural Variety of Mankind* (1775 and 1795), tr. Thomas Bendyshe (London: Longman, 1865), 141–143, 253ff, 272–273, 313; or Christian Wünsch's tenth conversation on the "difference of individual humans" in his *Unterhaltungen über den Menschen. Erster Theil. Über die Kultur und äusserliche*

Bildung desselben, 2nd ed. (Leipzig: Breitkopf, 1796): "Zehnte Unterhaltung: Verschiedenheit einzelner Menschen."

37 Beyerhaus, "Abbé de Pauw," 476.

38 "Au reste, c'est un bonheur inestimable pour la plus grande partie de l'Europe, d'avoir des terres qu'il faut sans cesse cultiver: cela entretient, pour peu que le gouvernement ne soit pas excessivement mauvais, l'amour du travail, & non l'amour de l'oisiveté, l'amour de l'ordre, & non celui du brigandage."

39 De Pauw, "Amérique," *Supplément à l'Encyclopédie, ou Dictionnaire raisonné des sciences, des arts et des métiers* (Amsterdam: Rey, 1776–1777), 1: 345.

40 Blumenbach, *On the Natural Variety,* 88.

41 Karl Gottlob Schelle, *Geschichte des männlichen Barts unter allen Völkern der Erde bis auf die neueste Zeit. Für Freunde der Sitten und Völkerkunde. Nach dem Französischen frei bearbeitet und mit einer Theorie der Haare nach ihren Naturzwecken versehen* (Leipzig: Weygand, 1797), 50.

42 See John Woodforde, *The Strange Story of False Hair* (London: Routledge and Kegan Paul, 1971), 66.

43 Max von Böhn, *Die Mode. Menschen und Moden im 18. Jahrhundert* (München: Bruckmann, 1963), 193.

44 Karl Zedler, *Grosses vollständiges Universal-Lexikon,* 46: 1718, 1747.

45 Friedrich Nicolai, *Über den Gebrauch der falschen Haare und Perrucken in alten und neuern Zeiten* (Berlin: n.p., 1801), 66ff. Also Schelle, *Geschichte des männlichen Barts,* 104.

46 See, for example, Eduard Fuchs, *Illustrierte Sittengeschichte vom Mittelalter bis zur Gegenwart. Das bürgerliche Zeitalter* (München: Langen, 1912) who contrasted the "Parasitenideal" of the aristocratic "Weibmann" with the new ideal of the "Kraftmensch," as it emerged during Romanticism (141f). See also Schelle, introduction to *Geschichte des männlichen Barts,* x, who advocates the reintroduction of the beard as a natural sign of wisdom, maturity, and distinction between men and women. Earlier attempts to return to the male ideal are, for example, the Saxon sculptor Balthasar Permoser's treatise on beards: *Der ohne Ursach verworffene und dahero von Rechts wegen auff den Thron der Ehren wiederum erhobene BARTH* . . . (Frankfurt am Main: n.p., 1714), or Henri Blanes, *Der Stutzer nach der Mode* (Paris: n.p., 1765).

47 See, for example, James J. Sheehan, *German History, 1770–1866* (Oxford: Clarendon Press, 1989), 23, who calls Prussia a "predator state" (23) and stresses the Prussian kings' "desire for mastery" (62), or colonial expansion (67f) toward the east. Ulrike Müller-Weil (*Absolutismus und Aussenpolitik in Preussen. Ein Beitrag zur Strukturgeschichte des Preussischen Absolutismus* [Stuttgart: Steiner, 1992]) describes in great detail Frederick's aggressive trade and conquest politics ("Arrondierungspolitik"), which relied, for example, on systematic undercutting of "weak" Poles and instrumentalization of his own subjects for his extensive population and colonization politics (see 313ff).

48 Quoted in Sheehan, *German History,* 67.

49 Hugh Honour, *The New Golden Land,* 131.

4   Racializing the Colony

1   "Bey meinem Aufenthalte zu Hessen-Cassel beobachtete ich viele dort lebende
    Neger und zergliederte mit Muse [*sic*] mehrere männliche und auch einen
    weiblichen Negerkörper."

2   For a balanced discussion of "race" in the late eighteenth century see Philip D.
    Curtin, *The Image of Africa: British Ideas and Action, 1780–1850* (Madison:
    University of Wisconsin Press, 1964), 28–57.

3   The conflation of race and gender is, for example, highlighted in Pernety's
    circular argument: (1) skin color depends on temperament; (2) dark brown skin
    and very white, pale skin are signs of melancholia and fear; (3) hence blacks
    and white women are melancholic and fearful; (4) they are fearful, weak, and
    lazy, because of their phlegmatic, humid temperament; (5) humid, phlegmatic
    temperament produces dark or very pale skin. . . . *Discours sur la physiog-
    nomie. La Connaissance de l'homme moral par l'homme physique* (Berlin:
    Decker, 1769); German tr. *Versuch einer Physiognomik oder Erklärung des
    moralischen Menschen durch die Kenntniss des physischen*, 3 vols. (Dresden:
    Walther, 1784), 1: 338–339.

4   On the preponderance of ideological and political over strictly scientific con-
    cerns, see Michael Weingarten, "Menschenarten und Menschenrassen. Die
    Kontroverse zwischen Georg Forster und Immanuel Kant," in *Georg Forster in
    seiner Epoche*, ed. G. Pickerodt et al. (Berlin: Argument, 1982), 117.

5   The first seven-volume edition, *Des Ritters C. von Linné vollständiges Natur-
    system, nach der 12. lateinischen Ausgabe, und nach Anleitung des hollän-
    dischen Houttuynischen Werks, mit einer ausführlichen Erklärung ausgefertigt
    von P. L. S. Müller* (Nürnberg, 1773–1776) was soon followed by a fourteen-
    volume edition (1777–1788) based on the thirteenth Latin edition, and a four-
    volume edition of the mineral realm, based on the twelfth Latin edition (1777–
    1779). All appeared in Nuremberg.

6   See, for example, Bitterli, "Die Überseebewohner im europäischen Bewusstsein
    der Aufklärungszeit," in *Fürst, Bürger, Mensch.*

7   Review in *Allgemeine Literatur-Zeitung*, 1, no. 4 (Jan. 6, 1785): 17–22; "Be-
    stimmung des Begrifs einer Menschenrace," *Berlinische Monatsschrift*, 6, no. 1
    (Nov. 1785): 390–417; "Mutmasslicher Anfang der Menschengeschichte,"
    Berlinische Monatsschrift 7, no. 1 (Jan. 1786): 1–27.

8   In the second edition of 1785 "Mohr" was changed to "Neger," possibly to
    avoid identification of the racialist term "Negro" with the cultural-religious
    term "Moor" that applied to the Muslims of southern Spain and northern
    Africa and to one of the three Magi. See Frank W. P. Dougherty, "Johann
    Friedrich Blumenbach und Samuel Thomas Soemmering: Eine Auseinander-
    setzung in anthropologischer Hinsicht," in *Samuel Thomas Soemmering und
    die Gelehrten der Goethezeit*, ed. Günter Mann and Franz Dumont (Stuttgart
    and New York: Fischer, 1985), 37.

9   For discussions of these debates, see Marita Gilli, "Georg Forster, das Ergebnis

einer Reise um die Welt," in *Europäisches Reisen im Zeitalter der Aufklärung,* ed. Hans-Wolf Jäger, 268–273; Londa Schiebinger, "More Than Skin Deep: The Scientific Search for Sexual Difference," *The Mind Has No Sex?;* Wolf Lepenies, "Georg Forster als Anthropologe und als Schriftsteller," *Akzente* 3, no. 6 (1984): 557–575; Frank W. P. Dougherty, "Johann Friedrich Blumenbach"; and Weingarten, "Menschenarten oder Menschenrassen."

10   See Andreas Käuser, "Anthropologie und Aesthetik im 18. Jahrhundert," in *Das 18. Jahrhundert* 14, no. 2 (1990): 196–206. Käuser argues convincingly that quasi-theories were, to contemporaries, just as acceptable as "real" science and had considerable popular impact. While his concept of "Wissensdiskurs der Popularphilosophie und Semitheorie" refers to mesmerism and Lavater's physiognomy, it applies just as much to Meiners's racialist theories of "racial" difference.

11   Critical interest in Christoph Meiners has been scarce. Only three longer texts, two on ethnography, the other on history of religion, focus exclusively on his contributions. See Alexander Ihle, *Christoph Meiners und die Völkerkunde* (Göttingen: Vandenhoek, 1931); Britta Rupp-Eisenreich, "Des choses occultes en histoire des sciences humaines: Le destin de la 'science nouvelle' de Christoph Meiners," *Ethnographie* 90–91 (1983): 131–183; and Herbert Wenzel, "Christoph Meiners als Religionshistoriker," Ph.D. diss. (Frankfurt an der Oder: Beholtz, 1917). Horst Fiedler's afterword to Georg Forster's reviews, *Georg Forsters Werke* (Berlin-Ost: Akademie Verlag, 1977), 11: 413–426, constitutes the only contemporary German discussion of Meiners's controversial contribution — an *East* German discussion. I have found few references to him in West German critical literature. Maybe post-Holocaust critics find it too embarrassing to engage seriously with one of the earliest and most vicious proponents of racism; maybe he is the "victim" of the tendency to re-create history by focusing on the great thinkers rather than on secondary figures (see Wenzel, introduction to *Christoph Meiners*).

12   See, for example, Christoph Girtanner's popularization of Kant's theories, which are dedicated to Blumenbach, quote Sömmerring, refute Forster, and reiterate, once again, all the known "facts" on the five human races: *Ueber das Kantische Prinzip für die Naturgeschichte. Ein versuch diese wissenschaft philosophisch zu behandeln* (Göttingen: Vandenhoek, 1796).

13   Urs Bitterli, *Die Entdeckung des Schwarzen Afrikaners. Versuch einer Geistesgeschichte der europäisch-afrikanischen Beziehungen an der Guineaküste im 17. und 18. Jahrhundert* (Zürich: Atlantis, 1970), 118, emphatically rejects any connection between late-eighteenth-century race theories and "modern racism." While I acknowledge the differences in meaning some of the categories have acquired in years of nationalist/biologistic/social Darwinist overlay, there is no doubt in my mind that we are witnessing here the beginnings of modern, that is, biological racism.

14   Immanuel Kant, "Von den verschiedenen Racen der Menschen," *Werke* (Berlin: Reimer, 1905) 2: 428–443. Page numbers in parentheses in the text refer

to this edition. As my text makes clear, I hope, de Pauw's and by implication Buffon's influence is much more pervasive and therefore merits to be considered a "first." Neither in the German translation of Buffon's *Natural History* nor in de Pauw does the term "race" appear. Buffon's translator uses "Gattungen," de Pauw's uses "Verschiedenheit." See also Weingarten, "Menschenarten und Menschenrassen"; or Thomas Saine, *Georg Forster* (New York: Twayne, 1972), 43–46.

15 Although "Weisse von brünetter Farbe" may be translated as whites with a tanned complexion, I believe he means brown-haired whites, since "brunette," like blond, is usually applied to hair — which is how Kant himself uses the term in the preceding paragraph.

16 Weingarten categorically denies any "racist" or "white supremacist" motivations: "It would be wrong to assume that Kant falls into the traps of any racism or exaggerated appreciation of Europeans" ("Menschenarten und Menschenrassen," 127). Whatever Kant's motivations may have been — and they may indeed have been guided by his a priori system of colors, the derivation of all other colors from a "white" origin — the fact is that his idea of the white as the primeval race was used to argue for white superiority.

17 A similar argument is eloquently made by David E. Stannard in *American Holocaust: Columbus and the Conquest of the New World* (New York: Oxford University Press, 1992), 14. In his elaboration on Kant, Christoph Girtanner, *Über das Kantische Prinzip für die Naturgeschichte*, 138, carries Kant's theory one step further, when he claims that the Indians' lack of adaptation to the new continent creates their particularly unadapted "Naturell" and their total lack of abilities and talents, which puts them even "below the level of the Africans." In this, Girtanner claims, Indians resemble slaves, Gypsies, and Jews (157).

18 *Über die natürlichen Verschiedenheiten im Menschengeschlechte* (Leipzig: Breitkopf und Härtel, 1798). The references in the text are to the translation by Thomas Bendyshe.

19 The translator's (?) footnote identifies the source of this reference as Kant's two essays in *Berliner [sic] Monatsschrift*, 1785, and *Teutscher Merkur*, 1788.

20 See "Über die natürlichen Verschiedenheiten," xi fn. "As to the other races, they are only for Blumenbach, transitional: that is, the American is the passage from the Caucasian to the Mongolian; and the Malay, from the Caucasian to the Ethiopian." The translator also quotes approvingly from an essay by a French anthropologist: "It is apparent that Blumenbach was more or less aware of three truths whose importance no one can dispute in anthropological taxinomy [sic], that is to say, the plurality of races of man; the importance of the characteristics deduced from the conformation of the head; and the necessity of not placing in the same rank all the divisions of mankind, which bear the common title of races, in spite of the unequal importance of their anatomical, physiological, and let us also add, psychological characteristics."

21 As Curtin (*The Image of Africa*) noted, Blumenbach "made a serious effort to correct the dominant tendencies of the science as a whole," moderating "his

own earlier racial chauvinism" (47). However, his voice was that of a minority, and his theories, taken out of context, had become part of the classificatory, hierarchical racist discourse.

22   Londa Schiebinger, *The Mind Has no Sex?* chap. 7.

23   I used the second edition, titled *Über die körperliche Verschiedenheit des Negers vom Europäer* (Frankfurt am Main and Mainz: Varrentrapp, 1785). References in the text are to this edition.

24   See his preface, entitled *Vorrede und Apologie für die erste Ausgabe*, xixff. For a discussion of Sömmerring's "recanting," see Dougherty, 37ff. The question, as Dougherty puts it, is not one of anatomical evidence, but of epistemological interest and interpretation. Why would Sömmerring feel the need to "prove" the closeness between the skull form of Africans and apes, if, as Andreas Mielke has recently pointed out, he could just as well have proven the relatedness of the European to the chimpanzee: both have thin lips and white skin. (*Laokoon und die Hottentotten*, 228).

25   Sömmerring, *Vorrede*, xvii.

26   Dougherty, "Johann Friedrich Blumenbach," 44; Schiebinger, "More than Skin Deep," 213; Curtin, *The Image of Africa,* 39–40. By the mid-1780s, the association between Africans and apes is so deeply ingrained that it even appears in self-proclaimed abolitionist texts. See, for example, Johann Ernst Kolb's introduction to his anthology *Erzählungen von den Sitten und Schicksalen der Negersklaven. Eine rührende Geschichte für Menschen guter Art* (Bern: Haller, 1789), where he repeatedly establishes that connection: black women have easy births, like "Orang-Outangs or other animals" (xvii); blacks have instinctive knowledge of herbal medicine, since the Creator has provided "all animals with the means for their preservation" (xix); blacks are cannibals and as such like a roasted joint of monkey as much as a roasted joint of human (xx).

27   J. G. Herder, "Ideen zu einer Philosophie der Geschichte der Menschheit," in *Sämmtliche Werke*, vol. 13, ed. Bernhard Suphan (Berlin: Weidmann, 1887). Unless otherwise stated, all page numbers in parentheses refer to this edition.

28   Marian Musgrave, writing on Herder's representation of blacks, is less harsh in her judgment. Despite his blindnesses, Herder "was saved" from racist bias, she thinks, "by a remarkable kind of 'people-orientation'" ("Herder, Blacks, and the 'Negeridyllen': A Study in Ambivalent Humanitarianism," *Studia Africana* 1 [1977], 89–99, quote from 92). Even more generous is Eberhard Müller-Bochat ("Afrika und Herders 'Stimmen der Völker' aus komparatistischer Sicht," in *Négritude et Germanité, l'Afrique Noire dans la littérature d'expression allemande* [Dakar: Nouvelles éditions africaines, 1983], 88), who declares that Herder's "intention" was one of brotherhood, humanity, and cosmopolitanism. Since I am not concerned with Herder as an individual but with how his formulations in this text serve to support a specific discourse on race, the question of Herder's own ambivalent humanitarianism is outside the scope of my argument. Uta Sadji ("Johann August von Einsiedel und Afrika," in *Négritude,* 80) corroborates my contention when she reports that Einsiedel, a friend

of Herder's who traveled to Africa, wrote back to him about the "Affenland, wie Ihrs nennt" — "the 'monkey land,' as you call it." Not the intentions, but the language seems to have gained currency.

29   Herder's admired model Johann Caspar Lavater had already described an "upright Moor" as exhibiting "heat and softness, sharp sensuality, constancy. Truly the element of earthly passions," in *Physiognomische Fragmente zur Beförderung der Menschenkentniss und Menschenliebe* (Leipzig: Weidmanns Erben und Reich, 1778), 309 (my translation). As Lavater (like Pernety before him) points out, this supposed sensuality associates Africans with women.

30   A few paragraphs later, Herder rejects all animal-human analogies (257)!

31   In his essay "Des coches," Montaigne had argued that the Indians, kindhearted, childlike innocents of considerable cultural skills, had been corrupted by the Spanish conquerors.

32   E.g., "deeply set small monkey eyes," "signaling cowardice and greed," "monkey-like," "sharp-filed front teeth."

33   Even in his critique of abstract classifications, Forster, for example, equates lighter skin with beauty and dark skin with ugliness: the natives of the Pacific islands are "of light brown color, well-proportioned, of beautiful stature, pleasant countenance, with wavy black hair and full beards" (all the attributes of beauty, according to Meiners), whereas the aborigines in New Zealand and New Guinea are described as "smaller, skinny black people with kinky woolly hair and uglier features," in "Noch etwas über die Menschenrassen," *Der Teutsche Merkur* (Weimar, Oct.–Nov., 1786), 4: 64–65. On Herder's "radical conflict" see Antonello Gerbi, *The Dispute*, 287ff.

34   Christoph Meiners, *Grundriss der Geschichte der Menschheit* (Lemgo: Meyer, 1785; Frankfurt ed., 1786; 2nd improved ed. Lemgo, 1793), introduction. The quote is from the 1786 edition, since I was unable to obtain the 1793 edition.

35   For a discussion of the German positions on slavery see Rainer Koch, "Liberalismus, Konservativismus und das Problem der Negersklaverei."

5   Patagons and Germans

1   "Der Mensch selbst, der Bewohner dieser kalten Region von Südamerika, zeigte zwei merkwürdige Phänomene: Das kalte nördlicher gelegene Binnenland bildete den Menschen zu jenen Kolossen aus, die unsern deutschen Ahnen glichen, wodurch Gallien und Rom in Erstaunen gesetzt wurden. . . . Der hierauf folgende südlichste Theil der neuen Welt, Feuer-Land, eine in viele Stücke zertrümmerte höchsttraurige erfrorne Insel, zeigte auch ihm ähnliche Bewohner. Alle Reisende nannten diese Pesheräs ein elendes, kleines hageres, schmutziges, dürftiges und stumpfsinniges Volk. Selbst die sogar mancher Thierart beiwohnende Neugierde schien ihnen die Indolenz entzogen zu haben: sie wünschten nicht einmal das merkwürdigste Gebäude der menschlichen Industrie, das europäische Schiff, zu betrachten" ("Rückblick auf die Neue Welt," my translation).

2   *Stolzes Brittannien du! du raubst von Osten und Westen*
    Köstlich duftendes Reis, das dich in Flammen verzehrt.
    Glänzender Phönix! Wir, die deutsche fleissige Biene,
    Sammlen auf jeglicher Flur Honig, und wissen nicht, wem?

3   See the repeated allusions to the topicality of the race question in light of the
    revolutions in Meiners's "Über die Natur der Afrikanischen Neger, und die
    davon abhangende Befreyung, oder Einschränkung der Schwarzen," *Gött-*
    isches historisches Magazin 6 (1790): 385–456, 390, 401.

4   See Bitterli, *Die Entdeckung des Schwarzen Afrikaners,* 19.

5   Sömmerring, *Über die körperliche Verschiedenheit des Negers vom Europäer,*
    xiii.

6   The extreme nature of Meiners's views could, of course, suggest that he is an
    aberration and that he therefore does not deserve to be given such prominence.
    Rupp-Eisenreich ("Des choses occultes," 90–91; 131–183), on the contrary,
    argues that he was extremely well received in France. My own research sug-
    gests that while he was controversial Meiners enjoyed considerable recognition
    among "middle-brow" circles. See Zantop, "The Beautiful, the Ugly, and the
    German: Race, Gender, and Nationality in Eighteenth-Century Anthropologi-
    cal Discourse," in *Gender and Germanness: Cultural Productions of Nation,*
    ed. Patricia Herminghouse and Magda Mueller (Providence, R.I.: Berghahn,
    forthcoming).

7   Not surprisingly, his theories received a belated "revindication" during the
    Nazi period (see Rupp-Eisenreich, "Des choses occultes," 133).

8   The tendency to see Germans as the epitome of European civilization was
    becoming en vogue, as Antonello Gerbi noted (*The Dispute,* 423); he accuses
    both Hegel and Friedrich Schlegel of Germanocentrism (see 423: "Hegel . . .
    needs to construct a system of cosmic, mythological, and geophysical relation-
    ships so compact and coherent, indeed so perfectly rational that its center turns
    out, as is only right, to be Germany!" or 445: "For him [Schlegel] the Germans
    are the bearers of the purest and highest traditions, and will be able to carry
    forward their educative task in all climates").

9   See "Über die Natur der Americaner," *Göttingisches historisches Magazin* 6
    (1790): 102–156; "Über die Natur der Afrikanischen Neger," 385–456; "Von
    den Varietäten und Abarten der Neger," *Göttingisches historisches Magazin* 6
    (1790): 625–645; "Historische Nachrichten über die wahre Beschaffenheit des
    Sclaven-Handels, und der Knechtschaft der Neger in West-Indien," *Götting-*
    isches historisches Magazin 6 (1790): 645–679.

10 "Über den Haar- und Bartwuchs der hässlichen und dunkelfarbigen Völker,"
    "Über die Farben, und Schattierungen verschiedener Völker," and "Über die
    Verschiedenheit der cörperlichen Grösse verschiedener Völker," all in *Göttin-*
    gisches historisches Magazin 1 (1792): 484–508, 611–672, 697–762, respec-
    tively. Page numbers in the text refer to this issue.

11 "Über die Natur der Afrikanischen Neger," 386.

12 "One may assert without hesitation that those apes which most resemble men

are more like the ugly Negroes than these are like Europeans" (430). All translations from Meiners are mine.

13   See, for example, the twisted argument with which Meiners tries to counter Blumenbach's critique of Sömmerring, 406–408. He admits that one cannot judge a people by one physical property alone and that one would have to examine many different specimens before making any conjectures. But since this is physically impossible (407), he has to resort to (selected) eyewitness reports by others, all of which support his contentions.

14   In one instance, Meiners talks about the Africans' lack of fear of death (411), in another, he speaks about their fear of death (417); in one, he affirms the women's lack of motherly love for their offspring — they even eat their children (437) — in another he claims that their often observed motherly love, a natural instinct, associates them with animals (453).

15   See, for example, Geoffrey Scammell, "The Other Side of the Coin: The Discovery of the Americas and the Spread of Intolerance, Absolutism and Racism in Early Modern Europe," paper delivered at the John Carter Brown Library conference "America in European Consciousness" (June 1991). Scammell convincingly argues that the identification of Africans with lust and bestiality and with "animals" to claim their natural predisposition for slavery dates back to the conquest and slave trade. The difference between earlier racism and later racism is that the latter provides a "scientific" rationale for it. Meiners's theories did not meet universal approval, as a somewhat catty remark by C. M. Wieland, suggests: "Meiners's hypothesis on human races. He himself with his black hair is a Mongol and has no backhead, as his conspicuous silhouette in Lavater's *Physiognomik* proves." However, as Wieland's reference to Meiners's "Mongol" skull formation indicates, racialist epithets had already become part of common discourse. See Thomas Starnes, *C. M. Wieland, Leben und Werk: aus zeitgenössischen Quellen chronologisch dargestellt* (Sigmaringen: Thorbecke, 1987), 2: 554. In a letter to Herder of 21 January 1787, and in a series of reviews, Georg Forster criticizes Meiners vehemently, while recognizing that his "horrible principles penetrate the public with power, and his judgment is constantly referred to" (Letter to Heyne, Sep. 7, 1789). His review of Meiners's race theories in *Allgemeine Literatur-Zeitung* (Jan. 8, 1791), although highly critical of their categorical nature and doubtful as to their universal applicability, shares Meiners's conviction that morality and reason have developed "most perfectly, as much as history tells us, undoubtedly among the inhabitants of our continent. . . . In Europe, the sciences and the arts have reached a stage of perfection nowhere else achieved; we are ahead of other peoples as to our moral mechanism . . . and finally we rule even in other parts of the earth and embrace with our more perfect knowledge the whole world" (51). Forster only takes issue with the supposed causes of that superiority, which, to him, are rooted in climate and environment, not inborn (Georg Forster, "Rezensionen," in *Werke* 11: 236–252).

16   For example: "From the irritability and the lack of elasticity connected with it

results, furthermore, their characteristic laziness" (418); "From the weakness and slipperiness of their firm parts, the true cause of their unusual irritability, and the consequences I have mentioned so far, I finally deduce the curious agility of the body and its limbs, proper to all Negroes, in addition to their inimitable speed and dexterity as runners" (419).

17   Despite reservations and public critique by Georg Forster and others, Meiners's theories became extremely popular. While their originator's name faded into oblivion, they led an underground existence throughout the nineteenth century, before they reemerged in the twentieth. See Rupp-Eisenreich, "Des choses occultes," 137, 145, 154–156.

18   Again, all the stereotypes about Indians—their alleged weakness, imbecility, depravity etc.—were by then well established. See Scammell, "The Other Side of the Coin."

19   "Purity of blood" had served as metaphor for racial purity (*pureza de sangre*) since sixteenth-century Spain. While the fear of contamination with Moorish or Jewish blood, as Scammell has shown, was pervasive throughout the sixteenth and seventeenth centuries, "blood," I would argue with Henry Kamen, lost its genealogical/class connotation in the eighteenth, gaining a biological connotation instead—which was then used to confirm cultural or economic superiority. See Henry Kamen, "America and Its Impact on Racial Attitudes and 'Blood Purity,'" paper presented at the 1991 "Conference on America in European Consciousness" (John Carter Brown Library).

20   "On the Colors and Shades of Different Peoples," 655ff, esp. 666.

21   See, for example, Otto W. Johnston, *The Myth of a Nation: Literature and Politics in Prussia under Napoleon* (Columbia: Camden House, 1989), introduction; or Bernd Fischer, *Das Eigene und das Eigentliche: Klopstock, Herder, Fichte, Kleist. Episoden aus der Konstruktionsgeschichte nationaler Intentionalitäten* (Berlin: Schmid, 1995).

22   Johnston, *The Myth of a Nation,* xiii.

23   Rudolf Ibbeken, *Preussen 1807–1813. Staat und Volk als Idee und Wirklichkeit* (Köln: Grote, 1970), 16.

24   To Girtanner, their hunting and meat eating associates them, again, with the Old Germans. *Über das Kantische Prinzip für die Naturgeschichte,* 187.

25   Herder, *Ideen,* 247.

26   Meiners, "Über die Ausartung der Europäer in fremden Erdtheilen," *Göttingisches historisches Magazin* 8 (1791): 209–268; quotes on 221, 230, and 244.

27   Johann Gottfried Herder, "England und Deutschland," in *Sämmtliche Werke,* ed. B. Suphan (Berlin: Weidmann, 1889), 29: 160. An analogous idea, yet transferred back onto the colonies, was expressed in Friedrich Bouterwek's "Morgenlied eines Negersklaven aus seinem Kerker," where the African slave laments: "The fruit produced by our sweat is not ours." *Musenalmanach* 32 (1788): 124–127. Clearly, the topos of unremunerated "slavery" could be transferred from continent to continent.

28   On national identity/national spirit based on prejudice see Karl Menges, "Vom

Nationalgeist und seinen 'Keimen'. Zur Voruteils-Apologetik bei Herder, Hamann und anderen 'Patrioten,'" in *Dichter und ihre Nation*, ed. Helmut Scheuer (Frankfurt: Suhrkamp, 1993), 103–120, esp. 107.

29   Bernd Fischer, *Das Eigene und das Eigentliche*, 228.

30   Johann Gottfried Herder, *Briefe zur Beförderung der Humanität* (Berlin and Weimar: Aufbau, 1971), 2: 234: "Von den spanischen Grausamkeiten, vom Geiz der Engländer, von der kalten Frechheit der Holländer, von denen man im Taumel des Eroberungswahnes Heldengedichte schrieb, sind in unsrer Zeit Bücher geschrieben, die ihnen so wenig Ehre bringen, dass vielmehr, wenn ein europäischer Gesamtgeist anderswo als in Büchern lebte, wir uns des Verbrechens beleidigter Menschheit fast vor allen Völkern der Erde schämen müssten. Nenne man das Land, wohin Europäer kamen und sich nicht durch Beeinträchtigungen, durch ungerechte Kriege, Geiz, Betrug, Unterdrückung, durch Krankheiten und schädliche Gaben an der unbewehrten, zutrauenden Menschheit, vielleicht auf alle Äonen hinab, versündigt haben!" (my translation).

31   *Der zweite Ruhm ist Mässigung. Es ruft*
Der Hindus und der Peruaner Not,
Die Wut der Schwarzen und der Mexikaner
Gebratner Montezuma rufen noch
Zum Himmel auf und flehn Entsündigung! —
O glaube, Freund, kein Zeus mit seinem Chor
Der Götter kehrt zu einem Volke, das,
Mit solcher Schuld- und Blut- und Sündenlast
Und Gold- und Demantlast beladen, schmaust!
Er kehrt bei stillen Äthiopiern
Und Deutschen *ein, zu ihrem armen Mahl.*
(215–225; my translation)

32   Curiously, France does not enter the equation as a "colonial" power. Herder's remarks about the French national character, despite his reservations about cultural predominance and German aping, are surprisingly benign. Maybe, the problematic nature of French-German relations at this point makes him proceed with utmost caution. (See letter 17 in *Humanitätsbriefe* 2: 334–338.)

33   Immanuel Kant, *Anthropology from a Pragmatic Point of View*, tr. Victor Lyle Dowdell (Carbondale: Southern Illinois University Press, 1978), 233.

Part III   Colonial Families

1   "Den Einwurf, dass ich als Deutscher einen fremden Helden und eine fremde Geschichte zu meinem Gegenstand genommen, halte ich kaum für nöthig zu beantworten. Die Entdeckung der neuen Welt, und die Eroberung eines so mächtigen Reichs, wie Mexico war, ist für alle Nationen wichtig. Wir Europäer sind auch durch die Religion, durch unsre Sitten und durch unser Staatssystem so mit einander verknüpft, dass wir uns alle mit einander für eine einzige Nation ansehn können. Die Eroberung geschah auch noch überdiess für einen Monarchen, der Spanier und Deutsche zugleich beherrschte" (tr. Walter Arndt).

2 On the "family" see also McClintock, *Imperial Leather,* 44–45, who, however, focuses on the emergence of the family of man metaphor in post-Darwinian England and therefore ignores the peculiarly German constellation.

3 See ibid., 45.

4 "Las maldades, matanzas, despoblaciones, injusticias, violencias, estragos y grandes pecados que los españoles en estos reinos de Sancta Marta han hecho e cometido contra Dios, e contra el rey, e aquellas innocentes naciones." From "Brevísima relación de la destruición de las Indias" (1542), in *Tratados de Fray Bartolomé de las Casas,* tr. Agustín Millares and Carlo and Rafael Moreno (México: Fondo de Cultura Económica, 1965) 1: 118–119. The English translation is taken from Bartolomé de las Casas, *The Devastation of the Indies: A Brief Account,* tr. Herma Briffault (New York: Seabury Press, 1974), 99. Curiously, it distorts the meaning of the Spanish passage by leaving out "e aquellas innocentes naciones."

5 "Digo, sagrado César, que el medio para remediar esta tierra es que Vuestra Majestad la saque ya de poder de padrastros y le dé marido que la tracte como es razón y ella merece; y éste, con toda brevedad, porque de otra manera, según la aquejan e fatigan estos tiranos que tienen encargamiento della, tengo por cierto que muy aína dejará de ser," etc. (119). Again, the translation leaves much to be desired: "que la tracte como es razón y ella merece" is not "with the reasonableness she deserves," but "who treats her as it is reasonable, and as she deserves it" (see 99).

6 Hegel, *Die Vernunft in der Geschichte,* 193.

6 Fathers and Sons

1 "Was mich so in die Welt hinaustrieb? — Will ich aufrichtig sein, so war der, der den ersten Anstoss dazu gab, ein alter Bekannter von uns allen, und zwar niemand anders als Robinson Crusoe. Mit meinen acht Jahren schon fasste ich den Entschluss, ebenfalls eine unbewohnte Insel aufzusuchen, und wenn ich auch, herangewachsen, von der letzteren absah, blieb doch für mich, wie für tausend andere, das Wort 'Amerika' eine gewisse Zauberformel, die mir die fremden Schätze des Erdballs erschliessen sollte."

2 The lasting impact of Robinson Crusoe and other Robinsonades on German readers is attested to in Heinrich Pleticha, ed., *Lese-Erlebnisse 2* (Frankfurt: Suhrkamp, 1978).

3 Jürgen Fohrmann, *Abenteuer und Bürgertum. Zur Geschichte der deutschen Robinsonaden im 18. Jahrhundert* (Stuttgart: Metzler, 1981). Fohrmann counts 128 separate German Robinsonades, which, of course, does not include translations and rewrites of the original (20).

4 Hermann Ullrich, *Robinson und Robinsonaden. Bibliographie, Geschichte, Kritik* (Weimar: Felber, 1898), 43–53.

5 There is ample documentation of the impact of Robinson Crusoe on German children's literature. See, for example, Sophie Köberle, *Jugendliteratur zur Zeit der Aufklärung. Ein Beitrag zur Geschichte der Jugendschriftenkritik* (Wein-

heim: Beltz, 1972); Wolfgang Promies, "Kinderliteratur im späten 18. Jahrhundert," in *Hansers Sozialgeschichte der deutschen Literatur,* ed. Rolf Grimminger (München: Hanser, 1980), 3: 765–831.

6 See, for example, Jeannine Blackwell, "An Island of Her Own: Heroines of the German Robinsonades from 1720 to 1800," *German Quarterly* 58, no. 1 (1985): 5–26, who mentions "over sixteen female castaways that appeared in German fiction, followed by at least three French, three Dutch, three British and one American variation on the genre."

7 See Egon Schmidt, *Die deutsche Kinder- und Jugendliteratur von der Mitte des 18. Jahrhunderts bis zum Anfang des 19. Jahrhunderts* (Berlin-Ost: Kinderbuchverlag, 1974), 73.

8 Joachim Heinrich Campe, *Robinson der Jüngere. Ein Lesebuch für Kinder* (1779; 63rd authorized ed. Braunschweig: Vieweg, 1862). References in the text refer to this edition. The translations are mine.

9 The popularity and profound impact of Campe's version is repeatedly alluded to by authors quoted in Pleticha (see epigraph for this section by von Kloeden). Justinus Kerner's remark that no other book ever created such reading pleasure for him as this one is symptomatic for many (35).

10 Elke Liebs, *Die pädagogische Insel: Studien zur Rezeption des 'Robinson Crusoe' in deutschen Jugendbearbeitungen* (Stuttgart: Metzler, 1977), 67.

11 See, for example, ibid.; Jürgen Schlaeder, "Die Robinsonade als frühbürgerliche Utopie," in *Utopieforschung,* ed. Wilhelm Vosskamp, 2: 280; and Jürgen Fohrmann, *Abenteuer und Bürgertum.* To Fohrmann, the island is "in principle superfluous," it has a purely didactic function (114). Egon Schmidt (*Die deutsche Kinder- und Jugendliteratur*) notes with regret Campe's "inhuman thinking," the "natural" class hierarchies the "progressive" educator Campe still believes in, his being guided by protocapitalist interests (65). The connection between capitalism and colonialism, however, escapes his attention. The only exception is Egon Menz, "Die Humanität des Handelsgeistes. Amerika in der deutschen Literatur des ausgehenden 18. Jahrhunderts," in *Amerika in der deutschen Literatur. Neue Welt-Nordamerika-USA,* ed. Sigrid Bauschinger, Horst Denkler, and Wilfried Malsch (Stuttgart: Reclam, 1975), 45–62.

12 By "colonializes" I understand the ideological indoctrination with colonialist ideas.

13 Krusoe boards a *Guineafahrer,* supposedly to make a fortune by trading toys and trinkets to the Africans, who "take such great pleasure in such things that they will give you for them a hundred times more in gold, ivory, and other things than they are worth" (16, my translation). There is no mention what these "other things" are, but a historically astute reader can imagine.

14 The German original adds a slightly different emphasis by using "zu den Seinigen" — to his own people ("als wäre er von einer langen Reise wieder zu den Seinigen zurückgekommen," 2: 4).

15 Daniel Defoe, *Robinson Crusoe,* critical ed., ed. Michael Shinagel (New York and London: Norton, 1975). All page numbers refer to this edition.

16 Unlike Hulme, I see less of a "masculinist ethos" at work than, as I stated in the

introduction to this chapter, a displacement of native men and women by feminizing and subjecting the native other. Peter Hulme, *Colonial Encounters,* 211.

17 The German term "Gastfreund" is ambiguous, since it denotes both "the host" and the "guest." While Freitag would be Robinson's "host," if the island were his, he is more Robinson's "guest," since Robinson considers himself the owner of the island, which has become "his" home.

18 Menz, "Die Humanität des Handelsgeistes," 56.

19 Johann Carl Wezel, *Robinson Krusoe* (Leipzig: Dyk, 1779–80; 2nd ed., ed. Anneliese Klingenberg, Berlin: Rütten and Loening, 1979), 156–157. For a characterization of Wezel's novel see Brent O. Peterson, "Wezel and the Genre of 'Robinson Crusoe,' " *Lessing Yearbook* (1988), 20: 183–204.

20 See Joachim Heinrich Campe, *Die Entdeckung von Amerika. Ein Unterhaltungsbuch für Kinder und junge Leute,* 3 vols. (1780–1781). Page numbers refer to the 8th ed. (Reutlingen: Mäcken, 1820), which I used. All translations are mine.

21 See *Robinson der Jüngere,* chap 1, 132; Campe, *Die Entdeckung* 1: 15–16, 224–225; 2: 6, 26–27, 36–37. Campe makes noticeable efforts, however, to diffuse any responsibility of Europeans by placing the guilt on the oppressed themselves. Thus he explains slave trading to the children by focusing exclusively on African tribal chiefs or kings who sell their own kinsmen, even children, into slavery "like beasts" (132). Europeans become accomplices, rather than culprits.

22 See Liebs, *Die pädagogische Insel,* 159–164.

23 See Pleticha, ed., *Lese-Erlebnisse,* or the individual memoirs.

7 Husbands and Wives

Portions of this chapter appeared previously as "Domesticating the Other: European Colonial Fantasies, 1770–1830," in *The Question of the Other/s,* ed. Gisela Brinker-Gabler (Albany: State University of New York Press, 1995), 269–283. Reprinted with permission of the State University of New York Press, © 1995.

1 Doris Sommer, *Foundational Fictions: The National Romances of Latin America* (Berkeley: University of California Press, 1991).

2 Hulme, *Colonial Encounters,* 246.

3 Jean Mocquet, *Voyages en Afrique, Asie, Indes Orientales et Occidentales, faits par Jean Mocquet, 1601–1614* (Paris: Gouvernement, 1830), 123–124: "She took her child and, tearing it in two, threw one half toward him on the sea, as if she wanted to say that this was his half, and the other half she took along, subjecting herself to the mercy of luck, full of sorrow and discomfort" (my translation). Hulme considers Mocquet the possible source for the later Inkle-Yarico story (256–257).

4 For the popularity of the Inkle/Yarico plot see Lawrence Marsden Price, *Inkle and Yarico Album* (Berkeley: University of California Press, 1937), esp. 139–140.

5   *Sooft der Morgen kommt: so macht Yariko*
    Durch neuen Unterhalt den lieben Fremdling froh,
    Und zeigt durch Zärtlichkeit, mit jedem neuen Tage,
    Was für ein treues Herz in einer Wilden schlage!
    — *1746, quoted in Price,* Inkle and Yarico Album, *76; my emphasis.*

6   This move is described in one of the handbooks of nineteenth-century colonial-
    ism, Wilhelm Roscher's *Kolonien, Kolonialpolitik und Auswanderung* (Leipzig
    and Heidelberg: Winter, 1848; 2nd ed. 1856; 3rd ed. with Robert Jannasch,
    1885) as the move from "conquest colony" [*Eroberungskolonie*] to "agricul-
    tural colony" [*Ackerbaukolonie*], which was established after the extinction of
    the native population, to "plantation colony" [*Pflanzungskolonie*] (33 of 2nd
    ed.). See also Hulme, *Colonial Encounters,* who terms these rewritings "con-
    cessionary narratives" (253).

7   Jean-François Marmontel, *Les Incas, ou la Destruction de l'Empire du Pérou,*
    2 vols. (Berne/Lausanne: Société Typographique, 1777). I am quoting from
    The Incas; or, The Destruction of the Empire of Peru (Alston, England: John
    Harrop, 1808); all page numbers in the text refer to this edition. Hulme men-
    tions the story of Cora and Alonzo only in passing because it is outside his
    Caribbean focus.

8   On the work's reception see Karl-Ludwig Löhndorf, *Marmontels Incas. Unter-
    suchungen zu ihrer Stellung in der Literatur der Aufklärung, ihrer Aufnahme
    und Nachwirkung* (Ph.D. diss., Bonn, 1980). According to Löhndorf the
    novel's central point is to promote enlightened tolerance (as opposed to re-
    ligious fanaticism). Although he does not state it outright, he considers the
    colonialist implications of the text (noted, for example, by Chinard in 1913) an
    anachronistic reading (see, for example, 179).

9   Enriquillo was the *cacique* whose successful, albeit short-lived, rebellion
    against the Spaniards Las Casas had described in his *Historia de las Indias,* 3:
    259–270. Marmontel, *The Incas,* 153–157.

10 See Price, *Inkle and Yarico Album,* 115. The most popular rewritings are
    Chamfort's comedy *La jeune Indienne* (1764); the opera *Inkle and Yarico* by
    George Colman the Younger (1787); the anonymous French story *Inkle &
    Iarico, Histoire américaine* (1778); *L'Héroïne américaine* (1786); Salomon
    Gessner, *Inkel und Yariko, zweyter Theil,* 1756 ("No heart can be so devoid of
    kindness that it would not be mightily affected by a change of heart, a shudder
    of remorse; in order that the ability for goodness may not be drowned out in
    your bosoms by the weeds of passion, let me tell you about Yariko's salvation
    and Inkle's remorse," Gessner's introduction, quoted in Price, 87); Friedrich
    Carl von Moser, *Ynkle und Yariko,* 1762: "[I]t seemed only fair that they would
    work things out and that their love would not longer be disturbed by secret
    reproaches," quoted in Price, 91.

11 This ending is proposed in the anonymous French story of 1778 mentioned in
    note 10.

12 August von Kotzebue, "Die Sonnen-Jungfrau" (1789) and "Die Spanier in
    Peru; oder, Rollas Tod" (1795), in *Theater* (Leipzig: Kummer, 1840), 2: 4–118

and 4: 205–318 respectively. Löhndorf, *Marmontels Incas,* and Price, *Inkle and Yarico Album,* 89–92, mention a trilogy, attributing *Ataliba, der Vater seines Volkes* (1794) to Kotzebue. Since Kotzebue's *Collected Works* only contain the two works mentioned and "Ataliba" is also listed as Schröder's work, I preferred not to deal with a "trilogy." See Löhndorf, *Marmontels Incas,* 309, and Price, *Inkle and Yarico Album,* 92.

13 Kotzebue is only one in many who treated the Cora-Alonzo love story or used the popular Inca/Atahualpa motif to promote his own productions. See Löhndorf, *Marmontels Incas,* 240–265. The particular popularity of Marmontel's *Les Incas* in Germany is mentioned by Schlosser (quoted in Löhndorf, 171).

14 See, for example, the introduction to the English translation/adaptation of *Die Spanier in Peru* by Richard B. Sheridan, who reports that the play had its opening night on May 24, 1799, in Drury Lane Theatre and ran for thirty-five nights in a row, throughout the theater season. Within a few months, twenty-nine editions of one thousand copies each were sold of the play (A. von Kotzebue, *Pizarro: A Play in Five Acts,* altered and tr. Richard B. Sheridan [New York: S. French, 1924]). There are seventy-eight entries alone for English translations of this play in the National Union Catalog. *Die Sonnen-Jungfrau* was almost equally popular and went through multiple translations and reeditions. Herbert Jacob ("Kotzebues Werke in Übersetzungen," in *Studien zur neueren deutschen Literatur,* ed. H.-W. Seiffert [Berlin: Akademie Verlag, 1964]) reports of the "unprecedented success of *The Spaniards in Peru,* "which surpassed that of all local and foreign authors" and lists 160 editions of his works in English between 1798–1800 alone (see 179). For an assessment of the popularity of "Die Sonnen-Jungfrau" see Lawrence Marsden Price, "The Vogue of Marmontel on the German Stage," *University of California Publications in Modern Philology* 27, no. 3 (Berkeley: University of California Press, 1944): 27–124, esp. 87ff.

15 See Jacob, "Kotzebues Werke," 175: "No German writer has had as strong an impact on the literature of almost all European nations in the nineteenth century as August von Kotzebue." In the six-volume edition of *The German Theatre,* tr. Benjamin Thompson (London: Vernor and Hood, 1806), three volumes alone are dedicated to Kotzebue (containing, among others, *The Virgin of the Sun, Pizarro,* and *Indian Exiles,* another translation of *Die Indianer in England*). Schiller is represented with two plays (*The Robbers, Don Carlos*), Goethe and Lessing with one each (*Stella, Emilia Galotti*), in volume 6, preceded by plays by Babo, Iffland, Schroeder, and Karl von Reitzenstein, most of whom are totally unknown today.

16 Price, *Inkle and Yarico Album,* 113. Price does not say, however, which works of Kotzebue's were performed; he only gives a number: sixty-nine. Nor is Julius Wahle more explicit (*Das Weimarer Hoftheater unter Goethes Leitung* [Weimar: Goethe-Gesellschaft, 1892]). While Wahle confirms — with obvious contempt — that Kotzebue's and Iffland's plays constituted the main fare on German stages for a long time (219), he does not specify whether the eighty-seven Kotzebue pieces performed under Goethe's direction included the *Virgin of the*

Sun or *Pizarro* (220). In view of their European reputation, it is, however, more than likely that they were included. Even if the numbers given by various researchers vary, Kotzebue's major role in nineteenth-century German literature remains undisputed.

17 I have changed or amended the rather free and overly sentimental English translation by Sheridan whenever necessary. "Don Alonzo Molina verliess die wilden Schaaren des Pizarro, weil er ihre Grausamkeiten verabscheute, weil er in jedem Indianer einen Bruder liebte. Das war brav! Ich will hingehen, sprach er, der Freund und Lehrer dieses gutmüthigen Volks zu werden. Ich will ihren Geist bilden, ihnen nützliche Künste mittheilen, ich will ihr Wohlthäter seyn. — Das war sehr brav!" (126).

18 "Was ich ihm [Las Casas] sagen würde? An seiner Hand würde ich die Fluren von Quito durchstreichen; sieh, wie alles grünt und blüht, wie hier die Pflugschaar unbebaute Felder durchwühlt, und dort eine reiche Saat unserer Hoffnung entgegenreift, das ist mein Werk. Sieh, wie Zufriedenheit auf jeder Wange lächelt, weil Gerechtigkeit und Milde barbarische Gesetze tilgten, das ist mein Werk. Sieh, wie schon hier und dort Einer und der Andere Blicke voll hoher Andacht emporhebt nach dem einzigen wahren Gott! das ist mein Werk. Und Las Casas würde mich in seine Arme schliessen, und eine Thräne, sanfter Wehmuth voll, würde Segen auf mich herabträufeln" (74–75).

19 In the Mysore Wars of 1769–1779, 1779–1783, and 1786–1799, the British East India Company tried to extend its control over most of the still independent southern Indian states.

20 Urs Bitterli, *Die Entdeckung des Schwarzen Afrikaners*, 80.

21 Helen Callaway, *Gender, Culture, and Empire: European Women in Colonial Nigeria* (Urbana: University of Illinois Press, 1987), 57.

22 By 1789, because of economic pressures from the "peripheral colonies" (Cuba, Venezuela, Chile, the Río de la Plata region, and New Granada), the Spanish Empire underwent major economic and administrative changes, which resulted first in the establishment of an internal free market and new viceroyalties and, eventually, the opening up to international competitors, especially the United States and England. For details see Mark A. Burkholder and Lyman L. Johnson, *Colonial Latin America*, 282–287.

23 Egon Menz, "Die Humanität des Handelsgeistes," 58–59.

24 I am playing with the categories established by Sigrid Weigel in her essay "Die nahe Fremde–Das Territorium des Weiblichen," in *Die andere Welt. Studien zum Exotismus,* ed. Thomas Koebner and Gerhart Pickerodt (Frankfurt am Main: Suhrkamp), 179–199.

25 Johann Gottfried Herder, "Ideen zur Philosophie der Geschichte der Menschheit," in *Sämmtliche Werke*, ed. B. Suphan, 13: 289.

26 See Helmut Schneider, "Der Zusammenbruch des Allgemeinen" (Sozialgeschichtliche Werkinterpretationen), in *Positionen der Literaturwissenschaft. Acht Modellanalysen am Beispiel von Heinrich von Kleists 'Das Erdbeben in Chili,'* 2nd ed., ed. David Wellbery (München: Beck, 1987), 115; Schneider does not, however, analyze the colonial implications of the story.

8   Betrothal and Divorce

A shorter, German version of this chapter appeared as "Verlobung, Hochzeit und Scheidung in St. Domingo: Die Haitianische Revolution in zeigenössischer deutscher Literatur (1792–1817)," in *"Neue Welt"/"Dritte Welt." Interkulturelle Beziehungen zu Lateinamerika und der Karibik,* ed. Sigrid Bauschinger and Susan Cocalis (Tübingen: Francke, 1994), 29–52.

1   "Es muss einen Deutschen freuen, wenn Tacitus seinen tapfern Vorfahren das Zeugniss giebt, dass das Schicksal der Knechte bey ihnen ungleich milder, und bey weiten nicht so unmenschlich und Naturwidrig, wie bey den stolzen Welteroberern war, die sich doch für gesittet und jene für Barbaren ausschrien" (my translation).

2   *Deswegen, liebe Muse! lass*
Die gute Feder ihn behalten!
Die guten Geister werden walten,
Und der Tirannen Menschheits-Hass
Dem sie, wer weiss, warum? so lange
Zusahn, besiegen! Sanskülott!
Wem ist vor deiner Herrschaft bange!
Mir nicht, Pariser Hottentott!
Wir trotzen Deinem Blutgesange!
Der Preusse lebt! und Gott, ist Gott!
— My translation

3   Roger Norman Buckley, ed. *The Haitian Journal of Lieutenant Howard, York Hussars, 1796–1798* (Knoxville: University of Tennessee Press, 1985), xx.

4   See C. L. R. James, *The Black Jacobins: Toussaint l'Ouverture and the San Domingo Revolution* (1938; 2nd rev. ed. New York: Bantam, 1963), and Patrick Bellegarde-Smith, *Haiti: The Breached Citadel* (Boulder, Colo.: Westview Press, 1990), 35–39.

5   Buckley, *Haitian Journal,* xl–xli, xlvii–l, 50. As Buckley reports, 16,000 German soldiers and twelve officers (nine of whom were aristocrats) fought with the York Hussars (xli). Between 1793 and 1794, the German states, with the exception of Prussia, collected £1,792,008 sterling in subsidy for "renting out" troops, 60 percent of which was collected by Hanover. "The German character of the regiment was to remain constant despite the vicissitudes of the regiment's early history," xlvii.

6   See Bellegarde-Smith, *Haiti,* who describes the new regimes as "military governments," authoritarian, hierarchical, patriarchal, that excluded women, 46.

7   *Minerva. Ein Journal historischen und politischen Inhalts,* ed. J. W. von Archenholz (Berlin, 1792), 123 and 296–319. Further reports on Saint-Domingue in *Minerva,* now published in Hamburg (1796), 519–527; (1805), 1: 133–157, 276–293, 434–464; 2: 71–158, 292–299, 343–354, 459–466; 3: 343–420; 4: 276–298, 392–408. See also the reports "Geschichte der Unglücksfälle von St. Domingue," *Französische Blätter* 3 (Basel, 1796): 297–328; "Zustand von Domingo. Ein Schreiben daher, an einen Freund in H," *Politisches Journal* 1

(1803): 82–85; *Europäische Annalen,* ed. E. L. Posselt (Tübingen, 1795), 1: 231–251; 3: 95–106, 183–188; (1796), 1: 290–296; 2: 20–31; (1797), 1: 980–1112; (1802), 1: 189–204; (1808), 1: 105–129; 3: 173–186. There were also many separate treatises on Saint-Domingue, plantation culture, and the black leaders.

In discussing the uprisings in Saint-Domingue, I spell the name of the island in three different ways, depending on what is being expressed: "Saint-Domingue" is the official historico-political term used for historical narrative. "St. Domingo" is the German term (from Sankt Domingo); it became the code word for race riots and bloody uprisings and is used to refer to imaginary configurations. "Santo Domingo" is the English translation as it appears in Kleist's *The Betrothal in Santo Domingo.*

8   See, for example, Joachim Campe, *Briefe aus Paris zur Zeit der Revolution geschrieben* (Braunschweig: Schulbuchhandlung, 1790; rpt. Hildesheim: Gerstenberg, 1977), vi.

9   See Gleim poem, printed in *Minerva,* vol. 1 (1794), 7. See also Andreas Mielke, *Laokoon und die Hottentotten,* 85; 253–254. German fears of French acts of savagery were expressed in leaflets such as "The cannibals' progress; or, the dreadful horrors of French invasion: As displayed by the Republican Officers and Soldiers, in their perfidy, rapacity, ferociousness and brutality, exercised towards the innocent inhabitants of Germany," tr. Anthony Aufrer (Massachusetts: Walpole, 1798). The congruence of scenarios was also perceived by prorevolutionaries.

10 On the overlapping of both revolutions in popular German writing see my essay "Crossing the Boundaries: The French Revolution in the German Literary Imagination."

11 *Minerva,* 1 (1792): 125–126 (my translation).

12 Even C. L. R. James's prorevolutionary history of the Haitian Revolution, *Black Jacobins,* includes a similar passage: "The slaves on the Gallifet plantation were so well treated that 'happy as the negroes of Gallifet' was a slave proverb. Yet by a phenomenon noticed in all revolutions it was they who led the way. Each slave-gang murdered its masters and burnt the plantation to the ground. . . . in a few days one-half of the famous North Plain was a flaming ruin. From Le Cap the whole horizon was a wall of fire. From this wall continually rose thick black volumes of smoke, through which came tongues of flames leaping to the eery sky. . . . The slaves destroyed tirelessly. . . . In the frenzy of the first encounters they killed all, yet they spared the priests whom they feared and all the surgeons who had been kind to them. They, whose women had undergone countless violations, violated all the women who fell into their hands, often on the bodies of their still bleeding husbands, fathers and brothers. 'Vengeance! Vengeance!' was their war-cry, and one of them carried a white child on a pike as a standard" (*Black Jacobins: Toussaint l'Ouverture and the San Domingo Revolution,* 87–88). As James is quick to point out, though, the atrocities committed by the black revolutionaries must be seen in the context of systematic repression and torture perpetrated against blacks in hundreds of years of slavery.

13 J. W. L. Gleim, "Die Fabel von zehn Tigern," *Minerva* (April 1795): 179.

14 Louis Dubroca, "Geschichte der Neger-Empörung auf St. Domingo unter der Anführung von Toussaint-Louverture und Jean Jacques Dessalines," *Minerva* 53 (1805), 1: 434–464 and 2: 71–158. On women's actual participation during the revolution see Bellegarde-Smith, *Haiti: The Breached Citadel*, 26. A revision of that negative picture is undertaken in *Minerva* 53 (1805), 4: 276–298 and 392–408, in Marcus Rainsford's account of Toussaint l'Ouverture. As the editor, Archenholz, writes: "The Negroes, whom we have hitherto considered exclusively as monsters, appear in a very different light here."

15 *Theatralische Sammlung*, vol. 35 (Vienna, 1792). I have quoted from this edition in the text.

16 In *Briefe zur Beförderung der Humanität*, 233–248. I have quoted from this edition in the text.

17 In *Sämmtliche Werke*, vol. 6 (Leipzig: n.p., 1828). All page numbers in parentheses refer to this edition.

18 I quoted from the English translation by David Luke and Nigel Reeves in *The Marquise of O- and Other Stories* (1978; Penguin, 1983), 231–269.

19 In *Theodor Körner's sämmtliche Werke*, ed. Karl Streckfuss (Berlin: Nicolai, 1838), 2: 9–68.

20 In *Kleine Erzählungen und romantische Skizzen*, ed. Anita Runge (Hildesheim: Olms, 1988), 27–73.

21 Lawrence Marsden Price, *Inkle and Yarico Album*, 86. For a discussion of the coupling of Indian and black in the imagination of German/European abolitionists, see Sander Gilman, *On Blackness without Blacks*, 35ff.

22 It was released in book form in England in 1796, translated twice into German in 1797, and abridged and edited "für die Jugend" in 1799. All page references are from the 1790 facsimile edition, reprinted by the Johns Hopkins University Press in 1988.

23 Gilman, *On Blackness*, 47. While allowed and much practiced during the earlier colonial days in Saint-Domingue, miscegenation became prohibited in the latter part of the eighteenth century. See Bellegarde-Smith, *Haiti: The Breached Citadel*, 37.

24 Gilman's wholesale characterization of the enlightened German audience as racist although abolitionist ("Rathelf's German audience would not have allowed a miscegenous relationship. But this same white, enlightened society would also not permit the existence of slavery in Germany," 47) does not hold in view of texts such as August Lafontaine's satire on Christoph Meiners, "Leben und Thaten des Freiherrn Quinctius Heymeran von Flaming" (Berlin: Voss, 1795–1796), in which Iglou, an African slave, makes Quinctius love and marry her; or C. C. Dussel's *Merkwürdige Reise der Gutmannschen Familie. Ein Weihnachtsgeschenk für die Jugend* (1795), in which the perfect German daughter Emilie falls in love with and marries the young ruler of Dahomey. "Happy" marriage/miscegenation was apparently imaginable in literature and acceptable to the readers, although the opposite was probably more frequent — as in all Romeo and Juliet rewrites.

25 "If we have to fall, if these moments are our last, let me die as your wife, let us say our vows as man and woman right here, before the eyes of the heavens! Let God be my witness, I am this noble man's wife, and even if the day of our union be the worst of all days, I am happy in his arms."

26 As Stedman informs us, sexual relationships between white women and their black slaves, or even freed blacks, were considered illegal and severely punished in Surinam.

27 Governor: "[T]he subject itself is not so new" (63). Omar's frequent allusions to the "Sun" as his goddess, his mother (34), can also be read within an Enlightenment context.

28 Döhner is borrowing from abbé Raynal. In his essay on the conditions of Saint-Domingue, Raynal had advocated a "humanization" of the treatment of slaves so that public and domestic government abide by the same rules (*Uebersicht der politischen Lage und des Handelszustandes von St. Domingo* [Leipzig: Haug, 1788], 117).

29 "Es ist nicht die weisse Farbe, was Euch empört—unsere Vorältern hielten sie einst für die Farbe der Götter—sondern die harte, grausame Art, womit einige von Ihnen die Unsern behandeln; nicht Alle, oder ist einer von des braven Fleris Sklaven unter euch, einer von einem deutschen Pflanzer! Keiner, und doch hetzt, und führt er [der Anführer] euch zum allgemeinen Mord, zur allgemeinen Zerstörung" (41). Unless otherwise noted, all translations of the texts in this chapter are mine.

30 "Unser Herr ist unser Vater! Wären alle Kolonisten wie Sie, edler Mann, entweder wäre der Aufruhr gar nicht, in so fern ich sie mir als Folge schrecklicher Behandlung denke, oder fremder Politik sollte es sehr schwer, wo nicht unmöglich geworden seyn, zufriedne Menschen zu empören" (23).

31 "Ja, Freyheit heisst die Binde vors Aug des Pöbels, der Dolch ins Herz des Vaterlandes-die Maske für Privat-Absicht und Eigennutz—ihr grässliches Gebrüll wird erstaunen vor Schrecken, wenn die Binde vom Aug fällt und sie sich sehn im Abgrund, in den man sie hineinstürzte" (58).

32 Kolb's remarks come close to Edward Long's infamous characterizations of blacks in *The History of Jamaica* (1774, esp. 2: 353) or to Christoph Meiners's. As proof to his "impartiality," however, Kolb includes an attack on Meiners's position on slave trade in an open letter by a certain Mr. Becker from Gotha, 224ff.

33 Kolb's text exhibits the same fascination with the supposedly naturally passionate disposition among people of color that Kotzebue's *Virgin of the Sun* and Döhner's play alluded to. In all three instances, the marriage is either consummated or staged "spontaneously," with only the sun/God as witness.

34 "Da trat/Ein Mann vor uns mit Blute nicht befleckt, / Und Güte sprach in seinen Zügen, die / Im Augenblick mit Zorn und Trauer, Wut / und Wehmut wechselten."

35 In fact, Kotzebue combines two of Kolb's stories, "Zimeo" and "Tragische Liebe zweyer Neger" (38–40).

36 In Gotthold Ephraim Lessing's "bourgeois tragedy" *Emilia Galotti* (1776), the

conflict between the "bourgeois" family of Odoardo Galotti and the prince is carried out over the "body" of Emilia, the pawn in this class struggle. In order to keep the prince from seducing Emilia by all possible means, father Odoardo stabs his daughter to death.

37 Most German slave dramas of the eighteenth century argue the same point. See Beverly Harris-Schenk, "Der Sklave: ein Bild des Schwarzen in der deutschen Literatur des 18. Jahrhunderts," *Akten des VI. Internationalen Germanisten-Kongresses,* ed. Heinz Rupp and Hans-Gert Roloff (Berne: Lang, 1980).

38 Harris-Schenk, "Der Sklave: ein Bild des Schwarzen," 36.

39 "Du hast mich frey gelassen, und ich bin dein Sklave auf ewig; mit gebundenen Armen hätte ich entlaufen können, aber du fesseltest mein Herz — ich weiche nimmer von dir!"

40 "Der Neger bedarf so wenig zur Freude. Gebt ihm einen Dudelsack und ein Glas unverfälschten Rhum, so arbeitet er Wochenlang ohne Murren. Das wusste Euer guter Vater wohl."

41 John: "Machen es denn die übrigen Nationen besser als wir Engländer?" William: "Leider nein! Der Spanier macht aus den Negern Gefährten seiner Faulheit; der Portugiese missbraucht sie zu seinen Ausschweifungen, der Holländer zu Schlachtopfern seines Geizes. Der Franzose beugt sie unter schwere Arbeiten, und versagt ihnen oft das Nothdürftige; aber er lacht doch zuweilen mit ihnen, und ihr Elend ist erträglicher. Der Engländer lächelt nie, lässt sich nie zu ihnen herab — "

42 See also Sigrid Weigel, "Der Körper am Kreuzpunkt von Liebesgeschichte und Rassendiskurs in Heinrich von Kleists Erzählung 'Die Verlobung in St. Domingo,'" *Kleist Jahrbuch* (1991): 186–201; Hans Jakob Werlen, "Seduction and Betrayal: Race and Gender in Kleist's 'Die Verlobung in St. Domingo,'" *Monatshefte* 84, no. 4 (Winter 1992): 459–471. Both papers, which were written simultaneously with this chapter, intersect in significant ways with my basic points.

43 "Congo Hoango war, bei dem allgemeinen Taumel der Rache, der auf die unbesonnenen Schritte des National-Konvents in diesen Pflanzungen auflodderte, einer der ersten, der die Büchse ergriff, und eingedenk der Tyrannei, die ihn seinem Vaterlande entrissen hatte, seinem Herrn eine Kugel durch den Kopf jagte. Er steckte das Haus, worein die Gemahlin desselben mit ihren drei Kindern und den übrigen Weissen der Niederlassung sich geflüchtet hatte, in Brand, verwüstete die ganze Pflanzung, worauf die Erben, die in Port au Prince wohnten, hätten Anspruch machen können, und zog, als sämtliche zur Besitzung gehörige Etablissements der Erde gleichgemacht waren, mit den Negern, die er versammelt und bewaffnet hatte, in der Nachbarschaft umher, um seinen Mitbrüdern in dem Kampfe gegen die Weissen beizustehen." *Erzählungen, DTV-Gesamtausgabe* (München: dtv, 1964), 126 (I have used the translation by David Luke and Nigel Reeves).

44 See Weigel, "Der Körper am Kreuzpunkt," 197.

45 I agree in principle with Ruth (Angress) Klüger's and Bernd Fischer's distinction

between Kleist and the narrator. A close reading of the text, of reactions by text-immanent "readers" and information provided in subordinate clauses reveals a very different perspective from the one Gustav holds, whose moral blindness causes the final disaster. See Ruth Angress, "Kleist's Treatment of Imperialism: 'Die Hermannsschlacht' and 'Die Verlobung in St. Domingo,'" *Monatshefte* 69 (1977): 17–33; Bernd Fischer, "Zur politischen Dimension der Ethik in Kleists 'Die Verlobung in St. Domingo,'" in *Heinrich von Kleist. Studien zu Werk und Wirkung,* ed. Dirk Grathoff (Opladen: Westdeutscher Verlag, 1988), 248–262. More recent discussions of the text agree with this premise, too. See Ray Fleming, "Race and the Difference It Makes in Kleist's 'Die Verlobung in St. Domingo,'" *German Quarterly* 65, nos. 3–4 (Summer/Fall 1992): 306–317; Roswitha Burwick, "Issues of Language and Communication: Kleist's 'Die Verlobung in St. Domingo,'" *German Quarterly* 65, nos. 3–4 (Summer/Fall 1992): 318–327.

46 "Toni fragte: wodurch sich denn die Weissen daselbst so verhasst gemacht hätten?-Der Fremde erwiderte betroffen: durch das allgemeine Verhältnis, das sie, als Herren der Insel, zu den Schwarzen hatten" (155).

47 "Der Wahnsinn der Freiheit, der alle diese Pflanzungen ergriffen hat, trieb die Negern und Kreolen, die Ketten, die sie drückten, zu brechen, und an den Weissen wegen vielfacher und tadelnswürdiger Misshandlungen, die sie von einigen schlechten Mitgliedern derselben erlitten, Rache zu nehmen" (155).

48 " . . . dass nach dem Gefühl seiner Seele, keine Tyrannei, die die Weissen je verübt, einen Verrat, so niederträchtig und abscheulich, rechtfertigen könnte" (156).

49 " . . . dass sie ja in diesem Falle ein vornehmes und reiches Mädchen wäre" (154).

50 On Kleist's ambivalent political views but his unrelenting "realism" when it comes to exposing structures of thought and discourse, see Bernd Fischer's summary remarks, "Zur politischen Dimension," 318. I am, however, skeptical as to his statement that "love" is the ideal in *The Betrothal,* in opposition to the hatred Kleist exposed in his later works.

51 Gustav's/Körner's racism is obvious, e.g., when Gustav says that he had expected Toni to have a "black heart" to match her skin, but is relieved to find her to be the "color of his people" (20).

52 Werlen, "Seduction and Betrayal," 469. The "monumental lie," namely the dehistoricization and depoliticization that Gustav's and Toni's story experiences in the memory of the Strömlis, is, I would argue, not Kleist's conclusion, but the Strömlis' — the colonizers who, because of their nationality and paternal kindness, believe they can remain outside the repressive slave system. They preserve the lie until the end and transform it into symbolic discourse.

53 *Doch was Ein Bube grausam hier verbrach,*
    Warum es rächen an dem ganzen Volk?
    Warum schuldloser Menschen Blut verspritzen,
    Weil sie nicht schwarz, wie eure Brüder sind;

> *Weil ihre Sonne güt'ger sie bedachte,*
> *Und klar die Farbe ihres mildern Tags*
> *Aus ihren weissen Zügen leuchtet?* (12)

54   *Der Männer blut'gen Grimm will ich verzeihen,*
> *Doch eines Weibes mörderische List*
> *Hat Gott verworfen als die höchste Schandthat.* (13)

55   As Babeckan had recognized: "Her heart is tied to her father's people" (29, my translation).

56   In Babeckan's words, "prepared quick poison in this milk / Five other jugs I'll send to the woods / And thus construct the house of freedom / And earn for me the citizen's crown" (44, my translation).

57   The association with Simon Bolívar, a Europe-educated Venezuelan, is not as far-fetched as it may seem if one remembers that Bolívar secured arms and supplies from Haiti, after promising Pétion to promote slave emancipation in South America. Bolívar offered those slaves freedom who were willing to fight on the side of the anticolonialists.

Part IV   Virgin Islands, Teuton Conquerors

1   "Ich verschaffte mir Campes Entdeckung von Amerika; ich las sie mit grossem Interesse und nicht ohne mannigfache Belehrung, auch wusste sich meine Phantasie die sonnenbeglänzten Landschaften der bis dahin in jungfräulicher Verborgenheit gelegenen Inseln sehr wohl vorzustellen."

2   *Noch war die Welt nicht ganz vertheilt!*
> *Noch manche Flur auf Erden*
> *Harrt gleich der Braut: die Hochzeit eilt!*
> *Des Starken will sie werden.*
> *Noch manches Eiland lockt und lauscht*
> *Aus Palmen und Bananen:*
> *Der Seewind braust, die Woge rauscht,*
> *Auf, freudige Germanen!*

3   G. W. F. Hegel, *Die Vernunft in der Geschichte,* 5th ed., 198ff. All references in the text refer to this edition. As Antonello Gerbi asserts, "the ambiguity in the word 'new' had never been used with greater shrewdness and abandon" (*The Dispute of the New World: The History of a Polemic, 1750–1900* [1955; rev. and enl. ed. Pittsburgh: University of Pittsburgh Press, 1973], 425).

4   Martín Fernández de Navarrete, *Die Reisen des Christof Columbus, 1492–1504. Nach seinen eigenen Briefen und Berichten veröffentlicht 1536 von Bischof Las Casas, seinem Freunde, und Fernando Columbus, seinem Sohne. Aufgefunden 1791 und veröffentlicht 1826 von Don M. F. von Navarette,* tr. Fr. Pr. (Leipzig: Hinrichs, 1826–1890). The information given in the German title is not quite correct, since Navarrete discovered the documents in 1790 in the library of the Duque del Infantado and published them in 1825.

5   *Die Geschichte des Lebens und der Reisen Christoph's Columbus,* tr. P. A. G. von Meyer (Frankfurt am Main: Sauerländer, 1828–1829). *Reisen der Ge-*

fährten des Columbus, tr. D. A. G. von Meyer (Frankfurt am Main: Sauerländer, 1831).

6   Irving had access to the collection in manuscript form and discussed his project with Navarrete himself. He also used the library holdings of the U.S. Consul in Madrid, the Jesuit College of San Isidro, the Royal Library, and the Duque de Veragua. Furthermore he had access to the papers of Juan Bautista Muñoz, whose 1793 *Historia del Nuevo Mundo* (German ed. tr. M. C. Sprengel, *Don Juan Baptista Muñoz' Geschichte der Neuen Welt* [Weimar: Landes-Industrie-Comptoir, 1795]) had already taken Columbus's log into consideration, but who had died before he could finish the work.

9   The German Columbus

1   *Muthig, mit kühnem Vertrau'n durchschiffte Columbus die Fluthen,*
Schaute mit trunkenem Aug' auf zu den Sternen der Nacht.
Doch nur dem leiblichen Blick erschloss er die Pforten des Weltmeers,
Schätze gewann er, ach! nur irdisch verderbliches Gold.
Siehe! da fährt durch Okeanos Reich ein zweiter Entdecker,
Humboldt! dem geistigen Blick hast Du erschlossen die Welt.
Schätze hobst Du herauf aus tieffstem Schacht der Erkenntniss,
Dass wir der Wissenschaft heiligen Hunger gestillt.
Seelen nicht losgekauft hast Du aus ewigem Feuer,
Aber die Geister befreit aus dem Gefängniss des Wahns. (Tr. Walter Arndt)

2   Mary Louise Pratt, *Imperial Eyes: Travel Writing and Transculturation,* 120.

3   See for example his *Essai politique sur le royaume de la Nouvelle-Espagne* (Paris, 1811), or his *Essai politique sur l'île de Cuba* (Paris, 1828).

4   Gerbi, *The Dispute of the New World,* 411ff.

5   Ibid., 408.

6   (Leipzig: Spamer, 1851). All quotations in the texts refer to this edition; all translations of this text are mine.

7   *Alexander von Humboldt's Leben und Wirken, Reisen und Wissen. Ein biographisches Denkmal von Dr. Herm. Klencke,* 7th ed. (Leipzig: Spamer, 1876), 486.

8   Editorial in *Deutsche Kolonialzeitung* 19 (1886): 553–554.

9   *Examen critique de l'histoire de la géographie du Nouveau Continent et des progrès de l'astronomie nautique au 15e et 16e siècles* (Paris: Gide, 1837), 3: 154: "Si le caractère d'un siècle est 'la manifestation de l'esprit humain dans un temps donné,' le siècle de Colomb, tout en étendant inopinément la sphère des connaissances, a imprimé un nouvel essor aux siècles futurs. C'est le propre des découvertes qui touchent à l'ensemble des intérêts de la société, que d'agrandir à la fois le cercle des conquêtes et le terrain à conquérir. Des esprits faibles croient à chaque époque l'humanité arrivée au point culminant de sa marche progressive; ils oublient que, par l'enchaînement intime de toutes les vérités, à mesure que l'on avance, le champ à parcourir se présente plus vaste, borné par un horizon qui recule sans cesse" (my translation).

10 See Ernst Wetzel, *Der Kolumbus-Stoff im deutschen Geistesleben* (Breslau: Priebatsch, 1935), who lists some twenty-eight Columbus texts, mostly plays, that appeared in the nineteenth century alone, not to mention the many travel narratives by Sealsfield, Gerstäcker, and Karl May or the innumerable Robinson Crusoe takeoffs mentioned in chapter 6.

10   The Second Discovery

1   *Steure muthiger Segler! Es mag der Witz dich verhöhnen,*
    Und der Schiffer am Steur senken die lässige Hand.
    Immer, immer nach West! Dort muss *die Küste sich zeigen,*
    Liegt sie doch deutlich und schimmernd vor deinem Verstand.
    Traue dem leitenden Gott, und folge dem schweigenden Weltmeer,
    Wär' sie noch nicht, sie stieg' jetzt aus den Fluten empor,
    Mit dem Genius *steht die* Natur *in ewigem Bunde,*
    Was der Eine verspricht, leistet die andre gewiss.
    (All translations in this chapter are by W. Arndt.)

2   "Columbus. Ein dramatisches Gedicht," in *August Klingemann's dramatische Werke* (Wien: Grund, 1820), 5: 124–432. All references in the text refer to this edition.

3   Karl Werder, *Columbus*, ed. Otto Gildmeister, after the second version of 1858 (Berlin: Fontane, 1893). Friedrich Rückert, "Cristofero Colombo oder die Entdeckung der Neuen Welt. Geschichtsdrama in drei Theilen," in *Poetische Werke*, vol. 10 (Frankfurt am Main: Sauerländer, 1882).

4   Karl Weickum, *Columbus. Dramatisches Gemälde in 5 Acten aus der Geschichte der Entdeckung Amerikas* (1873; 2nd rev. ed., Freiburg: Herder, 1893); or Rudolf Cronau, *Amerika. Die Geschichte seiner Entdeckung von der ältesten bis auf die neueste Zeit. Eine Festschrift zur 400jährigen Jubelfeier der Entdeckung Amerikas durch Christoph Columbus*, 2 vols. (Leipzig: Abel & Müller, 1892); Sophus Ruge, *Columbus*, 2nd ed. (Berlin: Hofmann, 1902).

5   See *Allgemeine Deutsche Bibliographie*, 16: 187–189. The entry emphasizes Klingemann's reputation in his own times: he was considered a "rival to Schiller" and was particularly successful with his plays *Martin Luther, Moses, Cromwell, Faust, Cortez,* and *Columbus*, which reveal his penchant for heroic "founding fathers."

6   "Noch schallet mir der Fluch des Sterbenden! O bin ich stark genug ihn abzuwenden / Von diesen Ländern? (Einen Entschluss fassend). Nun wohlan, es sey! Mit Kühnheit will ich denn mein Werk beginnen; Und wenn die Nachwelt diesen Zeitpunct richtet, So richte sie mich *selbst*, und nicht mein Schicksal!" (431)

7   In addition to Werder's and Rückert's play see Ludwig August Frankl, "Christoforo Colombo," in *Epische Gedichte* (Wien and Leipzig: Hartleben, 1880), 2: 99–155. Milo's play is summed up by Ernst Wetzel *Der Kolumbus-Stoff im deutsches Geistesleben*, 18–20; I could not locate a copy of the play.

8   See Wetzel, *Der Kolumbus-Stoff*, 20. Wetzel's division into "classic" and "Romantic" interpretations under the influence of Irving, and post-Romantic "realism" under the impact of Humboldt's scientific works, seems untenable, since both Irving's and Humboldt's works were published simultaneously.

9   *"Ja, und nicht durch Waffen oder*
Politische Klugheit, sondern durch die Künste
Des Friedens; durch die Weisheit einer
Academie, durch eines Fürsten Forschergeist,
Der es verstand, dem Aberglauben und
Dem Zweifel Königreiche abzuringen;
Der sich den Ocean zum Gegner nahm,
Ihm *Krieg erklärend um sein Kleinod Indien."* . . .
     "Wir leben in bedeutsamer Epoche.
Des Wissens Aufgab', umfangreicher nur
Wird sie mit jedem Fortschritt. Der Gesichtskreis,
Erweitert, rückt in immer breitere Ferne."

10   "Hab' ich doch verkauft, Was menschlich Antlitz trägt und was geformt / Nach deinem Bild, wie ich? . . . Ich wollt's ja nicht" (132).

11   *Was von Künsten ich erraffen konnte, was von Wissenschaft,*
Schien mir zu verborgnen Zwecken zu verleihn geheime Kraft.
Von den schönen Künsten lernt' ich allererst den Schreibestift
Kunstreich führen, dann des Malens und des Zeichnens Bilderschrift.
Meine Handschrift übt' und schmückt' ich, um mit schönster Züge Wahl
Ein Diplom mir selbst zu schreiben als des Weltmeers Admiral.
Künftig auch an hohe Häupter wollt' ich Brief' in hohem Styl
Mit Berichterstattung schreiben an der Welteroberung Ziel.
Aber Mal- und Zeichenkunst trieb dazu einzig meine Hand,
Auf Landkarten zu verzeichnen jedes unentdeckte Land;
Und mehr als der landerfüllte, war der leere Raum mir lieb,
Wo mir nach soviel Entdecktem mehr noch zu entdecken blieb.

12   "Ja, solchem Glauben wird nichts abgeschlagen; Wenn, was er glaubt, nicht wäre, würd es nun: Ja, wäre nicht die neue Welt vorhanden, Durch deinen Glauben wäre sie entstanden" (313).

13   "Wie kam's, dass Unheil meine Hände schufen, Wo Heil zu schaffen schien mein Geist berufen" (549).

14   "Sind sie wohl der Schöpfung Blume, deren dunkle Blätter wir?" (430).

15   De Pauw's condemnation of the "beardless savages" is also echoed by Sebastian, supposedly the most tolerant and open-minded of all Spaniards who accompany Colombo: "diese(r) von Natur versäumten, Missfarbigen, bartlosen Angesichter" (516).

16   "Muss sich nicht der Macht des Himmels unterwerfen Meer und Land. Deine nackten Krieger halten nicht vor ihren Waffen Stand. . . . Erkennt' ich ihren Vorzug vor den unsern, Und ihre Ueberlegenheit ob uns: . . . Dass diese Fremdling' einer andern Welt / Berufen sind, in unserer zu herrschen."

17 Isabella: *Frei über der Zerstörung Graus*
Erhebe deinen Blick!
In goldn'e Zukunft sieh hinaus,
Sieh deiner Welt Geschick!
America, von Blut gedüngt,
Europa blüht daselbst verjüngt.
Die wilden Stämme welken hin
Wie dein Pimentobaum,
Dem keine Pflege bringt Gewinn;
Für neu Gewächs wird Raum:
Sieh, freie Staaten wachsen da
Im blühenden America!
Anacaona: *Lass nicht betrüben deinen Sinn,*
Was du von ihr gehört!
Ich bin des Stammes Königin,
Der jetzo wird zerstört
Wie der Pimentobaum unbeklagt,
Weil er sich der Cultur versagt;
Doch sah' ich: eine Wurzel bleibt
Von dem Pimentobaum,
Der wieder seine Sprossen treibt
und füllet seinen Raum;
Zu Ehren wird dein Name da
Einst kommen in Colombia. (647)

18 The references to the "Pimentobaum" possibly allude to the tree of liberty referred to by Toussaint l'Ouverture upon his capture. According to Pamphile de Lacroix, upon boarding the ship that would take him to captivity, Toussaint l'Ouverture said: "By toppling me, they only felled the trunk of the blacks' liberty tree; its roots will burgeon again, though, because they are deep and many." *Mémoires pour servir à l'histoire de la révolution de Saint-Domingue* (Paris, 1819), 2: 203.

19 Hermann Theodor von Schmid, *Columbus. Trauerspiel in fünf Aufzügen* (1857; 2nd ed. Leipzig: Weber, 1875). Karl Kösting, *Columbus. Ein historisches Trauerspiel* (Wiesbaden: Niedner, 1863).

20 Schmid, *Columbus,* 126.

21 Karl Kösting (1842–1907), son of an official at the ducal court of Wiesbaden, wrote his play during a half-year stay in Stuttgart in 1862. Inaugurated on March 7, 1963, the play was surprisingly successful. It was adopted by several German stages and witnessed a second edition that same year. Kösting spent several years of study in Berlin, then lived in complete seclusion in Wiesbaden, Frankfurt, and Dresden, working as a free-lance playwright. His plays are completely forgotten today.

22 *Was hat mich mit geheimer Sympathie*
Allmächtig zu Columbus hingezogen,

Dass ich ihm freudig meine Seele lieh,
An der er lang und inniglich gesogen? —
Mein deutsches Volk, Volk ohne Gegenwart,
Dem nur sein Selbst und seine Zukunft eigen,
Das, flehend wandelnd durch den Völkerreigen,
Verkannt, geschmäht, auf die Erlaubniss harrt,
die Welt, die es im Geist trägt, zu gebären,
Sich selbst und seinen Kindern zu gehören,
Erkenne dich in dieses Dulders Bild!
Der, so wie du, der Menschheit Kampf gerungen,
Und, was sein Herz mit Siegesmuth erfüllt,
In zähem Streit dem Schicksal abgedrungen,
Den Eigennutz zu schnödem Dienst gezwungen,
Und der sein Sehnen spät und ganz gestillt.
O trinke Muth aus seinem muthgen Ringen,
Begeisterung aus seiner Siegerruh,
Verachte deiner Feinde feige Schlingen
Und steure furchtlos deinem Ziele zu!
Dein Schiller sang's mit heiligen Gewalten:
'Im Bund steht mit dem Genius die Natur,
Was er verspricht, das wird von ihr gehalten!'
Verfolge muthig deines Weges Spur!
Dein Indien, deine deutsche Freiheit suchend,
Durchsegle kühn den Zeitenocean,
Der Menschenfreiheit ewig grüne Jugend
Winkt, ein Amerika, am Ende deiner Bahn. (xi, xii)

23   " . . . an der er lang und inniglich gesogen" — the English translation could not
reproduce this image of Columbus "intimately and for a long time suckling the
poet's soul."

24   Perez: "Das Kind das Euer Geist gebar, Columbus, Müsst Ihr erziehen." Ferdinand: "Geboren habt Ihr, und mit Klang und Jubel / Ward die Geburt gefeiert"
(79).

25   *Ihr habt des Lebens Rose nur gesehn,*
Ich ihren Duft geathmet. Denn das Weib,
O Perez, ist des Lebens Duft, der Schatten
Des heissen Lebenstags, der goldne Hauch,
Der weich und warm des Manns zerklüftet Wesen
Wie Abendroth umfliesst. Wir Männer können
Verwunden nur, ihr sanftes Amt ist heilen (139).

26   *In Menschenherzen*
Wird sein Gedächtniss leben, ein Columbus
Wird Jeder heissen, der, wie er, ein Land
Dem Menschengeist entdeckt und neue Bahnen
Zum Freiheitstempel bricht. Einst kommt die Zeit,

Du bist dess Bürge, wo ein frei Geschlecht,
Dem finstern Bann des Formelzwangs entwachsen,
Zu dir und deinen Geistesbrüdern dankbar
Zurückwallfahrtet, eure Bilder kränzt
Und eure Feste triumphirend feiert,
Wohlthäter ihr der Menschheit!
Es werden Dichter eure Thaten singen,
Und manch erwachend Volk wird hoffend lauschen
Und stolz in seinem Pulsschlag euren fühlen. (157–158)

11   Colonial Fantasies Revisited

1   Another example is Heinrich Bulthaupt's play *Eine neue Welt* (Oldenburg, 1885), in which a Ludwig Beheim, who accompanies Columbus, occupies center stage. In his drive for new horizons, the proto-Protestant German Beheim, man of the future, displaces Columbus who is associated with Spanish cruelty, superstition, and the fanaticism of the Inquisition. See Ernst Wetzel, *Der Kolumbus-Stoff im deutschen Geistesleben,* 46–48.

2   G. A. Riecke, "Vorwort. An die deutsche Jugend!" In *Christoph Columbus, der Entdecker Amerikas. Ein Lesebuch für die männliche Jugend,* rev. ed. (Stuttgart: Ullrich, 1873), iv. In his concluding remarks, Riecke joins Humboldt in scolding the Spaniards and Italians for not appreciating Columbus's achievements (408). (All translations in this chapter, unless otherwise noted, are mine.)

3   See, for example, Rudolf Cronau, *Amerika. Die Geschichte seiner Entdeckung von der ältesten bis auf die neueste Zeit . . .* , 2 vols. (Leipzig: Abel and Müller, 1892), 1: 313, 314, 321; or Sophus Ruge, *Columbus,* 2nd ed. (Berlin: Hoffmann, 1902), 2.

4   See C. Herb, "Die Aussichten neuer Unternehmungen im tropischen Südamerika," *Beiträge zur Kolonialpolitik und Kolonialwirtschaft* 4 (1901–1902): 330, who designates the Germans the "successors" of the Spanish in South America. The conquest of a "German India" is advocated by A. Fick, "Ist die Welt vergeben?" *Deutsche Kolonialzeitung* 1 (1884): 77. While Fick apparently refers to India proper, the association with Columbus retains the term's ambiguity.

5   For the following see Woodruff Smith, *The German Colonial Empire* (Chapel Hill: University of North Carolina Press, 1978), 7ff.

6   Eugen von Philippovich at the annual meeting of the Deutscher Kolonialverein, in *Deutsche Kolonialzeitung* 4 (1887): 339.

7   Ibid.

8   For the controversy between a traditional, middle-class settlement colonialism and a more industry- and capital-oriented economic colonialism see Smith, *The German Colonial Empire,* 22f.

9   See, for example, C. Herb, "Die Aussichten neuer Unternehmungen," 330, where it is pointed out that "the(se) territories had to start from scratch again, as it were, but without the necessary support from Nature, whose virgin abun-

dance had already been destroyed"; see also the complaint in *Deutsche Kolonialzeitung* 2 (1885): 143, that "the earth in actual fact proves nothing like as rich as the never-ending panegyrics to the inexhaustible wealth of Brazil's virgin soil have sought to make the World believe."

10   A. Geffcken, "Die Auswanderungs- und Kolonisationsfrage," *Deutsche Kolonialzeitung* 1 (1884): 69–72. A. Fick, "Ist die Welt vergeben?" *Deutsche Kolonialzeitung* 1 (1884): 51–56, 75–80.

11   The idea that Germans are superior colonizers crops up everywhere: they are of superior racial quality; they are more respected by native governments; they are cleaner and more hardworking (H. C. Nebel, "New Germany," *Beiträge zur Kolonialpolitik und Kolonialwirtschaft* 1 [1899–1900]: 99–103); they have greater organizational talents, patience, and courage (H. Hübbe-Schleiden, "Deutsche Welt-Hegemonie," *Deutsche Kolonialzeitung* 8 [April 1980], n.p.).

12   Friedrich Ratzel, "Roscher's 'Kolonien, Kolonialpolitik und Auswanderung' in dritter Auflage," *Deutsche Kolonialzeitung* 2 (1885): 20.

13   Timotheus Fabri, "Unsere Überproduktion an geistiger Arbeitskraft und praktische Kolonisation," *Deutsche Kolonialzeitung*, Neue Folge 1, no. 24 (June 1888): 1.

14   See, for example, H. Faulhaber, "Deutschtum in Südbrasilien," *Beiträge zur Kolonialpolitik und Kolonialwirtschaft* 1 (1899–1900): 437–438. Faulhaber speaks of *Eingeborene*, natives, but means the "Romanic race," the good sides of which the German race absorbed and improved upon. Prof. Eggert, the manager of the Kolonialverein, in his annual address, advocates the acquisition of settlements in South America, since "the native" is so far removed from the German that miscegenation is not likely; Germans will remain "pure." *Deutsche Kolonialzeitung* 3 (1886): 300. Heinrich von Treitschke speaks of absorption of "inferior stock." *Politics*, tr. Blanche Dugdale and Torben de Bille (New York: Macmillan, 1916), 1: 121.

15   "Program," *Deutsche Kolonialzeitung* 1 (1884).

16   While the term "intercourse" is used by most contemporary translators, it does not have the same sexual connotations as in its modern usage. However, the metaphors describing this colonial relationship do.

17   Wilhelm Georg Roscher, *Kolonien, Kolonialpolitik und Auswanderung*, 2nd ed. (Leipzig: Winter, 1856), 75. Roscher develops what he considers a "Naturlehre der Kolonien," a natural science of colonialism (3).

18   Treitschke, *Politics*, 115–116.

19   Ibid., 113.

20   Treitschke, "First Attempts at German Colonization," in *Treitschke: His Doctrine of German Destiny and of International Relations*, tr. Adolf Hausrath (New York: Putnam's, 1914), 196.

21   Treitschke, *Politics*, 113, 114.

22   The purely German nature of the new colonies is stressed in all descriptions by German travelers that appear in the *Koloniale Beiträge* and the *Kolonialzeitung*. See for example von Berlepsch, "Deutsche Kolonien und koloniale Bestrebungen in Paraguay, Rio Grande do Sul und S. Paulo," *Deutsche Kolo-*

nialzeitung 3 (1886): 274. They continue a tradition started by Friedrich Gerstäcker, who visited German colonies and wrote about them in the 1860s and 70s. See *Achtzehn Monate in Süd-Amerika und dessen deutschen Colonien* (Leipzig: Costenoble, 1863) and *Die Colonie. Brasilianisches Lebensbild*, 4th ed. (Jena: Costenoble, n.d.).

23 Deutscher Kolonialverein, "Zur Jahreswende," *Kolonialzeitung* 3 (1886); I. R. Sernau, "Zur Frage der Auswanderung," *Kolonialzeitung* 3 (1886): 133–134. Eggert, address at the annual convention, *Kolonialzeitung* 3 (1886): 296.

24 Smith, *The German Colonial Empire*, 30.

25 Friedrich Fabri, "Koloniale Aufgaben," *Deutsche Kolonialzeitung* 2 (1885): 541, 542.

26 Richard Lesser, "Die Kolonialpolitik des Grossen Kurfürsten," *Deutsche Kolonialzeitung* 5 (1988): 199–200. The fantasy of the continuing loyalty of German-educated Africans forms part of the colonial legend until well into the twentieth century.

27 Heinrich Hübbe-Schleiden, "Deutsche Welt-Hegemonie." As a footnote indicates, even the editor(s) of the *Kolonialzeitung* seem to have had second thoughts about Hübbe-Schleiden's global claims: "The following thoughts by Dr. Hübbe-Schleiden will surprise some of our readers and provoke their criticism."

28 Treitschke, *Politics*, 120. As Treitschke knows, "youth has always been more radical than age, and here is the adequate explanation of the Democratic tendency in colonies" (115); or: "On the other hand these [agricultural colonies] are the colonies which are the most apt to turn against the parent State, and try to cut themselves loose from her" (116).

29 Walter Schatz, "Die Treue der Eingeborenen," in *Das koloniale Deutschtum. Ein Volkslesebuch*, ed. Gerhard Jacob (Bayreuth: Gauverlag Bayerische Ostmark, 1939), 73. See also Joachim Warmbold, *Germania in Africa: Germany's Colonial Literature* (New York: Peter Lang, 1989), 199ff.

30 Title of Luise Diel's book, *Die Kolonien warten. Afrika im Umbruch* (Leipzig, 1939).

31 Ibid., 100.

Epilogue

1 "Traulich und keineswegs ohne Grazie sass sie zu seinen Füssen, und als er sanft ihren roten Sammetrücken, wie die Herren vielleicht sich ausdrücken würden, mit lässiger Hand streichelte, dünkte er sich der Christofor Columbus zu sein, welchem sich der entdeckte Weltteil in Gestalt eines zarten Weibes anschmiegt" (Gottfried Keller, "Das Sinngedicht," *Sämtliche Werke*, ed. Jonas Fränkel [Bern: 1934], 11: 333; tr. W. Arndt; all subsequent quotes are taken from this edition).

2 "Nach der Heimath meiner Feinde, / Die Europa ist geheissen, / Will ich flüchten, dort beginn ich / Eine neue Carrière (*Historisch-kritische Gesamt-*

ausgabe der Werke, "Düsseldorfer Ausgabe," ed. Manfred Windfuhr [Hamburg: Hoffmann und Campe, 1992], 3, pt. 1: 75). All Heine translations in this chapter are from Hal Draper's *The Complete Poems of Heinrich Heine* (New York: Suhrkamp/Insel, 1982).

3   I am thinking here, above all, of the colonial novels and tales by Frieda von Bülow and Hans Grimm.

4   The quotes are taken from the cover of *Kolonie und Heimat* 8, no. 24 (1915) and from Wilhelm Wintzer, *Die Deutschen im tropischen Amerika* (1900), 48f.

5   Joachim Warmbold, *Germania in Africa: Germany's Colonial Literature,* 200. The quotes inside the quote are from H. S. Chamberlain, *Die Grundlagen des neunzehnten Jahrhunderts* (popular ed., 1906), and *Die Deutschen Kolonien. Jubiläumsausgabe zur vierzigjährigen Wiederkehr des Beginns der deutschen Kolonialgeschichte* (1924).

6   *People without a Space* [*Volk ohne Raum*] is the title of Hans Grimm's colonialist novel of 1928–1930. It became a slogan with Nazi ideologues who tried to justify Germany's expansionist politics with the nation's need for "more living space."

7   Heinrich Heine, "Vitzliputzli," 3, pt. 1, 56–75.

8   "Die Nordsee," *Heines Werke und Briefe in 10 Bänden,* ed. Hans Kaufmann (Berlin: Aufbau, 1961), 3: 112f.

9   E.g., "Über Polen," *Heines Werke,* 3: 569f; "Briefe aus Berlin," *Heines Werke,* 3: 504.

10   Joseph Kruse, "Heines Leihpraxis und Lektürebeschaffung," in *Die Leihbibliothek als Institution des literarischen Lebens im 18. und 19. Jahrhundert,* eds. Georg Jäger and Jörg Schönert (Hamburg: Hauswedell, 1980), 197–228.

11   This is also the main topos of Heine's epic poem, "Bimini" — the return to youth, to a state of innocence outside of history, can only be (re)created in and through the imagination.

12   "Dieses ist Amerika! / Dieses ist die Neue Welt! / Nicht die heutige, die schon / Europäisieret abwelkt" (56).

13   See, for example, in Juan Ginés Sepúlveda's "Apologia pro libro de justis belli causis" [*Tratado sobre las justas causas de la guerra contra los indios*] ([1550; 2nd ed. México: Fondo de Cultura Económica, 1941], 101).

14   Joachim Heinrich Campe, *Die Entdeckung von Amerika,* vol. 2, 118f.

15   " . . . ich bin jetzt dein und kann nicht anders, wie das Meer!"

16   While a real Don Correa supposedly stood as model, the associations between "correr," to run, to move, and Correa's movement between continents are all too obvious.

17   "Die französischen Militärs aber mochten den Tag nicht erwarten, ihre Neugierde und die Lust an den idealen Naturzuständen zu befriedigen; sie lockten schon vorher die wilden Rothäute über das Wasser."

18   "Wie würde das philosophische Paris erstaunen, dachte er sich, ihn mit diesem Inbegriff von Natur und Ursprünglichkeit am Arme zurückkehren und in die Salons treten zu sehen."

19   "Denke man sich also einen Komplex herrlich gewachsener riesiger Glieder vom sattesten Kupferrot und vom Kopf bis zu den Füssen mit gelben und blauen Streifen gezeichnet, auf jeder Brust zwei kolossale Hände mit ausgespreizten Fingern abgebildet, so hat man einen Vorschmack dessen, was noch kommt."

Bibliography

Sources

Albrecht, Johann Friedrich Ernst. "Die Kolonie. Schauspiel in 4 Aufzügen." *Die deutsche Schaubühne.* 1: 1–112. Augsburg, 1793.

Allgemeine deutsche Bibliothek. Berlin: Nicolai, 1763–1791 [*Neue allgemeine deutsche Bibliothek*, 1793–1806].

Allgemeine deutsche Biographie. Ed. Königliche Akademie der Wissenschaften. Leipzig: Duncker & Humblot, 1875–1912.

Allgemeine Literatur-Zeitung. Jena and Halle, 1785–1849.

Anson, Lord. *Des Admirals, Lord Ansons Reise um die Welt in den Jahren 1740, 41, 42, 43, 44.* Tr. Eobald Toeze. Leipzig: Vandenhoek, 1749.

Becher, Johann Joachim. *Politische[r] Discurs. Von den eigentlichen Ursachen des Auff- und Abnehmens der Stadt, Länder und Republicken. In Specie, wie ein Land volckreich und nahrhafft zu machen und in eine societatem civilem zu bringen.* 1668. 2nd ed. 1673; 3rd ed. 1688; rpt. of 3rd ed. Glashütten: Auvermann, 1972.

———. *Gründlicher Bericht von Beschaffenheit und Eigenschafft, Cultivirung und Bewohnung, Privilegien und Beneficien dess in America zwischen dem Rio Orinoque und Rio de las Amazones an der vest Kust in der Landschafft Guiana gelegenen . . . Landes . . .* Frankfurt am Main: Kuchenbecker, 1669.

Beiträge zur Kolonialpolitik und Kolonialwirtschaft. Ed. Deutsche Kolonialgesellschaft. Berlin: Süsserott, 1899–1903.

Berlepsch, Hans von. "Deutsche Kolonien und koloniale Bestrebungen in Paraguay, Rio Grande do Sul und S. Paulo." *Deutsche Kolonialzeitung* 4 (1887): 271–280.

Berlinische Monatsschrift. Ed. Friedrich Gedike and Johann Erich Biester. Berlin: Haude & Spener, 1783–1796. Continued as *Neue Berlinische Monatsschrift.* Ed. Johann E. Biester. Berlin: Nicolai, 1799–1811.

Bernoulli, Johann. *Johann Bernoullis Sammlung kurzer Reisebeschreibungen und anderer zur Erweiterung der Länder- und Menschenkenntniss dienender Nachrichten.* Berlin: Richter, 1781–1783.

Blanes, Henri. *Der Stutzer nach der Mode.* Paris: n.p., 1765.

Blumenbach, Johann Friedrich. "Einige zerstreute Bemerkungen über die Fähigkeiten und Sitten der Wilden." *Göttingisches Magazin* 6, no. 6 (1781): 409–425.

———. *On the Natural Variety of Mankind.* 1775 and 1795. Tr. Thomas Bendyshe.

London: Longman, 1865 [Original in Latin, 1771; German tr. *Über die natür lichen Verschiedenheiten im Menschengeschlechte*. Leipzig: Breitkopf and Härtel, 1798].

Bonneville, Zacharie de Pazzi de. *De l'Amérique et des Américains, ou Observations curieuses du Philosophe La Douceur, qui a parcouru cet hémisphere pendant la dernière guerre, en faisant le noble métier de tuer des hommes sans les manger.* Berlin: Pitra, 1771; new ed., 1772.

Borcke, Heinrich von. *Die brandenburgisch-preussische Marine und die Afrikanische Compagnie.* N.p., 1755; new ed., 1864.

Bouterwek, Friedrich. "Morgenlied eines Negersklaven aus seinem Kerker." *Musenalmanach* 32 (1788): 124–127.

Braunschweigische Anzeigen. Braunschweig: Meyer, 1745–present.

Buckley, Roger Norman, ed. *The Haitian Journal of Lieutenant Howard, York Hussars, 1796–1798.* Knoxville: University of Tennessee Press, 1985.

Buffon, Georges Louis Leclerc, comte de. *Herrn von Buffons allgemeine Naturgeschichte. Eine freye mit einigen Zusätzen vermehrte Übersetzung nach der neuesten französischen Ausgabe von 1769.* 7 vols. Tr. Heinrich Wilhelm Martini. Berlin: Pauli, 1771–1774.

Bulthaupt, Heinrich. *Eine neue Welt. Drama in 5 Akten.* Oldenburg: n.p., 1885.

Byron, John. *John Byrons, obersten Befehlshabers über ein Englisches Geschwader, Reise um die Welt, in den Jahren 1764 und 1765. Nebst einer genauen Beschreibung der Magellanischen Strasse, der Patagonischen Riesen, und der ganz neu-entdeckten Sieben Inseln in der Süd-See.* Frankfurt: Metzler, 1769.

Campe, Joachim Heinrich. *Briefe aus Paris zur Zeit der Revolution geschrieben.* Braunschweig: Schulbuchhandlung, 1790. Rpt., Hildesheim: Gerstenberg, 1977.

———. *Die Entdeckung von Amerika. Ein angenehmes und nützliches Lesebuch.* 3 vols. 1780–1781. 4th ed., Braunschweig: Schulbuchhandlung, 1791.

———. *Robinson der Jüngere. Ein Lesebuch für Kinder.* Hamburg: Commission Carl E. Bohn, 1779–1780. 8th ed., Reutlingen: Mäcken, 1820. 63rd authorized ed., Braunschweig: Vieweg, 1862. English edition: *The New Robinson Crusoe: An Instructive and Entertaining History. For the Use of Children of Both Sexes.* Tr. from the French. Boston: Thomas & Andrews, 1790.

Camper, Petrus. *Über den natürlichen Unterschied der Gesichtszüge in Menschen verschiedener Gegenden und verschiedenen Alters.* Tr. S. T. Sömmerring. Berlin: Voss, 1792.

The Cannibals' Progress; or, The Dreadful Horrors of French Invasion: As Displayed by the Republican Officers and Soldiers, in Their Perfidy, Rapacity, Ferociousness and Brutality, Exercised towards the Innocent Inhabitants of Germany. Tr. Anthony Aufrer. Massachusetts: Walpole, 1798.

Casas, Bartolomé de las. "Brevísima relación de la destruición de las Indias." 1542. In *Tratados de Fray Bartolomé de las Casas.* Tr. Agustín Millares and Carlo and Rafael Moreno. Mexico: Fondo de Cultura Económica, 1965.

———. *The Devastation of the Indies: A Brief Account.* Tr. Herma Briffault. New York: Seabury Press, 1974.

————. *Historia de las Indias.* Ed. Agustín Millares. Mexico: Fondo de Cultura Económica, 1965.

————. *Newe Welt. Warhafftige Anzeigung der Hispanier grewlichen, abschewlichen vnd vnmenschlichen Tyranney, von jhnen inn den indianischen Ländern, so gegen Nidergang der Sonnen gelegen, vnd die Newe Welt genennet wird, begangen . . .* Frankfurt am Main: n.p., 1797.

————. *Die Verheerung Westindiens. Beschrieben von Bischof Bartholomäus de las Casas.* Tr. D. W. Andreä. Berlin: Himburg, 1790.

Coyer, Gabriel François. *Ueber die Riesen in Patagonien. Ein Sendschreiben an den Herrn Doctor Maty, Sekretär der königlichen Societät in London, von dem Herrn Abt Coyer, Mitglied derselben Gesellschaft.* Tr. Samuel William Turner. Danzig: Wedel, 1769.

Cronau, Rudolf. *Amerika. Die Geschichte seiner Entdeckung von der ältesten bis auf die neueste Zeit. Eine Festschrift zur 400jährigen Jubelfeier der Entdeckung Amerikas durch Christoph Columbus.* 2 vols. Leipzig: Abel & Müller, 1892.

Cuneo, Michele. "Letter on the second voyage, 28 October 1495." *Journals and Other Documents on the Life and Voyages of Christopher Columbus.* Tr. and ed. S. E. Morison. 209–228. New York: Heritage Press, 1963.

Defoe, Daniel. *Robinson Crusoe.* Critical edition. Ed. Michael Shinagel. New York: Norton, 1975.

Deutsche Kolonialzeitung. Berlin: Deutscher Kolonialverein, 1884–1890.

Der Deutsche Merkur. Weimar: Im Verlag der Gesellschaft, 1773–1810 [1730–1789: *Der Teutsche Merkur;* 1790–1810: *Der Neue Teutsche Merkur*].

Döhner, Friedrich. "Des Aufruhrs schreckliche Folge oder: die Neger. Ein Original-Trauerspiel in fünf Aufzügen." 1792. 35: 3–94. In *Theatralische Sammlung.* Vienna, 1792.

Dubroca, Louis. "Geschichte der Neger-Empörung auf St. Domingo unter der Anführung von Toussaint-Louverture and Jean Jacques Dessalines." *Minerva* 53 (1805) 1: 434–464 and 2: 71–158.

————. *Leben des J. J. Dessalines oder Jacob's des Ersten Kaysers von Hayti. Nebst Darstellungen der Schreckensszenen, welche während des Aufstandes der Neger daselbst vorgefallen sind.* Tr. from the French by K. L. Müller. Leipzig: Hinrichs, 1805.

Eggert, Dr. Minutes of Annual Assembly. *Deutsche Kolonialzeitung* 3 (1886): 294–301.

Ehrmann, Theophil. "El Dorado." *Allgemeine geographische Ephemeriden.* Weimar: Landes-Industrie-Comptoir, 1808.

Engel, Johann Jacob. "Die Entzückung des Las Casas; oder, Quellen der Seelenruhe." *Die Horen* 1/2, no. 3 (1795): 70–79.

Europäische Annalen. Ed. E. L. Posselt. Tübingen: Cotta, 1795–1820. Continued as *Allgemeine politische Annalen.*

Fabri, Friedrich. *Bedarf Deutschland der Colonien? Eine politisch-ökonomische Betrachtung.* Gotha: Perthes, 1879.

————. *Fünf Jahre Deutscher Kolonialpolitik. Rück- und Ausblicke.* Gotha: Perthes, 1889.

———. "Koloniale Aufgaben." *Deutsche Kolonialzeitung* 2 (1885): 536–551.

Fabri, Timotheus. "Unsere Überproduktion an geistiger Arbeitskraft und praktische Kolonisation." *Deutsche Kolonialzeitung, Neue Folge* 1, no. 24 (June 1888): 1ff.

Faulhaber, H. "Deutschtum in Südbrasilien." *Beiträge zur Kolonialpolitik und Kolonialwirtschaft* 1 (1899–1900): 437–438.

Federmann, Arnold. *Deutsche Konquistadoren in Südamerika, mit einem Nachdruck der Indianischen Historia des Nicolaus Federmann d. J. von Ulm.* Berlin: Hobbing, 1938.

Federmann, Nikolaus. *Indianische Historia. Eine schöne kurzweilige Historia Nicolaus Federmanns des Jüngern von Ulm erster raise . . .* Hagenau: Bund, 1557.

Fick, A. "Ist die Welt vergeben?" *Deutsche Kolonialzeitung* 1 (1884): 51–56, 75–80.

Fischer, Caroline Auguste. "Wilhelm der Neger." *Kleine Erzählungen und romantische Skizzen.* Ed. Anita Runge. 29–73. Rpt., Hildesheim: Olms, 1988.

Förster, Friedrich Christoph. *Christoph Columbus, der Entdecker der neuen Welt. Ein Volksbuch zur Belehrung und Unterhaltung bearbeitet nach den besten Originalquellen.* Leipzig: Teubner, 1842.

Forster, Georg. "Noch etwas über die Menschenrassen." *Der Teutsche Merkur* 4 (Oct./Nov. 1786): 57–86.

———. Review of Göttingisches Historisches Magazin. In *Georg Forsters Werke.* Ed. Horst Fiedler. 11: 236–252. Berlin-Ost: Akademie Verlag, 1977.

Frankl, Ludwig August. "Christoforo Colombo." In *Epische Gedichte.* 2: 99–155. Wien: Hartleben, 1880.

Geffcken, A. "Die Auswanderungs- und Kolonisationsfrage." *Deutsche Kolonialzeitung* (1884): 69–72.

Gerstäcker, Friedrich. *Achtzehn Monate in Süd-Amerika und dessen deutschen Colonien.* Leipzig: Costenoble, 1863.

———. *Die Colonie. Brasilianisches Lebensbild.* 4th ed. Jena: Costenoble, n.d.

"Geschichte der Unglücksfälle von St. Domingue." *Französische Blätter* 3 (Basel, 1796): 297–328.

Girtanner, Christoph. *Ueber das Kantische Prinzip für die Naturgeschichte. Ein Versuch diese Wissenschaft philosophisch zu behandeln.* Göttingen: Vandenhoek, 1796.

Gleim, Johann Wilhelm Ludwig. "Die Fabel von zehn Tigern." *Minerva* (April 1795): 179.

Goehring, C. *Columbus. Die Entdeckung Amerikas, Deutschlands wackerer Jugend erzählt.* 2nd ed. Leipzig: Teubner, 1851.

Göttingische Anzeigen von gelehrten Sachen. Ed. Königliche Gesellschaft der Wissenschaften. Göttingen: Hager, 1753–1801. Continued as *Göttingische gelehrte Anzeigen, unter der Aufsicht der Gesellschaft der Wissenschaften,* 1802–1940.

Guyon, Claude Marie. *Geschichte derer Amazonen.* Tr. Johann Georg Krünitz. Berlin: Rüdiger, 1763.

Haebler, Konrad. *Die überseeischen Unternehmungen der Welser und ihrer Gesellschafter.* Leipzig: C. L. Hirschfeld, 1903.

Hallische gelehrte Zeitungen. Halle: Joh. Jac. Curt, 1766–1792 [also *Neue hallische gelehrte Zeitungen*].

Hantzsch, Viktor. *Deutsche Reisende des sechzehnten Jahrhunderts.* Leipziger Studien auf dem Gebiet der Geschichte 1, no. 4. Leipzig: Duncker & Humblot, 1895.

Hassert, Kurt. "Die Welserzüge in Venezuela. Das erste deutsche überseeische Kolonial-Unternehmen im 16. Jahrhundert." *Beiträge zur Kolonialpolitik und Kolonialwirtschaft* 3. Ed. Deutsche Kolonialgesellschaft. 297–317. Berlin: Süsserott, 1901–1902.

———. "Johann Joachim Becher, ein Vorkämpfer deutscher Kolonialpolitik im 17. Jahrhundert." *Koloniale Rundschau. Zeitschrift für Weltwirtschaft und Kolonialpolitik* (Berlin, 1918): 148–264.

Hegel, G. W. F. *Die Vernunft in der Geschichte.* 1815. Ed. Johannes Hoffmeister. 5th ed., Hamburg: Meiner, 1957.

Heine, Heinrich. *The Complete Poems of Heinrich Heine.* Tr. Hal Draper. Boston: Suhrkamp/Insel, 1982.

———. "Vitzliputzli." *Historisch-kritische Gesamtausgabe der Werke.* 3, part 1: 56–75. Hamburg: Hoffmann & Campe, 1992.

———. *Selected Prose.* Tr. Ritchie Robertson. London: Penguin, 1993.

Herb, C. "Die Aussichten neuer Unternehmungen im tropischen Südamerika." *Beiträge zur Kolonialpolitik und Kolonialwirtschaft* 4 (1902–1903): 329–330.

Herder, Johann Gottfried. *Briefe zur Beförderung der Humanität.* 3 vols. Berlin: Aufbau, 1971.

———. "England und Deutschland." *Sämmtliche Werke.* Ed. B. Suphan. 29: 160. Berlin: Weidmann, 1889.

———. "Ideen zur Philosophie der Geschichte der Menschheit" (1784). *Sämmtliche Werke.* Ed. B. Suphan. Vol. 13. Berlin: Weidmann, 1887.

Howard, Thomas Phipps. *The Haitian Journal of Lieutenant Howard, York Hussars, 1796–1798.* Ed. with an introduction by Roger Buckley. Knoxville: University of Tennessee Press, 1985.

Hübbe-Schleiden, D. J. U. *Deutsche Colonisation. Eine Replik auf das Referat des Herrn Dr. Friedrich Kapp über Colonisation und Auswanderung.* Hamburg: Friederichsen, 1881.

Hübbe-Schleiden, H. "Deutsche Welt-Hegemonie." *Deutsche Kolonialzeitung* 8 (April 1890): n.p.

Humboldt, Alexander von. *Ansichten der Natur mit wissenschaftlichen Erläuterungen.* Tübingen: Cotta, 1808.

———. *Essai politique sur le royaume de la Nouvelle-Espagne.* 5 vols. Paris: Schoell, 1811. Tr. as *Versuch über die politischen Zustände des Königreiches Neu-Spanien.* Tübingen: Cotta, 1809–1814.

———. *Essai politique sur l'île de Cuba.* Paris: Gide, 1828.

———. *Examen critique de l'histoire de la géographie du Nouveau Continent et des progrès de l'astronomie nautique au 15e et 16e siècles.* Paris: Gide, 1837. Tr. as

Kritische Untersuchungen über die historische Entwicklung der geographischen Kenntnisse von der Neuen Welt und die Fortschritte der nautischen Astronomie in dem 15ten und 16ten Jahrhundert. Berlin: Nicolai, 1852.

———. *Kosmos. Entwurf einer physischen Weltbeschreibung.* Tübingen: Cotta, 1845–1858.

———. *Voyage aux régions équinoctiales du Nouveau Continent, fait en 1799–1804.* Tr. as *Reise in die Äquinoctialgegenden des Neuen Continents.* Vienna: Strauss, 1825.

Hutten, Philipp. "Juncker Philipps von Huttens Zeitung aus India; aus seiner z. Th. unleserlich gewordenen Handschrift." *Historisch-literarisches Magazin,* ed. Johann Georg Meusel (1785): 51–117.

Ihle, Alexander. *Christoph Meiners und die Völkerkunde.* Göttingen: Vandenhoek, 1931.

Irving, Washington. *History of the Life and Voyages of Christopher Columbus.* 1827. New York: Carvill, 1828. German edition: *Die Geschichte des Lebens und der Reisen Christoph's Columbus.* 4 vols. Tr. P. A. G. von Meyer. Frankfurt am Main: Sauerländer, 1828–1829.

———. *Reisen der Gefährten des Columbus.* 3 vols. Tr. P. A. G. von Meyer. Frankfurt am Main: Sauerländer, 1831.

Jacob, Ernst Gerhard, ed. *Das koloniale Deutschtum. Ein Volkslesebuch.* Bayreuth: Gauverlag Bayrische Ostmark, 1939.

Jacobi, E. "Ein bayrisches Kolonialunternehmen im 17. Jahrhundert." *Beiträge zur Kolonialpolitik und Kolonialwirtschaft* 5 (Berlin: Süsserott, 1903): 184–192, 200–202.

Kant, Immanuel. "Anthropologie in pragmatischer Hinsicht." 1798. *Gesammelte Schriften.* Akademie Ausgabe. Ed. E. Cassirer. 7:117–335. Berlin: Reimer, 1907. Tr. as *Anthropology from a Pragmatic Point of View,* tr. Victor Lyle Dowdell. Carbondale: Southern Illinois University Press, 1978.

———. "Bestimmung des Begrifs einer Menschenrace." *Berlinische Monatsschrift.* Ed. F. Gedike and J. E. Biester. 6: 390–417. Berlin: Haude and Spener, 1785.

———. "Reflexionen zur Anthropologie." *Gesammelte Schriften.* Akademie-Ausgabe. Ed. E. Cassirer. 15: 55–654. Berlin: Reimer, 1913.

———. "Von den verschiedenen Racen der Menschen." 1775. *Gesammelte Schriften.* Akademie-Ausgabe. Ed. E. Cassirer. 2: 428–443. Berlin: Reimer, 1907.

———. *Critique of Pure Reason.* Tr. Norman Kemp Smith. London: Macmillan, 1973.

Katterfeld, A. "Joachim Nettelbeck als Vorkämpfer für eine Deutsche Kolonialpolitik." *Deutsche Kolonialzeitung* 3 (1886): 170–174.

Keller, Gottfried. "Die Berlocken." *Sämtliche Werke.* Ed. Jonas Fränkel. 11: 315–336. Bern and Leipzig: Benteli, 1934.

Kirchhoff, Alfred. "Die Neue Welt und das dortige Deutschtum." *Deutsche Kolonialzeitung* (1888): 110–112.

Kleist, Heinrich von. "Das Erdbeben in Chili." *Erzählungen. DTV Gesamtausgabe.* 4: 131–145. Based on *Sämtliche Werke und Briefe.* 2nd ed. Ed. Helmut Sembdner. München: dtv, 1964.

———. "Die Verlobung in St. Domingo." *Erzählungen.* 4: 146–178. München: dtv, 1964.

———. "The Betrothal in Santo Domingo." *The Marquise of O- and Other Stories.* Tr. David Luke and Nigel Reeves. 231–269. London: Penguin, 1983.

Klencke, Hermann. *Alexander von Humboldt. Ein biographisches Denkmal.* Leipzig: Spamer, 1851.

———. *Alexander von Humboldts Leben und Wirken, Reisen und Wissen. Ein biographisches Denkmal von Dr. Herm. Klencke.* Continued, much amended, and revised. 7th ed. Leipzig: Spamer, 1876.

Klingemann, August. "Columbus. Ein dramatisches Gedicht (1811)." *August Klingemann's dramatische Werke.* 5: 124–432. Wien: Grund, 1820.

Klöden, Karl Friedrich von. "Die Welser in Augsburg als Besitzer von Venezuela und die von ihnen veranlassten Expeditionen der Deutschen dahin." *Zeitschrift für Allgemeine Erkunde.* 433–455. Berlin: Reimer, 1855.

Klunzinger, Karl. *Der Antheil der Deutschen an der Entdeckung von Südamerika.* Stuttgart: Sonnewald, 1857.

Kolb, Johann Ernst. *Erzählungen von den Sitten und Schicksalen der Negersklaven. Eine rührende Geschichte für Menschen guter Art.* Bern: Haller, 1789.

Koloniale Monatsblätter. Ed. Deutsche Koloniale Gesellschaft, 1899–1914.

Kolonialpolitische Korrespondenz. Ed. Fritz Bley. Gesellschaft für deutsche Kolonisation. Berlin, 1885–1887.

Körner, Theodor. "Toni." 1812. *Theodor Körners sämmtliche Werke.* Ed. Karl Streckfuss. 10–68. Berlin: Nicolai, 1838.

Kösting, Karl. *Columbus. Ein historisches Trauerspiel.* Wiesbaden: Niedner, 1863. Also entitled "Die neue Welt." In *Ausgewählte Werke.* Ed. Fritz Kummer. Wiesbaden: Niedner, 1891.

Kotzebue, August von. "Die Indianer in England. Lustspiel in drey Aufzügen." 1789. In *August von Kotzebues Theater.* 2: 94–178. Wien: Lechner, 1831.

———. "Die Negersklaven. Ein historisch-dramatisches Gemälde in 3 Aufzügen." 1796. In *August von Kotzebues Theater.* 5: 155–244. Leipzig: Kummer, 1840.

———. "Die Sonnen-Jungfrau." 1789. In *August von Kotzebues Theater.* 2: 4–118. Leipzig: Kummer, 1840.

———. "Die Spanier in Peru; oder, Rollas Tod." 1795. In *August von Kotzebues Theater.* 4: 205–318. Leipzig: Kummer, 1840.

———. *Pizarro: A Play in Five Acts.* Altered and tr. Richard B. Sheridan. New York: S. French, 1924.

———. *Baron von Kotzebue's Dramatic Works.* Tr. Charles Smith. Vol. 3: "The Virgin of the Sun"; "Pizarro; or, The Spaniards in Peru"; "The East Indian." New York: Stephens, 1800.

Kratter, Franz. *Die Sclavin in Surinam.* Frankfurt: Esslinger, 1804.

Lacroix, Pamphile de. *Mémoires pour servir à l'histoire de la révolution de Saint-Domingue.* Paris: Pillet Ainé, 1819.

Lafitau, P. *Moeurs des sauvages amériquains comparées aux moeurs des premiers temps.* Paris: Sangrain & Hochereau, 1724.

Lafontaine, August. *Leben und Thaten der Freiherrn Quinctius Heymeran von Flaming.* Berlin: Voss, 1795–96.

Lavater, Johann Caspar. *Physiognomische Fragmente zur Beförderung der Menschenkenntniss und Menschenliebe.* Leipzig: Weidmanns Erben und Reich, 1778.

Lesser, Richard. "Die Kolonialpolitik des Grossen Kurfürsten." *Deutsche Kolonialzeitung* 1 (1884): 199–200.

Linnaeus, Carl. *Des Ritters C. von Linné vollständiges Natursystem, nach der 12. lateinischen Ausgabe, und nach Anleitung des holländischen Houttuynischen Werks, mit einer ausführlichen Erklärung ausgefertigt von P. L. S. Müller.* 7 vols. Nürnberg: n.p., 1773–1776.

Marmontel, Jean-François. *Les Incas, ou la Destruction de l'Empire du Pérou.* 2 vols. Berne/Lausanne: Société Typographique, 1777. English translation, *The Incas; or, The Destruction of the Empire of Peru.* Alston, England: John Harrop, 1808.

Meiners, Christoph. *Briefe über die Schweiz.* Tübingen: Cotta, 1791.

——. *Grundriss der Geschichte der Menschheit.* Lemgo: Meyer, 1785. Frankfurt ed., 1786. 2nd improved ed. Lemgo, 1793.

——. "Historische Nachrichten über die wahre Beschaffenheit des Sclaven-Handels, und der Knechtschaft der Neger in West-Indien." *Göttingisches historisches Magazin* 6 (1790): 645–679.

——. "Über die Ausartung der Europäer in fremden Erdtheilen." *Göttingisches historisches Magazin* 8 (1791): 209–268. Appendix to previous essay, 268–274.

——. "Über die Farben, und Schattierungen verschiedener Völker." *Neues Göttingisches historisches Magazin* 1 (1792): 611–672.

——. "Über den Haar- und Bartwuchs der hässlichen und dunkelfarbigen Völker." *Neues Göttingisches historisches Magazin* 1 (1792): 484–508.

——. "Über die Natur der Afrikanischen Neger und die davon abhangende Befreyung, oder Einschränkung der Schwarzen." *Göttingisches historisches Magazin* 6 (1790): 385–456.

——. "Über die Natur der Americaner." *Göttingisches historisches Magazin* 6 (1790): 102–156.

——. "Über die Verschiedenheit der cörperlichen Grösse verschiedener Völker." *Neues Göttingisches historisches Magazin* 1 (1792): 697–762.

——. "Von den Varietäten und Abarten der Neger." *Göttingisches historisches Magazin* 6 (1790): 625–645.

Minerva. Ein Journal historischen und politischen Inhalts. Ed. J. W. von Archenholz. Berlin: Unger, 1792–1805.

Mocquet, Jean. *Voyages en Afrique, Asie, Indes Orientales et Occidentales, faits par Jean Mocquet, 1601–1614.* Paris: Gouvernement, 1830.

Muñoz, Juan Bautista. *Historia del Nuevo Mundo.* 1793. German ed., *Don Juan Baptista Muñoz' Geschichte der Neuen Welt.* Tr. M. C. Sprengel. Weimar: Landes-Industrie-Comptoir, 1795.

Navarrete, Martín Fernández de. *Die Reisen des Christof Columbus, 1492–1504. Nach seinen eigenen Briefen und Berichten veröffentlicht 1536 von Bischof Las*

Casas, seinem Freunde, und Fernando Columbus, seinem Sohne. Aufgefunden 1791 und veröffentlicht 1826 von Don M. F. von Navarette [*sic*]. Tr. Fr. Pr. Leipzig: Hinrichs, 1826–1890.

Nebel, H. C. "New Germany." *Beiträge zur Kolonialpolitik und Kolonialwirtschaft* 1 (1899–1900): 99–103.

Nicolai, Friedrich. *Über den Gebrauch der falschen Haare und Perrucken in alten und neuern Zeiten.* Berlin: n.p., 1801.

Orellana, Antonio de. *Die kriegerischen Frauen, oder: historische Beschreibung einer neuentdeckten Insel.* Berlin: n.p., 1736.

Pauw, Cornelius de. "Amérique." *Supplément à l'Encyclopédie, ou Dictionnaire raisonné des sciences, des arts et des métiers.* 1: 343–354. Amsterdam: Rey, 1776–1777.

———. *Défense des recherches philosophiques sur les Américains par Mr. de P***.* Berlin: Decker, 1770.

———. *Défense des Recherches philosophiques sur les Américains. Nouvelle édition corrigée et augmentée.* Berlin: Decker, 1772. New edition: Berlin, 1777.

———. *Oeuvres philosophiques I–VII.* Paris: Bastien, 1795.

———. *Philosophische Untersuchungen über die Amerikaner, oder wichtige Beyträge zur Geschichte des menschlichen Geschlechts.* 2 vols. Tr. Carl Gottlieb Lessing. Berlin: Decker & Winter, 1769.

———. *Recherches philosophiques sur les Américains, ou Mémoires intéressants pour servir à l'Histoire de l'Espèce humaine par M. de P.***.* 2 vols. Berlin: Decker, 1768.

———. *Recherches philosophiques sur les Égyptiens & les Chinois par Mr. de P.***.* Berlin: Decker, 1773.

———. *Recherches philosophiques sur les Grecs.* 2 vols. Berlin: Decker, 1787–1788.

Pauw, Cornelius de, and Pernety, Antoine-Josephe. *Recherches philosophiques sur les Américains, ou Mémoires intéressants pour servir à l'Histoire de l'Espèce humaine par Mr. de P. Nouvelle Edition, augmentée d'une Dissertation critique par Dom Pernety; & de la Défense de l'Auteur des Recherches contre cette Dissertation.* 3 vols. Berlin: Decker, 1770.

Permoser, Balthasar. *Der ohne Ursach verworffene und dahero von Rechts wegen auff den Thron der Ehren wiederum erhobene BARTH/Bey jetzigen ohnbärtigen Zeiten sonder alle Furcht zu männigliches Wohl und Vergnügen ausgefertiget vor und von B. P. Königl. Pohl. und Churf. Sächs. Hoff-Bildhauer. Zu Druck gebracht Durch Barbatium Schönbart.* Frankfurt am Main: n.p., 1714.

Pernety, Antoine-Josephe. *Discours sur la physiognomie. La Connoissance de l'homme moral par l'homme physique.* Berlin: Decker, 1769.

———. *Dissertation sur l'Amérique et les Américains, contre les Recherches philosophiques de Mr. de P. Par Dom Pernety.* Berlin: Decker, 1770.

———. *Examen des Recherches philosophiques sur l'Amérique et des Américains et de la défense de cet ouvrage.* 2 vols. Berlin: Decker, 1771.

———. *Journal historique d'un voyage fait aux Îles Malouïnes en 1763 & 1764 pour les reconnoître & y former un établissement; & deux voyages au Détroit de Magellan, avec une Relation sur les Patagons.* 2 vols. Berlin: Bourdeaux, 1769.

————. *Versuch einer Physiognomik oder Erklärung des moralischen Menschen durch die Kenntniss des physischen.* 3 vols. Dresden: Walther, 1784 [tr. of *Discours sur la physiognomie*].

Peters, Carl. *Die Gründung von Deutsch-Ostafrika.* Berlin: Schwetschke, 1905.

Petit, Pierre. *Traité historique sur les Amazones.* Leyden: Langerak, 1718.

Pfeiffer, Hans Ernst. *Unsere schönen alten Kolonien.* Berlin: Weller, 1941.

Rainsford, Marcus. "Toussaint Louverture. Eine historische Schilderung für die Nachwelt." *Minerva* 53, no. 4 (1805): 276–298, 392–408.

Ratzel, Friedrich. "Roscher's 'Kolonien, Kolonialpolitik und Auswanderung' in dritter Auflage.'" *Deutsche Kolonialzeitung* 2 (1885): 19–22.

Raynal, Thomas Guillaume François. *Histoire philosophique et politique des établissements des deux Indes.* Amsterdam: n.p., 1770 [tr. as *Uebersicht der politischen Lage und des Handelszustandes von St. Domingo.* Leipzig: Haug, 1788].

Reichard, Heinrich August Ottokar. *Über den gesetzlichen Zustand der Negersklaven in Westindien.* Leipzig: Weygand, 1779.

Riecke, G. A. *Christoph Columbus, der Entdecker Amerikas. Ein Lesebuch für die männliche Jugend.* Rev. ed. Stuttgart: Ullrich, 1873.

Robertson, William. *History of America.* Alston, England: Walton, 1800.

Roscher, Wilhelm Georg. *Kolonien, Kolonialpolitik und Auswanderung.* 2nd ed. Leipzig: Winter, 1856. 1st ed. 1848. 3rd ed. with Robert Jannasch, 1885.

Rückert, Friedrich. "Cristofero Colombo oder die Entdeckung der Neuen Welt. Geschichtsdrama in drei Theilen." *Poetische Werke.* 10: 288–648. Frankfurt: Sauerländer, 1882.

Ruge, Sophus. *Columbus.* 2nd ed. Berlin: Hofmann, 1902.

Schatz, Walter. "Die Treue der Eingeborenen." In *Das Koloniale Deutschtum. Ein Volkslesebuch.* Ed. Gerhard Jacob. Bayreuth: Gauverlag Bayrische Ostmark, 1939.

Schelle, Karl Gottlob. *Geschichte des männlichen Barts unter allen Völkern der Erde bis auf die neueste Zeit. Für Freunde der Sitten und Völkerkunde. Nach dem Französischen frei bearbeitet und mit einer Theorie der Haare nach ihren Naturzwecken versehen.* Leipzig: Weygand, 1797.

Schiller, Johann Friedrich. "Columbus." *Musenalmanach für das Jahr 1796.* P. 197. Neustrelitz: Michaelis, 1796.

Schmid, Hermann Theodor von. *Columbus. Trauerspiel in fünf Aufzügen.* 1857. 2nd ed., Leipzig: Weber, 1875.

Schnabel, Johann Gottfried. *Die Insel Felsenburg* (alternate title: *Wunderliche Fata einiger See-fahrer, absonderlich Albert Julii . . . entworfen von dessen Bruders-Sohnes-Sohnes-Sohne, Mons. Eberhard Julio . . . dem Drucke uebergeben von Gisandern.* Nordhausen: J. H. Gross, 1731–1743. Rpt., Frankfurt am Main: Minerva-Verlag, 1973.

Schück, Richard. *Brandenburg-Preussens Kolonialpolitik unter dem Grossen Kurfürsten und seinen Nachfolgern (1647–1721).* Leipzig: Grunow, 1889.

Sernau, I. R. "Zur Frage der Auswanderung." *Deutsche Kolonialzeitung* 3 (1886): 133–134.

Simonsfeld, Heinrich. *Die Deutschen als Colonisatoren in der Geschichte.* Hamburg: Richter, 1885.

Sömmerring, Samuel Thomas von. *Über die körperliche Verschiedenheit des Mohren vom Europäer.* Frankfurt am Main: Varrentrapp, 1784. 2nd ed. with changed title, *Über die körperliche Verschiedenheit des Negers vom Europäer,* 1785.

Sprengel, Matthias Christian. *Vom Ursprung des Negerhandels. Ein Arbeitsprogramm.* Halle: Hendel, 1779.

Springer, Johann Christoph Erich von. *Physikalische Untersuchung, ob auch patagonische Riesen möglich, und die Erzählungen davon wahr sind.* Leipzig: Hilscher, 1769.

Stedman, Colonel Gabriel. *Narrative of a Five Years Expedition against the Revolted Negroes of Surinam.* 1790. Rpt., Baltimore: Johns Hopkins University Press, 1988.

Stetten, Paul von. *Bartolme Welser. Lebensbeschreibung zur Erweckung und Unterhaltung bürgerlicher Tugend.* Augsburg: n.p., 1778–1782.

Thompson, Benjamin, tr. *The German Theatre.* 6 vols. London: Vernor & Hood, 1801.

Topf, Hugo. *Deutsche Statthalter und Konquistadoren in Venezuela.* Hamburg: Verlagsanstalt und Druckerei A.-G. (formerly J. F. Richter), 1893 [Sammlung gemeinverständlicher wissenschaftlicher Vorträge, H 163].

Treitschke, Heinrich von. "First Attempts at German Colonization." *Treitschke: His Doctrine of German Destiny and of International Relations.* Tr. Adolf Hausrath. 195–216. New York and London: Putnam's, 1914.

———. *Politics.* 2 vols. Tr. Blanche Dugdale and Torben de Bille. New York: Macmillan, 1916.

"Über die vielen Reisebeschreibungen in unseren Tagen." *Berlinische Monatsschrift* 4 (1798): 319–332.

Vallentin, Wilhelm. *Das Deutschtum in Südamerika.* Berlin: Paetel, 1908.

Weickum, Karl. *Columbus. Dramatisches Gemälde in 5 Acten aus der Geschichte der Entdeckung Amerikas.* 1873. 2nd rev. ed. for the fourth centenary, Freiburg: Herder, 1893.

Werder, Karl. *Columbus.* Ed. Otto Gildmeister "after the second version of 1858." Berlin: Fontane, 1893.

Wezel, Johann Carl. *Robinson Krusoe.* Leipzig: Dyk, 1779–1780. 2nd ed., ed. Anneliese Klingenberg. Berlin: Rütten und Loening, 1979.

Wieland, C. M. "Über die vorgebliche Abnahme des menschlichen Geschlechts." *Sämmtliche Werke.* 31: 213–252. Leipzig: Göschen, 1821.

Wintzer, Wilhelm. *Die Deutschen im tropischen Amerika (Mexico, Mittelamerika, Venezuela, Kolumbien, Ekuador, Peru und Bolivien).* München: J. F. Lehmann, 1900.

Wünsch, Christian. *Unterhaltungen über den Menschen: Erster Theil: Über die Kultur und äusserliche Bildung desselben.* 1780. 2nd ed., Leipzig: Breitkopf, 1796.

Zachariae, Friedrich Wilhelm. *Cortes.* Braunschweig: Fürstliche Waisenhaus Buchhandlung, 1766.

Zedler, Johann Heinrich. *Grosses vollstandiges Universal-Lexikon, 1732–1763.* 68 vols. Rpt., Akademische Drucks- und Verlagsanstalt Graz, 1961.

Zimmermann, Eberhard August Wilhelm von. *Geographische Geschichte des Menschen und der allgemein verbreiteten vierfüssigen Thiere.* Leipzig: Weygand, 1778–1783.

———. "Rückblick auf die neue Welt." In *Taschenbuch der Reisen, oder unterhaltende Darstellung der Entdeckungen des 18ten Jahrhunderts.* 8: 3–104. Leipzig: Fleischer, 1809.

———, ed. *Taschenbuch der Reisen, oder unterhaltende Darstellung der Entdeckungen des 18ten Jahrhunderts, in Rücksicht der Länder-, Menschen- und Productenkunde. Für jede Klasse von Lesern.* 18 vols. Leipzig: Fleischer, 1802–1819.

"Zur neuesten Geschichte von St. Domingo. Actenstücke zur Geschichte der Revolution in St. Domingo." From the French. *Minerva. Ein Journal historischen und politischen Inhalts.* 53 (1805): 133–157, 276–293.

Critical Literature

Althusser, Louis. *For Marx.* Tr. Ben Brewster. London: Verso, 1979.

Andersen, Benedict. *Imagined Communities. Reflections on the Origin and Spread of Nationalism.* London: Verso, 1983.

Angress, Ruth (Klüger). "Kleist's Treatment of Imperialism: 'Die Hermannsschlacht' and 'Die Verlobung in St. Domingo.'" *Monatshefte* 69 (1977): 17–33.

Appiah, Kwame Anthony. "Race." In *Critical Terms for Literary Study.* Ed. Frank Lentricchia and Thomas McLaughlin. 274–287. Chicago: University of Chicago Press, 1990.

Arciniegas, Germán. *Los Alemanes en la conquista de América.* Buenos Aires: Losada, 1941.

Armstrong, Nancy. "The Occidental Alice." *Differences: A Journal of Feminist Cultural Studies* 2, no. 2 (1990): 3–40.

Baginsky, Paul Ben. *German Works Relating to America, 1493–1800.* New York: New York Public Library, 1942.

Bald, Detlef, Peter Heller, et al. *Die Liebe zum Imperium. Deutschlands dunkle Vergangenheit in Afrika. Zur Legende und Wirklichkeit von Tanzanias deutscher Kolonialvergangenheit.* Übersee-Museum Bremen, 1978.

Barker, Francis, et al. *Europe and Its Others: Proceedings of the Essex Conference on the Sociology of Literature, July 1984.* Colchester: University of Essex Press, 1985.

Barker, Martin. "Biology and the New Racism." In *Anatomy of Racism.* Ed. David Theo Goldberg. 18–37. Minneapolis: University of Minnesota Press, 1990.

Bauschinger, Sigrid, Horst Denkler, and Wilfried Malsch, eds. *Amerika in der deutschen Literatur. Neue Welt-Nordamerika-USA.* Stuttgart: Reclam, 1975.

Bellegarde-Smith, Patrick. *Haiti: The Breached Citadel.* Boulder, Colo.: Westview Press, 1990.

Beyerhaus, Gisbert. "Abbé de Pauw und Friedrich der Grosse, eine Abrechnung mit Voltaire." *Historische Zeitschrift* 134 (1926): 465–93.

Bhabha, Homi. "The Other Question: The Stereotype and Colonial Discourse." *Screen* 24, no. 6 (Nov./Dec. 1983): 18–36.

——. "Difference, Discrimination and the Discourse of Colonialism." In *The Politics of Theory*. Ed. Francis Barker et al. Colchester: University of Essex Press, 1983.

Bitterli, Urs. *Cultures in Conflict: Encounters between European and Non-European Cultures, 1492–1800*. Tr. Ritchie Robertson. Stanford: Stanford University Press, 1989.

——. *Die Entdeckung des Schwarzen Afrikaners. Versuch einer Geistesgeschichte der europäisch-afrikanischen Beziehungen an der Guineaküste im 17. und 18. Jahrhundert*. Zürich: Atlantis, 1970.

——. *Die Entdeckung und Eroberung der Welt. Dokumente und Berichte*. 2 vols. München: Beck, 1980.

——. "Die Überseebewohner im europäischen Bewusstsein der Aufklärungszeit." In *Fürst, Bürger, Mensch: Untersuchungen zu politischen und soziokulturellen Wandlungsprozessen im vorrevolutionären Europa*. Ed. Friedrich Engel-Janosi et al. 186–214. München: Oldenbourg, 1975.

Blackwell, Jeannine. "An Island of Her Own: Heroines of the German Robinsonades from 1720 to 1800." *German Quarterly* 58, no. 1 (1985): 5–26.

Bley, Helmut. "Unerledigte Kolonialgeschichte." In *Deutscher Kolonialismus. Materialien zur Hundertjahrfeier 1984*. Ed. Entwicklungspolitische Korrespondenz. 9–16. Hamburg: Gesellschaft für entwicklungspolitische Bildungsarbeit, 1983.

Boerner, Peter. "Die grossen Reisesammlungen des 18. Jahrhunderts." In *Reiseberichte als Quellen europäischer Kulturgeschichte*. Ed. Antoni Maczak and Jans Jürgen Teuteberg. Wolfenbüttler Forschungen 21: 65–72. Wolfenbüttel: Herzog-August-Bibliothek, 1982.

Bohle, Ernst Wilhelm. Foreword to *Unsere schönen alten Kolonien* by Hans Ernst Pfeiffer. Berlin: Weller, 1941.

Böhme, Helmut. "Thesen zur Beurteilung der gesellschaftlichen, wirtschaftlichen und politischen Ursachen des deutschen Imperialismus." In *Der moderne Imperialismus*. Ed. W. Mommsen. 31–59. Stuttgart: Kohlhammer, 1971.

Böhn, Max von. *Die Mode. Menschen und Moden im 18. Jahrhundert*. München: Bruckmann, 1963.

Brauner, Sigrid. "Cannibals, Witches, and Evil Wives in the 'Civilizing Process.'" In *"Neue Welt"/"Dritte Welt": Interkulturelle Beziehungen Deutschlands zu Lateinamerika und der Karibik*. Ed. Sigrid Bauschinger and Susan Cocalis. 1–28. Tübingen: Francke, 1994.

Briesemeister, Dietrich. "' . . . allerhand iniurien Schmehkarten pasquill vnd andere schandlose ehrenrürige Schriften vnd Model.' Die antispanischen Flugschriften in Deutschland zwischen 1580 und 1635." *Wolfenbütteler Beiträge* 4 (1981): 147–190.

Brinker-Gabler, Gisela, ed. *The Question of the Other(s)*. Binghamton: State University of New York Press, 1995.

Broyles, Yolanda Julia. *The German Response to Latin American Literature*. Heidelberg: Winter, 1981.

Bucher, Bernadette. *Icon and Conquest: A Structural Analysis of the Illustrations of de Bry's Great Voyages*. Tr. Basia Miller Gulati. Chicago: University of Chicago Press, 1981.

Burkholder, Mark A., and Lyman L. Johnson. *Colonial Latin America*. 2nd ed. New York: Oxford University Press, 1994.

Burwick, Roswitha. "Issues of Language and Communication: Kleist's 'Die Verlobung in St. Domingo.'" *German Quarterly* 65, nos. 3–4 (Summer/Fall 1992): 318–327.

Callaway, Helen. *Gender, Culture, and Empire: European Women in Colonial Nigeria*. Urbana: University of Illinois Press, 1987.

Chamberlain, H. S. *Die deutschen Kolonien, Jubiläumsausgabe zur vierzigjährigen Wiederkehr des Beginns der deutschen Kolonialgeschichte*. N.p., 1924.

Chatillon, Marcel. "Europas Blick auf die erregenden Zustände in Saint-Domingue." In *Schwarze Freiheit im Dialog: Saint-Domingue 1791–Haiti 1991*. Catalogue of an exhibition. Ed. C. Hermann Middelanis. Bielefeld: University of Bielefeld, 1991.

Church, Henry Ward. "Corneille de Pauw, and the Controversy over his 'Recherches philosophiques sur les Américains.'" *PMLA* 51, no. 1 (March 1936): 178–206.

Conze, Werner. "Einheit und Vielfalt in der deutschen Geschichte." In *Ploetz. Deutsche Geschichte. Epochen und Daten*. Ed. Werner Conze and Volker Hentschel. 2nd ed. 9–25. Freiburg: Ploetz, 1979.

Crosby, Alfred W. *The Columbian Exchange: Biological and Cultural Consequences of 1492*. Westport: Greenwood Press, 1972.

Curtin, Philip D. *The Image of Africa: British Ideas and Action, 1780–1850*. Madison: University of Wisconsin Press, 1964.

———. *Imperialism*. New York: Harper & Row, 1971.

Dougherty, Frank W. P. "Johann Friedrich Blumenbach und Samuel Thomas Soemmering: Eine Auseinandersetzung in anthropologischer Hinsicht." In *Samuel Thomas Soemmering und die Gelehrten der Goethezeit*. Ed. Günter Mann and Franz Dumont. 35–56. Stuttgart: Fischer, 1985.

Drechsler, Horst. *Let Us Die Fighting: The Struggle of the Herero and Nama against German Imperialism, 1884–1915*. Tr. B. Zöllner. London: Zed Press, 1980.

Fabian, Johannes. *Time and the Other: How Anthropology Makes Its Object*. New York: Columbia University Press, 1983.

Fick, Carolyn E. *The Making of Haiti. The Saint Domingue Revolution from Below*. Knoxville: University of Tennessee Press, 1990.

Fiedler, Horst. Afterword to *Georg Forsters Werke*, by Georg Forster. 11: 413–426. Berlin-Ost: Akademie Verlag, 1977.

Fieldhouse, David K. *Die Kolonialreiche seit dem 18. Jahrhundert*. Fischer Weltgeschichte vol. 29. Frankfurt am Main: Fischer, 1965.

Fischer, Bernd. *Das Eigene und das Eigentliche: Klopstock, Herder, Fichte, Kleist. Episoden aus der Konstruktionsgeschichte nationaler Intentionalitäten.* Berlin: Schmid, 1995.

——. "Zur politischen Dimension der Ethik in Kleists 'Die Verlobung in St. Domingo.'" In *Heinrich von Kleist. Studien zu Werk und Wirkung.* Ed. Dirk Grathoff. 248–262. Opladen: Westdeutscher Verlag, 1988.

Fleming, Ray. "Race and the Difference It Makes in Kleist's 'Die Verlobung in St. Domingo.'" *German Quarterly* 65, nos. 3–4 (Summer/Fall 1992): 306–317.

Fohrmann, Jürgen. *Abenteuer und Bürgertum. Zur Geschichte der deutschen Robinsonaden im 18. Jahrhundert.* Stuttgart: Metzler, 1981.

Friede, Juan. "Das Venezuelageschäft der Welser." *Jahrbuch für Geschichte von Staat, Wirtschaft und Gesellschaft Lateinamerikas* 4 (1967): 162–175.

——. *Los Welser en la conquista de Venezuela.* Caracas: Ed. Edime, 1961.

Friede, Juan, and Benjamin Keen, eds. *Bartolomé de las Casas in History.* DeKalb: Northern Illinois University Press, 1971.

Friesen, Gerhard K., and Walter Schatzberg, eds. *The German Contribution to the Building of the Americas.* Studies in Honor of Karl J. R. Arndt. Hanover, N.H.: University Press of New England, 1977.

Frost, Alan. "The Pacific Ocean — The Eighteenth Century's 'New World.'" In *Captain James Cook: Image and Impact.* Ed. Walter Veit. 5–49. Melbourne: Hawthorn Press, 1979.

Fuchs, Eduard. *Illustrierte Sittengeschichte vom Mittelalter bis zur Gegenwart. Das bürgerliche Zeitalter.* Munich: Langen, 1912.

Geggus, David P. *Slavery, War, and Revolution: The British Occupation of Saint Domingue, 1793–1798.* Oxford: Clarendon Press, 1982.

Gerbi, Antonello. *The Dispute of the New World: The History of a Polemic, 1750–1900.* 1955. Rev. and enl. ed. Pittsburgh: University of Pittsburgh Press, 1973.

Gilli, Marita. "Georg Forster, das Ergebnis einer Reise um die Welt." *Europäisches Reisen im Zeitalter der Aufklärung.* Ed. Hans-Wolf Jäger. 251–274. Heidelberg: Winter, 1992.

Gilman, Sander. *On Blackness without Blacks: Essays on the Image of the Black in Germany.* Boston: Hall, 1982.

——. "The Figure of the Black in German Aesthetic Theory." *Eighteenth-Century Studies* 8 (1975): 373–391.

Griep, Wolfgang. "Reiseliteratur im späten 18. Jahrhundert." In *Hansers Sozialgeschichte der Literatur vom 16. Jahrhundert bis zur Gegenwart.* Ed. Rolf Grimminger. 3: 739–764. München: Hanser, 1980.

Griep, Wolfgang, and Hans-Wolf Jäger, eds. *Reisen im 18. Jahrhundert. Neue Untersuchungen.* Heidelberg: Winter, 1986.

——. *Reise und soziale Realität am Ende des 18. Jahrhunderts.* Heidelberg: Winter, 1983.

Grosser, Thomas. "Der mediengeschichtliche Funktionswandel der Reiselektüre in den Berichten deutscher Reisender aus dem Frankreich des 18. Jahrhunderts." In *Europäisches Reisen im Zeitalter der Aufklärung.* Ed. Hans-Wolf Jäger. 275–310. Heidelberg: Winter, 1992.

Häcker, Otto. *Ulm, die Donau- und Münsterstadt im Lichte der Vergangenheit.* Stuttgart: Steinkopf, 1940.

Hanke, Lewis. *All Mankind Is One: A Study of the Disputation between Bartolomé de las Casas and Juan Ginés de Sepúlveda in 1550 on the Intellectual and Religious Capacity of the American Indians.* De Kalb: Northern Illinois University Press, 1974.

Harbsmeier, Michael. "Reisebeschreibungen als mentalitätsgeschichtliche Quelle: Überlegungen zu einer historisch-anthropologischen Untersuchung frühneuzeitlicher deutscher Reisebeschreibungen." In *Reiseberichte als Quellen europäischer Kulturgeschichte.* Ed. Antoni Maczak and Jans Jürgen Teuteberg. Wolfenbüttler Forschungen. 21: 1–32. Wolfenbüttel: Herzog-August-Bibliothek, 1982.

Harris-Schenk, Beverly. "Der Sklave: ein Bild des Schwarzen in der deutschen Literatur des 18. Jahrhunderts." *Akten des VI. Internationalen Germanisten-Kongresses.* Ed. Heinz Rupp and Hans-Gert Roloff. Bern: Lang, 1980.

Hendricks, Margo, and Patricia Parker, eds. *Women, "Race," and Writing in the Early Modern Period.* New York: Routledge, 1994.

Honour, Hugh. *The European Vision of America.* Cleveland: Cleveland Museum of Art, 1975.

———. *The New Golden Land: European Images of the Americas from the Discoveries to the Present Time.* London: Allen Lane, 1976; New York: Pantheon, 1976.

Huber, Siegfried. *Entdecker und Eroberer. Deutsche Konquistadoren in Südamerika mit zeitgenössischen Erlebnisberichten und Dokumenten.* Olten: Walter, 1966.

Hulme, Peter. *Colonial Encounters: Europe and the Native Caribbean, 1492–1797.* New York: Routledge, 1989.

———. "Polytropic Man: Tropes of Sexuality and Mobility in Early Colonial Discourse." *Europe and Its Others.* Ed. Francis Barker et al. 1: 17–32. Colchester: University of Essex Press, 1985.

Humbert, Jules. *L'Occupation allemande du Vénézuela au XVIe siècle.* Bordeaux: Féret & Fils Editeurs, 1905.

Ibbeken, Rudolf. *Preussen 1807–1813. Staat und Volk als Idee und Wirklichkeit.* Köln: Grote, 1970.

Jacob, Herbert. "Kotzebues Werke in Übersetzungen." In *Studien zur neueren deutschen Literatur.* Ed. H.-W. Seiffert. 95–163. Berlin: Akademie Verlag, 1964.

Jäger, Hans Wolf, ed. *Europäisches Reisen im Zeitalter der Aufklärung.* Heidelberg: Winter, 1992.

James, C. L. R. *The Black Jacobins, Toussaint l'Ouverture and the San Domingo Revolution.* 1938. 2nd rev. ed., New York: Bantam, 1963.

Jameson, Fredric. *The Political Unconscious. Narrative as a Socially Symbolic Act.* Ithaca: Cornell University Press, 1981.

Jantz, Harold. "Amerika im deutschen Dichten und Denken." *Deutsche Philologie im Aufriss 3.* Ed. Wolfgang Stammler. 2nd ed., Berlin: Schmidt, 1967.

Johnston, Otto W. *The Myth of a Nation: Literature and Politics in Prussia under Napoleon*. Columbia, S.C.: Camden House, 1989.

Kamen, Henry. "America and Its Impact on Racial Attitudes and 'Blood Purity.'" Paper presented at 1991 Conference on America in European Consciousness. John Carter Brown Library at Brown University, Providence, R.I.

Käuser, Andreas. "Anthropologie und Aesthetik im 18. Jahrhundert." *Das 18. Jahrhundert* 14, no. 2 (1990): 196–206.

Keen, Benjamin. "Introduction: Approaches to Las Casas, 1535–1970." *Las Casas in History*. Ed. Juan Friede and Benjamin Keen. De Kalb: De Pauw University Press, 1976.

Kellenbenz, Hermann. "Deutsche Plantagenbesitzer und Kaufleute in Surinam vom Ende des 18. bis zur Mitte des 19. Jahrhunderts." *Jahrbuch für Geschichte von Staat, Wirtschaft und Gesellschaft Lateinamerikas* 3 (1966): 141–163.

———. "Die Brandenburger auf St. Thomas." *Jahrbuch für Geschichte von Staat, Wirtschaft und Gesellschaft Lateinamerikas* 2 (1965): 196–217.

Kleinbaum, Abby Wettan. *The War against the Amazons*. New York: McGraw-Hill, 1983.

Köberle, Sophie. *Jugendliteratur zur Zeit der Aufklärung. Ein Beitrag zur Geschichte der Jugendschriftenkritik*. Weinheim: Beltz, 1972.

Koch, Rainer. "Liberalismus, Konservativismus und das Problem der Negersklaverei. Ein Beitrag zur Geschichte des politischen Denkens in Deutschland in der ersten Hälfte des 19. Jahrhunderts." *Historische Zeitschrift* 222 (1976): 529–548.

Koebner, Thomas, and Gerhard Pickerodt, eds. *Die andere Welt. Studien zum Exotismus*. Frankfurt am Main: Athenäum, 1987.

Kolodny, Annette. *The Lay of the Land: Metaphor as Experience and History in American Life and Letters*. Chapel Hill: University of North Carolina Press, 1975.

Körner, Karl Wilhelm. *La independencia de la América española y la diplomacia alemana*. Buenos Aires: Universidad de Buenos Aires, 1968.

Kruse, Joseph. "Heines Leihpraxis und Lektürebeschaffung." In *Die Leihbibliothek als Institution des literarischen Lebens im 18. und 19. Jahrhundert*. Ed. Georg Jäger and Jörg Schönert. Hamburg: Hauswedell, 1980.

Laermann, Klaus, Hans Joachim Piechotta, Uwe Japp, and Ralph-Rainer Wuthenow, eds. *Reise und Utopie. Zur Literatur der Spätaufklärung*. Frankfurt am Main: Suhrkamp, 1976.

Le Goff, Jacques. "Mentalities: A History of Ambiguities." In *Constructing the Past: Essays in Historical Methodology*. Ed. J. LeGoff and Pierre Nora. 166–180. Cambridge: Cambridge University Press, 1985.

Lepenies, Wolf. "Georg Forster als Anthropologe und als Schriftsteller." *Akzente* 3, no. 6 (1984): 557–575.

Liebs, Elke. *Die pädagogische Insel. Studien zur Rezeption des 'Robinson Crusoe' in deutschen Jugendbearbeitungen*. Stuttgart: Metzler, 1977.

Löhndorf, Karl-Ludwig. *Marmontels Incas: Untersuchungen zu ihrer Stellung in der Literatur der Aufklärung, ihrer Aufnahme und Nachwirkung.* Ph.D. diss., Bonn, 1980.

McClintock, Anne. *Imperial Leather: Race, Gender and Sexuality in the Colonial Contest.* New York: Routledge, 1995.

McLynn, Frank. *Hearts of Darkness: The European Exploration of Africa.* New York: Carroll & Graf, 1992.

Magdoff, Harry. *Imperialism: From the Colonial Age to the Present.* New York: Monthly Review Press, 1978.

Mason, Peter. *Deconstructing America: Representations of the Other.* London: Routledge, 1990.

Menges, Karl. "Vom Nationalgeist und seinen 'Keimen.' Zur Vorurteils-Apologetik bei Herder, Hamann und anderen 'Patrioten.'" In *Dichter und ihre Nation.* Ed. Helmut Scheuer. 103–120. Frankfurt am Main: Suhrkamp, 1993.

Menz, Egon. "Die Humanität des Handelsgeistes. Amerika in der deutschen Literatur des ausgehenden 18. Jahrhunderts." In *Amerika in der deutschen Literatur. Neue Welt-Nordamerika-USA.* Ed. Sigrid Bauschinger, Horst Denkler, and Wilfried Malsch. 45–62. Stuttgart: Reclam, 1975.

Mielke, Andreas. *Laokoon und die Hottentotten. Oder über die Grenzen von Reisebeschreibung und Satire.* Baden-Baden: Koerner, 1993.

Mommsen, Wolfgang J. *Theories of Imperialism.* Tr. P. S. Falla. 1980. Rpt., Chicago: University of Chicago Press, 1982.

Morison, S. E., tr. and ed. *Journals and Other Documents on the Life and Voyages of Christopher Columbus.* New York: Heritage Press, 1963.

Mörner, Magnus. "Europäische Reiseberichte als Quellen zur Geschichte Lateinamerikas von der zweiten Hälfte des 18. Jahrhunderts bis 1870." In *Reiseberichte als Quellen europäischer Kulturgeschichte.* Ed. Antoni Maczak and Jans Jürgen Teuteberg. Wolfenbüttler Forschungen vol. 21: 281–314. Wolfenbüttel: Herzog-August-Bibliothek, 1982.

Mosse, George. *Nationalism and Sexuality: Respectability and Abnormal Sexuality in Modern Europe.* New York: Fertig, 1985.

——. *Toward the Final Solution: A History of European Racism.* New York: Fertig, 1978.

——. "Was die Deutschen wirklich lasen: Marlitt, May, Ganghofer." In *Popularität und Trivialität.* 4th Wisconsin Workshop. Ed. Reinhold Grimm and Jost Hermand. Frankfurt am Main: Athenäum, 1974.

Müller-Bochat, Eberhard. "Afrika und Herders 'Stimmen der Völker' aus komparatistischer Sicht." In *Négritude et Germanité, L'Afrique Noire dans la littérature d'expression allemande.* 84–93. Dakar: Nouvelles éditions africaines, 1983.

Müller-Weil, Ulrike. *Absolutismus und Aussenpolitik in Preussen. Ein Beitrag zur Strukturgeschichte des Preussischen Absolutismus.* Stuttgart: Steiner, 1992.

Musgrave, Marian. "Herder, Blacks, and the 'Negeridyllen': A Study in Ambivalent Humanitarianism." *Studia Africana* 1 (1977): 89–99.

Naber, J. P. l'Honoré, ed. *Reisebeschreibungen von deutschen Beamten und Kriegs-*

leuten im Dienst der niederländischen West- und Ostindischen Kompagnien 1602–1797. 3 vols. Haag: Nijhoff, 1930.

Opitz, Alfred. "Durch die Wüste, Lichter tragend . . . Sozialgeschichte und literarischer Stil in den Reiseberichten über die Iberia um 1800." In *Reise und soziale Realität*. Ed. Wolfgang Griep and Hans-Wolf Jäger. 188–217. Heidelberg: Winter, 1983.

Pagden, Anthony. *European Encounters with the New World: From Renaissance to Romanticism*. New Haven: Yale University Press, 1993.

Palmer, Phillip M. "German Works on America, 1492–1800." *University of California's Publications in Modern Philology* 36: 271–412. Berkeley, 1952.

Pavel, Thomas. "Thematics and Historical Evidence." In *The Return of Thematic Criticism*. Ed. Werner Sollors. 121–145. Cambridge: Harvard University Press, 1993.

Pelz, Annegret. *Reisen durch die eigene Fremde. Reiseliteratur von Frauen als autogeographische Schriften*. Köln: Böhlau, 1993.

Peterson, Brent O. "Wezel and the Genre of 'Robinson Crusoe.'" *Lessing Yearbook* 20 (1988): 183–204.

Pleticha, Heinrich, ed. *Lese-Erlebnisse 2*. Frankfurt am Main: Suhrkamp, 1978.

Pollock, Sheldon. "Deep Orientalism? Notes on Sanskrit and Power Beyond the Raj." In *Orientalism and the Postcolonial Predicament: Perspectives on South Asia*. Ed. Carol A. Breckenridge and Peter van der Veer. 76–133. Philadelphia: University of Pennsylvania Press, 1993.

Pratt, Mary Louise. *Imperial Eyes: Travel Writing and Transculturation*. New York: Routledge, 1992.

Price, Lawrence Marsden. *Inkle and Yarico Album*. Berkeley: University of California Press, 1937.

——. "The Vogue of Marmontel on the German Stage." *University of California Publications in Modern Philology* 27, no. 3. Berkeley: University of California Press, 1944.

Promies, Wolfgang. "Kinderliteratur im späten 18. Jahrhundert." In *Hansers Sozialgeschichte der deutschen Literatur*. Ed. Rolf Grimminger. 3: 765–831. München: Hanser, 1980.

Rabasa, José. "Allegories of the 'Atlas.'" In *Europe and Its Others*. Ed. Francis Barker, Peter Hulme, et al. 2: 1–16. Colchester: University of Essex Press, 1985.

Rama, Angel. *Transculturación narrativa en América Latina*. Mexico: Siglo Veintiuno, 1982.

Rein, Gustav Adolf. *Europa und Übersee, Gesammelte Aufsätze*. Göttingen: Musterschmidt, 1961.

Richter, Dieter. "Das Bild der Neapolitaner in der Reiseliteratur des achtzehnten und neunzehnten Jahrhunderts." In *Europäisches Reisen im Zeitalter der Aufklärung*. Ed. Hans-Wolf Jäger. 118–130. Heidelberg: Winter, 1992.

Rupp-Eisenreich, Britta. "Des choses occultes en histoire des sciences humaines: Le destin de la 'science nouvelle' de Christoph Meiners," *Ethnographie* 90–91 (1983): 131–183.

Sadji, Uta. "Johann August von Einsiedel und Afrıka." In *Négritude et Germanité; l'Afrique Noire dans la littérature d'expression allemande.* 75–82. Dakar: Nouvelles éditions africaines, 1983.

———. "Der Negersklavenhandel auf der deutschen Bühne des 18. Jahrhunderts." In *Images de l'Africain de l'antiquité au XXe siècle.* Ed. Daniel Droixhe and Klaus Kiefer. 95–101. Frankfurt am Main: Lang, 1987.

Sagarra, Eda. *An Introduction to Nineteenth-Century Germany.* Harlow: Longman, 1980.

Said, Edward. *Culture and Imperialism.* New York: Knopf, 1993.

———. *Orientalism.* New York: Random House, 1979.

———. "Orientalism Reconsidered." In *Europe and Its Others.* Ed. Francis Barker et al. Colchester: University of Essex Press, 1985.

Saine, Thomas. *Georg Forster.* New York: Twayne, 1972.

Scammell, Geoffrey. *The First Imperial Age: European Overseas Expansion c. 1400–1715.* London and Boston: Unwin Hyman, 1989.

———. "The Other Side of the Coin: The Discovery of the Americas and the Spread of Intolerance, Absolutism and Racism in Early Modern Europe." Paper delivered at the John Carter Brown Library Conference, "America in European Consciousness" (Providence, June 1991).

Schiebinger, Londa. *The Mind Has No Sex? Women and the Origins of Modern Science.* Cambridge, Mass.: Harvard University Press, 1989.

Schlaeder, Jürgen. "Die Robinsonade als frühbürgerliche Utopie." In *Utopieforschung.* Ed. Wilhelm Vosskamp. 2: 280–298. Stuttgart: Metzler, 1982–1985.

Schmidt, Egon. *Die deutsche Kinder- und Jugendliteratur von der Mitte des 18. Jahrhunderts bis zum Anfang des 19. Jahrhunderts.* Berlin-Ost: Kinderbuchverlag, 1974.

Schmitt, Albert. "The Elusive Philipp von Hutten: Colonizer in Venezuela." *Yearbook of German-American Studies* 13, no. 3 (1978): 63–71.

Schneider, Helmut. "Der Zusammenbruch des Allgemeinen" (Sozialgeschichtliche Werkinterpretationen). In *Positionen der Literaturwissenschaft. Acht Modellanalysen am Beispiel von Heinrich von Kleists 'Das Erdbeben in Chili.'* Ed. David Wellbery. 2nd ed. 110–129. München: Beck, 1987.

Sheehan, James J. *German History, 1770–1866.* Oxford: Clarendon Press, 1989.

Siebenmann, Gustav. "Das Lateinamerikabild der Deutschen. Quellen, Raster, Wandlungen." *colloquium helveticum* 7. Bern: P. Lang, 1980.

Smith, Duncan. " ' . . . beschreibung eyner Landtschafft der Wilden/Nacketen/Grimmigen Menschfresser Leuthen': The German Image of America in the Sixteenth Century." In *The German Contribution to the Building of the Americas.* Ed. Gerhard K. Friesen and Walter Schatzberg. 1–19. Hanover, N.H.: University Press of New England, 1977.

Smith, Woodruff. *The German Colonial Empire.* Chapel Hill: University of North Carolina Press, 1978.

Solbrig, Ingeborg. "American Slavery in 18th-Century German Literature: The Case of Herder's Neger-Idyllen." *Monatshefte* 82, no. 1 (1990): 38–49.

Sollors, Werner, ed. *The Return of Thematic Criticism*. Cambridge, Mass.: Harvard University Press, 1993.

Sommer, Doris. *Foundational Fictions: The National Romances of Latin America*. Berkeley: University of California Press, 1991.

Spitta, Silvia. *Between Two Waters: Narratives of Transculturation in Latin America*. Houston: Rice University Press, 1995.

Stannard, David E. *American Holocaust: Columbus and the Conquest of the New World*. New York: Oxford University Press, 1992.

Starnes, Thomas. *Christoph Martin Wieland, Leben und Werk: aus zeitgenössischen Quellen chronologisch dargestellt*. Sigmaringen: Thorbecke, 1987.

Stepan, Nancy Leys. "Race and Gender: The Role of Analogy in Science." In *Anatomy of Racism*. Ed. David Theo Goldberg. Minneapolis: University of Minnesota Press, 1990.

Stewart, William E. *Die Reisebeschreibung und ihre Theorie im Deutschland des 18. Jahrhunderts*. Bonn: Bouvier, 1978.

Stokes, Eric. "Late Nineteenth-Century Colonial Expansion and the Attack on the Theory of Economic Imperialism: A Case of Mistaken Identity." *Historical Journal* 12 (1969): 285–301.

Stoler, Ann Laura. *Race and the Education of Desire: Foucault's History of Sexuality and the Colonial Order of Things*. Durham, N.C.: Duke University Press, 1995.

Theweleit, Klaus. *Male Fantasies*. Tr. Stephen Conway. Minneapolis: University of Minnesota Press, 1987.

Tietz, Manfred. "Amerika vor der spanischen Öffentlichkeit des 18. Jahrhunderts. Zwei Repliken auf de Pauw und Raynal: die 'Reflexiones imparciales' von Juan Nuix y Perpiñá und die 'México conquistada' von Juan de Escoiquiz." In *Iberoamérica. Historia-sociedad-literatura. Homenaje a Gustav Siebenmann*. Ed. José Manuel López de Abiada and Titus Heydenreich. 989–1016. München: Fink, 1983.

Timm, Uwe. *Deutsche Kolonien*. München: Autorenedition, 1981.

Townsend, Mary Evelyn. *The Origins of Modern German Colonialism, 1871–1885*. New York: Columbia University Press, 1921.

Trexler, Richard. *Sex and Conquest: Gendered Violence, Political Order, and the European Conquest of the Americas*. Ithaca: Cornell University Press, 1995.

Trotter, David. "Colonial Subjects." *Critical Quarterly* 32, no. 3 (1990): 3–37.

Ullrich, Hermann. *Defoes Robinson Crusoe*. Leipzig: Reisland, 1924.

———. *Robinson und Robinsonaden. Bibliographie, Geschichte, Kritik*. Weimar: Felber, 1898.

Volberg, Heinrich. *Deutsche Kolonialbestrebungen in Südamerika nach dem Dreissigjährigen Kriege. Insbesondere die Bemühungen von Johann Joachim Becher*. Köln: Böhlau, 1977.

Wahle, Julius. *Das Weimarer Hoftheater unter Goethes Leitung*. Weimar: Goethe-Gesellschaft, 1892.

Warmbold, Joachim. *Germania in Africa: Germany's Colonial Literature.* New York: Peter Lang, 1989.

Weber, Gaby. *'Krauts' erobern die Welt. Der deutsche Imperialismus in Südamerika.* Hamburg: Libertäre Assoziation, 1982.

Weigel, Sigrid. "Der Körper am Kreuzpunkt von Liebesgeschichte und Rassendiskurs in Heinrich von Kleists Erzählung 'Die Verlobung in St. Domingo.'" *Kleist Jahrbuch* (1991): 186–201.

——. "Die nahe Fremde — das Territorium des 'Weiblichen.' Zum Verhältnis von 'Wilden' und 'Frauen' im Diskurs der Aufklärung." In *Die andere Welt. Studien zum Exotismus.* Ed. Thomas Koebner and Gerhart Pickerodt. 179–199. Frankfurt am Main: Athenäum, 1987.

Weingarten, Michael. "Menschenarten oder Menschenrassen. Die Kontroverse zwischen Georg Forster und Immanuel Kant." In *Georg Forster in seiner Epoche.* Ed. G. Pickerodt et al. 117–148. Berlin: Argument, 1982.

Wellbery, David, ed. *Positionen der Literaturwissenschaft. Acht Modellanalysen am Beispiel von Heinrich von Kleists "Das Erdbeben in Chili."* 2nd ed. München: Beck, 1987.

Wenzel, Herbert. *Christoph Meiners als Religionshistoriker.* Ph.D. diss. Frankfurt an der Oder: Beholtz, 1917.

Werlen, Hans Jakob. "Seduction and Betrayal: Race and Gender in Kleist's 'Die Verlobung in St. Domingo.'" *Monatshefte* 84, no. 4 (Winter 1992): 459–471.

Wetzel, Ernst. *Der Kolumbus-Stoff im deutschen Geistesleben.* Breslau: Priebatsch, 1935.

Wintzer, Wilhelm. *Die Deutschen im tropischen Amerika.* München: Lehmann, 1900.

Wittkower, Rudolf. "Marvels of the East: A Study in the History of Monsters." *Journal of the Warburg and Courtauld Institutes* 4 (1942): 159–197.

Woodforde, John. *The Strange Story of False Hair.* London: Routledge & Kegan Paul, 1971.

Wuthenow, Ralph-Rainer. *Die erfahrene Welt. Europäische Reiseliteratur im Zeitalter der Aufklärung.* Frankfurt am Main: Insel, 1980.

Young, Robert. *Colonial Desire: Hybridity in Theory, Culture and Race.* London: Routledge, 1995.

——. *White Mythologies: Writing, History, and the West.* London: Routledge, 1990.

Zamora, Margarita. *Reading Columbus.* Berkeley: University of California Press, 1993.

Zantop, Susanne. "The Beautiful, the Ugly, and the German: Race, Gender, and Nationality in Eighteenth-Century Anthropological Discourse." In *Gender and Germanness: Cultural Productions of Nation.* Ed. Patricia Herminghouse and Magda Mueller. Boston: Berghahn, forthcoming.

——. "Crossing the Boundaries: The French Revolution in the German Literary Imagination." In *Representing Revolution: Essays on Reflections of the French Revolution in Literature, Historiography, and Art.* Ed. James Heffernan. 213–233. Hanover, N.H.: University Press of New England, 1992.

——. "Dialectics and Colonialism: The Underside of the Enlightenment." In *Impure Reason: Dialectic of Enlightenment in Germany.* Ed. W. Daniel Wilson and Robert C. Holub. 301–321. Detroit: Wayne State University Press, 1993.

——. "Domesticating the Other: European Colonial Fantasies, 1770–1873." In *The Question of the Other/s.* Ed. Gisela Brinker-Gabler. 269–283. Albany: State University of New York Press, 1995.

——. "Verlobung, Hochzeit und Scheidung in St. Domingo: Die Haitianische Revolution in zeitgenössischer deutscher Literatur (1792–1817)." In *"Neue Welt"/"Dritte Welt": Interkulturelle Beziehungen Deutschlands zu Lateinamerika und der Karibik.* Ed. Susan Cocalis and Sigrid Bauschinger. 29–52. Tübingen: Francke, 1994.

Index

Acéphales, 35, 55
Albrecht, J. F. E.: *Die Kolonie,* 38
Amazons, 35, 45, 55–56, 229 n. 30
Anatomy: as racial marker, 70, 72, 84, 234 n. 24
Andreä, D. W., 25
Anson, Lord, 33
Anthropology: eighteenth-century, 43–80 passim, 232 n. 10
Anticolonialism. *See* Colonial suspicion
Anti-Semitism, 3. *See also* Jews; "Race(s)"
Arciniegas, Germán, 221 n. 43
Aristocracy: decadence of, 44, 62–63
Arminius: cult of, 200
Armstrong, Nancy, 212 n. 16

Beards, 62–63, 70. *See also* Hair
Becher, Johann Jakob, 24
Bellegarde-Smith, Patrick, 142
Beyerhaus, Gisbert, 60
Bhabha, Homi, 4, 5, 212 n. 15
Bildungsreise, 32
Bismarck, Otto von, 1, 193, 199
Bitterli, Urs, 232 n. 13
Black Legend (*leyenda negra*), 23, 25, 39, 219 n. 22
Blood: and ethnicity, 88–90, 97; purity of, 238 n. 19
Blumenbach, Johann Friedrich, 62, 67, 70–73, 74, 76, 78–79, 84, 85, 92, 229 n. 34, 233 n. 20 and n. 21
Böhn, Max von, 62
Bolívar, Simon, 160, 252 n. 57
Bonneville, Zacharie de Pazzi de ("Le Philosophe la Douceur"), 47, 63

Bouterwek, Friedrich, 238 n. 27
Buffon, G. L. L., comte de, 13, 43, 163, 227 n. 11, 233 n. 14
Bülow, Frieda von, 203, 261 n. 3
Bulthaupt, Heinrich, 258 n. 1
Byron, John, 33

Campe, Joachim Heinrich, 4, 121, 133, 138, 169, 198, 206, 241 n. 11, 242 n. 24; *Die Entdeckung von Amerika,* 116–120; *Robinson der Jüngere,* 13, 14, 102–120, 127, 197
Camper, Pieter, 73
Cannibalism: in literature, 109, 124, 143, 204; as metaphor for colonial relations, 11, 16, 45, 204, 206
Casas, Bartholomé de las, 18, 22–30, 34, 100, 123–125, 138, 165, 176, 179, 180, 205, 216 n. 2, 219 n. 20, 220 nn. 23 and 24
Charles V, 25
Colonial desire, 13, 211 n. 4. *See also* Colonial relations; Colonial romance
Colonial guilt, 22, 25–30, 95
Colonialism: and anticolonialism, 47, 82; British, 245 n. 19; European, 5, 12, 21, 36, 39, 96–97; French, 26; and gender, 50–65, 137, 185–190, 199, 212 n. 16, 215 n. 33, 225 n. 5, 226 n. 11; German, 1, 8, 17, 18–30, 64–65, 106–120, 138, 148, 189, 192–201, 213 n. 22, 217 n. 6, 218 nn. 8 and 9, 222 n. 46, 223 n. 13, 243 n. 6, 259 n. 22; as German mission, 193; German propensity for, 23, 29, 40, 96, 97, 99, 101, 120, 199,

Colonialism (*cont.*)
201, 259 n. 11; vs. imperialism, 8,
214 nn. 23 and 24; intellectual, 41;
latent vs manifest, 2; models of, 193,
258 n. 8; as a natural drive, 16, 194;
as a pedagogical project, 106–120,
198–199; Prussian, 64, 199, 217 n.
6, 230 n. 47; Spanish, 11, 21, 245 n.
22
Colonial legend, 7, 201, 203, 213 n. 22,
260 n. 26
Colonial relations, metaphors for, 100–
101, 196; birthing, 186; brotherhood, 108–120, 121, 133, 148, 197;
conquest, 9, 100–101, 128–132,
136, 146; daughter colony, 2, 197;
divorce, 156, 160, 163; family, 2, 90,
99–165, 197, 240 n. 2; father-child,
101, 103–120, 188–189; friendship,
112; love, 13, 60–61, 121–140,
145–165; marriage, 2, 9, 13, 100–
101, 121–140, 145–165, 202, 205;
master-slave, 5, 132, 142–161 passim; natural surrender, 9, 52, 125,
131; rape, 9, 195, 196, 197; virgin
land/island, 2, 13, 128–140 passim,
162–165, 167, 168, 172, 186, 196,
197, 259 n. 9. See also Cannibalism;
Slavery
Colonial romance: Cora and Alonzo
(*see also* Kotzebue; Marmontel),
123–140, 168, 200, 207, 244 n. 13,
244 n.13; Inkle and Yarico, 6, 122–
126, 146, 243 n. 10; John Smith and
Pocahontas, 6, 122; Krusoe and
Freitag (*see also* Campe), 108–120,
121, 126, 163, 168, 197, 200, 207;
Prospero and Caliban, 6; Robinson
and Friday (*see also* Defoe), 6, 13.
See also Columbus
"Colonial suspicion," 15, 203–209
Colony: as island, 108, 113–120; as
metaphor, 7, 37
Columbus: as a literary figure, 108,
116–117, 169, 173–192, passim,

196, 197, 200, 202, 208, 254 n. 10
(chap. 9), 254 n. 7 (chap. 10), 255 n.
8, 258 nn. 1 and 2
Condamine, Charles Marie de la, 33
Conquest: and gender, 46–65, 228 n.
21; Germans and, 118, 216 n. 3; as
metaphor, 49. *See also* Colonialism;
Colonial relations
Cook, James, 33
Cora and Alonzo. *See* Colonial romance
Cortés: as literary figure, 116
Coyer, Gabriel François, 55
Curtin, Philip, 231 n. 2, 233 n. 21

Defoe, Daniel: *Robinson Crusoe*, 37,
102–103, 104, 105, 106, 109, 110,
218 n. 9
Degeneracy: of New World Indians,
50–65, 227 n. 11
Dessalines, Jean-Jacques, 142
Discovery: of Germany's "India," 184–
190, 258 n. 4; as metaphor, 13, 49,
168–172, 173–190. *See also* Colonialism; Colonial relations
Disease: as metaphor, 50, 58, 62. *See
also* Degeneracy; Syphilis
Döhner, Friedrich, 147–149, 152, 153,
154, 159, 160, 161, 249 n. 28, 249 n.
33

Ehrmann, Theophil, 221 n. 35
Engel, J. J., 25
Ethnic identity, 80, 82, 90. *See also* Na-
tionalism; "Race(s)"
Ethnocentrism. *See* Germanness; Race
Eurocentrism, 41

Fabri, Friedrich, 195, 198, 215 n. 28
Family. *See* Colonial relations
Fantasy: collective imagination, 3; and
the colonial movement, 192–201;
"colonial stereotype," 5; colonial
"Urfantasy," 2; counter-fantasy, 204–
209; definition of, 3; desire, 4, 13,
35, 152, 172; effect of, 203; vs. fic-

tion and myth, 3; male fantasy, 3,
207; myth transfer, 55; political un-
conscious, 4; of redress, 146
Fichte, Johann Gottlob, 94
Fick, A., 193, 194, 195, 219 n. 17, 258
    n. 4
Fischer, Bernd, 94, 250 n. 45
Fischer, Caroline Auguste, 159, 160–
    161
Forster, Georg, 33, 67, 76, 232 n. 12,
    235 n. 33, 237 n. 15
Forster, Johann Reinhold, 33
Frederick II ("the Great"), 64, 230 n.
    47. See also Colonialism: Prussian
French Revolution. See Revolution(s)
Frézier, Amédée François, 33
Friede, Juan, 23, 218 nn. 10 and 11,
    219 n. 15, 222 n. 44

Geffken, A., 193, 194
Gender. See Colonialism: and gender;
    "Race": and gender
Gerbi, Antonello, 48, 64, 167, 236 n. 8
Germanen (Old Germans), 91–97, 200,
    238 n. 24
Germanness, 22, 24, 45, 87–97, 101,
    165, 185, 199, 218 n. 10, 236 n. 8.
    See also Ethnic identity; National
    character; Nationalism
Germany's India. See Discovery
Gilman, Sander, 248 nn. 21 and 24
Girtanner, Christoph, 232 n. 12, 233 n.
    17, 238 n. 24
Goethe, Johann Wolfgang, 127, 180,
    244 n. 16
Grand Tour, 32
Grimm, Hans, 203, 261 n. 6
Grosser, Thomas, 32
Guyon, Claude Marie, 56, 229 n. 30

Haebler, Konrad, 28
Hair, 52, 59, 62–63, 70–73, 111, 230
    n. 46. See also Beards
Haitian Revolution. See Revolution(s)
Hantzsch, Viktor, 22, 27, 219 n. 18

Hassert, Kurt, 22, 27, 220 n. 27
Hegel, G. F. W., 14, 163–165, 167, 214
    n. 27, 236 n. 8
Heine, Heinrich, 15, 204–206
Herder, Johann Gottfried, 67, 74–79,
    85, 93–97, 99, 120, 152, 153, 154,
    198, 234 n. 28, 235 nn. 29 and 30
"Hermann der Cherusker," 200
Hottentots: as embodiment of "ugli-
    ness," 11
Hübbe-Schleiden, D. J. U., 22, 195
Hübbe-Schleiden, H., 199
Hulme, Peter, 6, 44, 212 n. 6, 213 n.
    16, 241 n. 16
Humboldt, Alexander von, 165, 166–
    170, 178, 180, 202, 205
Hutten, Philipp von, 26

Ibbeken, Rudolf, 90
Iffland, August Wilhelm, 244 n. 16
Imaginary. See Fantasy
Imagination. See Fantasy
Imperialism. See Colonialism
Inkle and Yarico. See Colonial romance
Irving, Washington, 165, 178, 252 n. 5,
    253 n. 6

James, C. L. R., 247 n. 12
Jesuits, 35, 48
Jews, 15, 82–83, 89, 90. See also Anti-
    Semitism; Race

Kamen, Henry, 238 n. 19
Kant, Immanuel, 41–42, 67–70, 72,
    74, 76, 78, 85, 96, 99, 120, 154, 232
    n. 13, 233 nn. 15, 16, and 17
Kayser, Paul, 222 n. 46
Keller, Gottfried, 15, 204, 206–209
Kleist, Heinrich von, 15, 96, 139, 204,
    251 n. 50; Die Verlobung in St. Do-
    mingo, 154–158, 250 n. 45
Klencke, Hermann, 168–170
Klingemann, August, 173, 254 n. 5;
    Columbus, 174–178, 182
Klöden, Karl von, 26

Klopstock, Friedrich Gottlieb, 48
Klüger, Ruth (Angress), 250 n. 45
Klunzinger, Karl, 27
Koch, Rainer, 40
Kolb, Ernst, 149–154, 234 n. 26, 249
    nn. 32 and 33
Körner, Theodor: *Toni*, 158–159, 160,
    161, 251 n. 51
Kösting, Karl, 184–190, 197; biogra-
    phy, 256 n. 21
Kotzebue, August von, 174, 175; *Die
    Indianer in England*, 127, 134–140;
    Die Negersklaven, 152–154, 159; re-
    ception, 127, 244 nn. 14, 15, and 16;
    Die Sonnenjungfrau and *Die Spanier
    in Peru, oder: Rollas Tod*, 13, 126–
    140, 147, 249 n. 33
Kraft, Johann Daniel, 24

Lafitau, P.: *Moeurs des sauvages améri-
    quains*, 55
Las Casas, Bartolomé de. *See* Casas,
    Bartolomé de las
Lavater, Johann Caspar, 235 n. 29
Lennox, Sara, 3, 212 n. 7
Lessing, Gotthold Ephraim, 153, 249 n.
    36
Leyenda negra. See Black Legend
Long, Edward, 249 n. 32
Love. *See* Colonial relations

Malinchismo, 53
Marmontel: *Les Incas*, 13, 123–126,
    127, 138, 139, 164, 175, 243 n. 8
Masculinity, 90, 99. *See also* Colonial-
    ism: and gender
McClintock, Anne, 6, 212 nn. 6 and 8,
    213 n. 17, 225 n. 2, 240 n. 2
Meiners, Christoph, 14, 39, 67–68, 79,
    82–94, 99, 119, 198, 235 n. 33, 237
    nn. 13 and 14; reception, 232 n. 11,
    236 n. 6, 237 n. 15, 238 n. 17, 248 n.
    24, 249 n. 32
Miscegenation, 84, 89, 101, 195, 211
    n. 4, 259 n. 14; as metaphor, 158

Monogeny vs. phylogeny, 70
Monsters, 57, 59, 228 n. 22. *See also*
    Acéphales; Amazons; Cannibals; Pa-
    tagon Giants
Montaigne, Michel de, 76, 235 n. 31
Morison, Samuel Eliot, 44
Mosse, George, 213 n. 17, 215 n. 35
Musgrave, Marian, 234 n. 28
Myth. *See* Fantasy

National character, 94–97, 238 n. 28;
    English, 94–97; German, 94–97, 99,
    119; Spanish, 94
Nationalism: German, 90, 169, 176
Native Americans. *See* "Race(s)";
    Racism
Natural order, 61
Naumann, Friedrich, 16
Navarrete, Martín Fernández de, 165,
    252 n. 4, 253 n. 6
Neocolonialism, 13, 37, 136–138,
    171–172
New World: allegories of, 44–45; theo-
    ries of, 163–165
Nicolai, Friedrich, 63

Occidentalism, 9, 10
Orellana, Antonio de, 56
Orientalism, 4, 5, 212 n. 16

Patagon Giants, 15, 35, 55–56, 58, 76,
    81–97, 228 nn. 24 and 25, 229 n. 27
Patriarchy, 5, 104–106, 123. *See also*
    Colonial relations
Pauw, Corneille de, 13, 14, 46–65, 68,
    74, 82–83, 87, 92, 99, 163, 164,
    167, 182, 227 nn. 11 and 13, 233 n.
    14, 255 n. 15; biography, 226 nn. 1
    and 4; reception, 227 n. 6
Pavel, Thomas, viii
Pernety, Antoine, 47, 58–65, 229 n. 34,
    235 n. 29
Peters, Carl, 7, 193, 195, 215 n. 28,
    219 n. 17
Philippovich, Eugen von, 192, 193

Physiognomy, 71–72, 83–97. *See also* Beards; Hair; Lavater; "Race(s)"; Racism; Skull
Pizarro: as literary figure, 116
Political unconscious. *See* Fantasy
Pollock, Sheldon, 213 n. 21
Postcolonial theory: Germany, 3, 6, 212 n. 7
Pratt, Mary Louise, 166, 172, 212 n. 6
Prospero and Caliban. *See* Colonial romance

Rabasa, José, 225
"Race(s)": Africans, 15, 66, 73–75, 83–87, 149–150, 198, 231 n. 8, 234 nn. 26 and 28, 235 n. 29; American Indians, 15, 40, 45, 66, 73, 75, 83–87, 90–97; Arabs, 15; and beauty, 88–90, 235 n. 33; and climate, 74–75; comparative theories of, 66–80, 81–97, 229 n. 36; eighteenth-century race theory, 43–95, 231 nn. 2 and 4, 233 n. 14; and gender, 43–65, 66, 160, 235 n. 29; Germans, 15, 77–78, 80, 87–97; Gypsies, 15, 82, 89, 90; Jews, 15, 82–83, 89, 90; Slavs, 89. *See also* Racism
Racism, 213 n. 17, 233 nn. 16, 17, 20, and 21, 234 nn. 24 and 28, 235 n. 29, 259 n. 14. *See also* Race
Rainsford, Marcus, 248 n. 14
Ratzel, Friedrich, 194
Raynal, Thomas Guillaume François, 48, 176, 249 n. 28
Reiselust, 32, 171
Revolution(s): and the family, 145–161; French, 15, 82, 142–144; and gender, 144–161, 248 n. 14; Haitian, 15, 79, 81, 141–142, 155, 246 n. 4, 247 nn. 9 and 12 (German involvement in Haitian Revolution, 246 n. 5); Latin American, 137, 183; metaphoric overlap of French and Haitian, 15, 79–80, 83, 90, 139, 142–161

Riecke, G. A., 192, 258 n. 2
Robinsonade, 102–104, 108, 143, 240 nn. 2, 3, and 4, 241 nn. 6 and 11
Robinson and Friday. *See* Colonial romance
Robinson Crusoe: impact on German children's literature, 240 n. 5, 241 n. 9. *See also* Colonial romance; Defoe
Roscher, Wilhelm Georg, 194, 196, 197, 219 n. 17, 243 n. 6
Rousseau, Jean-Jacques, 59, 104–105
Rückert, Friedrich, 173, 178–183

Said, Edward, 4, 5, 7, 15, 212 n. 16, 214 n. 23
Saint-Domingue. *See* Revolution(s): Haitian
Savage: noble vs. ignoble, 59, 112, 117, 118, 132–134
Scammell, Geoffrey, 237 n. 15, 238 nn. 18 and 19
Schelle, Karl Gottlob, 62
Schiller, Friedrich, 21, 48, 173, 219 n. 17
Schlegel, Friedrich, 236 n. 8
Schmid, Hermann Theodor von, 184
Schnabel, Johann Gottfried: *Die Insel Felsenburg,* 37, 218 n. 9
Seubert, Adolph, 18, 21, 27
Simonsfeld, Heinrich, 218 n. 8
Size: as racial marker, 88–97. *See also* Meiners; "Race(s)"; Racism
Skin color: as racial marker, 66, 70, 81–97, 111. *See also* "Race(s)"; Racism
Skull shape: as racial marker, 72, 75, 77. *See also* Anatomy; Physiognomy; Sömmerring
Slave dramas, 250 n. 37. *See also* Colonial relations: master-slave; Colonial romance
Slavery, 5, 28, 83, 141, 157, 235 n. 36; abolitionism, 248 nn. 21 and 24; as metaphor, 6, 13, 37, 75, 80, 110, 207, 238 n. 27; slave trade, 148, 150, 151, 218 n. 15, 222 n. 44, 241 n. 13

Smith, John, and Pocahontas. *See* Colonial romance
Smith, Woodruff, 192, 198, 214 n. 24
Sommer, Doris, 122
Sömmerring, Thomas Samuel von, 67, 73–80, 83, 85, 231 n. 8, 234 n. 24
Sonderweg: German, 8, 213 n. 21, 225 n. 2
South America: in German literature, 35, 223 n. 14 and 16; German predilection for, 38, 10, 11, 215 nn. 29 and 30; as imaginary site, 9, 10
Stedman, Gabriel, 6, 146, 249 n. 26
Stetten, Paul von, 26
Strength: as racial marker, 70. *See also* Meiners; "Race(s)"; Racism
Syphilis, 50, 227 n. 10. *See also* Degeneracy; Disease

Theweleit, Klaus, 3
Toussaint l'Ouverture, 142, 256 n. 18
Townsend, Mary, 1–2
Transculturation, 216 n. 3
Travel literature, 32–43; German, 33–43, 222 n. 5; theory, 222 n. 3

Treitschke, Heinrich von, 196, 197, 199, 260 n. 28
Trivialliteratur, 16, 215 n. 35
Trotter, David, 4

Vitzliputzli, 204–206
Voltaire, 59

Wanderlust. See Reiselust
Warmbold, Joachim, 203, 215 n. 30
Wars of Liberation: German, 200
Weickum, Karl, 191
Weigel, Sigrid, 213 n. 18, 245 n. 24
Welser (merchants), 12, 18–30, 108, 202, 218 n. 10, 219 n. 21
Werder, Karl, 173, 178–183
Wezel, Johann Carl, 242 n. 19
Wünsch, Christian Ernst, 67–68, 71–72, 92

Young, Robert, 5, 6, 211 nn. 4 and 8

Zimmermann, E. A. W. von, 11, 93

About the Author

Susanne Zantop is Professor of German and Comparative Literature at Dartmouth College and Chair of the Department of German Studies. She is the author of *Zeitbilder: Geschichte und Literatur bei Heinrich Heine und Mariano José de Larra*. She is also the editor of *Bitter Healing: German Women Writers from 1700 to 1830* (with Jeannine Blackwell) and *Paintings on the Move: Heinrich Heine and the Visual Arts*.

Library of Congress Cataloging-in-Publication Data
Zantop, Susanne, 1945–
    Colonial fantasies : conquest, family, and nation in precolonial
Germany, 1770–1870 / Susanne Zantop.
    p.   cm. — (Post-contemporary interventions)
Includes bibliographical references and index.
ISBN 0-8223-1960-8 (alk. paper). —
ISBN 0-8223-1968-3 (pbk. : alk. paper)
    1. German literature — 19th century — History and criticism.
2. Nationalism — Germany — History.   3. German literature — 18th
century — History and criticism.   4. National characteristics,
German, in literature.   5. Imperialism — Germany — History — 19th
century.   6. Imperialism — Germany — History — 18th century.
7. Military history in literature.   8. Nationalism in literature.
9. Colonies in literature.   10. Family in literature.   I. Title.
PT363.N27Z36   1997
830.9'358 — dc21   96-54617